Switzerland

William Martin, who died in 1934 at the age of forty-six, wrote in the French historiographical tradition. This short history of Switzerland, which, in the French, had six editions since it was first published in 1929, is an analytical reconstruction of the central events and forces in each main period of the country's past. Critics have remarked that the book reads as if it had been written yesterday. An extensive section by the distinguished Swiss historian and journalist Pierre Béguin updates the book to 1966, and the final chapters in this edition have been revised by Professor Hans Binswanger of St. Gallen and Dr. Mayrzedt of the Swiss Institute of International Economics to bring it up to date for 1970.

Switzerland

from Roman times to the present

by William Martin
With additional chapters
by Pierre Béguin
translated from the French
by Jocasta Innes

Praeger Publishers
New York · Washington

BOOKS THAT MATTER

Published in the United States of America in 1971
by Praeger Publishers, Inc., 111 Fourth Avenue,
New York, N.Y. 10003

First published in French under the title *Histoire de la Suisse*

Library of Congress Catalog Card Number: 75-134530

Printed in Great Britain

Contents

Chapter I

Roman, Barbarian and Medieval Switzerland

Switzerland is a political rather than geographic entity, and its unity is primarily a moral one so that there can be no Swiss history, properly speaking, before the founding of the Confederation. Nevertheless men lived, people suffered, for many centuries on the land we now call Switzerland, and traditions were formulated then which were to influence the later course of the nation's history, and which, in some instances, are still with the Swiss today.

We know nothing about the first inhabitants of the country. The discovery, here and there, at Wildkirchli (Appenzell), Kesserloch and Schweizerbild (Schaffhausen), of ancient caves, bones and implements is not really knowledge because all these remains tell us is that humanity here went through the same evolutionary stages as in the rest of Europe—the age of hewn stone, or Paleolithic, of polished stone, or Neolithic, and the Bronze and Iron Ages. However, since civilization invariably tends to move upwards from river mouths to their sources, the development of Europe's mountain areas noticeably lags behind that of the maritime regions. Thus the Bronze Age, beginning around the year 2000, lasted till about 650 B.C. in this part of the world, which was long after iron came into general use among its neighbours.

The lakeside settlements date from the Neolithic period. More than 160 of these have been found on the shores of Lakes Neuchâtel, Bienne, Murten, Zurich and Constance, as well as in Northern Italy. Archaeologically speaking, these are important discoveries, but they are of little historical interest because they tell us next to nothing about these lakeside people, what their origins were or what race they sprang from. All we know is that these were relatively civilized people of pastoral habits. The lakeside period ended, roughly speaking, with the coming of the Bronze Age.

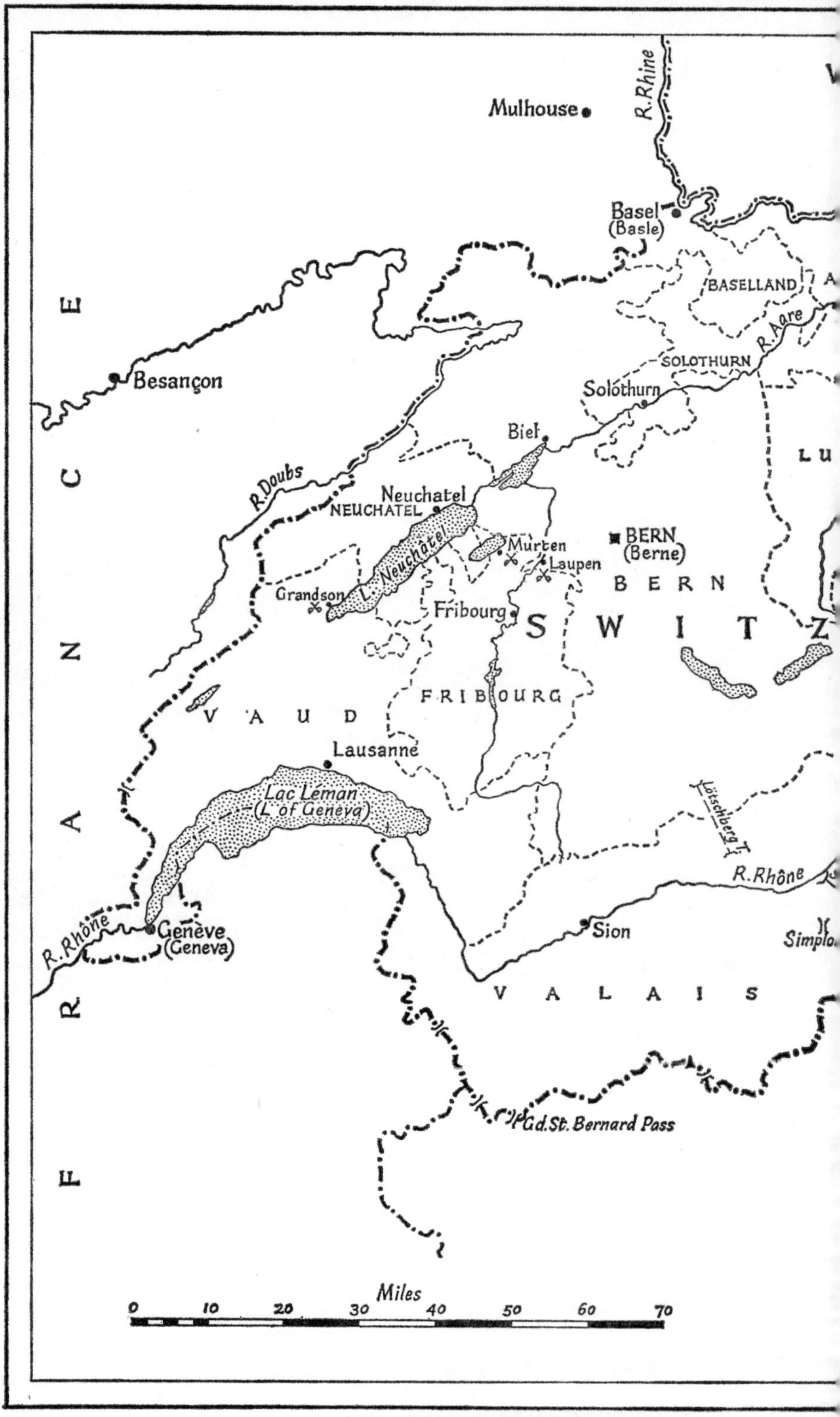

Mulhouse
R. Rhine
Basel
(Basle)
BASELLAND
SOLOTHURN
R. Aare
Solothurn
Besançon
F R A N C E
Biel
R. Doubs
Neuchatel
NEUCHATEL
L. Neuchâtel
Murten
Laupen
BERN
(Berne)
B E R N
Grandson
Fribourg
S W I T Z
F R I B O U R G
V A U D
Lausanne
Lac Léman
(L. of Geneva)
Lötschberg T.
R. Rhône
Genève
(Geneva)
Sion
Simplo
V A L A I S
Gd. St. Bernard Pass
Miles
0 10 20 30 40 50 60 70

GERMANY
SCHAFFHAUSEN
haffhausen
Rhine
Konstanz
(Constance)
Boden See
(L. Constance)
THURGAU
Frauenfeld
ZÜRICH
Zürich
L. Zürich
St Gallen
Herisau
Appenzell
APPENZELL
ST GALLEN
LIECHTENSTEIN
AUSTRIA
ZUG
Morgarten
SCHWYZ
L. Lucerne
Nafels
Glarus
GLARUS
Stans
Altdorf
R. Rhine
Chur
RLAND
URI
GRAUBUNDEN
Albula P.
Tunnel
Umbrail Pass
Stelvio Pass
St. Gotthard Pass
Splügen Pass
Bernina Pass
Val Levantina
Gries Pass
TICINO
Bellinzona
Val Tellina
Lake Maggiore
Lake Como
Como
ITALY
Lombardy Plain
Milan

The next five centuries are a closed book to us and we are not sure of the date when the Helvetians, the race which was to give the country its first name and introduce it to history, first made their appearance. They are thought not to have arrived much before the beginning of the first century—that is about fifty years before the Roman conquest. Julius Caesar was responsible for naming them, and thus ushering them into history. These men, who were little more than nomads and complete strangers to this part of the world, became the ancestors of modern Switzerland.

The Helvetians, who settled between the Rhine, Alps and the Jura mountains, were a Celtic tribe and took part in Gaul's political life, which consisted at that time of incessant civil wars. In this way they became involved, perhaps almost without realizing it, in the great struggle between the Arvernes and the Eduens in the first century B.C. The Eduens had an ambassador at Rome and their own intelligence system. The Arvernes, who occupied what is now the Auvergne, wanted independence for Gaul. Precisely what prompted the Helvetians to prepare a large-scale migration into South-West Gaul around the year 62 we do not know. They had spent scarcely forty years in this region and presumably had not formed any great attachment to it. It seems likely, however, that the move was inspired by Arverne emissaries, for we know that it gave rise to anxiety among the Eduens. The Eduen representative in Rome, Diviaticus, spread sombre rumours round the capital about Helvetian plans, which he interpreted as a projected attack on the Narbonne region of Gaul. The Romans took note of these rumours. In 58, just as the Helvetians were about to get under way after lengthy preparations for departure, Julius Caesar arrived posthaste from Rome to stop them crossing the Rhône and prevent them entering Narbonne. It was the Helvetians who brought about, quite involuntarily, the Roman conquest of Gaul.

We have only Julius Caesar's account of the battle which followed, and he is a partial witness. One rather curious fact emerges, and this is that the Helvetians, despite a victory over the Romans at Bibracte (Autun), eventually went back to their own country where they were rapidly assimilated, like all the other peoples of Gaul, into the Latin civilization.

Under Roman domination, Switzerland as we know it now was neither an independent nor a united province, but it shared in the unprecedented prosperity which Imperial Rome bequeathed to its conquered peoples, and which became a source of pride as well as material benefits to them.

Roman rule was not as peaceful in Helvetia as in the rest of Gaul; it was a military occupation. For much of the history of Roman Helvetia, from around 100 till 250 or thereabouts, the Rhine formed the boundary of the Empire. Switzerland was a March, or border country. Hence the large garrisons, notably at Vindonissa (Windisch), where there was a legion of 5,000 men, the XIIth followed by the XXIst, and at Augusta-Rerica. Hence too the strategic roads: one of these came from Northern Italy via the Julier and Septimer passes to Chur, and followed the Rhine valley as far as Vindonissa where it joined the road from Aosta via the St Bernard, Martigny (Octodurum), Avenches (Aventicum) and Solothurn (Solodurum) passes. Towns sprang up round the garrisons along these roads. Some of these, like Avenches, were very prosperous and opulent villas mushroomed.

As the centuries passed Helvetia's situation as a military zone was to have three consequences.

First, it could not escape the internal struggles which repeatedly divided the army against itself. In 69 A.D. the Rhine legions rose in revolt against the Emperor Galba, proclaiming their own leader Vitallius Emperor instead, and swept through Helvetia ravaging the towns which were loyal to Galba, Aventicum, the capital, in particular. This uprising did not have any lasting consequences. For reasons which are not very clear Emperor Vespasian and his Flavian successor seem to have taken a particular interest in Aventicum. While this dynasty ruled, Helvetia was specially favoured and the quantity of Flavian coins found in the soil testifies to her prosperity.

The second result of Helvetia's frontier position was the rapid spread of Christianity which seems to have taken place there. The Christian faith, as we know, was spread throughout the Empire by the Roman legions. So it is not surprising that we should find traces of Christianity in Helvetia from the second century, that the first persecutions should have fallen upon the Theban legions quartered at Agaune (St Maurice in Valais), and that the first Christian communities should have been set up along the military routes.

The third, last, and most serious consequence of its geographical situation was that Helvetia became one of the first

Roman territories to suffer the shock of barbarian invasion. In 260 A.D. the Germans made the first breach in the 'lines' between the Danube and the Rhine, where the Roman population had grown used to living in safety. This invasion only touched on Gaul but it ruined Helvetia. The people fled from Augusta-Rerica and Aventicum, which were burned and sacked. Now that the Danube frontier had been breached, Switzerland found itself once again in direct contact with the barbarians, and it never regained its former prosperity. In one century Aquae Sextiae (Baden) was destroyed no fewer than three times.

However, it was not until the end of the fifth century that the Germans, making use of the great roads built by the Romans for the defence of their Empire, invaded and engulfed the northern region of Helvetia. Around the same time the Burgundians installed themselves, with the consent of the Gallo-Romans, as allies of the Empire, in Savoy and the Leman basin.

The linguistic configuration of Switzerland, which has remained the same, with a few fluctuations, throughout its history, dates from this double invasion with its twofold characteristics. The Burgundians did not appear in the guise of enemies of the Empire, but quite the contrary. It is mistaken to suppose that the Roman army was made up of Romans; it was always full of barbarians. Gradually their numbers increased. The Empire meanwhile, in accordance with its inherent policy, sought every means of splitting up these tribes which were not bound by any real solidarity, setting one against another, making alliances with some against the rest. Thus the Burgondes became the allies of the Roman people and later, under attack from a neighbouring tribe, entered the Gallo-Roman territory as allies and refugees. They mingled with the population there and exerted a certain influence over them while submitting to their authority; to a certain extent at least they adopted their language and customs. It is through these Burgondes that the Roman civilization left deep imprints, despite successive barbarian invasions, on the western part of the country.

The Burgundians went no further than the region around the lakes of Neuchâtel and Murten, where they found themselves face to face with the Germans, their unconquerable foes.

The Germans were conquerors. They came as enemies. They reduced the population, most of whom had fled, to submission and did not mingle with it. They built new villages, retaining their Germanic customs and language. They destroyed the last vestiges of Roman civilization in the land they conquered, but gave it in return the sense of local autonomy from which Swiss federalism evolved.

The Germans, an agricultural people, occupied the high Swiss plateau and did not descend into the valleys. The Rhaetian Alps escaped the invasion and the Latin civilization and language were preserved there almost intact. This is how the islet of French Switzerland came into being—whereas the Ticino region continued to share the destiny of Northern Italy for many centuries longer.

The rule of the Germans and Burgundians had lasting effects on the country, particularly upon its language, and yet it did not last more than a century. The rule of the Franks, on the other hand, which lasted three hundred years, only made a superficial impression because it was a purely military and political occupation.

Making use in their turn of the Roman strategic roads, the Franks invaded the country and conquered the people who had settled there and in so doing lost their military aptitudes. The Frankish army, which had seen long service under Rome, took upon itself the task of maintaining and rebuilding the political unity of Gaul for the profit of its kings after the fall of the Western Empire. The army advanced slowly, building fortified towns at widely spaced intervals, and bequeathed its conquered subjects the Frankish civil law (*droit public*), allowing them to retain their own penal and property laws. In 534, after defeating the Germans, Clovis's sons put an end to the Burgundian kingdom which had latterly achieved a certain splendour, particularly under Gondebaud, who died at Geneva in 516. In 538 they annexed to their empire the eastern part of Switzerland, a region populated by Rhaeto-Romans, which had formed part of the Ostrogothic kingdom of Theodoric in Northern Italy.

For some three centuries after that, the territory which is modern Switzerland followed the fortunes of the Frankish monarchy, a remote province unable to exert any influence on events at a time when communications were difficult and unreliable. The Carolingian dynasty took the place of the Merovingian dynasty. Following a revolt in Germany against the oppressive measures of the Palace Mayors, a system of centralization succeeded the system of local autonomy which had hitherto held sway in the three great administrative sub-divisions of Burgundy, Germany and the Rhaetian Alps.

What is owed to the Franks? Christianity first of all, which created the moral climate. Secondly, feudalism, which gave rise to a system of political organization.

The Franks introduced Catholicism to the Aryan Burgundians. They also managed to impose the Christian faith, after a struggle, on the pagan Germans.

Christianity entered the country under several guises and by many routes. It made its first appearance with the Roman legionaries; a second, under its Aryan form, with the Burgundian invasion. In the sixth and seventh centuries missionaries arriving, somewhat inexplicably, from Ireland, evangelized the country. St Fridolin, founder of the Abbey of Säckingen and the apostle of Glarus, on whose coat-of-arms he still figures, may be legendary but St Colomban, St Gallen, St Sigisbert and St Pirmin certainly existed. These apostles spread the Christian faith with great zeal, not only throughout the territory of modern Switzerland but beyond its frontiers, notably in the Vorarlberg, where the name of St Gallen remains an object of veneration to this day.

Thus in the early Middle Ages the Christian atmosphere in which Switzerland was to evolve was created. Mighty abbeys, some of which began as modest hermitages, date from this period. St Maurice was founded in 515 by the last Burgundian king, Sigismund. The seventh century saw the construction of St Gallen, Romainmôtier, Moutier-Grandval, St Ursanne, St Imier and probably Disentis. Reichenau and Pfäfers were founded by St Pirmin at the beginning of the eighth century, Fraumünster in Zurich by King Louis the German in 853, and Einsiedeln by St Meinrad at about the same time. In this century, a territorial redistribution of the old Roman episcopal seats gave rise to the bishoprics of Sion, Lausanne, Basle, Constance and Chur, which have played such a prominent role in Swiss history.

The political unity which the Franks restored to Switzerland did not last. The subdivision between Burgundian and German territories was soon re-established. Were it not for the fact that the Franks created the feudal setting which gave rise, in the natural course of events, to Confederalism, one might reasonably argue that they had less influence over Swiss history in the three centuries of their occupation than the Burgundians and Germans in one.

The custom among Frankish kings was not to bequeath the crown to their eldest son, but to share out their lands equally among all their sons. The early death of his brother Carloman left Charlemagne in control of a powerful empire. But soon after his reign, at the death of his son Louis the Debonair, his kingdom split into three parts. In 843 the Treaty of Verdun, one of the most important in the history of Europe, gave France to Charles the Bald, Germany to Louis the German and the imperial crown to their eldest brother, Lothar, who also acquired a long strip of land which came to be known as Lotharingia and which ran from the North Sea as far as Italy and was bounded by the Rhône on its western frontier and by the Aar to the east. This sharing out of the empire meant that Switzerland found itself divided once again. Louis the German retained the German lands as far as the Aar while Lothar held the Burgundian territory—including the southern Alpine valleys—which were thus united for the first time by political ties to the rest of Switzerland.

This arrangement did not last long, however. With the death of Lothar in 855 Lotharingia was the first to disintegrate. In 888 Rudolph founded the only national dynasty Switzerland has ever had. He had himself proclaimed and crowned king at St Maurice of the realm known to history as the Second Kingdom of Burgundy, which comprised the whole of what is now French Switzerland as far as Basle together with lands beyond the Jura and in Savoy. His reign, like that of his son Rudolph II and grandson Conrad I, was unusually peaceful and enlightened for this period of history. Good Queen Bertha, Rudolph II's wife and Conrad's mother, was one of the daughters of Duke Burckhardt of Germany and a native of German Switzerland. The deep impression she made upon the common people has lasted till this day. Unfortunately the Rudolphian dynasty failed to establish a lasting hold upon their kingdom and the system of divided inheritance—the weak point in the political system inherited from the Franks—caused the Second Kingdom of Burgundy to be swallowed up by the Empire again after a few generations of royal rule and one hundred and fifty years of existence.

Germany meanwhile had gone through similar upheavals. Louis the German was deeply attached to Switzerland and preferred to reside there. But his crown reverted to Louis the Child in 900 and the weakening of royal power was followed by an upsurge of independent kingdoms on all sides. The Frankish kingdom of the East was destroyed. In 1030, after long and wearisome conflict, Germany was restored to the German Empire at almost the same time as Burgundy and Italy. The political unity of the country was restored yet again. From now on Switzerland's history is intermingled with Germany's.

Shortly afterwards the terrible quarrel between Henry IV and Pope Gregory III over the rights of investiture broke out. In Switzerland, the opposing factions found themselves thrown together and the dispute became a war with everyone at each other's throats. This led to the emergence, for the first time in Swiss history, of the ecclesiastical and feudal powers who were to be the real rulers of this country for many centuries to come. The Emperor's supporters included the Counts of Lenzburg, the Abbot of St Gallen, and the Bishops of Basle and Lausanne. The Pope's numbered the Abbots of Constance and Reichenau, the noble Houses of Rheinfelden, Toggenburg, Kiburg and, most important of all, Zähringen. The power of this last dynasty in particular, heirs to the Counts of Rheinfelden, dates from this period. During the twelfth century their glory was to eclipse all others and pave the way for the founding of the Habsburg dynasty.

The Zähringen, though nominally deputizing for the Emperor, were in reality the rulers of Burgundy, on both sides of the Jura, though their dominance was challenged by the hostile Bishop of Lausanne in French Switzerland and by the growing power of the House of Savoy which had established itself in north Leman. They were great builders of fortresses and founders of cities: Fribourg, Burgdor, Thun, Laupen, Gümmenen, Murten, Yverdon, Moudon and Berne among others. Their policy was both far-sighted and liberal, and they blazed a trail for the emancipation of city communes which was to play so decisive a role in the founding and development of the Confederation. Furthermore it was under their rule that Switzerland was finally separated from Swabia and the Rhine became a natural frontier.

When Duke Berchthold V died without heirs in 1218 the extent of his possessions to the west can be traced, approximately, by the fortresses of Gruyères, Romont and Murten, all the land to the south of this boundary rendering homage to the Counts of Savoy. Berthold's vast possessions were shared out and one part of them passed to the Counts of Kiburg, and then, when this family became extinct, to the Habsburgs.

Other dynasties which wielded great power in the country deserve a mention too—secular lords like the Montforts and Werdenbergs in the Rhine valley, the Rapperswills, Wadenswills, d'Eschenbachs and Regensbergs in the Zürichgau, the Homberg-Tiersteins and Froburgs in the Jura, Ringgenbergs and Weissenburgs in the Oberland, Rarognes, Gruyères, Grandsons and Genèves in Western Switzerland. Then there were the powerful ecclesiastics like the Abbots of St Gallen, Pfäfers, Dissentis, Zurich, Romainmôtier, St Maurice, Rheinau, Einsiedeln, Muri, Schaffhausen, Engelberg and Wettingen, the Bishops of Basle, Constance, Chur, Sion, Lausanne and Geneva. But none of these could rival the importance of the noble house issuing from the Rheinfeldens and descending through the Zähringens, Lenzburgs and Kiburgs, to Rudolph of Habsburg in the twelfth century. Rudolph's territorial possessions were without equal in the land, and they were to find their only check in the ambition of certain towns and the resistance of some peasant communities.

It is often, and wrongly, supposed that the Middle Ages was a period of apathy for the population at large, disturbed only by the feuding of noble families. Nothing could be further from the truth. It was in fact a time of seething activity on the moral, political, economic and even intellectual fronts.

The Middle Ages was the era of great monastic houses, when St Gallen produced its celebrated artists and scholars, men like Ratpert, Notker, Tutilo, and the Ekkehard family. It was the age of great cathedrals, notably those of Basle and Zurich. These magnificent buildings testify to the collective enterprise of the city burgesses, and bespeak their solidarity, wealth and powers of organization as much as their religious faith. It was the age of the great fairs, of rapidly expanding trade which brought together merchants from different countries and forged links between the various cities, thereby laying the foundations for the emancipation of the cities as well as the formation of states. Above all, it was the age of the Crusades, the time of St Louis, Richard the Lionheart and Philippe le Bel, the astonishing period when a prophecy of St Bernard's was enough to set a mighty army of knights, burgesses and men-at-arms marching for the East. It is hard for us nowadays to conceive what the Crusades meant to Europe at that time, the immense upheaval they caused and the great changes they wrought in men's customs and ideas.

It is impossible to understand the birth of the Swiss Confederation properly unless one realizes that it was one of the distant consequences of the Crusades.

Chapter II

The First Alliance
(1218-1291)

All the great events of history can be attributed to both distant and immediate causes. The birth of the Swiss Confederation cannot be explained solely in terms of the situation of the forest cantons any more than it can be explained solely in terms of the decay of feudalism. General causes can pave the way for events but it is immediate ones which precipitate them.

By the thirteenth century, feudalism, which had been in existence for at least four hundred years, was an ageing institution. Although things evolved slowly during the Middle Ages, enough time had passed for the feudal system to undergo profound changes. The needs which had given birth to it were forgotten while its abuses, arising gradually over the years, were growing worse. Feudalism in fact no longer answered its original purpose, nor rendered its original services. The burdens it imposed on the people, on the other hand, were becoming heavier to bear, and some of them had become intolerable.

Feudalism, in the beginning, had been essentially a response to the need of security. The Emperor, source of all temporal power, appointed certain officials to maintain order throughout his territories; hence the right to bear arms, build strongholds, administer justice and maintain law and order, all functions peculiar to the order of chivalry.

Gradually the spirit of feudal institutions changed. Their original purpose was overlaid by the notion of privilege. Responsibilities became hereditary, the number of overlords multiplied and as happens with all decaying aristocracies, the ranks of chivalry closed and became exclusive. Formerly, free men who bore arms and tilled the land were on an equal footing with the barons. They married their daughters, moving easily between one class and the other and acting as links between castle and domain.

Developments in military science deprived the free men, who

made up the infantry, of their chief function. Once exempt from military service nothing remained to distinguish them from the serfs; the fiction whereby they were equal to the barons, which had made intermarriage possible, gradually faded from men's minds. A new class arose, of nobles with serf origins, a ministerial class analogous to the Roman freed-men, and these rapidly gained ascendancy over the free men. This led to mutual antipathy. The free men left the countryside, to which they were not bound like the serfs, for the towns in ever increasing numbers. Factories sprang up, trade prospered, the bourgeoisie grew rich. And all this was happening at precisely the time when the baronial class was becoming impoverished as a result of extravagance and the division of inherited lands.

Feudal privileges were no longer seen in the context of social services but had acquired the character of acknowledged rights. As a result of division of inheritance, sales, dowries, pledges and other mutations, these rights, instead of remaining in the hands of one family over a considerable length of time, became extremely mobile. The emotional tie between serf and overlord, between the lord and the populace whose labours he safeguarded from the fastness of his keep, grew steadily weaker. The serfs no longer knew their lord; the nobles no longer shared in their vassals' lives. Absenteeism, which, together with exclusiveness, is the ruling vice of a moribund aristocracy, was rife in the feudal world. The old bonds of loyalty weakened and disappeared.

This process was hardened by the fact that the barons, now both poorer and more numerous, no longer kept the peace throughout their lands but instead became a source of trouble and danger along the highways. As the traffic thickened along these roads the baron became the terror of the merchant. His privileges, which had been the price for performing a service, seemed exorbitant now that that service was no longer performed.

From this time on the middle class and peasantry struggled to free themselves from this feudal class, whose usefulness was no longer apparent, but whose misdeeds were so evident. They called on the powerful nobles to help them in this struggle against lesser dynasties of tyrannical and unscrupulous barons. In this way, various important dynasties were founded, in the course of the thirteenth century, with the assistance of townspeople and peasantry, some of which survive to this day.

The Crusades speeded up this process. They impoverished the barons, who spent recklessly on equipment for themselves and their men-at-arms, and aggravated absenteeism and the instability of feudal land ownership. They opened up new markets for trade. Finally, and most importantly, they gave new horizons to the peoples of Europe and introduced new ideas to the West.

This, then, was the state of society in the thirteenth century. Throughout this time the whole of Europe was seething with political activity. This was in fact the first of Europe's great revolutionary centuries. The move towards emancipation began in Italy. As early as 1183 Frederick Barbarossa was forced to recognize the existence of the Lombard free cities at the Treaty of Constancia. In 1215 Magna Carta was promulgated in England. In Germany, Cologne, Mainz, Strasbourg, Speyer, Worms, Nuremberg, Ulm, Augsburg, achieved independence one by one; the Hanseatic States were formed in 1241.

The movement towards communal emancipation, which convulsed Italy, Germany, and Flanders, was bound to influence events in Switzerland, as it lay directly on the road between Italy and Flanders. Basle won its franchise in 1264, St Gallen in 1272, and Solothurn in 1280.

The exact date of the opening of the St Gothard route is not known for certain. For many centuries, the Trou d'Uri and the Schöllenen had remained impassable. In Roman times the Upper Valais was part of the Rhaetian Alps, and it was the people of the Upper Valais who colonized the Rhine valley and the Vorarlberg. It was probably towards the end of the twelfth century that a bridge over the Reuss was built, at Schöllenen, but it certainly was not till the first or second quarter of the thirteenth century that this route acquired any real commercial importance. At all events, towards 1230 a significant proportion of the population of Uri was turning from agriculture to transport as a means of livelihood, and the same held true of the Levant valley.

This would perhaps explain the fact that the high Reuss valley should have been among the first to undergo Italian influences; the development of city communes was widespread at this time throughout Northern Italy and particularly in the Levant.

Some writers have argued against these influences and by the same token denied the importance of the opening of the

Gotthard highway for the founding of the Swiss Confederation.

Two points, however, must be made clear. The question of Italian influence is in reality a secondary one. It may be that the example followed unconsciously by the forest cantons came from the North rather than the South; it is likely that the people of Uri were following no particular example and that similar causes tended to have similar results in Switzerland, as elsewhere. Beside the question, however, of why the Swiss decided to free themselves, is the far more important one of how they managed to do so successfully. Free towns were springing up all over Italy and Upper Germany at this time with the purpose of establishing and defending their rights against the barons; they were to be found throughout Ossola, the Levant, Mendrisotto, Val Benio, at Chiavenna and Como. Thus the forest cantons had no monopoly of the concept. But how many of those free towns exist today? The originality of the Swiss lay not so much in making the pact but in making it for eternity—and in making it endure. And this they owe in good measure to the St Gotthard pass and its commercial importance.

The St Gotthard was not of course the only pass from Germany into Italy in use during the Middle Ages; the Brenner and Julier passes were better known and more frequented. As a result, however, of the active trading between the free towns of Lombardy and Germany it soon gained considerable economic importance. In addition to this the Emperors came to place a high value on its possession for political reasons. The Hohenstaufens' policies were dominated by their Italian ambitions; to be severed from Italy, or for the communication route between Germany and Italy to fall into enemy hands, would have been a great loss for them and even—because of their frequent visits to this part of the Alps—a considerable danger.

There were not many of these Alpine routes and none was entirely safe for them. With the incessant feuding between Guelfs and Ghibellines going on in all the Italian towns, with the attendant plots, intrigues, conspiracies and betrayals, the better routes were open to the threat of sudden attack. The Emperors had entrusted the Rhaetian passes to the Bishops of Chur, and those of the Valais to the Bishops of Sion, only to suffer the disappointment of seeing these ecclesiastical vassals go over to the enemy. They were obliged to keep the entrances to these passes under their own authority, turning them into

Imperial free ways. This was their policy with regard to the people of Uri, who guarded the St Gotthard.

The Uri region belonged, by virtue of a gift made by Louis the German in 853, to the Fraumünster monastery at Zurich. This situation suited the inhabitants. Ecclesiastical serfs were a privileged class during the Middle Ages, scarcely distinguishable from free men. The Uri region constituted a single 'rural association' (*Markgenossenschaft*) under the terms of the old German law. All the valley's inhabitants, whatever their social position, were members of this association with the responsibility of administering the 'allmend'. The association would meet in a general assembly; it elected its own leaders and used a seal emblazoned with a bull's head. This association united the whole valley, and gave it a political structure. The functions of the Markgenossenschaft might be purely economic but there was nothing to prevent them expanding from one day to the next and changing their character with ease.

Feudal common law was based on a very clear distinction between the rights of the ruler and his obligations to those under him. A monastery which ruled a certain region did not administer the law throughout that region. It merely collected the taxes and dues and left the duty of administering the law to a noble, the 'protector'. The 'protector' was the representative of the judiciary. In Uri the obligation to protect belonged to the Emperor, who delegated it personally to an imperial 'protector', in exchange for other feudal rights. The complexity of these arrangements, and the constant confusion during the Middle Ages between the notions of common and private law is quite bewildering to modern minds, accustomed to consistency.

On the death of Berchthold V of Zähringen, the Imperial Protector in Uri, in 1218, the obligation to protect was pledged by the Emperor—against what dues we do not know—to Count Rudolph the Elder of Habsburg, which proves that Frederick II either had no suspicion of the importance of the St Gotthard pass at this time, or that he had no reason to fear the Habsburgs, a loyal and unassuming family. He was probably influenced by both considerations.

This state of affairs, however, did not last long. The Habsburgs' power increased. They became, together with the Kiburgs—a house which soon became extinct—the most powerful family between the Alps, the Rhine and the Jura.

As they grew more powerful their loyalty to the Emperor diminished. It was already possible to foresee the time when Rudolph the Elder's successor would go over to the enemy camp.

Meanwhile the feud between Emperor and Pope, which seemed to have subsided in 1218, flared up again in 1228. In 1229 Frederick II was excommunicated. Como, the town commanding the southern access to the St Gotthard pass, via Bellinzona and the Levant, was now in papal hands. Had Frederick II allowed the Habsburgs to keep control of the Uri region he would have run the risk of finding the St Gotthard closed to him and its keys in Guelph hands.

The St Gotthard's importance was growing with every year that passed and it carried a huge volume of traffic. So much so, in fact, that the local people had little trouble in collecting together enough money to buy back those rights which the Emperor had pledged to the Habsburgs. These rights would have gradually led to Habsburg rule in the area. So long as the necessary money was available, however, there was nothing to stop the people buying them back.

Thus, on 26 May 1231, the people of Uri obtained a charter from King Henry VII, who administered the Empire on behalf of his father Frederick II, which stated that they had purchased the valley from the Habsburgs with their own money. Affixed to the charter was the imperial seal ordering it to be put into immediate effect. This charter is the foundation-stone of the Confederation. All the other franchises were based on this one.

Freedom is contagious. It was not long before the joyful emancipation of the people of Uri had repercussions among their neighbours of Schwytz.

Individually speaking, the Schwytzois had started off on a rather better footing than the Uranese. Most of them were free men, though this was not now the privilege it had once seemed. The valley itself, however, was in a less fortunate position than the Uri valley because it was not under direct Imperial rule. Various feudal lords had established themselves there over the years, and royal and seigneurial rights overlapped and intermingled in what strikes the modern eye as an almost impenetrable tangle. However, by the thirteenth century, all these various rights had come, by way of inheritance, into the hands of the Count of Habsburg.

The men of the Schwytz valley, like those of Uri, formed one corporation with its 'allmend', assemblies and leaders. The valley was densely populated—with as many inhabitants in the Middle Ages as there are now—and had difficulty in feeding all its inhabitants. The Schwytzois had made several attempts to encroach on the neighbouring lands belonging to the Convent of Einsiedeln, but had been prevented from doing so by the Habsburgs, protectors of the convent. A good number of the Schwytzois had been forced to emigrate. Being free men, and consequently men-at-arms, they had taken service abroad, fighting for the Pope or the Emperor. They brought back with them new notions of autonomy, freedom, independence. The corporation's assemblies, convoked to take economic action, were beginning to simmer with new political ideas. The forest cantons' love of independence has been attributed to their remoteness from the rest of the world, but it was precisely when they stopped being so cut off that the move towards independence began.

The Emperor was excommunicated in 1239. The following year Count Rudolph the Silent, heir to Rudolph the Elder, and uncle of the future Emperor Rudolph, suddenly went over to the Pope's side. As ruler of Schwytz and Unterwald, he forbade the Emperor access to the St Gotthard. The Emperor on the other hand, could stop the passage of grain needed to feed the valley. The situation was both a threat and a golden opportunity for the Schwytz. They did not waste a moment. A delegation set off at top speed to Faenza, which the Emperor Frederick II was besieging, to assure him of their unshakeable loyalty. The Emperor's response was to take the Schwytz valley under his own and the Empire's special protection.

The Faenza Charter (December 1240) is not as clear cut, juridically speaking, as its predecessor of May 1231. It did not establish direct Imperial control over Schwytz because this would have been a breach of feudal custom on the part of the Emperor, who had no rights to the region. However, the people of Schwytz paid no heed to these subtleties. They believed in the Emperor's promise. And when this was revoked by Rudolph of Habsburg in 1274, the population believed themselves to be the victims of malpractice.

The 1231 Charter gave the independence movement legal foundations. The Act of 1240 gave it a political character. The request made by the people of Uri was not directed against the Count of Habsburg, since it consisted of a straightforward repurchase in conformity with feudal law. The Schwytz move, on the other hand, had a revolutionary aspect—it was undertaken in opposition to the feudal lord, though it remained loyal to the Emperor. The immutable policy of the old Confederation, which was to back the Emperor against the feudal lord, or the distant power against the nearer one, dates from this period of Swiss history.

The immediate effect of the Faenza Charter was to unleash trouble throughout the forest cantons. There were risings in Schwytz and Sarnen—united for the first time in a common purpose—against the Count of Habsburg-Laufenburg in 1240, and again in 1241. As the Count had gone over to the Emperor's side again, in August 1241, on the death of Pope Gregory IX, this revolt proved abortive. The subjects of Murback Abbey, who supported the Pope, then came out in revolt at Lucerne and Nidwald. They even received help from the people of Uri, who favoured the papal cause at that time because Como and Lucerne, the two exits of the St Gotthard, were temporarily in Guelph hands. The forest cantons, in short were, deeply divided among themselves. So their first alliance could not possibly have occurred, as was long held to be the case, at this time. It can only have taken place after the second Schwytz and Sarnen revolt against the Habsburgs, in 1247.

The great interregnum began in 1254. The House of Hohenstaufen was extinct. The quarrel with the Pope died down. Authority everywhere was relaxed. Insecurity grew and the parties came closer together.

The regions, like Uri, which were under direct Imperial rule made the most of this Emperor-less time—*die schreckliche kaiserlose Zeit*—to enjoy what was in effect total autonomy.

Meanwhile, the Habsburgs were losing ground. Rudolph died in 1249. His two sons were ineffectual rulers, and thanks to the general weakening of authority, their subjects, the people of Schwytz and Unterwald, began acquiring independent habits, creating local customs. They soon built up a pleasant new freedom of action for themselves, the 'ancient liberties' which would be mentioned in the future alliance. The collective thinking which would give rise to the Confederation twenty years later, was moulded during this interregnum period, between 1250 and 1270.

In 1273 everything suddenly changed. Eberhard of Habsburg-Laufenburg, who was childless, sold all his rights in Schwytz, Unterwald, Zug, Lucerne and Aargau to his cousin

Rudolph III, of the senior branch of the family. Almost immediately, this same Rudolph of Habsburg was elected Emperor, under the title of Rudolph I.

This was one of the most important events in Swiss history. For the first time the three forest cantons found themselves united under one leader, and for the first time too Imperial power and feudal rights were in the same hands. It was many centuries since the forest cantons had known what it was to have such a strong ruler, and they had never been part of a great kingdom such as Rudolph's was to become when the defeat and then the death of the King of Bohemia, in 1278 and 1282, brought him immense acquisitions in Austria.

At first the three valleys received the news of Rudolph's election joyfully. As the staunch leader of the Ghibelline party in the country he was personally popular. In 1257 he had been invited to arbitrate in the long-standing feud between Izzelins and Grubas at Schächental, a proof of the trust in which he was held. He hastened to pay formal recognition to the rights of the people of Uri. And the fact that Imperial and feudal power were in the same hands augured well for the Schwytzois and the people of Unterwald, since it placed them under direct Imperial rule. Though he refused to recognize or confirm the Faenza Charter, Rudolph gave the Schwytzois his solemn assurance in 1281 that they would be brought to justice only before him, his sons or their own *Landammänner*. This was one of the privileges which people in the Middle Ages valued most highly since it guaranteed them a fair hearing in law and autonomy at one and the same time.

Unfortunately this promise could not be, and was not, fulfilled. Rudolph ruled over half of Europe and he did not have time to come and dispense justice beneath the lime tree of Altdorf. As for his sons, the eldest, Albert, was made Duke and then Prince of Austria, the second died in 1281, and the youngest was born in 1271. Little by little, through force of circumstances, the forest cantons found themselves invaded by functionaries in direct violation of the repeated Imperial promises of 1231, 1240, and 1281. Some of these functionaries, or bailiffs, were not even free men by birth, and were thus their social inferiors. In spite of charters, privileges and long-established custom, the situation of the three valleys was becoming identical—the Imperial valley of Uri and the free men of Schwytz were under the same administration as the lay and ecclesiastical serfs of Unterwald. The same bailiffs ruled the valleys, in the name of the Emperor here and in the name of the Count there. Furthermore, the burden of taxation was doubled and then tripled during Rudolph's reign to meet the cost of distant wars and the incessant buying up of feudal rights. Nothing makes foreign functionaries more unpopular than heavy taxation. Last, and perhaps worst of all, a toll-system was installed at the St Gotthard pass, a direct threat to the grain imports needed to feed the valleys.

Throughout this time the Habsburgs, their appetite whetted by devouring so much land, continued to expand their sway. In 1283 the family acquired rights in the Urseren valley, in 1285 in Glarus and Einsiedeln, in 1291 in the Convent of Murbach at Lucerne and in Unterwald. The forest cantons felt themselves hemmed in, shut off, oppressed on all sides by a great lord whom they were beginning to think of as an enemy.

It was the combination of all these factors which led to the conspiracy which gave birth to the first federal Pact. In 1289 the Schwytzois made a last attempt to win direct Imperial rule for themselves. They sent a troop of 1,500 men to help the Emperor in the siege of Besançon. The attempt failed. Rudolph thanked them warmly and conferred upon them the honour of bearing the Imperial standard, a red cross on a white ground, which was soon to become the symbol of Swiss liberty. But the Schwytzois did not want symbols, they wanted a reality. When the oath of loyalty was sworn at Grütli, and when, in the course of the following year, revolt and uprisings broke out throughout the forest cantons, details of which remain imprinted on popular memory till this day, it was the men of Schwytz, and the old Landammann Stauffacher in particular, who took charge.

For years, historical criticism, misled by a few wrong dates and implausible facts, has tended to view such events as the oath of Grütli, the seizing of the castles and the incident between the bailiffs and William Tell as pure legend. However, recent work shows that these tales contain a high degree of probability, and they enable us to reconstruct the sequence of events infinitely better than dry nineteenth-century logic ever succeeded in doing.

The 1291 Pact disappeared from the records for a long time. Historians did not learn of its existence till the end of the eighteenth century. By this time, popular tradition, which set the Oath of Grütli and the other events of the liberation of the forest cantons in 1307, was so firmly entrenched that at first no one paid any attention to a document which seemed to contradict the accepted facts. Later, when historians recognized the significance of the 1291 Federal Pact they were inclined to dismiss the traditional version wholesale as 'legend'. Professor Karl Meyer of Zurich University was the first to attempt, to our knowledge, a synthesis of the two versions, an attempt in which he has been largely successful. Verisimilitude, in the historian's view, is not sufficient proof. On the other hand, Professor Meyer's theory is a strikingly plausible one even while it cannot be conclusively proved to be correct.

Nothing was so contrary to the medieval way of looking at things as novelty. The law was immutable and could only be changed by common consent of rulers and subjects. Looked at from this angle the period was the most democratic in history. However, the presence of bailiffs in the valleys was contrary to established custom, and hence to the law. In the eyes of the people the exorbitant taxes they levied and the sentences they passed were nullified.

The men who met secretly in the meadow at Grütli—and whose oath still lives in the noble name of 'confederates' which the Swiss have chosen for themselves—made a vow among themselves that they would no longer accept a judge who was either a foreigner or who had bought his position. We know that the symbol of the law-court at this period was a hat on a pole. What could be more natural than that the conflict between the bailiffs and conspirators should have broken out on this very occasion?

It hardly matters whether Gessler was really called Conrad of Tillendort, or that Tell is only a nickname. The important thing is that an Austrian bailiff should have been killed by a man from the Uri valley. This explains why, on 19 February 1291, Rudolph should have been moved, without apparent reason, to renew the promise made to his subjects ten years earlier, and subsequently broken, that he would never again send them judges who were not free men. It was an intolerable humiliation for free men in the Middle Ages to have judgement passed on them by men who were not their equals.

This is how all revolutions begin, with the isolated actions of a few individuals. The forest cantons were exceptionally lucky—deservedly so, one might add—in having leaders at hand in this decisive stage in their history who had been trained for their political task in the management of the corporation's affairs, administration of justice, and discussion of community interests, as in the case of Glaris and Einsiedeln.

Rudolph Stauffacher had been *Landammann* several times at Schwytz. The fact that his name disappears from the public registers after 1281 suggests that he retired in the face of crushing opposition. Werner von Attinghausen was a nobleman from Uri, Fürst a rich landowner from the Schaechental. The Silenen, Hunnos, Ab Ibergs, all those who swore the oath at Grütli were undoubtedly the leaders of their people, which explains why the people did not hesitate to follow them when the time came. And if the people of Unterwald played only a minor role in this first declaration of independence it is merely because they had no corporation, or *allmend*, and no unity, and therefore were without leaders.

There is a strongly personal air about this revolt. It was the work of a few forceful personalities—a point tradition was quick to seize upon.

Rudolph of Habsburg died at Speyer, on 15 July 1291. A fortnight later, by which time the news had scarcely reached the valleys, the Pact which had been secretly sworn at night on the shores of the lake had already been transformed into an official alliance, publicly signed and sealed at the beginning of August. It was vital to take advantage of this interval of interregnum.

There has always been much debate as to whether or not the Pact of August 1291 had a revolutionary character. The question has received different answers according to the spirit of the times. In the eighteenth century, and under the Restoration, the liberation of the forest cantons was seen as the most romantic of revolutions. On the other hand, the nineteenth century interpreted it as the action of loyal subjects who respected law and custom and were inspired by a passion for conservatism. A recent author has even gone so far as to assert that the Pact of 1 August was directly inspired by the Habsburgs themselves and drawn up in their Chancellery.

In the end all this is merely a semantic debate. Taken on its own, the alliance of three communities, of which one at least had no autonomy whatsoever, was something unheard of and therefore revolutionary. This alliance was certainly contrary to existing law as far as the people of Nidwald were concerned, though not for the people of Uri. As for the Schwytz, it did not conflict with their allegiance to the Emperor, but it did conflict with their allegiance to the Habsburgs.

Similar distinctions need to be made with regard to the contents of the Pact. Certain clauses of a judicial nature show a markedly conservative tendency, their aim being to uphold certain customs and re-affirm old privileges. But these privileges were not all undisputed. The challenging spirit is there beneath all the apparent faithfulness to tradition. Finally, there are other clauses, like the one which forbids all appeal to the seigneurial judge, which break with tradition, their aim being radically to limit feudal rights and to replace them by a system of justice administered by the elected *Landammann.* Cunningly framed, these are essentially political and revolutionary clauses.

This tendency can be seen from the fact that the plot had to be kept secret while the Emperor lived. It shows up still more clearly in the policy subsequently adopted by the Waldstaetten. Till this time the Swiss, although fundamentally in favour of the Empire, had not displayed any radical resistance to the Habsburgs. After 1 August 1291, all this was changed. The century which followed was taken up with a life and death struggle for independence against the House of Habsburg.

Chapter III

The Growth of Freedom
(1291-1394)

This was a time of confused ambitions. There was such a rash of town enfranchisements, rebellions and ephemeral alliances that the 1 August Pact passed unperceived. After it had been proclaimed, nothing happened. Rudolph's son, Albert of Austria, was busy with the election of the new Emperor and paid no attention to it.

The forest cantons were the only ones to act upon it. On 16 October 1291 they sent the *Landammänner* of Schwytz and Uri, Conrad Ab Iberg and Arnold de Silenen, to Zurich to enrol them in the great coalition formed shortly after Emperor Rudolph's death by the towns of Zurich and Berne, the Bishop of Constancia, the Abbot of St Gallen, the Count of Savoy, the Countess of Rapperswill and a great many lords from Swabia. This alliance met with defeat on the battlefield (Winterthur, 12 April 1292) but its policies were those of the forest cantons throughout the fourteenth century, and it became the nucleus for that other coalition which has been inaccurately christened the Confederation of the Eight Cantons.

The most characteristic feature of the forest cantons' policy during this decisive period of Swiss history was its consistency and tenacity. Many of their allies see-sawed successfully in their allegiances, Zurich and Berne in particular. But the forest cantons held fast to one simple, almost down-to-earth idea, and this idea proved their salvation. Rather, they had only one enemy, and it was this that saved them.

Though the interests they represented were local and limited, the forest cantons saw their history as dominated by the vicissitudes of the Imperial throne. Every time Imperial power came, directly or indirectly, into Habsburg hands—during the first years of Adolph of Nassau's reign (1292–1298) under Albert of Austria (1298–1308), and at the end of Henry VII's reign (1308–1313), the forest cantons stayed buried in their valleys, doing nothing to remind the great ones of the world of their existence. But each time the Habsburgs found themselves in opposition to the Emperors, the forest cantons hurried to the latter to extract confirmation or extensions of their franchise.

Thus Emperor Adolph confirmed the Imperial mandate over the Schwytzois and the people of Uri on 30 November 1297; Henry VII accorded the same favour to the people of Unterwald on 3 June 1309, just after the assassination of Albert I by his nephew; and on 17 July 1315, on the eve of the Battle of Morgarten, Emperor Louis of Bavaria lifted the ban imposed on the forest cantons by his rival, Frederick the Handsome.

The first big quarrel between the forest cantons and the Habsburgs did not break out over a clearly defined point of civil law (*droit public*) however, but over a disputed boundary wall. As we have already mentioned, the boundaries between Schwytz territory and the lands of the Convent of Einsiedeln were never exactly defined and this led to constant conflict during the thirteenth century. These disputes grew more acrimonious as time passed, for a variety of reasons. One of these, no doubt, was that the Schwytzois felt themselves in a stronger position now they had the support of their Confederates behind them. Another was the fact that the convent was now under the direct protection of the Habsburg family. But the principal reason must certainly have been the tariff war waged by Habsburg agents against the forest cantons on the Lake of Lucerne. By hindering the flow of food imports into the valleys, this tariff system more or less forced their inhabitants to come up for air in another direction.

A new raid by the Schwytzois on Einsiedeln, bolder and more challenging than the earlier ones, finally snapped the Habsburgs' patience. Convinced as they were of their own strength and rights they had tolerated the forest cantons' provocative behaviour for almost twenty-five years, suffering them to make friends with their enemies, to plot against them whenever the chance arose, and even publicly to support the murderers of Emperor Albert I in 1308.

Seen from our own historical perspective, and knowing the outcome of the Battle of Morgarten and its consequences, this battle strikes us as a war between one State and another. But this is not how it appeared to Duke Leopold of Austria as he rode out of Zug at the head of his knights in the morning of 15 November 1315, on his way to Schwytz by way of the eastern shores of Lake Aegeri. In his eyes the Schwytz were subjects in revolt and he was leading a punitive expedition against them.

Unfortunately for him the expedition was disastrous. The Battle of Morgarten, memory of which is very much alive although we do not know its precise location, threw all the knighthood of Upper Germany into mourning. In one stroke, the forest cantons passed from obscurity to recognition as a power in the world. The rebellion became a revolution; the alliance became a State. It was the first time a power other than the Empire had risen up against the Habsburgs. The very fact of its existence would serve to crystallize opposition, even to create it where necessary; it would be the centre of every alliance and the Habsburgs would have to reckon with it. A century later there was nothing left of the Habsburg possessions between the Rhine and the Alps, and this is due to the Battle of Morgarten.

The victory had immediate consequences. The first, and most important, was to strengthen the bonds uniting the forest cantons. Their triumph, they felt, had brought them more danger than strength. On 9 December 1315, they swore a new alliance. It replaced the 1291 Pact, which deserves to be described as the foundation-stone of the Confederation, erasing it from men's memories for almost five centuries. The Brunnen Pact, for the most part a translation into German of the chief clauses of the 1291 Pact, introduces one new and highly important clause—the prohibition of separate alliances. This clause was the one which kept the forest cantons united in difficult times, assured their collaboration and guaranteed that they would always remain, despite changing fortunes and internal divisions, the nucleus and heart of the Confederation.

Success came to the rescue of the victors. Emperor Louis of Bavaria had always avoided declaring himself wholeheartedly on the side of the forest cantons. But on 26 March 1316, he declared the Dukes of Austria to have forfeited all the domains, property and rights they owned in the three valleys and on 29 March he confirmed the letters patent of 1240, 1297 and 1309, by which the forest cantons had acquired direct Imperial rule.

The position of the three valleys in law was clearly defined from this time on. It was based on an Imperial Act which would never be challenged. The Habsburgs themselves gave it implicit recognition when they signed an armistice on 19 July 1318, which was to be renewed many times in the years to come.

In their eyes the war had been a police operation. But the peace rested, fairly and squarely, upon a treaty between State and State.

As invariably occurs in the wake of revolution, the political liberation of the valleys led to profound changes in the social structure of the population. The Charter of 26 March 1316 confers upon all free men the privilege of direct appeal to the Emperor. Seven years later serfdom was abolished and all the inhabitants of the valleys became free men. Thus the forest cantons managed to introduce a reform, painlessly, in the early years of the fourteenth century, which their neighbours would not achieve for many centuries yet and then only at the cost of terrible struggles.

The results of the Battle of Morgarten were not confined to the relations between the forest cantons and the Habsburgs. They manifested themselves in their dealings with the Emperor too. Till now the Emperor had been the sole power capable of opposing the Habsburgs. This was no longer the case. Henceforth the adversaries of the Dukes of Austria were to turn to the forest cantons: Berne and Glarus, in 1323, Zurich and the Rhine towns in 1327 and 1329, and finally, Lucerne, in 1332. The forest cantons gained new assurance in their dealings with the Emperor. Without disputing his sovereignty they nevertheless began to circumscribe it. The reservations they made on swearing the oath to Count Jean of Arberg on 7 October 1323 are characteristic. They would have seemed unthinkable before Morgarten. One cannot help wondering whether it was only the Habsburgs who suffered defeat, or whether this mighty blow did not strike at the roots of Imperial power in Switzerland at the same time.

Secure as their position might be in law and in fact, the forest cantons remained economically vulnerable so long as their natural centre, Lucerne, was in the hands of their foes.

A rural community cannot survive or prosper without a market where it can sell its produce. Every town has been founded in answer to this need. Since the opening of the St Gotthard pass, Lucerne had become the essential trading centre for traffic entering and leaving through the pass. Throughout the thirteenth century, Lucerne was in close alliance with the valleys and generally supported them in their struggles. The Habsburgs had acquired the rights of the Monastery of Murbach over Lucerne and in 1291 the burgesses of that town joined in the great alliance which followed Emperor Rudolph's death. After its defeat, however, the old order was re-established. While the forest cantons were adopting an increasingly aggressive attitude towards the Habsburgs, the latter's power over the town steadily grew. Lucerne market was closed to the produce of the valleys on several occasions, notably in 1314, on the eve of the Battle of Morgarten.

This was an intolerable situation for the forest cantons. It meant that the lake, which was essential to their communication system, was unsafe for them. They had already been obliged to fortify the shores at several points. The Habsburgs, who controlled the Lucerne market and owned navigation rights on the lake, were in a position to paralyse food imports into the valleys at any moment and shut off the traffic through the St Gotthard.

However, the burgesses of Lucerne suffered just as grievously. The 1314 tariff war, which closed down their market for many long months, had ruined them. One party among them sympathized with the forest cantons in their struggle against the Habsburgs. This was the democratic party, supported by the town guilds which existed in most of the free towns at this period. In 1327 the forest cantons formed a new anti-Habsburg alliance with Berne and Zurich, and a new tariff war seemed imminent. At this point the burgesses of Lucerne entered into a conspiracy against the ducal civil servants (28 January 1328). On 21 October 1330, shortly after the Peace of Haguenau had strengthened the Habsburgs' position, the conspiracy finally won the support of the majority of Lucerne's citizens. It came out into the open and seized control of the town.

This move soon produced the results the forest cantons had been waiting for. The Lucerne revolt, directed against the Habsburgs, was forced to seek outside support. The natural place to find it was in Schwytz, Uri and Unterwald. On 7 November 1332, Lucerne entered into a perpetual alliance with the valleys, modelled on the Brunnen Pact. Once the independent towns of Gersau, Weggis and Vitznau had joined the alliance, the Lake of Lucerne was truly a lake of the Four Cantons as its French and German names imply (Lac des Quatre-Cantons and Vierwaldstätte See), a hyphen instead of a barrier and a bond cementing the new alliance.

This event, which was one of cardinal importance to the

Swiss, is largely due to the bold policy pursued by the *Landammann* of Uri. Hans von Attinghausen, son of one of the founders of the Confederation, reigned—the word is not too strong—over Uri from 1330 till 1356. His chief ambition was to make the St Gotthard into a great highway for traffic from distant lands, but to make this possible he had first to ensure the safety of both entrances to the pass. With this in mind he negotiated a treaty with the Republic of Como, mistress of the Levant, on 12 August 1331, and an alliance with Lucerne on 7 November 1332.

It is inaccurate to speak of Lucerne's entering the Confederation, as is often done. There was no Confederation at that time. The people of Lucerne would have been deeply astonished—as would the people of Berne, and Zurich twenty years later—if they had been told that they were henceforth part of a new State. All they were interested in was forming a new alliance—the latest in a long line of similar pacts. They did not know, and probably did not even stop to think, whether this alliance would be temporary or enduring. Their one aim was to make sure that help would be forthcoming against a threatening overlord, and guarantee the success of their fairs.

But man's ability to see into the future is limited. Though the allies who entered into the 1332 Pact had only limited aims in mind, they achieved far-reaching results. Hitherto, the forest cantons' alliance had been founded on a simple community of interests, without wider horizons or a world view. Had it kept this character it would have fallen easy prey to conquest, like the similar alliances formed at around the same time in the Levant and Ossola.

However, by introducing an urban element into the alliance, Lucerne entirely changed its character, paving the way for the entry of powerful cities like Berne and Zurich, enlarging its scope, and giving it the necessary solidity to weather the centuries.

There is a really striking parallel between the circumstances which led to Lucerne's alliance with the forest cantons in 1332, and those which induced Zurich to take a similar step twenty years later.

The townspeople of Zurich, like those of Lucerne and most other free towns of this period, were divided by a feud between the ruling families and the artisans. With the growth of trade and exchange, and the development of industry, the guilds had acquired wealth, power and efficiency out of all proportion to their influence in the State. As often happens, it was a member of the ruling families who because the leader of the malcontents. In 1336, he succeeded in overthrowing the aristocracy and drawing up a constitution modelled on the Strasbourg one of 1334, which, while apparently democratic, ensured that real power remained with the *Bürgermeister*.

The members of the old city administration left Zurich. As they had close ties of blood and self-interest with the neighbouring nobility they had little difficulty in persuading the latter to attack the town. Zurich found itself involved in a war which was to drag on for thirty years, with brief periods of respite, and absorb all its strength and resources.

Henceforth Rudolph Brun was obsessed with one idea—he must save the town's democratic constitution and to do this he needed allies. A choice offered itself. He could form an alliance with the Swabian towns, the forest cantons, or with Austria. He explored all three possibilities one after the other, and even, at times, all three at once. But the Swiss alliance was the only one which endured: not by chance, but because the Swiss alone were able to meet the real political and economic requirements of the situation.

After all, though they might enter into fleeting relations (notably in 1339) with Southern Germany, it was not to be expected that Zurich, with its corporative administration, would find solid support among this great league composed of rival towns and nobles sympathetic to their enemies. Austria was equally undependable, because Austria was overlord of most of the feudal states with which Zurich was at war. Clearly, the natural ally for Zurich, with her commercial interests, was the forest cantons.

Though Lucerne was the trade centre closest to the St Gotthard entrance, Zurich was the chief focus for trans-Alpine traffic, the place where it all converged and from which it set out. Lucerne corresponded to Como and Zurich to Milan. This situation still holds true today.

As well as being the chief trading centre, Zurich was also important for its silk industry, whose raw materials were all supplied by the South. It was essential that Zurich's relations with Northern Italy should be kept open. Thus, Zurich's relations with her northern neighbours were based on rivalry, while her relations to the south were founded on mutual commercial interests. This in itself is enough to explain the alliance.

In 1350 a new conspiracy sparked off more fighting between the town and the neighbouring feudal lords. But this time Zurich's enemies enjoyed the support not only of the Habsburgs, but of Emperor Charles IV, who was currently friendly towards the Habsburgs. In his hour of need Brun turned to the forest cantons who were the solid nucleus for all anti-Habsburg alliances. The forest cantons, for their part, were certain that their war with the Dukes of Austria was far from ended, and the Emperor's pro-Habsburg policy caused them great anxiety, so they welcomed the opportunity Brun's approaches offered for strengthening and enlarging the Confederation, and completing the task begun by the alliance with Lucerne. On 1 May 1351, a pact was signed between Zurich, Lucerne and the forest cantons.

This alliance differed from the preceding ones. Its provisions were both more elastic and more precise. On the one hand, Zurich entered into the pact as an equal, an equal with certain claims to superiority. She reserved the right to decide her own foreign policy, and this was soon—Brun's first alliance with Austria took place in 1356—to introduce a troublesome element into the Confederation. But on the other hand the forest cantons were moved, for the first time, to look beyond the narrow horizons of their own valleys. They were not content with mutual guarantees of freedom and possessions: they went further. They set the boundaries within which this mutual help and assistance was to be forthcoming. These boundaries delimited their sphere of interests, and indicated their territorial ambitions for the emergent Confederation, both then and in the future. These ambitions were extensive—the boundary followed the course of the Aar as far as the Rhine, continued upstream along the Rhine to the Thur, where it branched off, and then via Trons in the Grisons mountains, took in Mont Piottino, the Deischberg and finally rejoined the Grimsel. It took in huge territories still quite foreign to the forest cantons but where they were already intending to extend their influence—the Oberland, Aargau and Thurgau, and the Levant. The Zurich alliance is the first Imperialist treaty concluded by the Swiss Confederation.

The first result of the alliance was to involve the forest cantons in Zurich's war with Austria—a war lasting, with a few interruptions, till 1368. During this war the forest cantons made their first conquests: Glarus and Zug.

Unlike Lucerne and Zurich, who joined the alliance of their own free will, and for purely political reasons, Glarus and Zug were conscripted by force of arms, and not without some show of resistance, particularly in the case of Zug. The forest cantons' cunning—a cunning which deserted them in the next century—was to enter into alliances with conquered states instead of simply subduing them. This policy led to the federative shape of Switzerland today. However, these alliances did not last long. The forest cantons themselves abandoned them after a few weeks, after the so-called Peace of Brandenburg (1 September 1352) which was really no more than a truce. It is quite erroneous to set the date of the entry of Glarus and Zug into the Confederation as 1352, because it did not become definitive in Zug's case till 1365 when the forest cantons took advantage of Rudolph's IV's death and his son's minority to renew their attack, and in the case of Glarus, until 1388, before the Battle of Näfels.

However, the 1352 alliances did contain the seed of a new idea which was to prove highly important in the development of federal law; this was the principle of the superiority of towns over the countryside. This idea is not stated explicitly. But it is implicit in the fact that the terms of the alliance were more favourable to Zug than Glarus, in spite of the fact that Glarus had welcomed the Confederates as liberators whereas the people of Zug offered them some resistance.

The preponderance of urban elements in the alliance was accentuated the following year with the Berne Treaty of 6 March 1353.

Berne's history and origins were quite different from Lucerne's and Zurich's. Towns are invariably founded and developed in accordance with certain laws: in answer to the needs of passing traffic, at the crossroads of two major highways, or to exploit the wealth of the surrounding countryside. Berne, however, exists in defiance of all these laws. It was founded in 1191 by Berthold V of Zähringen on a site with many military advantages but few economic ones, on a curve of the Aar river. To begin with it was a colony of knights, but gradually peasants, both free and otherwise, who had been driven from the countryside by hard times, came and settled there. The town's administration remained solidly in the hands of the knights, and as a result the town has tended to follow a rather high-handed policy, even down to the present day.

At a time when townspeople everywhere were obsessed with making money and getting rich, the citizens of Berne had one ambition, which was to acquire land, and subjects with the land. Berne was not so much a free town, in the contemporary sense of the word, as a feudal power. The system of 'outside citizens'—'*Ausbürger*'—associated part of the lesser nobility in the neighbourhood with the growing prosperity of the town. In so doing, however, the Bernese alarmed the great nobles, who sensed a rival and a potential enemy in this bustling, wealthy, rapacious city. When Berne seized the Oberland and Hasli in 1334 Freiburg became the leader of a feudal coalition opposing her. But this coalition was defeated at Laupen on 21 June 1339, and the victory only spurred the town to further acquisitiveness.

The democratizing spirit at work in all the towns at this time made itself felt in Berne, too. In 1350 municipal power passed from the nobles to the burgesses, and it is tempting to explain the alliance with the forest cantons as a consequence of this upheaval, as was the case with Lucerne and Zurich.

The situation here, however, was quite different. Internal changes had no effect on the town's external policy, which remained closely linked with the Habsburgs out of fear of the Count of Savoy. In 1351 and 1352 the Bernese sent more troops against Zurich and it is hard to see why they should have changed their attitude so abruptly, from one year to the next.

In seeking an alliance with the forest cantons the Bernese seem to have been influenced by two considerations. The first was their growing rivalry with Zurich, and their fear that she would become dangerously strong as a result of her Swiss alliance. The second, and most important, was the anxiety which the proximity of their possessions in the Hasli to the free valleys of Unterwald caused the people of Berne. The people of Unterwald had more than once made overtures to their Hasli neighbours across the Brunig. It seems likely that the Bernese, following a policy which is not without historical precedent, tried to avert this danger by making friends with their potential foes, the forest cantons—and in the same stroke neutralizing the people of Unterwald, whom they feared, by invoking the help of the people of Uri and the Schwytzois. The manœuvre, as it turned out, was successful.

This alliance did not have the same significance to the two contracting parties. To the forest cantons it meant a considerable expansion of their sphere of influence in a totally new direction. In their alliances with Lucerne and Zurich they had kept within the limits of organic growth, all along the approaches to the St Gotthard, Berne, on the other hand, was a Burgundian town, whose activities were all orientated westwards, towards Solothurn, Bienne, Neuchâtel and Vaud. The forest cantons must have been deeply convinced of the dangers threatening them to have sought to increase their resources by such a radical extension of their field of action.

As it happened, though they could not have foreseen such a development then, the alliance with Berne completely altered the evolution of the Confederation.

The Bernese probably had no idea that they had just made a decisive move. Their relations with Austria were unchanged to begin with. Proof of this is the fact that the Bernese remained neutral during the war which was to decide the future of the Confederation—the Battle of Sempach—until after victory had been declared.

Since 1350 the struggle with Austria, provoked by the Zurich alliance, had gone on with only brief truces, in 1352, 1355, and 1368. Both sides were convinced of the need to pursue this war, which had proved indecisive so far. The new Duke, Leopold III, who had just succeeded his brother Rudolph IV in Switzerland, had reverted to his ancestors' sticky-fingered habits and the Swabian towns and princes had been forced to enter into a new alliance against him. It was concluded at Constancia, and Berne, Zurich, Zug, Solothurn and Lucerne all became signatories on 21 Feburary 1385.

War was inevitable—since both sides wanted it. With the passing of time the forest cantons had grown used to their new liberties. To their liberties in law, which were still threatened, they had added a good number of actual liberties which had not been legally conferred upon them, but which they were equally tenacious of. In the long run they could not stand the constant threat posed by the ambitions of the neighbouring Dukes of Austria.

The latter, meanwhile, were uneasy about this new power springing up in the midst of their possessions, setting a dangerous example to all their subjects and making the countries concerned increasingly difficult to rule. They could accept all these 'alliances' which did not have the precise or threatening meaning we tend to ascribe to them now. But now the forest cantons were really on the move, while the Habsburgs were bent on invasion, and there was bound to be a collision sooner or later between these two expanding powers.

The people of Lucerne provided a pretext for the war by signing a treaty with the townspeople of Sempach, a Habsburg possession. The pretext was well chosen because it was bound to involve the forest cantons, who had been reluctant to keep to the Treaty of Constancia.

The war which followed was decisive in the relations between Switzerland and Austria on the one hand, and Swabia on the other. It was undoubtedly the great war of independence without which Switzerland's very existence would have been unimaginable.

The Confederates were victorious at Sempach on 9 July 1386, thanks to the legendary heroism of Arnold of Winkelried and the tactical superiority of infantry over cavalry. Duke Leopold III was killed in the battle. The Confederates immediately renewed their 1352 alliance with Glarus. This resulted in a new Austrian expedition determined to bring the people of Glarus back into line. This second campaign ended on 9 April 1388 with the bloody defeat of Näfels, the tactics and vicissitudes of which are reminiscent of Morgarten.

At the same moment the League of Constancia broke up. The richest and most powerful towns, like Nuremberg, left their allies in the lurch at the last moment and these were defeated by the Austrians in two pitched battles, at Doffingen on 24 August and Worms on 6 November. These two battles, which the Swiss seem to have forgotten, had as much impact on the course of Swiss history as Sempach or Näfels. The definitive separation between the Confederation and Swabia dates from this time. The alliance with the Swabian towns had not helped the forest cantons in any way. The defeated towns submitted to their new master. Austria was in a position to consolidate her rule over the countries beyond the Rhine at the very moment when the Seven Year Pact of 1 April 1389, and the Twenty Year Pact of 16 July 1394, put an end—permanently as it turned out—to her rule over the countries between the Rhine and the Alps, though not to her efforts to reconquer them.

After Sempach, as after Morgarten, the Confederates made use of their victory to strengthen the ties uniting them.

This is the period when their alliances began to assume the appearance and form of a Confederation. Their Diets, infrequent to begin with, took place more often. They began to settle questions of private and public law in concert. The 1370 Priests' Charter and the Sempach Covenant, 1393, are framed along the lines of international treaties. Among other things, they succeeded in laying down a unified code of legislature for use in all the cantons. The aims of the Priests' Charter were primarily economic, the protection of traffic along the highroads, always an urgent preoccupation in the Middle Ages. The Sempach Covenant contained some clauses dealing with the rights of war which are truly remarkable for those times.

The victory at Sempach tightened Berne's hitherto somewhat elastic links with the Confederation, and it had a similar—though indirect—result where Zurich was concerned. In fact there could be no better proof of the progress in confederate ideas and solidarity than the events which took place in Zurich in July 1393. Thirty years earlier Brun had been able to make alliances with Austria, as his successors had done many times since, without objections being raised. But when the Zurich administration signed a new alliance with the Habsburgs on 4 July 1393, soon after the Sempach Covenant, the news provoked an outcry among the townspeople which erupted in revolt on 26 July 1393. The alliance with Austria was torn up and the democratization of Zurich was complete.

This date marks the real coming of age of the Confederation. On 10 August 1393 the alliances were solemnly sworn again throughout all eight cantons, but this time a solid reality lay behind the formal ratification. A new state was born. Its gestation had taken a hundred years.

The fourteenth century was a troubled period throughout Europe, torn by wars, revolutions and civil catastrophes. The Hundred Years War in France, dynastic wars in Germany, urban rivalry in Italy had ruined the Continent. Switzerland had not been spared. The plague, an inevitable consequence of war in the Middle Ages, ravaged the country in 1348 and 1351. In 1356 an earthquake destroyed Basle and laid waste to Aargau. In 1375 the country was overrun by bands of mercenaries, turned into armed unemployed by a lull in the Anglo-French war, under the leadership of the notorious Enguerrand de Coucy. And finally fire destroyed Berne twice, first in 1380 and again three years later.

However, seen as a whole, this dark century which spread so much destruction elsewhere proved a constructive one for Switzerland. After the peace had been signed with Austria on 16 July 1394, the Confederation was almost alone in Europe in having military strength and territorial resources at its command. It was only a shadow of the great State that was to be forged, by steel and flame, during the following century. But everything in politics is relative. The Swiss could raise an army of 80,000 men thanks to a system of compulsory service. They were in a strategically powerful position, occupying the heart of Europe, with countries drained of money and men on all sides. They were well placed to impose on their neighbours.

The great years of the Confederation are bounded by the Battle of Sempach on the one hand, where infantry triumphed over cavalry, and the Battle of Marignano on the other, where artillery triumphed over infantry. For a hundred and twenty years Switzerland was to be the greatest military power in Europe.

Chapter IV

Switzerland, A Great Power
(1400-1516)

Switzerland's territorial expansion in the fifteenth century did not follow a logical, preconceived plan. It came about under pressure of economic necessity and followed a strategy which was as yet unconscious. In this respect Swiss history differs from that of the great monarchies. Kingdoms were the creation of individuals carrying through premeditated plans of action—though the wisdom and prescience of kings can sometimes be overestimated. Switzerland's evolution was haphazard, shaped by circumstances and collective feeling rather than reason and will.

The Confederation had its share of great statesmen in the fifteenth century, as the names of Nicholas of Diesbach of Berne, Hans Waldmann of Zurich, Cardinal Schiner of Valais, Ital Reding of Schwytz, Nicholas of Flue of Unterwald and many less famous bear witness. But seen as a whole, Swiss history is an anonymous affair, a collective rather than individual enterprise. Swiss history, in short, was made by the Swiss.

The Confederates, to begin with at any rate, were not looking for wealth, glory or natural frontiers—a meaningless concept to people with little geographical sense—in their conquests. They increased their empire rather the way a peasant adds to his property. They would covet a neighbour's field, the one lying nearest their own. And since this field in nine out of ten cases belonged to the Habsburgs, they were forced to smash the ring which enclosed them from Fribourg to Lake Constance, Bodan to the St Gotthard.

The scantily productive mountain cantons, and the towns with next to no agricultural land, which made up the Confederation at that time, depended for food on the neighbouring countryside and this depended, in its turn, on the Dukes of Austria. The latter had only to close their frontiers to cut off the Confederates' food supplies and ruin their markets. This threat, which was not very serious during the fourteenth century when the ducal administration was poorly organized, became more ominous as time went on. Thus the very reasons which led towns like Lucerne and Zurich and regions like Glarus to join the Confederation, were bound to force them to extend their territory in order to feed themselves. Zurich could not exist without Aargau and Thurgau, Schwytz without the March and Toggenburg, Uri without the Levant, Berne without the lands to the south and west, towards Fribourg, Bienne and Solothurn.

Economic considerations were not the only motive for the Confederates' expansion. They were a determining factor in most cases, but one which came to be backed up by strategy. The Swiss were collectors of trade centres already; now they began collecting fortresses. To say, as many historians do, that Aargau was conquered because the Emperor quarrelled with the Duke of Austria at the Council of Constance is to miss the main point. The Confederates seized Aargau because it lay between Berne and Zurich and threatened their military communication lines. They needed Aargau for defence reasons as much as for food. Thurgau in the east played the same role in the defences of Zurich as Aargau to the west.

But fortresses do not defend themselves. At each point they were forced to strike through as far as the Rhine, and sometimes further, with bridgeheads like Mülhausen and Rottweil. In this way they gradually reached their natural frontiers to the north, and in some instances, overstepped them.

A frontier, however, is unsafe where it can be side-stepped. To hold the Rhine meant acquiring the upper reaches of the river—held by the Grey League—and the Jura—the Bishopric of Basle. From there the logical step was to seize Neuchâtel and Vaud.

What of the south? No one today imagines that mountain peaks are natural frontiers. The people of Uri already knew this. The real frontiers are the passes which seal off the valleys. The key to the St Gotthard is the Bellinzona gorge to the south, the St Maurice to the west and the Luziensteig to the east. This explains the conquest of the Levant and Ossola and the alliances with the people of the Valais and the League.

It has often been said that Swiss policy in the fifteenth century was dictated by the ambition of the leaders and the greed of the soldiery. But this is not the case. Foreign gold played a much smaller part in it than has been supposed. It was a policy inspired by the most elevated national interests. If this inspiration failed them at times it is because there was not one Swiss policy, but many. The cantons thought of themselves as independent entities. Each one acted according to its own best interests and there was no one to co-ordinate all these efforts and subordinate them to the common good.

The fifteenth century is the moment when the absence of a leader had a fatal impact on the country's destiny. There was a lack of balance between the Confederation's military power, which made it a power to be reckoned with in Europe, and a valuable ally, and its internal institutions, which were characterized by a spirit of everyone for himself, unrestrained self-seeking on the part of the cantons, and a lack of solidarity and public spirit. Their political power could have welded them together. Instead, the reverse happened, and internal strife finally destroyed their political power.

Each canton had its own policy; this was reasonable enough but they tended to be restricted and mutually contradictory. The Schwytz, faithful to the tradition of the early forest cantons, set themselves up as champions of popular rights against the nobles, be these Swiss or Austrian. They supported the people of Zug against the city of Zug, the people of Toggenburg against the Count, and the people of Appenzell against their Abbot. Zurich, meanwhile, was busily supporting the town of Zug against its people, the Count of Toggenburg against his subjects and the Abbot of St Gallen against the people of Appenzell.

The seeds of dissension and misunderstanding were being sown in the name of freedom on which the Confederation was based. Occasionally it was a convergence of ambitions which led to trouble between the cantons. The March and Toggenburg, for instance, were the granaries supplying Schwytz on the one hand, hemmed in by its mountains, and Zurich on the other, hemmed in by its walls. Sometimes it was divergent aims which led to strife. Uri was at war with Savoy in Ossola at the very moment when Berne was seeking the support of the Savoyards in the Vaud countryside. Thus everyone tugged this way and that as he saw fit without a moment's thought for the rest.

Things were scarcely any better in the heart of the Confederation itself, at the Diets, now being held so often as to be an almost permanent institution. Trouble between the towns and countryside, which had begun in the previous century, was growing. The towns had grown bigger and richer. Berne alone, with her allies, and a territory almost as large as the actual canton itself, was too powerful to be challenged by the local peasantry. Equality in the Diets was a word rather than a fact. The country people sensed this and it infuriated them. Feuds started up in this fiercer age which make our own look like parlour games. On many occasions the Confederation came within an ace of breaking up. It almost certainly would have had it not been for the near miraculous influence of Brother Nicholas.

These feuds were the more unfortunate and dangerous in that Switzerland's conquests, in the process of making her into a great nation and the Confederates into a great military power, were inevitably dragging her into European politics and the struggle for power. The Swiss entered this arena under the worst possible conditions, without a recognized leader, disunited, without a common purpose or shared ideas. The Confederates even carried their quarrels on to the battlefield. This is why they eventually broke up.

Thus the history of the fifteenth century falls quite naturally into three chapters. The first deals with the conquests. The conquests provoked internal dissension on the one hand, and the great European wars on the other which led finally to the Battle of Marignano and put an end to the growth of the Confederation.

1. *The Conquests*

At the dawn of the fifteenth century a moral revolution took place among the Confederates. Until this time, they had all, with the exception of the Bernese, felt their liberties threatened. They had united to defend them. They were neither revolutionaries nor democrats—these words had no meaning at that time—but subjects in opposition to the great ones of the world. They were full of the spirit of resistance.

The alliance with Berne, a power in her own right, with subjects of her own, changed this situation to some extent. The policy of expansion of the towns, the institution of 'outside citizens', the victory at Sempach and the peace treaty with the Austrians which the Confederates had negotiated as between equals, hastened the process and the change was evident by the beginning of the next century.

The Confederates would no longer hesitate to contract alliances with feudal powers, even with the Dukes of Austria. They would enter into treaties—like the one between the citizens of Zurich and Count Toggenburg on 20 September 1400—directed against feudal subjects and designed to keep them in check. An action like this would have been impossible before Sempach. It was a sign of the times. The Confederates then went a step further. They took barons—like the Sax-Misox—under their protection and rule. The people's triumph had made lords of them. Yesterday's rebels are today's government and the world looks very different to them.

In this way the Confederates were led quite logically, and almost unconsciously, to adopt an expansionist policy. They acquired subjects and treated them as they had been treated themselves, not harshly, but in the manner laid down by feudal tradition. They were insistent upon their rights as they had once been insistent upon their liberties. The spirit remains the same but the point of view is different.

The word 'conquest' horrifies modern readers. But first it needs to be clearly defined. The Confederates extended their territory by two different methods, one military, the other political, that is, by straightforward conquest and by treaties.

Contrary to what might be supposed there is no great difference between these two ways of acquiring territory. Both maintain the law as it is, making no new juridical departures.

Generally speaking, and allowing for a few rare exceptions, the Swiss tended to make alliances with self-governing communities which might be classed as independent States. When they encountered a subject community however, they conquered it and kept the sovereign rights for themselves.

The Confederates struck up alliances with feudal lords—the Abbots of St Gallen and Dissentis, the Margrave of Bade, Count Toggenburg, the Barons of Sax-Misox, for instance—and with free towns, Fribourg, Bienne, Solothurn, Basle, Mülhausen, Rottweil, St Gallen, Schaffhausen—with communities in revolt like Appenzell, and with Confederations modelled on themselves like the Rhaetian Leagues and the Dixains of the Upper Valais. These alliances differed widely from each other in almost every respect except one—they were all contracted with independent or sovereign bodies.

The conquests were no less varied. Some, like the conquest of Aargau, were made with the consent and even encouragement of the Emperor. Thurgau was taken with the approval of the Pope. Others again were carried out at the request of the subjects themselves, as happened in the Levant. Whatever the circumstances, though, the conquered populace never had to suffer anything beyond the usual losses inflicted by war. The Confederates simply stepped into the shoes of the dispossessed overlords. There is not one instance where the subjects' existing liberties were curtailed. Their rights were invariably recognized, and in some cases extended.

The northern Italian valleys exerted a positive fascination over the Confederates. Uri, in particular, stubbornly pursued a policy of conquest to the south for almost two centuries, from 1330 to 1515. They were unsatisfied with anything less than total success and undiscouraged by failure. They had to contend with the Milanese, France, Venice, the Pope, and Emperor, and all too frequently with the uncomprehending attitude of the other Confederates who could not see the point of these distant and costly expeditions. Nothing would put them off, however. At one point they attained their ambition and came very close to making it last.

The beauty of the Italian countryside, the gentle climate and the attraction every Northerner feels towards the sun, are not sufficient explanation for such stubborn persistence. The real explanation is to be found elsewhere: they wished to ensure protection for traffic through the St Gotthard pass.

The alliance with the other forest cantons, Lucerne and Zurich, had ensured the safety of the northern entrance to the pass. Now Uri was obliged to repeat the process with the southern entrance, but unfortunately under less propitious conditions. The small peasant republics of Northern Italy which had served as a model and inspiration for the forest cantons in the thirteenth century had not been able to hold on to their independence. The democratic state of affairs which in Switzerland often drifted towards oligarchy had foundered in tyranny in Lombardy. The cities had fallen into the hands of magistrates—the Rusca family at Como, the Visconti in Milan—and they had then subjugated the rural free towns.

The southern valleys of the St Gotthard were conquered by Como, and then absorbed, with her, by Milan between 1135 and 1340. From then on all southbound traffic through the Alps depended on the Dukes of Milan, who could hinder it by tolls and other interferences.

Uri was faced with a choice between two policies. She could negotiate with Milan, or seize her territory. She tried both, one after the other. In 1335 the people of Uri signed a concordat with the Milanese, which renewed the earlier treaties of 1315 and 1331, and promised them exemption from toll-levies on the St Gotthard as far as the gates of Milan. However, this concession, which put the people of Uri in a better position than the Milanese themselves, was clearly extravagant and in the long run the only way to maintain it would be by force.

The Duke of Milan, Gian Galeazzo Visconti, died on 4 September 1402. His heirs were all minors. The news created great unrest throughout the Duchy and particularly in the high Levant valley. Uri took advantage of this state of affairs to move into the Levant, with some help from Unterwald. They had previously entered into relations with the people of Levant in 1331. Now, on 19 August 1403, they received the homage of the valley's inhabitants. The people of the Levant remained unswervingly loyal to them right through the old regime and until as late as 1815.

The date is an important one in Swiss history, for three reasons. Firstly, this was the first time the Confederation assumed sovereign rights over another people. Secondly, the Confederation had assimilated a population of a different race and language, and was therefore no longer purely Germanic. Lastly, this conquest would certainly entail others.

Having once conquered the Levant it became necessary to defend her. To the west, the forest cantons negotiated a treaty, on 3 June 1403, with the 'peasantry of the Valais', which was a model for many similar treaties to come. In 1410, after various raids on the Levant by the people of Ossola, Uri troops seized this valley as well and reduced the population to subjection.

To the east, Glarus negotiated a treaty with the Grey League, on 24 March 1400. This federation had been formed five years earlier on the upper reaches of the Rhine. On 21 August 1407, Uri and Unterwald signed a further treaty with the Barons of Sax-Misox, sovereigns of the Val Blenio and Val Mesocco, and lords of Bellinzona fortress. In this way they made themselves masters of the various passes—Lukmanier, Greina, St Bernard—which debouched on to the Lombardy plain and were potential rivals to the St Gotthard; and of the key strategic point where the valleys converged, Bellinzona and its two castles.

Unfortunately, these triumphs proved precarious. In the Levant the Confederates had been welcomed by the whole population, as liberators. However, to raise support in Ossola, they were forced to set themselves up as leaders of the Guelph faction, thus incurring the hostility of the Ghibellines, supported at one moment by the Duke of Milan, and at another by the House of Savoy. They were driven out of Domo d'Ossola in 1414, but succeeded in recapturing it in 1416. In 1418, Emperor Sigismund formally ceded Ossola, with the Val Maggia and Val Versasca, to the Confederates. On 1 September 1419, the Barons of Sax-Misox were forced to follow suit with the town of Bellinzona.

The Confederates were not long in possession. On 4 April 1422, the Duke of Milan launched a sudden attack and seized Bellinzona.

On 30 June, Confederate troops who had hurried to the defence of the fortress were cut to pieces at Arbedo. This defeat led to the recapture of all the valleys to the south of the Alps.

The Confederates were already in disagreement over these far-flung expeditions. Many cantons saw them as colonial wars. Zurich wished to remain on good terms with the Duke of Milan, because her trading interests were affected by the war. Berne wanted to bring about friendly relations with the Count of Savoy because of her designs on Vaud, and she feared that the occupation of Ossola, where the Savoyards had ambitions, if not rights, was inimical to this policy. For one reason or another the people of Uri were alone in grasping the importance of these Italian conquests.

After several fruitless attempts to reconquer their Italian possessions the Confederates were forced to renounce all their transalpine claims at the Treaty of Bellinzona, 21 July 1426, in exchange for certain trade concessions and exemption from tolls on the Milan highway—all of which points to the real issue at stake in their Italian forays.

They had fallen into a trap. The Uranese soon discovered that there could be no guarantee of safe trading on Milanese territory. Meanwhile the people of the Levant, oppressed by crushing taxes, were in constant revolt against the Duke's administration. So the Uranese were once again welcomed with open arms when—in defiance of Zurich—they took possession of the Levant again in 1440 and demanded that it be assigned to them as security against further violation of the treaty by the Duke of Milan. They took advantage of the death of the last Visconti in 1447 and the strife which broke out in Milan between the Ambrosian Republic and Francesco Sforza, who aspired to the ducal throne, to force the latter to sign over the Levant to them a second time, as well as giving them important customs concessions between the St Gotthard and Milan.

The pact between the Confederates and the Sforza family, ratified by the Treaty of Lodi, 17 April 1450, survived in its broader outlines for more than half a century and was confirmed on several occasions. It ran into difficulties only once, after the Burgundian wars, when the Confederates made another attempt to seize Bellinzona to punish the Milanese leaders for having given help and arms to Charles the Bold. Once again the Northern Italian valleys resounded to the famous Swiss war cry 'Liga! Liga!' met by the answering cry of the Milanese 'Duca! Duca!'

This expedition was not wholly successful, but it was not altogether fruitless because after the victory of Giornico (28 December 1478) the Duchess of Milan, Bonne de Savoie, formally ceded all rights in the Levant to the Uranese.

This was how things stood when the Italian wars began in the early years of the sixteenth century—of which we shall have more to say later.

The Uranese policy in Italy was in line with the economic aims of their first alliance, but it overstepped them both geographically and morally, whereas the activities of the Schwytz were an expression of their political acumen.

The revolt by the people of Appenzell against the Abbot of St Gallen is one episode of this struggle, just as the revolt of the people of Glarus had been twenty years earlier. The Abbot's subjects had many grievances against him, but the decisive one was the news that the Abbot was planning to recognize the sovereignty of the Dukes of Austria in the hopes of putting an end to the disturbances in his territory. Such an extension of Austrian power not only threatened the rights of the people of Appenzell but the safety of the entire Confederation. So the Schwytz did not hesitate to go to the assistance of Appenzell, despite opposition from Zurich.

The men of Appenzell defeated the St Gallen army and its

Swabian allies at Voegelinsegg on 15 May 1403 and went on to inflict a bloody defeat on the Abbot, and Frederick IV of Austria, at Stoss on 17 June 1405.

The news set off a chain reaction through all the states bordering the Rhine, from Lake Constance upwards as far as Lake Zurich, together with the Thur valley. Towns like St Gallen, Feldkirch and Bludenz, the peasantry of Appenzell, Rheintal, Glarus, Fussach, Hochst, Rankweil, Walgau, Montafon, and Lichtenstein, and even a few feudal lords like Count Rudolph of Werdenburg, banded together in a confederation on 15 September 1405, calling itself the *Bund ob dem Bodensee*. This movement gathered strength on both sides of the Rhine, penetrating as far as the Tyrol. It was a positive *jacquerie*. Appenzell became the rallying cry of liberation.

The movement, however, was political rather than social and this was the cause of its downfall. It was the prestige of Appenzell, considerable at this juncture, which cemented the alliance, rather than mutual aims or policies. When Appenzell's army suffered defeat at Bregenz on 13 January 1408—Bregenz being the one town which remained loyal to the Emperor—the League dissolved as speedily as it had been formed. Still, this great drive towards independence was not without results. On 24 November 1411, the Confederates signed a treaty with the people of Appenzell, and on 14 December 1412 a further treaty with St Gallen.

The mortal feud which sprang up two years later at the Council of Constance between Emperor Sigismund and Frederick IV of Austria gave the Confederates an unexpected legal pretext for seizing Aargau, which lay like a wedge driven between the territories of Berne, Zurich and Lucerne, and endangered their economic and military supply routes. On 5 April 1415, the Emperor banished Frederick from the Empire, declaring forfeit the feudal rights of the Dukes of Austria over all territory not as yet under direct Imperial jurisdiction. This immensely important proclamation put an end, once and for all, to the feudal system in Switzerland.

The Confederates paused briefly before breaking the fifty year truce they had just cemented with the Austrians. First to go into action were the Bernese, then Zurich, anxious not to let her rival steal a march on her, followed by Lucerne and the forest cantons. The people of Uri alone kept apart, occupied as they were with events in Ossola (1414–1416). In less than a month the Swiss succeeded in conquering the whole of Aargau with hardly any bloodshed. Nearly four hundred fortresses, Aarburg, Aarau, Lenzburg, Brugg, Sursee, Munster, Maienfeld, Knonau, Mellingen, Bremgarten and Baden among them, either surrendered or were taken in battle. Ignoring the protests of the Emperor, who had meanwhile made peace with Duke Frederick, the Confederates divided out this rich plunder among themselves. Berne retained the region between Zofingen and Brugg, Lucerne took Sursee, Zurich kept Knonau and the counties of Baden and Freiamt came under joint jurisdiction.

The crisis which convulsed the Confederation at Count Toggenburg's death, in 1436, and paralysed it for almost fifteen years, gave rise to a whole new series of acquisitions between Lake Walenstadt and Lake Constance. The end of the civil war also gave the Confederation a tremendous new lease of life.

All the neighbouring countries had followed the fortunes of this war with passionate concern. They more than once concluded that the end of the Confederation was in sight, and were anxiously aware of the gap this would create in Upper Germany. The war between the cantons, and the foreign invasion which it precipitated, were indications of what would happen if and when the Confederation finally fell apart.

The Confederation's eventual mastery of the crisis, from which it emerged more solidly united than ever, aroused considerable admiration among its neighbours. Everyone realized that this Confederation was not just another ephemeral alliance. Henceforth any town, state or noble with rights or liberties to defend against the Habsburgs—Emperors again since 1438—looked for help and protection from the Confederates.

In this way God makes good come of evil.

The civil war finally ended on 13 July 1450, with the Declaration of Einsiedeln. On 17 August 1451, Zurich, Lucerne, Schwytz and Glarus signed a treaty with the Abbot of St Gallen. On 15 November 1452, the alliance with the people of Appenzell who had faithfully discharged their obligations to the Confederates during the war was strengthened. On 1 June 1454 they made a treaty with Schaffhausen. And in 1458 a fruitless and unsatisfactory expedition against Constance, which marred Swiss relations with the city for a long time to come, did at least result in the conquest of the Austrian town of Rapperswill and an alliance with Stein-am-Rhein (16 December 1459).

In September 1460 all these scattered possessions were joined to the old Confederate territory by the purchase of the Rheintal and the conquest of Thurgau and part of the Vorarlberg (Bregenz and Dornbirn). This last move was made at the instigation of the Pope, who had temporarily fallen out with the Emperor, Frederick III of Habsburg.

The conquest of Thurgau, the logical corollary to the conquest of Aargau, was the signal for a new leap ahead by the Confederates. They sealed a close alliance with the Swabian town of Rottweil, on 18 June 1463, and another with Mülhausen on 17 June 1466. These were two outposts which would have become advance guards if the bulk of the army had followed up the move. The Confederates no sooner reached the Rhine than they realized that the only way to secure their position was to extend it beyond the river.

These various alliances between the Swiss and the townships were naturally extremely unpopular with the neighbouring feudal landlords, against whom they were chiefly aimed, for any hostile moves on their part would lead to reprisals by the Swiss expeditionary forces. Thus, in 1455, the Confederates were led to invade Klattgau and Hegau to punish offences against Schaffhausen. Similar reasons provoked the Swiss attack on the Alsatian nobility in 1468, shortly after the Mülhausen alliance. They took the Sundgau and the Black Forest and came very near—Swiss territorial history is like a roll-call of missed opportunities—to taking permanent possession of them. However, the Confederates failed at Waldshut, as they generally did when besieging a stronghold. The usual quarrelling broke out among them and on 2 August 1468, they were forced to accept the Peace of Waldshut which put a full stop to their conquests north of the Rhine and any further expansion in that direction.

The Swiss alliance with Mülhausen was nevertheless a turning point in the history of the Confederation. By giving them a stake in Alsace it was to lead them some years later into a war with the Duke of Burgundy, a war which witnessed the highwater mark of Confederate power and glory even while it paved the way for their undoing.

2. *Internal Discord*

Unfortunately, while the Confederate army was going from

strength to strength on the battlefield, the internal growth of the federation was paralysed by rivalry and civil wars.

This phenomenon is not too hard to understand. The cantons were sovereign states and exceedingly jealous of their autonomy. They might feel a certain solidarity where foreign powers were concerned, but they were not inspired by any feelings of patriotism. To the modern Swiss, with five centuries of evolution behind them, all these separate alliances, the feuding in the Diets and on the battlefield, seem almost criminal. This was not at all how their ancestors saw them, a few enlightened spirits excepted. The Confederation was in fact no more than an alliance—and nobody is surprised, today, when allies are not in complete agreement, or even when they come to blows over certain issues.

All the trouble which broke out within the Confederation during the fifteenth century was grounded in one factor—social and political opposition between towns and country.

The opposition was social first and foremost. For the towns, the fifteenth century was a period of growth and prosperity. They derived greater benefits from most of the Confederate triumphs than the countryside. This was the case with the conquest of Aargau, for instance, which enriched Berne, Zurich and Lucerne, and again, with the Burgundian wars, which were mainly profitable to Berne. These conquests added to the wealth, and hence the importance, of the urban aristocracies. The peasant democracies, on the other hand, felt themselves ignored in the sharing of the booty.

The countryside took the brunt of war. It was ravaged on several occasions. The countrypeople saw their wealth diminished while the towns waxed fat, and this disturbed the balance of power at the heart of the Diets.

Impoverishment of the countryside had two consequences: emigration and agrarian troubles. Military fervour, due to the wars, led to many countrymen becoming mercenaries, but here again the peasant soldier would find his Confederates from the towns placed above him. Foreign service accentuated rather than diminished the contrasts in wealth and outlook.

It was a political movement as well. Aristocracies had sprung up in the towns which sought to establish their domination over the countryside, and more often than not succeeded, since the countryside was much less organized. These aristocracies were made up, for the most part, of former feudal lords who had been accepted as burgesses and brought their old way of looking at things to their new position.

The countrypeople, on the other hand, remained true to the spirit of the early Confederates, which was not so much democratic as popular. Instinctively, in their political wrangles, the towns would tend to side with the lords and nobles, while the country supported the subjects.

This was precisely the issue over which the Confederates sharply divided in 1404. The town of Zug had acquired the right of criminal jurisdiction over the external bailliages, and was trying to force them to submit to her sovereignty. The Schwytzois, guardians of the pure democratic and peasant doctrine, instantly promised the bailliages their support against the town. If necessary they were even prepared to fight on their behalf, in direct violation of federal law. The Schwytzois were right, perhaps, in taking this stand. But they thereby gave a passionate and unlawful twist to the feud which helped to poison dealings between urban and peasant communes and encourage future conflict.

A few years later, soon after the conquest of Ossola, the Confederation became embroiled in a conflict which brought them within a hairsbreadth of civil war. It will be recalled that the forest cantons made treaties, in 1403, with various free towns in the Valais. In 1414, the Baron de Rarogne came out against the Confederates, sending troops under the Count of Savoy, to drive the Swiss from Ossola. The peasantry rose against him, and the forest cantons supported and helped them.

But the Barons de Rarogne were allies of Berne, and the Valais peasants were permanently at odds with the Oberland peasantry over pasturage rights. Furthermore, the Bernese were not in the least interested in expeditions in Ossola, in fact they were strongly opposed to them, and so they hastened to support the Rarogne family and the Bishop of Sion against their rebellious subjects. The quarrel was finally settled by arbitration in 1420, but not till a lot of blood had been spilled in the Valais.

These feuds, however, are as nothing beside the great civil war which broke out between Zurich and the Confederates, after Count Frederick VII of Toggenburg's death on 30 April 1436.

The Count's territories around Lake Zurich were as tempting to the Schwytzois as to the people of Zurich. They were accessible and to some extent necessary to both as a source of food supplies. Hence both Schwytz and Zurich were continually striving, during the Count's lifetime, to establish better relations with him and gain some legal foothold over his possessions. The Count happily fell in with this double game, seeing it as a guarantee of peaceful rule.

After his death this fine inheritance, extending from Lake Constance to the Albula and Lake Zurich to Feldkirch, fell prey to ten different claimants, the Count's widow and relations, the Brandis, Aarburgs, Montforts, Werdenburgs, Raezuns, Maetsch and Rarogne families—not to mention the Emperor, the Duke of Austria, the Count's subjects and the Confederates. Thus Zurich and the Schwytzois found themselves face to face, both armed with legal and moral justifications, and both in search of allies.

At the start of the dispute it would have been hard to say which side was in the right. Zurich lost no time in putting herself in the wrong, however, by closing her markets to the people of Schwytz and Glarus. This was tantamount to an economic blockade against the two cantons, and in this year of poor harvests, was enough to cause hardship and even famine.

Schwytz took a grave enough view of the move to retaliate, on 4 November 1439, with a declaration of war. Nothing could better illustrate Zurich's importance at the time, as economic centre of the forest cantons. If another example were needed to clarify the real reasons for Zurich's entry into the Confederation, this would be the clinching one.

The war was brief. Zurich, defeated, accepted the Peace of Lucerne on 1 December 1440. However, this powerful city did not feel that she had exhausted her opportunities or resources. Her submission was never final and the war soon started up again.

It was a genuine war of secession. Zurich aspired to independence. The Confederates would not allow her to break with the permanent alliance she had made with them. Zurich clung to the idea of an alliance. The Confederates put themselves on the footing of a State. This, the very existence of the Confederation, was the real issue at stake—not a few possessions more or less in Toggenburg. 'Every civil war,' it is said, 'is a war of ideas in which interests play a part.'

Zurich turned away, morally speaking, from the Confederates. When the Imperial throne came into Habsburg hands again, in 1438, she struck up an alliance with Emperor Frederick III.

The people of Zurich did not flinch, in their zeal, from any of the consequences of their actions. They approved the Emperor's refusal to confirm Swiss liberties, promised to restore Aargau to him and to create a new Confederation rivalling the forest cantons. They exchanged the white cross for the ducal insignia of the peacock's feather. On 29 September 1442, Frederick was received at Zurich with all the honours due to his rank, amid popular rejoicing.

But the Empire's purely platonic intervention did not materially assist Zurich. After the battle of Saint-Jacques-sur Sihl, 22 July 1443, she found herself tightly blockaded by Confederate troops.

This led to the first ever foreign intervention in Swiss affairs. Whenever the Swiss are divided against themselves, foreigners have always seized the opportunity to increase their influence over them. This is one of the many respects in which the Zurich war resembles the Sonderbund war.

Charles VII, King of France by grace of Joan of Arc, had reconquered most of his kingdom. On 28 May 1444, he signed a truce with the English. It was a similar truce which had inflicted the mercenary marauders of Enguerrand de Coucy upon Switzerland, sixty years earlier. Charles was enchanted to see an opportunity now for getting his son and his soldiers out of the way, by means of a political operation which he had every reason to hope would be crowned by success.

He was not averse to helping the Emperor, thus placing him in his debt. But his real purpose, apart from the freeing of Zurich, was the capture of Basle, which commanded Alsace.

The battle of Saint-Jacques-sur-la-Birse, 26 August 1444, was an unmistakable victory for the French. The French succeeded in lifting the siege of Zurich. But the victory proved so costly that the Dauphin Louis hurriedly withdrew his army to the other side of the Jura. The French drew some profit from this campaign, but fortunately, it was all indirect. Charles VII took two Imperial towns, Toul and Verdun, under his protection, but not Basle, as he had hoped, and still less the Confederation.

The Confederation was right to preserve the memory of Saint-Jacques, because this defeat strengthened the country and united it more than many a resounding victory. And it had the practical side-effect, compared with the conquest of Zurich, that it forced both sides to display moderation and magnanimity.

The glorious defeat of Saint-Jacques ended the war, with a moral victory for the Confederation. On 28 October 1444, they made peace with France at Ensisheim, in Alsace. In June 1446, they agreed on a temporary truce among themselves pending the verdict of Einsiedeln in 1450, which was to settle their bitter dispute with a compromise.

The Confederation had triumped over its first attempted secession. She had joined battle with Zurich as a full-grown nation bent on defending her existence and territorial integrity. She had undermined the intrigues and ambitions of France and the Emperor. This triumph earned her great prestige, many territorial accessions and, for a while at least, some degree of internal cohesion.

Unfortunately the Confederation would have to pay a high price for this success. It was, as has been noted, the spoils of the Burgundian wars which led to the demoralization of Switzerland towards the end of the fifteenth century. The gravest symptoms of this were corruption in public life, abuse of foreign titles and pensions and a disturbing increase in enlistment in the mercenary armies. It would be more precise, however, to set this demoralization down to the protracted civil war and the resultant impoverishment of towns and countryside.

Zurich was ruined. The silk industry, mainstay of its wealth for so long, was destroyed. Flax and wool weaving were on the decline.

The conquerors were equally badly off, morally and economically. Agriculture was either at a standstill, or badly neglected, and industry ruined by the impoverishment of the peasantry. Thus the Swiss had to emigrate in huge numbers in search of the resources lacking in their own country. This migration took the form of military service abroad. It was a job rather than a calling, but a job with demoralizing effects.

A taste for warmongering and gold bred corruption among the leaders and anarchy among their subjects. The soldiers returning home with their pay, and their arms, found their families poor and discontented. This occasioned a whole series of civil disturbances—uprisings in Berne in 1470 and 1471, at Entlebuch in 1478, at Zurich in 1489, when *Bürger-*

meister Waldmann lost his life, and in that same year, an attack by St Gallen on Rorschach, whose Abbot was engaged in building a new monastery destined to rival St Gallen. It was a time of seething unrest and brutality all round. Leaders had forfeited the trust of their subjects, and subjects lost the respect of their leaders.

One among all these outbursts of popular discontent was to prove more serious, in its scope and consequences, than the rest. During the 1477 Carnival, the *Folle Vie* expedition succeeded in terrorizing Switzerland from Lake Lucerne as far as Lake Geneva. The expedition started as a wild joke on the part of a few hot-heads but developed into a looting expedition against the towns, Geneva in particular, in debt to the Confederates since the Burgundian wars. As it crossed the Emmenthal countryside, the expedition gradually attracted a raggle-taggle following of the poorer and more violent elements of the population, and was soon engaged in nothing more or less than downright robbery.

This episode was taken seriously enough for five towns, Zurich, Berne, Lucerne, Fribourg and Solothurn, to negotiate a separate alliance on 29 May 1477. The alliance was formed against the peasant cantons, who were further enraged to discover that two of the five towns—Solothurn and Fribourg—were not even members of the Confederation, whereas Lucerne was forbidden under federal law to make a separate alliance at all.

Once more the Confederates were on the brink of war. A separatist movement started up at Entlebuch against Lucerne, which was openly supported by the forest cantons. It was under these circumstances that the Diet met to discuss, on the one hand, the dissolution of the five town alliance, and, on the other, the inclusion of Fribourg and Solothurn in the Confederation.

The expression 'admission into the Confederation', pejorative with regard to the fourteenth century, is now the correct one. It was no longer a question of alliances. Fribourg and Solothurn had been allies of the Confederation for some time, and followed a common policy to a certain extent. But they were now seeking promotion, and thus for the first time a clear distinction between the notions of allies and confederates emerges.

It is not to be wondered at that the question, arising in the form it did, should have led to heated debate. The opposition of town and country was as serious in the fifteenth century, as the feuds between Catholics and Protestants later, or the language split today. Problems like these, as we know, were a heavy burden on the Confederation throughout her history. Already, in 1451, Uri and Unterwald had come out strongly against an alliance with St Gallen. The admission of two new urban cantons would threaten the equilibrium between the urban—Zurich, Berne, Lucerne and Zug—and rural—Uri, Schwytz, Unterwald, Glarus—members of the Confederation as represented in the Diet, and thus the balance between aristocratic and popular interests.

The astonishing aspect of the affair, however, is not that the Stans Diet which met from 22–30 November 1481 to discuss the admission of Fribourg and Solothurn, should have had a session so stormy that it often looked as though the Confederation would collapse, but that they should at last have arrived at an agreement whereby the rural cantons swallowed their doubts and fears and Fribourg and Solothurn were received into the Confederation on 22 December 1481.

This happy outcome was, as we know, largely due to the mediation of Brother Nicholas of Flue. Brother Nicholas has often been compared to Joan of Arc. The comparison seems a little exaggerated, yet it must be conceded that his role in the Stans Diet was a decisive, if not strictly speaking, miraculous one, and that it spared the Confederation a second civil war.

Before becoming a hermit Flue had been a politician and his great achievement lay in finding a formula which both parties would accept. The towns abandoned their separate alliance and the rural cantons agreed to the admission of Solothurn and Fribourg, under certain restrictive conditions. It was entirely thanks to Nicholas's disinterest, conviction and grandeur of spirit, that the solution proved acceptable.

Simultaneously with the admission of Solothurn and Fribourg the Stans Diet drew up an act designed to complete the Sempach Covenant. This act—the Stans Covenant—governed relations between the Confederates till the French Revolution, and is often regarded as the first Swiss constitutional law.

This return to harmony was celebrated by peals of church bells throughout Switzerland. Unfortunately, however, this new state of affairs was not to prove so solid under duress. Internal feuds, Switzerland's running sore, broke out again during the great European wars which the Confederation would have to support. And they led, after the Battle of Marignano, to the crisis of the Reformation.

3. *The European Wars*

The *Folle Vie* escapade which led to the last great crisis in the Confederation was a direct consequence of the Burgundian wars.

The fighting which broke out between the Swiss and Charles the Bold in 1474 was inevitable—in so far as any historical event can be considered independent of individual human wills and desires. It was necessitated by the very nature of things. Some Swiss historians, and not only the lesser ones, have tried to explain the war in terms of the effect of French gold on the Bernese aristocracy. But this is wilful blindness. The Burgundian wars were caused by the prevailing state of affairs throughout Europe and the Confederation, as inevitably as the Swabian war and the Italian wars some years later.

The situation only puzzles us now because certain words no longer have the meaning they had then. When we say 'Switzerland' we think of a small country, and when we say 'Burgundy' we think of a French province. But, at that time, Burgundy and Switzerland were two great powers.

The end of the fifteenth century saw the formation of modern States. They crystallized in a certain pattern, which now hypnotizes us to such an extent that it seems the only one possible. But this was by no means the case. The Duchy of Burgundy had all the elements of a great State and the fact that it vanished from the map is chiefly because Duke Charles did not have a son.

As for Switzerland, she was a great military power. As the only country with compulsory military service and a national army, she had more manpower at her disposal than any of her neighbours, not to mention a superb infantry which was literally invincible, thanks to the spirit which inspired it. It was technical progress which defeated this army in the end, the development of artillery and changes in military science which this produced.

Charles the Rash—or rather the Bold—was not the violent, greedy and imprudent figure that popular legend paints for us. He seems to have been, on the contrary, an attractive personality somewhat ahead of his time, and a great politician who came very near to being a great sovereign.

His hereditary possessions included the Low Countries,

Flanders, Artois, Burgundy and the Franche-Comté. These territories were split by Champagne and Lorraine and his one idea was to unite them.

Besides this, Charles the Bold had hopes of succeeding to good King René, now an elderly man, and thus acquiring Provence. Like all the princes of his day he had designs on the Milanese, who were only separated from his kingdom by Savoy. This then was his ruling ambition—to reassemble these scattered fragments, welding them into a great nation under one leader, and restore the ancient Kingdom of Lotharingia which stretched from Amsterdam to Marseilles and from the Somme to the Po.

Nowadays we are obsessed by the idea of natural frontiers, and nationalities, and this plan strikes us as chimerical. Nevertheless, it could have succeeded and the existence of a great buffer state between France and Germany would have drastically altered the course of European history.

But Charles the Bold made the serious error of not weighing up the opposition with sufficient care. There was Louis XI, who held Champagne, the Emperor, suzerain of Alsace and Lorraine, and the Swiss, whose expansion stretched to the west and south. The whole policy of Charles the Bold should have concentrated on keeping his foes divided, which would not have been too difficult. But he did not give enough time to it and he failed. Louis XI's policy, on the other hand, was to form alliances with everyone who felt menaced by the Duke's power and ambitions, and in this he was successful.

The Bernese were neighbours of Burgundy, via Franche-Comté. As their own aspirations lay to the west they were hardly likely to remain indifferent to Burgundy's growing power. Allies of Bienne since 1352, Solothurn and Neuveville since 1388, the Count of Valangin since 1401, Fribourg since 1403, of the Count and town of Neuchâtel since 1406, and possessing many sovereign rights in Seeland, on Lake Bienne, the Bernese were confronted from Basle to Lake Geneva by the Jura Mountains, and they saw them not only as a barrier but as an objective. They had also struck up a rather shaky alliance with Savoy, in the hopes of securing the Vaud canton, which was a link in their communications with Valais, and where they had their intelligence system at work. It was on this corner of land that the ambitions of the Bernese were bound to conflict with the openly avowed designs of Charles the Bold.

It is no coincidence that the Burgundian wars should have broken out around Grandson and Murten, for these were what the fighting was about.

Savoy at that time was governed by Queen Yolande of France, sister of Louis XI. It was torn by court intrigues and dynastic struggles.

A worthy sister to Louis, Yolande was playing Louis off against Charles. But she did not fool the Duke of Burgundy. Savoy was absolutely necessary to the realization of his grand design, and if he chose to attack the Swiss from the Vaud canton it was primarily with the idea of prolonging his stay there and gaining a foothold in Savoy.

Alsace, which belonged to the Empire, had been surrendered as a pledge to the Duke of Burgundy. He administered the country and was confidently expecting to add her to his possessions. The Confederate alliance with Mülhausen and their conquest of Sundgau in 1468 had revealed the Confederates' interest in this country, which dominated Basle and was one of the gateways to the Swiss plateau. As master of Alsace, Franche-Comté and the Vaud canton, Charles the Bold would have completely encircled Berne and held her at his mercy.

The conflict between the Swiss and the Charles the Bold was not a mere dispute over land, however. There were bigger issues at stake. The Swiss were the greatest military power of the day. Duke Charles could hardly contemplate building up a great nation, whose elongated shape made it easy to sever, with a power he could not trust on one flank. The war between the Confederates and the Duke was a war to the death because it was literally a fight for existence.

French diplomacy did not play the vital role in this affair so long attributed to it. It was limited to making clear to the Swiss where their best interests lay, and to acting as intermediary between the Swiss and Austrians in the hope of achieving better relations between them.

The year 1474 was characterized by intense diplomatic activity. On 30 March the Swiss signed a treaty 'in perpetuity' with the Austrians at Constance. This was a real alliance, which seemed to put an end to two hundred years of war, and was received with outbursts of joy and enthusiasm up and down the country.

Soon afterwards the Confederates allied themselves with the Bishops of Basle and Strasbourg and with four Alsatian towns:

Basle, Colmar, Schlettstadt and Strasbourg. On 4 April, Duke Sigismund of Austria renounced the St Omer treaty linking him with the Duke of Burgundy. Finally, on 6 June, the King of France entered the grand coalition which now mustered all the great powers of the day, the Empire, Switzerland and France.

Alsace was in revolt against Burgundy. The Emperor ordered Duke Charles to evacuate the country. When he refused, he summoned the Swiss to arms. On 25 October 1474, Berne declared war.

The Swiss soon found themselves fighting the war unaided. On one pretext or another their allies all managed to keep out of the fighting. However, this did not stop them from winning the most resounding victory in Swiss military history, and destroying one of the great nations of the West in a few months.

The Swiss entered Franche-Comté soon after their declaration of war. On 13 November they won their first victory at Héricourt, taking Blamont, Pontarlier and various other strongholds. The following year they twice invaded Vaud canton, as far as Geneva, which they took. The outcome of all this was that Charles the Bold marched to attack them in the spring of 1476. He suffered defeat at Grandson on 2 March 1476. Reassembling his army in the Lausanne region, he then marched on Berne. He was intercepted by the Swiss at Murten, and his army totally routed. Finally, on 5 January 1477, he was killed in tragic circumstances at Nancy, in a battle with Swiss troops bent on reconquering the capital of their ally, René of Lorraine.

These brilliant victories won glory and booty for the Swiss, but not much real advantage. And this was their own fault. This is one of the darker pages of Swiss history.

They had certainly achieved the main purpose of the war, which was to free Alsace, check Burgundy's expansion and keep her hands off the Vaud canton. But they had overreached themselves. By handing Burgundy over to France, and the Low Countries and Franche-Comté to Austria, the Burgundian wars had simply created new, and more threatening, dangers along the frontiers of the Confederation than the ones which they had just escaped.

How had this happened? Through jealousy and greed, it must be confessed.

First, jealousy. The Bernese had shown little sympathy for the Confederation's plans for expansion southwards. The forest cantons found the notion of expansion westwards equally incomprehensible. Berne, alone, stood to gain by such a move and none of the Swiss—Zurich least of all—wanted Berne to get any more powerful, or her already overwhelming influence in the Confederation any greater.

Then, greed. The Swiss, though traditionally frugal, were not above coveting worldly goods. Wealth, in the fifteenth century, was immensely alluring to them.

There are many examples of this, but the outstanding one is their almost criminally short-sighted surrender of Franche-Comté to Austria, for which they received in return the derisory sum of five million francs. Despite the fact that this magnificent province was a rich source of wheat, salt and wine, the Confederates hardly thought twice before handing it over to Austria, their traditional foe, who already contained them on all sides. The Swiss retained for themselves only the theoretical rights of a protectorate.

The victors then relinquished Vaud canton, which they were in no danger of losing, and which they were only to reconquer after much fighting and bloodshed.

The Confederates' only territorial acquisitions from the Burgundian wars were the admission of Solothurn and Fribourg into the Confederation, a treaty between Berne, Fribourg and the Bishop of Geneva, 14 November 1477, and a few bailliages.

Nevertheless, the renown these victories conferred on the Confederates, and an idea of their prestige in Europe at that time, can be gauged from the alliance proposed to them by Matthias Corvin, King of Hungary, in 1479, which they accepted. This alliance against Austria was based on the sensible principle of a counter-weight. Although they had renewed their perpetual alliance with Austria on 13 October 1477, the Swiss cannot have had many illusions about the future. Their continued existence and their independence had depended, for more than a hundred and fifty years, on the rivalry between the Habsburgs and the Emperors. But since 1438 the Imperial throne was in Habsburg hands. In these circumstances it was a danger rather than safeguard for the Swiss to belong to the Empire.

Frederick III's reign proved this clearly. For the first time in their history the Confederates knew what it was to be the target of the Emperor's unrelenting hostility. His refusal to confirm their traditional liberties, his attitude during the war with Zurich, his appeal to the Armagnacs, his treachery during the Burgundian wars—all these reasons estranged the Swiss from the Empire.

Sooner or later their relations would have to be clarified—and settled by main force.

As often happens, it was not Frederick III who pushed his policy through, but his son Maximilian I, with whom the Swiss had no quarrel.

This was the period when the great States throughout Europe were creating, by means of an administrative structure, the foundations of a tax system, armies, and a legal code. France, Spain and England had already accomplished the main part of this transformation. Germany alone lingered in feudal ways.

No sooner was he on the throne than Maximilian I resolved to reform the Empire, sweeping away the anarchy which tore it apart and giving it the solidity of a real State. All reforms meet with some resistance. And since nothing can be done without money, the Emperor managed to get the Diet of Worms to agree to an Imperial tax, the *Gemeinpfennig*, 1495.

The creation of this tax clearly involved a crucial point of law. With the formation of territorial States, a notion quite foreign to the Middle Ages, the whole concept of sovereignty had undergone profound modifications. Feudal sovereignty was a real right—a bond between a person and his land. Modern sovereignty is a public right. If the Swiss had paid the tax demanded of them, they would have accepted a transformation in the sovereignty imposed upon them. They would have become, not subjets of the Empire, but Germans—especially as Maximilian claimed exclusive recruiting rights on Confederate territory. The question of Swiss independence had never been posed so clearly or dramatically. The Swiss refused to pay the tax.

Realizing war was now inevitable they went in search of allies. They could no longer count on the Swabian towns which had often combined with them against the Habsburgs in the fourteenth century, but now displayed extraordinary animosity towards the Confederates. The 'papplarts' expedition, and futile disputes over certain feudal rights in Thurgau had alienated even the closest and most loyal of them, Constance; Rottweil alone remained firmly attached to the Swiss cause.

The Grey League, however, feeling themselves increasingly threatened by Austria's encroachment in the Tyrol and her designs on their own territory, negotiated alliances with the Confederates on 21 June 1497 and 13 December 1498.

These alliances were the immediate cause of the Swabian war, which was brief and devastating. It was the first really national war in Swiss history, accompanied by polemic, reprisals and bursts of collective savagery beyond the frontier; a national war in its consequences as well. In less than six months, the Swiss, thanks to the tactical advantage which their central position gave them, destroyed the Swabian League, which the Emperor had created to oppose them, and the Imperial power into the bargain. The battles of Hardt (20 February 1499), Bruderholz (22 March), Frastanz (20 April), Calven (24 May), Dorneck (22 July) and the invasions of the Black Forest, the Klettgau, Hegau and Vorarlberg, are less vivid in popular memory for some reason than the great military feats of the Burgundian and Italian wars. Nevertheless, these wars stand out among those fought by the Swiss as the most dearly won, decisive and glorious.

The Basle Peace Treaty, of 22 September 1499, finally severed Switzerland's links with the Empire. For this reason it deserves to be included among Switzerland's most important charters of independence. From this time on Switzerland need pay homage to no one. She had no obligations abroad. Moreover, the Swabian war had actually brought her two new members—Basle on 13 July and Schaffhausen on 1 August 1301. Gradually, to the north, what was to be Switzerland's definitive frontier was taking shape. But the Vorarlberg, which Swiss armies had so brilliantly reconquered for the second time, slipped through their hands again—and this time for good, much as the Franche-Comté had already done.

Peace was no sooner re-established to the north than war broke out again to the south. Having wrested her independence from the Empire, Switzerland once again set out to make conquests in Italy; which merely goes to show that power imposes obligations and victories entail dangers.

A clear distinction needs to be drawn, where the Italian wars are concerned, between the role played there by Swiss fighting as mercenaries and Swiss fighting on their own behalf. There were Swiss in Louis VII's armies, and in those of Ludovico il More, Duke of Milan. All of this does not mean that there was not a central Swiss policy towards Italy, despite many contradictions and changes of fortune.

To sum up briefly how things lay at the end of the fifteenth century—the Swiss possessed the Levant quite legitimately but had lost all their other Italian conquests. They had not lost hope of recapturing Bellinzona, however, which was still the key to the St Gotthard, both from an economic and military point of view, and whose population gave evidence of lively support for their former conquerors.

When Louis XII asked the Swiss for help in conquering the Duchy of Milan from Ludovic Sforza, they stipulated Bellinzona, Lugano and Lucarno as the price for their collaboration. When Louis XII failed to keep his word, the Swiss entered Italy on their own account, seized Bellinzona and laid siege to Arona, where Louis XII finally yielded. Bellinzona became Swiss, as did the Val Blenio, where the Confederates were warmly welcomed (11 April 1503).

This new acquisition soon involved them in further fighting They were too near Milan, at Bellinzona, and too powerful to stand aside from the struggles for possession of the Duchy A powerful alliance was formed against France, headed by Pope Julius II, and numbering the young Maximilian Sforza, the Empire, Spain, England and the wealthy Venetian Republic among its adherents. At this the Swiss realized they were no longer free to abstain. They had to choose. The choice they made was the only reasonable one under the circumstances. Cardinal Schiner's advice played no more part in their decision than French gold had played in the Burgundian wars. Their decision was dictated by the realities of the situation.

On the one hand stood France, mistress of Milan, and barely a hundred miles from Bellinzona; on the other an imposing but bizarre coalition of foreign princes. If France were victorious the Swiss would be exposed to threat of attack in their South Alpine possessions. However if the 'Holy League' were to win, in which they would be the single fighting element, they stood to gain. This, in fact, was what happened.

In March 1512, a deputation from the Diet was received with great honour in Venice. Throughout that spring the Confederate contingents were assembling. They only had to show their faces in Northern Italy to carry all before them. They were victorious at Pavia (14 June) and on 20 June they entered Milan. By the end of the month the French had retreated across the Alps and the Confederates were in possession of Domo d'Ossola, Locarno, Lugano and Mendrisio.

Meanwhile the Grisons took the Adda valley, and the fiefs of Bormio and Chiavenna which they held till 1797. Wherever they went, driving out the French, the Swiss were acclaimed as liberators by the people.

On 29 September the young Duke Maximilian Sforza formally assigned all these territories to the Confederation. He agreed to be reinstated in his Duchy under conditions which made him little more than a bailiff. He rode into his capital on 29 December 1512. Ulrich von Hohensax and the other Swiss army leaders handed the keys of the city to him under the Porta Tricinese.

The King of France made another attempt to seize Milan the following year. But the French army was crushed at Novara, on 6 June 1513, during a battle in which the odds all seemed at first to be against the Confederates.

Now, for a brief space of time, the Swiss were at the pinnacle of their material power and military glory. They did not hesitate before attacking France on her own territory. Foreign wars were a solution to their internal problems which, at that time, were many and threatening—the year 1513 had seen revolts in Berne, Solothurn and Lucerne. The Confederates entered Burgundy and marched on Dijon. But the army's morale, which reflected that of the Swiss people in general, was so bad that its leaders preferred to negotiate and a peace treaty was signed on 13 September which gave the Swiss virtual possession of the Duchy of Milan and neutralized the Franche-Comté.

The Confederates' mistake, at this point, was to assume that the war was over. They organized their conquests and created six bailliages in Italy, two of them in Ossola. On 13 December 1513 they received Appenzell into the Confederation as the thirteenth canton. On 19 January 1515, they renewed their close alliance with Mülhausen and prepared to rest on their laurels.

However, it should have been obvious that the French had by no means relinquished the struggle. The Holy League was disbanding. The Swiss had sole responsibility for keeping the peace in Italy, and they were constantly falling out among themselves. When François I, who succeeded Louis XII on 1 January 1515, launched a campaign against them the Swiss were taken by surprise. They dispatched an army at top speed to defend Milan. But there was rioting in the city itself against

Duke Maximilian and the army leaders kept up their quarrelling even under fire from the enemy cannon.

While part of the Confederate forces were busy negotiating the shameful Treaty of Gallarate with François I on 8 September, the rest carelessly allowed themselves to be led into a military trap on 14 September.

The Swiss were beaten at Marignano, despite prodigious feats of heroism, by the combination of the enemy's superior arms and tactics and their own lack of a common purpose.

The battle of Marignano, which barely qualified as a defeat, was nevertheless catastrophic for the Swiss. The battle demonstrated the superiority of artillery over the Swiss infantry, which had triumphed over enemy cavalry at Morgarten, Sempech and Murten. Swiss military supremacy was ended. And at this same moment rival ambitions among the Confederates prevailed over a common aim.

It is probably exaggerated to claim that the policy of neutrality and abstention which the Confederation practised from then on stems entirely from this defeat. If the Reformation had not rendered any common policy among the cantons impossible for a long time to come, Swiss abstention would no doubt have been only temporary. As it was, they continued to push back their frontiers, in 1519, 1525, 1526 and 1536. Marignano was not the cause of Swiss neutrality. But it was certainly the end of the period of glorious conquest. The Swiss, discouraged by their own lack of unity, lost faith in themselves. From that time they stuck rigidly to Nicholas of Flue's famous dictum: 'Don't meddle in foreign wars.'

The demoralization was not immediately apparent, however; on 24 September 1515, just after their defeat, the Swiss tore up the Gallarate treaty and refused to negotiate with the King of France.

There were various attempts the following year to form a new coalition against the King of France. But the King's diplomacy was adept at exploiting their internal divisions, and fomenting the mood of discouragement which followed defeat. A peace treaty was signed on 29 November 1516. The Swiss retained Lugano, Locarno, Mendrisio, Val Maggia, Valteline, Bormio and Chiavenna conquered in 1512. But they lost Ossola and the town of Milan, and this time for good.

This Peace Treaty, which completed the Austrian Treaty of 1511, has come to be known as a 'Perpetual Alliance'. In fact it lasted more than two hundred and fifty years. It was the foundation of the Confederation's foreign policy, under the old regime, and was of considerable service to Switzerland by providing a common bond between the various members of the Confederation at times of crisis.

On the eve of the Reformation, in a still fragmented Europe, Switzerland had claims over all the territory she now owns, together with Valteline, Mülhausen, Rottweil and the Franche-Comté. Public federal law had been created, and the changes that would be made throughout the old regime would be confined to secondary issues which would be gradually accentuated and elaborated. For two hundred years the Confederation affords the astonishing spectacle of a young and flourishing organism whose growth has been stopped dead, and which can only crystallize.

Chapter V

The Collapse of National Unity (1519-1603)

To assert that the Battle of Marignano put a stop to Switzerland's expansion and checked her natural evolution is in fact to enter the field of conjecture. No one knows what the lasting effects of Marignano would have been if, three years after it was fought, on 1 January 1519, Ulrich Zwingli had not entered the pulpit in Zurich's Grossmünster to preach Reform.

From then on the Confederation was to be divided against itself for many centuries. It ceased not only to play the part of a great power in Europe, but even her natural role there. The Diet was too absorbed by internal strife to evolve a foreign policy. Swiss armies enlisted under foreign standards and no longer fought to consolidate their own nation. The Swiss people were so preoccupied by denominational matters that they lost track of their collective interests.

It is pointless trying to allot blame for this collective abasement. Catholics insist that, had it not been for the Reformation, Switzerland would have continued to forge ahead. When they tried to obtain sanctions at the 1524 Diet against Zurich—the only reformed canton at that time—they no doubt believed they were acting in the national interest.

However the Reformers did not create the Reformation; it started elsewhere and imposed itself upon them. The Catholic Church is just as much responsible for the Reformation as those who put it into effect. She was later to acknowledge the need for reform by reforming herself. In any case the Reformation, in the beginning, was a powerful incentive to national expansion. It was Catholic resistance which prevented the impulse being carried through.

The division created by the Reformation, which had such dismal consequences for Switzerland, is all too apparent. The historian's task is to look for reasons rather than apportion blame.

We need to show just why the Reformation should have

come about. But that alone is not enough. We must also determine why it should have emerged as a divisive force, why it ran into difficulties, why it prevailed here and not there, and why it should have created internal frontiers which seemed much higher to the Swiss people of the time than the shared ones separating Switzerland from her neighbours. Finally, we must explain the real miracle of this tale which is not division, but union. The astonishing thing, considering the intense hatreds which the Reformation engendered, is not that the Swiss failed to achieve anything in unison, but that they stayed together despite these hatreds. The amazing thing is that the Confederation emerged whole.

This will be the framework of the following chapter. We shall first of all study the birth of the Reformation, the reasons for its success in some cantons and the resistance it met with in others. Then we shall show the repercussions it had upon the inner life of the Confederation, the mediatory role played by the mixed and neutral cantons, and by the shared bailliages, which, after provoking two civil wars, imposed a degree of collaboration upon Catholics and Reformed. Finally, in a third section, we shall examine the Confederates' foreign policy during the sixteenth century, the denominational alliances which divided them and the French alliance which brought them together. Thus we shall see the gradual emergence of a policy of neutrality, which was not preconceived so much as dictated by events, and which did not spring from the defeat at Marignano, as is often claimed, but from the divisions of the Reformation.

1. *Causes of the Reformation*

A Protestant pastor once said: 'I cannot see how a whole population can be converted.' This thought emanates from the idea of religious conversion as a phenomenon of conviction and an essentially personal experience. It underlines the mistaken assumptions which tend to obscure the real nature of the Reformation, at least in the beginning.

The Reformation appears to us now as a purely religious movement which seized hold of souls rather than minds. This indeed is the meaning the word 'reformation' has acquired over the centuries. But to begin with, at least, the great movement of ideas, which Zwingli was the first to disseminate in Switzerland, had a much more universal character, at once political, social, moral and religious.

Grave abuses had insinuated themselves into the administration of the Catholic Church. The clergy's moral and material privileges attracted a large number of people into its ranks who were without religious zeal or conviction and accepted the advantages of ecclesiastical life without its obligations. The ministry of the Church had become a highly paid and comfortable job, which imposed a heavy burden on the people: in two ways—by the taxes, dues and various duties which the clergy collected, and by the exaggeration of ritual practices, feasts, periods of fasting and so on.

These abuses were widely recognized. The Councils and prelates had made frequent attempts to check them. But these efforts towards reform within the Church met with stubborn resistance from entrenched tradition and were not supported energetically enough by the Papacy. Hence the preaching of Zwingli and his friends found a sympathetic echo among the humanists, among a large number of enlightened Catholics—and even among the leaders of the two largest Swiss dioceses, the Bishops of Basle and Constance, Christopher von Uttenheim and Hugo von Landenburg. If Zwingli had pressed for reform within the church and nothing more he could probably have counted on the support of the majority of Confederate governments.

The mass of Swiss people were pious and punctilious churchgoers but it does not follow that the civil authorities tamely submitted to orders from the Church. The great services rendered by Confederate armies to the Holy See had left Swiss magistrates conscious and proud of their power. Religion was treated as a State matter and the governments knew how to hold their own against encroachments by the clergy far better than was later to be the case. Paradoxically enough, it was the Reformation which drove the remaining Catholic administrations into the hands of the Church. However, this was not yet the position in the early years of the sixteenth century. There was endless discussion between the spiritual and temporal powers about monastic property and wealth. When the monk Samson appeared in Switzerland selling indulgences the canton governments instantly protested to Rome. This traffic was promptly abolished. These steps taken by the Zurich government aroused much less commotion at the time than might have been expected. No one was surprised that the State should intervene in a matter of ecclesiastical discipline because religious and civil affairs were closely intermingled, both in spirit and in fact.

Zwingli, who stamped his personality on the Swiss Reformation, was not a disciple of Luther. When Zwingli began his apostolate, he had never heard of the preacher of Wittenberg. Luther's influence over Zwingli is confined to one thing—it was Luther who showed Zwingli that it was possible to break with the Church, a hitherto unheard-of audacity. But that was all. Zwingli was not a monk absorbed in philosophical speculations. He was a military chaplain and a statesman.

The Reformation, in his case, was not the fruit of long hours of solitary meditation in the silence of a cell. It had been borne in upon him on the Italian battlefields, in his contacts with the soldiery, amid the dead and wounded, and the fluttering of military banners, and at the sight of the corruption inseparable from war and victory. This was why Zwingli began by preaching against military service abroad, against pensions, the tithe system, immorality, priests and wealth. His preaching was anti-clerical rather than anti-Catholic. He appealed to the people's instincts, and his fellow-citizens and adversaries saw him as a partisan rather than as an apostle.

In the early sixteenth century Switzerland had suddenly grown rich. After a long period of poverty, and the Zurich crisis, she had amassed the rich spoils of Burgundy and Italy in less than fifty years. Mercenary service abroad had been followed by a sudden influx of money into the country, and this led to profound economic and social changes. The moral outlook of the people which till then had been rough but sound, was becoming corrupt. At least this was the view of the old folk and puritans. Luxury had arrived and with it, social distinctions, almost unknown in patriarchal societies.

Zwingli strikes us now as an innovator, which in fact he was, in matters of religion. He was even, in one sense of the word, a revolutionary, in that he more than once set the anonymous, envious mob against the army officers with their pensions and the priests with their tithes. In this sense he was the real founder of the Anabaptist movement, which was more or less communist in spirit. They claimed to have pushed his teachings to their logical conclusions, but Zwingli fought them pitilessly.

But one can make out an equally good case for Zwingli as a reactionary. He preached a return to the values of the good old days. Following in the footsteps of Nicholas of Flue, with whom he has a striking moral affinity, he preached that the Swiss should go back into their history, stop trying to play a role in Europe and retire among their mountains to lead simple, healthy lives.

Zwingli's doctrine soon developed more dogmatic overtones. From a party leader he became, in his own eyes, a reformer. He set theology above discipline and politics. It was then that he entered into a violent dispute with Luther—who later thanked God for his death—over the dogma of the real presence. It was then too—as usually happens—that the people stopped understanding him and merely followed his teaching blindly.

His adversaries, meanwhile, were unaware of the change. They simply ignored it. In their eyes Zwingli was still nothing but a demagogue and agitator who undermined the social order, sapped military discipline and incited the people to loot the monasteries and refuse to pay tax. The Catholic cantons saw Zwingli as a sort of Lenin.

This was the misunderstanding the Reformation had to contend with in Switzerland. To its followers it was a religion, a faith worth dying for, but to its adversaries it was merely politics. This misconception explains the ferocity with which both sides set about fighting and destroying each other.

Zurich, at the beginning of the sixteenth century, seemed an unlikely place to be the cradle of the Reformation. Religious and social conditions there were no different from any of the other towns, where the new doctrine did not make headway until much later. In 1522, three years after Zwingli's arrival at the Grossmünster, the Zurich government made no bones about dispatching a contingent to the pontifical army in spite of all his preaching against foreign military service. In the battle of Bicoque the Zurich contingent found themselves fighting fellow-countrymen from different cantons who had enlisted in the French army. This incident was to influence Zurich's future decisions by creating a strong revulsion against foreign service and the policies of the Pope. At the same time it aroused fierce resentment against Zurich in the forest cantons, who were allies of France.

The Reformation was born in Zurich. This central fact must be borne in mind because it is the key to the whole mystery. Zurich was not a Confederate State like the others. The generation which fought at St Jacques had only just passed away. Memories of the Diet of Stans were still vivid. Zurich was the traditional enemy of Schwytz. The mere fact that the Reformation was first triumphantly expounded in Zurich was enough to make the forest cantons close their ears.

In any case the abuses which Zwingli inveighed against, whether secular or ecclesiastical, were not felt so strongly in the rural districts as in the towns. The clergy there were autochthonous, living among the people. Scarcely anything separated peasants and peasants' sons. These deeply pious but far from mystical people had no conception of the great abuses rife in the Church. When one talked to the forest cantons of the troubles of the Church of Christ, they did not understand.

But they understood perfectly well when one spoke to them of suppressing military service abroad, and they were furious. Mercenary service in industrial and commercial towns was restricted to a relatively small class of people, mostly officers, who derived both honour and profit from it. And it was a simple matter to rouse the people against them. In the country, however, mercenary service was the only means of livelihood of a large section of the population. Switzerland can only scrape by on the proceeds of her agriculture. The profits modern Switzerland draws from her industries are owed to the steady stream of emigration in preceding centuries. We must remember that Switzerland in the sixteenth century was an overpopulated country. Her population, we are told, was only slightly smaller than that of England. Thus emigration was a social necessity. Switzerland then was in an analogous situation to certain regions of Italy today. The only emigration possible was military emigration. François I had 163,000 Swiss under his command. There were generally 20,000 Swiss serving in the French army, and some 60,000 in other European armies. The money which flowed into the country as a result ran into millions—36 million pounds from the French recruits alone between 1594 and 1605. The Confederates did not grow rich on this money—they needed it to survive. The central cantons who had to import almost all their foodstuffs had no other resources with which to pay their bills. What Zwingli was asking of the forest cantons—at least this is how it was interpreted to them—was that they should either die of hunger or have no more children.

Other differences should also be mentioned: the fact that the bourgeois, intellectual class who made up the Reformation's following in the cities did not exist in the rural areas; the absence of those feudal and ecclesiastical overlords whose unpopularity drove many of the towns to embrace the new teaching. All these reasons contributed to the forest cantons' implacable resistance to the doctrines of Reform. A few of its preachers managed to infiltrate Schwytz and Uri but the populace rose up against them. The same thing happened in Zug and Lucerne, which was the forest cantons' natural outlet and whose policies were inseparably intermingled with theirs. Thus we see a spontaneous regrouping of the five cantons who had led the war against Zurich eighty-five years earlier.

Only two of the mountain cantons were penetrated by the Reformation, and their conversion was only partial. These were Glarus, where Zwingli had exercised his calling before going to Zurich and where he had many friends, and Appenzell, which seized on the Reformation as a new weapon in its struggle against the Abbot of St Gallen.

There was every reason why the towns should espouse the new doctrines—corruption of the clergy and the effects of mercenary service were more in evidence there, they had a much more numerous class of leisured, cultured people, the preachers spoke to them directly, and the fairs, which were a powerful means of disseminating ideas and propaganda, were held frequently in them. Most of the towns adopted the new doctrine and used it to crush what was left of the old feudal powers. In their eyes the Reformation was the completion of the long process of emancipation which had freed them from medieval servitude. Only Lucerne and Zug remained untouched, because of their links with the forest cantons. Evangelical communities were formed at Fribourg and Rottweil, but too late to make much impact on the bourgeoisie before the strong Catholic counter movement which followed hard on the second Kappel war. Solothurn likewise, which had been briefly converted, was snatched out of Protestantism by a *coup d'état*, 30 October 1533, which was a direct result of this war.

With these few exceptions all the towns, allies and Confederates alike, eagerly followed the example set by Zurich within the next ten years—St Gallen, Constance, Schaffhausen, Basle, Mülhausen, Strasbourg, Bienne, Berne. The Reformation made its chief impact everywhere on the popular elements, led by a few intellectuals. It entered the towns via the guilds. The ruling families, on the other hand, who drew most of their revenue from mercenary service, were refractory to begin with. Fribourg, for instance, remained Catholic because of the opposition of the ruling caste. The same thing almost happened at

Berne, which was the aristocratic town par excellence, and where the Reformation was finally imposed on the Petit Conseil by the Two Hundred.

By far the most important collective conversion was that of Berne, in 1528. It took place at a slow, reflective and moderate pace, unlike Zurich, and was brought about by a series of considerations in which practical politics as well as theology played a part. Practical considerations included the need to prevent Zurich assuming too much importance as head of the Protestant party, and, more important still, the inspiration, which gradually came to Berne, of using the Reformation as a weapon against Savoy, whose Leman possessions Berne coveted. Politically, this was an adroit step, and shows how profitable the Reformation might have been to Switzerland, if she had adopted it universally and known what use to make of it.

Basle was Switzerland's only university town. Thanks to Erasmus and Holbein it was one of the centres of European humanism, and the university's influence there was considerable though indirect. Officially, the university, founded by Pope Pius II in 1460, stayed loyal to its protector and eschewed the Reformation. Most of the professors emigrated to Freiburg-im-Breisgau, after the bourgeoisie had adopted the new doctrine and the university closed its gates. Erasmus himself left Basle full of resentment. The great humanist, and translator of the Bible, had nevertheless done as much as anyone to create an atmosphere in which the principles of the Reformation would be understood and welcomed, as preached by the eloquent and learned Oecolampadius.

In St Gallen, as in Appenzell, the determining factor was undoubtedly the old rivalry between the middle class and the monastery. The bourgeois found a weapon against their abbot in the Reformation. And much the same thing happened in the other episcopal cities. The bishops who had been the natural protectors of the bourgeoisie against feudal oppression for many centuries had ended by making common cause with the feudal elements against the bourgeoisie.

Geneva is a typical example of this. The episcopacy had been in the hands of the House of Savoy since the mid fifteenth century. Its sons and bastards succeeded each other on the episcopal throne. The last was John of Savoy (1513). In 1523 a puppet of the Duke's, Pierre de la Baume, succeeded him.

At this time, following Geneva's alliance with the cantons,

relations between the Duke and the bourgeoisie became extremely strained. The Genevese saw the Reformation, which was just reaching them from Berne, as a means of tightening their alliance with the Swiss on the one hand and protecting themselves from the Duke and his bishop on the other.

The new teaching, or rather the administrative form of it, spread from the towns into the surrounding countryside. In some cases this happened quite spontaneously because of the natural prestige and influence of towns as centres of enlightenment as well as trade. Sometimes this happened as the result of an administrative decision. No State believed in the sixteenth century that religion could be an individual matter. Every ruler felt he had the right to impose his will in a matter which pertained to public order.

The Reformation fanned out from Zurich, Schaffhausen, Constance and St Gallen, penetrating swiftly into Thurgau, Appenzell, Toggenburg, Rheintal and the country round Sargans. Basle's influence was felt in the Jura, Berne's and Zurich's in Aargau. Berne succeeded finally in imposing the new doctrine on all her possessions, though she met with fierce resistance in Oberland and Hasli, whose peasantry took up arms against the new faith, supported by the people of Unterwald.

One of Berne's subject possessions, since the Burgundian wars, was the fief of Aigle; Farel set out from there in 1526 to convert the Savoyard territory round Lake Geneva, paving the way for the magnificent campaign of 1536. The Reform had already bitten deep into these regions before the conquest, and from there it rapidly spread to the Vaud region, the Bernese part of Gruyères, Lower Valais and Chablais.

If we add the fact that two out of the three Rhaetian leagues had gone over to the Reformation—the Gotteshaus and the Ten Jurisdictions—we will have a pretty comprehensive picture of Switzerland's denominational lay-out towards 1530, after the first invasion of the new doctrine.

Four of the thirteen cantons which regularly took part in the Diet belonged to the new movement. These were Zurich, Basle, Berne and Schaffhausen. Six more were deeply hostile to the new movement—Lucerne, Zug, Fribourg, Schwytz, Uri and Unterwald. The remaining three—Glarus, Appenzell and Solothurn—were hesitant or divided in their allegiance, and they played the role of mediators. Most of the members of the various alliances were Reformed, being urban communities.

The Valais was not an altogether reliable adherent of the Catholic cause.

During the sixteenth century, however, this situation changed in a direction favourable to the Church, as a result of two events which had a strengthening effect on Catholicism. These were the consequences of the second war of Kappel, and the movement towards reform within the Church itself.

2. *The Religious Wars*

It is hard for us now to conceive of the intense hatreds which divided Catholics and Reformed during the sixteenth century, hatreds nourished on memories of the old conflicts of the previous century. To the Evangelists the Catholics were not merely pagans and idolators, but monsters of corruption, the puppets of Austria and traitors to their country. The Catholics, for their part, saw the Protestants as heretics and atheists—at a time when crimes of conscience were punishable by death—and destroyers of the social order. The communistic Anabaptist movement which swept Zurich in 1525 lent colour to this legend in spite of the persecution to which it was subjected. Debates in the Diet would soon have been an impossibility had it not been for the mediation of the mixed or neutral cantons.

As we know, of the five States admitted to the Confederation since the Stans Diet, the last three—Basle, Schaffhausen and Appenzell—in particular had been admitted only on the express understanding that they remained neutral during any disputes which might arise among the Confederates. On the whole this stipulation was respected. Furthermore, Glarus, which was not a party to this contract, undertook to maintain parity between the denominations of her own accord. Thus a block of Deputies grew up in the Diet whose aim, far from inciting hatreds and violent solutions, was to preach calm and moderation.

The existence of jointly administered bailliages also helped foster a degree of collaboration among the Confederates. It will be recalled that the Swiss were in the habit, since the capture of Aargau in 1415, of regarding their conquests as joint assets. These regions were governed by bailiffs, appointed by each of the cantons in turn, who gave an account of their administration to the Diet. The systems of government in the bailliages varied greatly but they all had this in common, that they depended on a degree of collaboration from several cantons.

With things as they were this collaboration must have been difficult to achieve. Catholics and Protestants could not agree about the nature of the Reformation. The only point on which they agreed was that religion was the business of the government. The people of Zurich believed that God's will and the public interest demanded that they should help the spread of the new doctrine, whereas the forest cantons were convinced that every possible measure, even death, should be used to prevent its dissemination. It followed that the joint bailliages, while imposing some co-operation on the Confederates, would inevitably foster new troubles and conflicts. On two occasions these led to civil war.

Zwingli, the authoritarian ruler within his own canton, preached moderation in the joint bailliages—a contradiction which shows what happens when principles run up against the facts. This did not mean toleration for the individual—a notion much too advanced for that time. A man was not free to practise the religion of his choice. But each parish was allowed to cast a majority vote—'by the most' as they say in French Switzerland—for the denomination which it would follow. Zwingli realized that restriction, rather than freedom of worship, could only help his cause in a predominantly Catholic region, especially as the bailiffs appointed by Zurich did not go out of their way to assist the process of collective conversion.

This was the thinking which brought about the first peace treaty of Kappel.

It is quite wrong to talk of the first 'war' of Kappel, incidentally, because the only war existed in Zwingli's imagination. He saw the freedom to preach the new doctrine, even in the forest cantons, as a means of converting the whole of Switzerland to the Reformed faith. The Catholic cantons were unprepared for war and had no desire for it. The neutral cantons—including Berne, who did not want to go to war either—seized on this to play a mediatory role with Zurich. So peace was concluded, on 16 February 1529, without there ever having been a war.

Zwingli was disappointed. He had not obtained the right to preach in the Catholic cantons, but only in the jointly held bailliages. Adherents of the old faith were equally disappointed, however, because the freedom to preach and proselytize meant prompt conversion in the bailliages round about Zurich.

Aargau, quite apart from any religious considerations, was important both strategically and politically as the seat of the Diet and a communication route between Berne and Zurich on the one hand, and Lucerne and Solothurn on the other. The forest cantons hemmed in by Reformed Zurich and Berne, half-converted Glarus and Toggenburg, by the Protestant Leagues and the unpredictable Valais, were forced to rely on the joint bailliages of Aargau and the Ticino as their means of communication with the outside world.

Under these circumstances neither Zwingli nor his adversaries could be expected to regard the Peace of Kappel as final. In fact, both parties saw it as a truce. The only historic significance of the first Kappel 'war' is that it prepared the ground for, and triggered off, the second.

Zwingli's activity during the next two years was deliberately provocative. It is almost as though the great Reformer knew he had not much time left. He tried to squeeze the last drop out of the peace settlement, and a few more besides, which were the drops he would have liked it to contain. A man of Zurich as well as a Protestant, he was anxious to secure the political and moral hegemony for Zurich which she had tried to win for herself in her battles with the Confederates the century before. He abandoned every Confederate precaution in Thurgau and Toggenburg, and set out to interpret freedom for Protestants in such a way as to impose an intolerable tyranny on Catholic consciences.

Zwingli was being perfectly logical. He wanted war and was not afraid to show it. 'This peace is a war,' he wrote. His thinking, ever more religious and denominational, could no longer tolerate delays in the triumph of the truth.

Unfortunately for him, his authoritarian temperament did not make him enemies only among his religious opponents. He entered into bitter conflict with Luther and made a point of repudiating the Evangelical cities of southern Germany. Even in Zurich, opposition to him was growing among the bourgeoisie. On 25 July 1531, Zwingli anticipated Calvin's famous gesture and handed in his resignation to the Council. He was asked to stay, but under conditions which made it clear to him that he was not going to be allowed to make more trouble.

These internal problems, which were one of the chief contributory factors to the second Kappel war, temporarily paralysed all preparations for it. Zwingli made the mistake of so many rulers; he wanted a diversionary war but failed to organize it properly. He felt that victory would be the only means of regaining his authority, but he did not have the means to enforce his policy.

This war, which was to arrest the spread of the Reformation in Switzerland and contain the Evangelical creed, was forced upon the Catholics. On 16 May 1531 Zurich decided to close its markets to the forest cantons—in other words to run a blockade against them. To understand what this meant, it must be pointed out that there was not a single wheat field throughout the whole of Uri and Schwytz under the old regime. For the second time in one century, this measure, which aimed at starving the inner cantons till they pleaded for mercy, forced them to attack in self-defence. And for the second time, Zurich, which had taken the offensive, was completely routed. In a few days, in two battles, at Kappel and Gubel, on 11 and 23 October 1531, the Catholic forces completely crushed their opponents from Zurich. Zwingli was killed, on 11 October, before Kappel on the boundary between Zug and Zurich. The second national peace treaty, which was vastly more important than the first, was signed on 20 November.

The Catholic cantons refrained from abusing their success—which was precarious in any case since Berne had abstained from the battle. But they made good use of it. The principle of the denominational status quo was instituted, to the detriment of Protestants alone. No parish in the joint bailliages was to be allowed to adopt the Reformed faith. But it was permissible for reformed parishes to return to the old faith.

More important still, the prestige of this victory greatly enhanced the Catholic cause. Catholic bailiffs in the bailliages were free to act as they pleased while Reformed bailiffs had their hands tied. Catholicism won back ground in Gaster, Rapperswil, Sargans, Toggenburg and the Rheintal, as well as in Thurgau and the territories of the St Gallen Abbey. The Catholic cantons brutally dispersed the Evangelical community in Lucarno, and its members—among them the Pestalozzi, Orelli and Muralt—sought refuge in Zurich. In Glarus the Reform movement was halted, and likewise in Fribourg. Finally, on 30 October 1533, Solothurn was won back to Catholicism by a bold seizure of power which the Reformed towns did not dare oppose.

What was significant about this second national peace treaty was not so much the amount of ground reconquered by Catholicism, which was negligible, as the fact that it left Switzerland permanently divided between the two denominations. If the war had turned out differently it is possible that even the mountain cantons would have eventually fallen to the Reformation. As it was that hope was permanently extinguished.

Instead of pacifying the contestants, the peace treaty merely enraged them. It had created a political equilibrium which did not correspond to the real strength of the two parties. In the federal Diet the Catholics now disposed—thanks to Solothurn's reconversion—of seven out of thirteen votes. Yet Berne, Basle and Zurich on their own were vastly more powerful than the Catholics. It is always dangerous for a State when a gap yawns between the law and the realities.

Both parties gradually fell into the habit of holding separate Diets. The first Catholic Diet was held at Beckenried on 8 April 1524. These meetings grew more and more frequent. Denominational alliances became standard practice. Far from restoring unity to the Confederation, the Peace of Kappel ruptured it once and for all.

The Catholic position was further consolidated during the next few decades by the process of reform taking place within the Church itself. When the Reformation was first launched the Church, in spite of a few isolated efforts to put a stop to the more striking abuses, had been caught unawares. For about twenty-five years or so the Reformation had a striking moral and intellectual advantage over the defenders of the traditional faith.

But the Church lost no time in profiting by the lesson given to it, and one might well ask whether the Reformation's greatest service was not to the Catholic Church. The Council of Trent and the founding of the Jesuit Order were direct consequences of the Reformation. Without it they would have been inconceivable and it would be fair to say that they proceeded from a similar state of mind, from the same search for moral purity and spiritual enlightenment.

From the middle of the sixteenth century the Church was determined to show the world that schism and the one true evangelical life were not inseparable, and to some extent she succeeded. The calendar reforms she instituted, for instance, aroused violent controversy and actually set the Protestants against scientific progress.

The apostolic activities of such men as St Charles Borromeo, R. P. Canisius, St François de Sales, would have been inconceivable, or useless, if the Church had not taken herself in hand. Events like the introduction of Jesuits to Lucerne and Fribourg, and of Capuchin monks in the other Catholic cantons, the founding of the nunciature at Lucerne and of the Helvetic College at Rome, were events which testified to the progress of the Restoration.

From the mid-sixteenth century on the Church had once more recovered her momentum. She reconquered positions which had seemed irretrievably lost—Constance, the Valais, Chablais. In 1564 Glarus split off into two separate communities. In 1597 Appenzell became two half-cantons. By then the impetus of the Reformation, which had lasted barely twenty-five years, was definitely checked.

3. *The Confederates' Foreign Policy*

At the onset of the Reformation Swiss military prestige was, if not intact, still very considerable. It was only forty years or so since the Confederate armies had destroyed the greatest military power of the day in the Burgundian wars, and only twenty years since they inflicted a crushing defeat on the Emperor in the Swabian wars. Ten years earlier they had entered Milan as conquerors, trailing Duke Maximilian Sforza behind their banners, and for many years now they had completely dominated Northern Italy.

A single defeat had not undermined these triumphs. People are slow to catch on to radical innovations. Developments in artillery warfare might have challenged the supremacy of the Confederate army, but the Swiss infantryman was still the finest fighter in Europe. One campaign, in 1536, won them the whole of Northern Savoy. Parodoxical as it may seem it was between the years of 1536–1564, before Chablais, Genevois and Gex were restored to the House of Savoy, that Switzerland, already decadent from the political point of view, achieved her greatest territorial triumphs.

From Hungary to England, the Princes all sought an alliance with Switzerland. Internal strife forced the Swiss into a policy of neutrality. This actually increased, rather than lessened, their military importance as well as the opportunities for deploying it. The only trouble was that the country no longer derived any advantages from these enterprises, apart from pecuniary ones.

As we know, most of the federal alliances reserved the right for the cantons to make separate alliances with foreign powers. They made great use of this right during the sixteenth century and it was this, even more than civil war, which came within an ace of destroying the Confederation altogether.

On 8 April 1524, the Catholic cantons concluded the first denominational alliance with each other, a veritable Sonderbund. On 25 June 1528, it was the turn of Berne and Zurich to enter into a 'Christian' pact, first of a great network of similar alliances which was to take in St Gallen, Constance, Bienne, Mülhausen, Basle, Schaffhausen, Strassburg and others. The Catholics replied to this by concluding a 'Christian alliance' with Austria at Waldshut on 22 April 1529.

After this, the two policies followed widely divergent paths—determined to a certain extent by geography. The Protestant policy was expansionist, the Catholics' to preserve the territorial status quo.

Like the French Revolution in the eighteenth century, the Swiss Reformation in the sixteenth century led to a policy of imperialism via conversion. All the countries bordering on the Confederation were Catholic. Believing in their apostolic mission, the Swiss Protestants felt obliged to spread the word among them. The easiest way to do this was to conquer—or at the least make alliances—with them. Temporal and spiritual interests coincided, so that nationalism was an expression of religious faith.

After the second Kappel war stopped the spread of conversion within the country, the only direction in which the Swiss Reformation could expand was outwards, enlarging national and religious frontiers simultaneously. It had to do this to survive. And it needed to make up the ground it had lost by enlarging the Confederation, bringing in new allies and, if possible, new Confederates. Everything combined to set the Protestants on the path of conquest.

Zurich on the one hand, Berne on the other, both energetically pursued this policy.

Zwingli's ambitions went further than the Christian alliance which linked St Gallen, Mülhausen and Bienne to the Confederation as members of an evangelical community. He roped in Constance, the virtual capital of Thurgau, as well, and

Strassburg. Zwingli's doctrine dominated the South German towns and the way seemed open for a political alliance. In 1530 he persuaded Philip of Hesse to enter the Christian alliance. He envisaged this as the beginning of a great series of alliances which would take in Württemberg, the German towns, and if possible Venice and France: in other words, all the world powers who had reason to fear the Empire.

This grand design was doomed to failure because it was unrealistic. Memories of the Swabian war and Luther's influence were much too powerful for the German towns to contemplate making pacts with their traditional enemies and Luther's adversary. Zwingli, on his side, was not prepared to make the dogmatic concessions which his policy demanded. On 28 December 1530, the German towns—including Constance and Strassburg—joined together in the League of Schmalkalden. The Swiss were excluded from this just as they had been from the Swabian League the century before. When Emperor Charles V decided to destroy the League in 1545, the Protestant Swiss towns were so paralysed by opposition from the Catholic cantons that they sat by and watched the destruction without raising a finger to help. Strassburg, even Constance, the key to Thurgau, were shamefully abandoned by the Swiss. It is one of the darkest passages in Swiss history.

This war turned out disastrously for the Reformation. The Confederation lost Constance, which was deprived of its Imperial protection and dragged forcibly back into the lap of the Church. The same thing happened to Strassburg. It was useless for Berne and Zurich to make a new evangelical alliance with the Margrave of Baden in 1612. By then the proselytizing force of Protestantism in Southern Germany was destroyed, and with it the magnetic power of the Confederation.

Luckily Berne's policies had met with more success along the western frontiers of Switzerland.

The Burgundian wars left Berne in possession of the fief of Aigle, together with the bailliages of Murten, Grandson, Orbe and Echallens, which she administered jointly with Fribourg. The two cantons also had rights over Gruyères, and over the Vaud region, which belonged to Savoy and to the Bishop of Lausanne. Since 1512 the Swiss had been in occupation of Neuchâtel, a county belonging to the Orléans-Longueville. At length, in 1526, Berne and Fribourg entered into alliance with Lausanne and Geneva.

Guillaume Farel, the great Reformer in French Switzerland, was a native of Dauphiné. He began his preaching at Aigle in 1526, under the protection of the Berne authorities. A man of weak physical build but unconquerable moral strength, he covered all the bailliages over which Berne ruled. He even appeared in what was strictly speaking Savoyard territory and in the four valleys of Piedmont. He preached in the Bishopric of Basle, in St Imier and Moutiers-Grandval, and he evangelized Neuchâtel in 1529 before Switzerland restored it to its Counts. Finally, in October 1532, he made his first appearance at Geneva.

The theme of his preaching was strictly religious, a fact which should be borne in mind if we are to have an undistorted view of events. All the same he had chosen the right time and place to speak.

Geneva was an old episcopal town. During the middle ages she had submitted to the twofold authority of the bishop, and the feudal lord, the Count, later Duke, of Savoy. He was the heir to the Counts of Geneva, who held the right of *vidomnat* over the town, or what was then called the right of attorney, or the right to administer common law (*basse justice*).

For many centuries the Bishop had played his natural role, protecting the bourgeoisie against the feudal powers. However, during the fifteenth century, a cunning stroke brought the episcopal throne into the hands of the Dukes of Savoy and since then it had been occupied either by members of their family, or their puppets.

Thenceforth the bourgeoisie were defenceless, at the mercy of their rulers' schemes and forced to look elsewhere for an ally against the Dukes.

Possession of Geneva was a historical necessity to the House of Savoy. Geneva was the natural trading centre for the whole of Northern Savoy. Strategically speaking she was the key to the Vaud region. Geneva represented prosperity and security to that entire region of the Duchy. The Dukes of Savoy had pressing reasons for seeking to tighten their hold on Geneva, reasons which overruled the wishes of its citizens. As feudalism crumbled around them they sought to transform their rights into territorial sovereignty.

The bourgeoisie, for their part, were quite aware of the Savoy policy. They turned to the one power capable of standing up to the House of Savoy—Switzerland. Immediately after the Burgundian wars Geneva took stock of the political situation and tried to make an alliance with the Confederates. In 1519 the efforts of the Eidguenot party, led by Philibert Berthelier, met with partial success—a citizens' treaty was signed with Fribourg. But this alliance came up against opposition from the Diet, the Bernese, who had been excluded from it, and from the supporters of Savoy—the Mamelukes—who were a force in the town. It had to be abandoned.

All the same Geneva managed to obtain a new alliance with Fribourg and Berne in 1526. Berne, at this point, had not officially declared itself for the Reformation. This alliance was highly unpopular with the House of Savoy, which retaliated by endless raids on Geneva's territory and all sorts of brigandry against its fairs and merchants. The 1530 treaty of St Julien notwithstanding, it was clear that a serious dispute was brewing which must end with the submission of Geneva or the defeat of the Duke.

These were the circumstances attending the arrival of Farel, then Froment, in the town—at the express recommendation of the Bernese authorities. This was enough to earn them the goodwill of the section of Genovese who realized at once that the best way to secure Geneva's independence would be to use religion to distance her from the Bishop and the Dukes of Savoy, while bringing her closer to the Confederates.

The Reformation made rapid progress in Geneva. All the same the final decision between Church and Reform was difficult to make and several years passed before it was reached. To break with Catholicism meant breaking with Fribourg too, and losing all hope of being admitted to the Confederation. To reject the Reformation meant coming into conflict with Berne—and in all probability falling into the hands of Savoy. This last consideration was the most persuasive in the end. But the Reformation did not finally triumph in Geneva till 21 May 1536, a time when the republic of Berne was actually at war with Savoy over Geneva's independence, and when the town had a Bernese garrison. To quibble any longer would have been dangerous. *Periculum in mora*. Geneva's adoption of the Reformation was, to a certain extent, a declaration of war against Savoy.

In 1534 Duke Charles III resorted to an old ruse. He closed his frontiers against Geneva, in violation of the 1530 treaty, and sought to starve the town with a blockade. That there was no immediate reaction was only because the Bernese were afraid that, in attacking Savoy, they might run foul of France. In 1535, however, the King and the Duke fell out over a matter relating to Italy. The Bernese opened their campaign at once—chiefly to prevent Geneva falling into the hands of France. So, indirectly, it was Geneva who secured the Vaud region for Switzerland! Conversely, it was the nearness of Berne which proved Geneva's surest safeguard.

Time was running out. Berne declared war on the Duke of Savoy on 16 January 1536. Almost immediately Hans-Franz Naegli conquered the whole of the Vaud region at one stroke, together with the Bishopric of Lausanne, the Gex region, Chablais, part of Faucigny and the Genevois. The Bernese, who conferred the abolition of serfdom on their conquered territories by way of a celebratory gesture, were warmly received by the population. On 2 February, Bernese troops entered Geneva amid general acclaim. The men of Valais, then Fribourg entered the war. Within a few weeks all the Duke's possessions in Leman were in Swiss hands.

This was a conquest of vital importance, far outweighing the capture of Ticino. It seems improbable, in view of the tendency of modern nationalism to create great states founded on a single language, that Switzerland would have kept her identity if she had remained purely a Germanic country. The Bernese were almost certainly unaware of the national implications of their conquest of the Vaud region, for a diversity of language was nothing new at the time. But the victory gave new vigour to the Confederation, and may even have saved its life.

This was something the Catholic cantons refused to admit. They saw the conquest of Northern Savoy as a gigantic rape of Church lands, rather than a valuable acquisition to their country. Bitterly and persistently they came out, on ten different occasions, against Berne and Geneva and for Savoy. This attitude died hard. As late as 1798 the Catholics continued to insist that Federal territory ended at Murten.

Calvin's presence there, and the theocratic administration which the French reformer imposed on the town, were factors which contributed to Geneva's growing European renown. Under its new spiritual leader, Geneva, capital of French Protestantism, sanctuary and university city, underwent a profound transformation. This did not happen without some stiff resistance on the part of the bourgeoisie, however, who resented seeing newcomers take over power in their administration. The

Berne Councils had to intervene between Calvin and his adversaries on several occasions, usually taking the latter's part. The Catholic cantons, meanwhile, never stopped protesting in the Diets against the alliance between Berne—and since 1584, Zurich—with Geneva. In their view this introduced the town into the federal system and made Switzerland, after a fashion, the centre of the Reformation.

By the treaty of Cateau-Cambrésis, 3 April 1559, the Duke of Savoy recovered all his possessions which had been in French hands for more than twenty years and which included Savoy, Bresse and Bugey. This unexpected turn of events was a terrible blow for Geneva, because it completely changed the balance of power in the Leman basin. So long as the Duke of Savoy, as France's enemy, was occupied with the task of regaining control of his hereditary states, he had not paid much attention to the Savoy possessions now in Swiss hands. Now that the new Duke Emmanuel-Philibert, self-declared liberator of his country, was safely back in command in Chambéry, Annecy and Bourg, it would not be long before he cast about for ways of recapturing Lausanne, Gex, Thonon and Geneva, especially since some of the Catholic cantons had entered into a treaty with him, on 11 November 1560, which recognized the whole of the Vaud region as the Duke's legitimate property.

To Berne and Geneva this alliance was nothing less than a betrayal. It was bad enough for the Duke to regain the regions conquered by France. But now the Bernese saw themselves faced with another war in which their own Catholic confederates would be fighting side by side with the Duke. They felt compelled to capitulate. They have been criticized for this decision but it is arguable whether there was any other course open to them. The Treaty of Lausanne, 30 October 1564, restored the bailliages of Gex, Ternier and Thonon to the Duke of Savoy, in return for the formal relinquishment of the Vaud region. With the Treaty of Thonon, 3 March 1569, the people of Valais in their turn surrendered the region of Chablais between St Gingolph and the Dranse, including the Vallée d'Abondance. They retained only the bailliage of Monthey, St Maurice and the Val d'Illiez. The frontiers created by these treaties have scarcely altered since.

The Lausanne Treaty left Geneva, once more embedded in Savoy lands, at the mercy of the Duke. In this emegency the people of Geneva looked for help from another quarter—by tightening their bonds with the Swiss. They asked to be admitted into the Confederation as a canton. This request was twice refused by the Diet, in 1572, and again in 1573. The Catholic cantons went further. They promised the Duke explicitly on 26 October 1574 that they would forbid any alliance between their evangelical Confederates and Geneva. Such an undertaking was a breach of federal law. Finally, on 8 May 1577, they consolidated their alliance with the Duke, which was to be renewed subsequently on several different occasions, most notably the accession of Charles-Emmanuel in 1581.

From now on the House of Savoy was to oscillate between two policies—an Italian policy and a Transalpine—or, as it was then called, a Burgundian—policy. It was widely recognized that Charles-Emmanuel, Philip II's son-in-law, ally of Spain and the League, was resolved to prosecute his ancestors' Burgundian policy against the King of France. This, necessarily, involved re-possessing Geneva.

So began a long diplomatic and military war between Savoy and Geneva, which was to drag on for more than twenty years, ending, soon after the *Escalade*, with the peace of St Julien. The first people the Genevans turned to were their traditional protectors—the Swiss. They managed to renew their alliance with Berne, on 30 August 1584, and make Zurich a party to it. But they failed to soften the inflexible hostility of the Catholic cantons. The latter refused another request by Geneva to be admitted to the Confederation and went on to consolidate their Savoyard policy with the Borromeo League of 1586 and a Spanish alliance in 1587.

Geneva found herself abandoned to the enemy. She was a prey to continual attack, too weak to hold her own and obliged to rely on imports for food. She now turned toward the Duke of Savoy's traditional enemy, the King of France. The King, fortunately, recognized that Geneva's independence was his own surest safeguard against the ambitions of Savoy.

As a policy this was a dangerous one for Geneva to adopt, although the policy had a precedent in Berne's Solothurn Treaty of 8 May 1579. It was not as risky then as it was to prove later, since the King of France was not a neighbour of theirs.

On 19 April 1589, the Genevans signed a treaty with M. de Sancy, Henri III's ambassador, which promised them considerable territorial gains. This was a reasonable stipulation. Geneva could not survive the constant threat of blockade.

This would have meant famine. The only way to guarantee her independence was to move back her frontiers, and thus become self-supporting.

In 1589, thanks to the war which had broken out between France and Savoy, the Genevans re-occupied the Gex region, Chablais and Faucigny. They wanted to make sure that their city, which was not playing a leading role in world politics, had an adequate territorial base. They would most likely have succeeded if Henri IV had kept the promises made by Henri III, and if the Swiss had not deserted them. Unfortunately, Henri IV was playing a double game. Geneva got nothing from the Treaty of Vervins (1598), nor from the Treaty of Lyons, 17 January 1601—neither security nor land. The Genevans were forced to surrender the Gex region, their granary, to their ally the King of France, despite the fact that they had occupied it for more than ten years and that Henri IV himself had said: 'I have no more right to this country than I have to Castile.' In return for this territory, which was the price of their independence, the Genevans had to be content with certain economic concessions granted to them by the letters patent of 25 May 1602. These were the origin of free zones. But it was a meagre return for a kingdom. In 1602 the Swiss renewed their treaty with the King of France without making the slightest effort on behalf of the Genevans. They were probably happy that French territory now lay adjacent to their own frontiers.

The Duke of Savoy took his cue from this general desertion of Geneva to make a last all-out attempt to capture the city. St Francis of Sales had just succeeded—between 1594 and 1598—in re-converting Chablais, evangelized by Berne, to Catholicism. This was a region where the reform had seemed deeply rooted. Charles-Emmanuel decided the time was ripe to take Geneva by storm. He attacked on 12 December 1602—the night of the *Escalade*. He came very close to succeeding—amid the acclaim of the whole Catholic world, the Confederates included. The capture of Geneva would have been an event of international significance. It would have been a death blow to the Reformation in the French-speaking countries, and in all likelihood throughout Europe. However, the *Escalade* was a failure, for reasons which remain obscure. The peace of St Julien, 21 July 1603, finally put an end to Savoy designs on the capital of Calvin's Reformation.

The attitude of the Catholic cantons towards Geneva reflected their systematic policy, which in turn proceeded from their denominational and economic situation.

Swiss territory was circumscribed from Stelvio to Montbéliard by the Empire. Spain owned the Franche-Comté and the Duchy of Milan. Savoy lands stretched from the Jura to the Ticino. If one subtracts the Valteline frontier and the Venetian Republic, Switzerland emerges surrounded on all sides by her hereditary foes.

Any policy aiming at maintaining the territorial status quo for denominational reasons would be forced to seek an alliance with Switzerland's enemies. This in fact was the substance of Catholic policy during the sixteenth century. In so doing the Catholic cantons turned their back on all their national traditions. It was this Catholic policy, and not the Reformation, which halted the growth of Switzerland.

It should be added though that the Catholic cantons had some justification for acting as they did. Denominational passions were not their only motive. They were driven, one might almost say coerced, to adopt this policy by their own geographical position and economic dependence, as a glance at the map will prove. The forest cantons, Lucerne and Zug were surrounded by the territories of the Protestant cantons. They could not expect to get provisions from there, nor were they self-supporting. Their one outlet and market was Lombardy. Thus an alliance with the Habsburgs was a vital necessity for them, at least during periods of internal tension.

On 2 April 1592 the five cantons signed a treaty with Austria at Waldshut whereby they promised to surrender any future conquests outside the Confederation to the Emperor. The cancellation of this treaty was one of the conditions imposed by the first peace of Kappel. Still, the bonds between the Catholic cantons and the Empire remained, and with time they grew closer and closer. It reached the point where the magistrates of Lucerne did not hesitate to style themselves 'subjects of the Empire', thus denying the Swabian war and the heroic efforts of the fifteenth century.

On 16 June 1557 the Catholic cantons added a Spanish alliance to the Austrian one. On 11 November 1560 they became the allies of the Duke of Savoy, and on 10 April 1565 of the Pope. They had woven a net round the country from which Switzerland was never to extricate herself. All these treaties were confirmed several times.

On 5 October 1586 the seven Catholic cantons struck up a close mutual alliance—the Golden League or Borromeo League—whose aim was to make the status quo introduced by the second Kappel Peace a permanent reality throughout the Confederation. This meant maintaining an artificial instead of a real balance of power.

This is why the Catholic cantons were forced to seek allies abroad and find them among the Confederation's natural enemies. This was why they abandoned the Rhaetian Leagues, in 1531 and 1532, to the attacks of an adventurer, the Châtelain de Musso. Between 1545 and 1548 they prevented the Protestant cantons from helping Strassburg and Constance who were at war with the Empire. In 1572, 1573, 1582, they refused to accept Geneva, and in November 1584 they refused to accept Strassburg, into the Confederation. On 13 June 1585 the Catholic cantons officially recognized the League at the risk of sabotaging the Diet's whole French policy. On 4 October 1586, they denounced the Mülhausen alliance. The following year the people of Solothurn went to the lengths of attacking a contingent from Berne which had been sent to relieve the town.

This is why the Catholic cantons renewed their alliances with Spain and Milan in 1587, 1588, 1604 and again in 1624, right in the middle of the Thirty Years War; why they voluntarily set themselves up as guardians of Franche-Comté on behalf of Spain and why they undertook to guarantee the territory of all their neighbours. One could quote dozens more examples. Even when the Catholic cantons allied themselves with the Bishop of Basle on 28 September 1579 they did not do so to increase federal territory but merely to stop the Bishop's subjects from siding with the Protestant cantons.

Such was the blindness which resulted from sectarian passions during the sixteenth century.

4. *The Principles of Union*

A degree of unity was kept up in the field of foreign policy despite these disputes, by two ideas which seem contradictory in theory to modern eyes but which in practice complemented each other very well—neutrality and the French alliance.

It is quite wrong to imagine that neutrality came as a revelation on the battlefield of Marignano and that the Swiss adopted it unanimously. Swiss neutrality was something different. It evolved from the Confederates' inability in the sixteenth century to act in unison. It is not an idea but a fact, not a principle so much as a negation.

Neutrality, at first, was a matter of Swiss internal policy. As we know, the last cantons to be admitted into the Confederation were bound by the terms of their federal charters to remain neutral in any disputes which might arise among the Confederates. In this clause lay the seed of the policy of neutrality which the Swiss have adopted ever since.

The Diet was led through force of circumstances to foster as neutral as possible an atmosphere among its members in order to avoid irremediable collisions. This neutrality towards the two parties tearing the country to pieces naturally extended to the allies of these parties abroad. These were the great powers at war in Europe. The Diet could not make a choice between the Empire, Spain, Savoy and the Pope, who were the allies of the Catholic cantons, and the Protestant princes supported by the Reformed cantons. Equally, it could not make a choice between Austria, with whom it entered into alliance in 1511, and France, to whom it was bound by the alliance of 1516. In other words, it was neutral.

This neutral policy was first put into practice between 1545 and 1547, during the war between Charles V and the Schaalkalden League. And a shameful policy it was—against all the country's best interests, and a violation of Swiss obligations towards Strassburg and Constance. But it was during the Thirty Years War (1618–1648) that neutrality was to find its most definitive expression.

Neutrality alone would not explain the federation's continuing unity. Neutrality is a negative concept—it does not divide but it cannot unite. The real bond between the members of the Confederation during the sixteenth century was the alliance with the King of France, which involved both Catholic and Protestant cantons.

The French alliance first came about after Marignano and was renewed by all François I's successors. It was sworn with particular solemnity under Henri IV, on 31 January 1602. Zurich, which abstained for some time out of loyalty to the preaching of Zwingli, joined the alliance in 1614.

The French alliance was vitally important to Switzerland because the two countries had so many interests in common. There was more in it for France than the recruitment of soldiers in the Swiss cantons, and for the Confederates, than the economic benefits earned by their concessions, together with freedom to trade on French soil. This was part of the story, to be sure, but there was more to it than that.

French policy at that time was dominated by the struggle against the Empire and against Spain—the two branches of the House of Habsburg. Essentially this struggle was a worthwhile fight against a hegemony threatening to upset the balance of power so deeply rooted in European instincts.

France was vitally concerned, throughout this long struggle, not to let the Confederation, or in other words the Alpine routes, fall into the hands of the enemy. Switzerland, which had belonged to the Empire until the Swabian war, and still thought of herself as a German country, remained bound to the Habsburgs by close alliances. There was always the danger that she might come under the Emperor's influence again, if not his rule. This was what French diplomacy was principally concerned to prevent.

To put it another way, it was in France's interest to keep Switzerland independent, which meant the Swiss had to be united, because nothing threatens a country's independence so much as internal strife.

This explains why the French alliance alone of all the alliances undertaken at that time was non-denominational. There were times when the Kings of France made use of soldiers recruited in the Catholic cantons against the Protestants. Louis de Pfyffer, 'the King of the Swiss', and his contingents played a decisive role at Jarnac, Moncontour and Meaux. The Swiss Catholics even went so far as to support the League, and meddle in the Kingdom's internal affairs. Nevertheless, France remained the ally of all the cantons. It was in her interest to calm denominational feuds, unlike Austria and Spain, who worked to foment them. French ambassadors exerted a consistently pacifying role in Switzerland.

What made this policy at once practicable and fruitful was the fact that France, while internally a Catholic nation, played the role of a Protestant power abroad. This double game underwent reverses but it remained the essential policy of French kings, the policy of Richelieu and Henri IV, dictated by the traditional opposition towards Spain and the Empire. France, as an ally of Venice and Sweden, was at the heart of every European alliance against the Empire. Her policy was exactly the same as a Protestant nation's would have been in her place.

An elder daughter of the Church, France inspired confidence throughout the Catholic cantons by her internal policy. But the foreign policy of the Most Christian King inspired equal confidence among the Protestant cantons. Thus for Switzerland in the sixteenth and seventeenth centuries the French alliance provided an element of national unity, the bond which stopped the Confederation from falling apart.

Chapter VI

The Search for Internal Stability (1607-1718)

By the first years of the seventeenth century, from the time of the *Escalade* and the St Julien treaty, the frenetic period of the Reformation had passed. The reciprocal positions of both parties as well as their territorial possessions were defined once and for all.

This is not to say that the astounding phenomenon of the Reformation did not influence the country's history for a long time to come. Religious passions were aroused more than once in the first half of the seventeenth century, by events of the Thirty Years War abroad, and by the bloody battles which took place in the Rhaetian Leagues. But it was no longer a matter of one party triumphing over the other, the victory of one religion over another. Henceforth it would be a case of colliding sympathies rather than clashing interests. This is why the unity of the country was not seriously threatened during the Thirty Years War, despite appearances and verbal disputes. It explains how the Congress of Westphalia was able to inscribe the Confederation's independence and sovereignty, at that very moment, and for the first time, in European law.

We cannot agree with the authors who suggest 1648 as the time when the Reformation ended. However important it may have been to Switzerland's national life, the Peace of Westphalia was something which happened abroad: it was not a stage in Swiss history. The Peasants' War and the first war of Villmergen were direct consequences of the Thirty Years War. There is an organic connection between these events.

The second half of the century, from the Peasants' War to the second war of Villmergen, was a time of transition from religous to political conflict. This was the period when the towns established their supremacy over rural areas, when a patrician class emerged, when the divine right of magistrates was confirmed. But it was also the period when the Protestant party made two supreme efforts to translate the real balance of power in the cantons into Confederate law.

By the end of this period the Protestant victory has destroyed the artificial equilibrium created by the Kappel treaty. It is now that we see the patrician regime in full flower. This is the beginning of the rule of Berne.

1. *The Thirty Years War*

The Thirty Years War put Switzerland in one of the most difficult situations of her history. There were many reasons for this.

Firstly, the war activated the divergent sympathies of the Swiss people to a degree unparalleled even by the 1914–18 war.

For thirty years Catholic and Protestant princes were at war for the same causes which divided the Swiss. The antagonists were allied to one or other of the two Swiss parties—Spain and Austria with one faction, Baden and Venice with the other—with the result that the cantons felt themselves involved in the war, in spirit at least. Switzerland had not yet grown as far away juridically and morally from the Empire as she was to later. As a German-speaking nation she could not be indifferent to Germany's fate, and it was in Germany that the fighting was going on. In short, the Thirty Years War, because of its nearness and its long duration, was to have extensive repercussions throughout a divided Switzerland. A victory for one side or the other would strengthen the position of Catholics or Protestants in the Diet. Any new development in the war influenced the Confederation's internal politics, and on more than one occasion the country hovered on the brink of civil war.

It may be imagined that neutrality was not always easy or practicable for the Swiss, even within the very elastic boundaries of the word as it was then understood. Such things as recruitment of mercenaries, or foreign armies in transit, were not seen as infringements of neutrality. In fact this question of foreign armies in transit occupied a great deal of time in the Diet during this period.

When, however, an ambassador from Gustavus-Adolphus came to the Diet on 16 December 1631, to suggest an alliance with Sweden, the proposal was turned down despite the sympathies of the Protestant party and the anti-Austrian traditions of the Swiss. When the Swedish army occupied Stein-am-Rhein in its campaign against Constance, the townspeople instantly blamed Zurich, with some justification. When the Duke of Saxe-Weimar marched into the territory of the Bishop of Basle, ally of the Catholic cantons, the latter accused Berne of complicity in the scheme.

In spite of all this, however, the Thirty Years War was more beneficial than otherwise to the unity of the Confederation. The Swiss were brought up short by the spectacle of war-ravaged Germany, and the threat posed by their own geographical proximity. In 1647 they signed the Defence Treaty of Wil, a first attempt at military organization on a federal scale. In spite of relatively minor infringements of a still shaky neutrality, one might say that the Confederation emerged from these thirty years with honour—were it not for the fact that they abandoned the Three Leagues who were their allies to their fate, and thus opened up the way to foreign occupation.

To fully understand the tragic events which took place on the territory belonging to the Grey Leagues from 1607 to 1639, one must bear in mind their geographical position. Grison territory bordered on the Venetian Republic via the Valteline. Tyrol and the Duchy of Milan, which is to say Austria and Spain, who were allies, were separated by the lands belonging to their enemy, Venice, and by the territory of the Grey Leagues. This gives one some idea of the immense strategic importance both parties attached to the possession of the Grison lands, or at least, of the Valteline. In Franco-Venetian hands it was a door shutting off communications between Spain and Austria. In Spanish hands it was a corridor for communications between them. There were moments when the whole fate of the war seemed to depend on this tiny, almost inaccessible strip of land.

This is not the place to go into the machinations of the various ambassadors to the Leagues, assisted by an archaic and complicated political regime, or the coups d'état, revolutions, murders and massacres which left a bloody trail through Grison territory for thirty years. Broadly speaking, the Protestants, led by the Salis family, supported the Franco-Venetian party; the Catholics, led by the Planta family, sided with the Empire. It is a sombre story, filled with digressions. All we need to know is that the troubles were sparked off by the alliance between the Leagues and the Venetian Republic of 1602, and that they were fomented by the Hispano-Catholic party. In 1620, after an appalling massacre of Protestants at Tirano, the Spanish occupied Valteline and imposed the Roman faith on the whole population.

Soon after Richelieu's arrival on the scene, French troops were sent to capture the Valteline from Spain. But they had no intention of returning it to the Grisons, whose energy, force, will-power and talents were rightly held in suspicion by the French. On the contrary, French troops, under the leadership of Duke Henri de Rohan, threatened to take over the country. This led to a new revolt by the national party, led by Colonel Jurg Jenatsch, ferryman and condottiere and one of the most singular characters of the time. The Grisons, who had sent for the French to chase out the Spanish, now had to send for the Spanish to chase out the French.

The Treaty of Westphalia happily put an end to the Thirty Years War and to the dangers and plots which threatened to spread to the Confederation from Grison country. The Catholic cantons failed once again to recognize the importance of the event, and opposed the sending of a delegation to Münster and Osnabrück. However, Jean-Rodolphe Wettstein from Basle, deputy for the Protestant cantons, managed to get Switzerland included in the treaty with the help of the French. The Confederation's independence of the Empire, which hitherto existed only as a fact, was formally recognized and sanctioned by the rest of Europe. Furthermore, Valteline was restored to the Grisons.

On the other hand the alliance with Rottweil, abrogated in 1632, was not renewed. Alsace, for whom Confederates had died in the Burgundian wars, became French. Strasbourg and Mülhausen, towns without lands, found themselves bottled up in French territory and at the mercy of the French government as far as food imports and trade were concerned. Alsace retained a provisional tariff system, but the Treaty of Westphalia had paved the way for the reunion of these two advance-posts of the Confederation with France. Strasbourg capitulated in 1681, but Mülhausen managed to hold out for as long as the old Confederation itself lasted.

The Treaty of Westphalia cut short the centuries-old relationship between Switzerland and the Empire. The Confederation had originally been founded in opposition not to the Empire, but to the Habsburgs, with the Emperor's support. The second stage of this relationship, coinciding with the Habsburg seizure of the Imperial throne, ended with the

Swabian War. The third stage, which begins with the Basle Treaty, sees the Confederation independent of the Empire in fact if not in law, with Basle remaining subject to Imperial authority. The Treaty of Westphalia cleared away these last vestiges of subjection.

This important event, which came at the lowest ebb of Confederate fortunes to set the seal on three centuries of fighting for independence, throws light on the deep community of interests which existed between France and Switzerland at that time. It is not the policy of neutrality we have to thank for the fortunate outcome of the Treaty of Westphalia for Switzerland, but the French alliance. The King of France had a political as well as a military motive in finally separating the Confederation from the Empire. His political aim was to weaken the Emperor and remove the Swiss from his sphere of influence, while his military aim was to be able to call on Swiss mercenaries against the Habsburgs when the need arose. Because France wanted Switzerland free, it was at last able to recognize her independence.

By assuring national cohesion throughout this critical time the French alliance preserved the existence and independence of the country from the Empire. Thanks to this alliance, the Treaty of Westphalia, which determined the balance of power in Europe for the next century and a half, came as the crowning achievement of French royal policy where the Swiss were concerned and the fulfilment of the Confederation's real aims.

2. *The Overthrowing of Alliances*

The Thirty Years War had considerable economic and social consequences for Switzerland. Alongside a Germany so ravaged and despoiled that it would take her more than a hundred and fifty years to recover, Switzerland, which had been spared and enriched by the war, was a sight to inspire envy among her contemporaries. The writers of the time picture the prosperity of the country in idyllic terms. The earnings of the mercenaries, combined with the profits Swiss industry and agriculture had made from supplying the belligerents during these terrible years, had given the Swiss people a comfortable standard of living in contrast to the general poverty around them.

It is not far-fetched to discover the foundations of Switzerland's current prosperity as far back as the Thirty Years War. The events of the time, by destroying the German economy and stimulating national production, gave the Confederation a head start over her neighbours which she has never entirely lost. This explains how a country in the worst possible natural conditions, without raw materials, or maritime outlets, was able to play such a considerable role in the European economy.

But, as always happens after a great war, the Thirty Years War was followed by a severe economic crisis whose effects were the more serious in that they followed a period of comparative prosperity. A whole generation had been born and brought up in times of plenty. It had forgotten—because one rapidly grows accustomed to good fortune—hard times and poor returns.

The price of commodities, which had risen considerably, fell sharply once the products of Swabia and Bavaria reappeared in Swiss markets. The price of land fell. The neighbouring countries, Austria in particular, who had to rebuild finances crippled by war, raised their customs duties. Finally, a monetary crisis, caused by the depreciation of exchange values and complicated by a poorly organized credit system, placed the peasants in a position where they were unable to meet the mortgage obligations which they had contracted in the years of prosperity.

These economic phenomena, inevitable consequences of great wars and all too familiar to our generation, were further complicated by social phenomena. At the very time when the soil no longer yielded fat profits to the peasantry, their sons, who had been away from the country for so long, suddenly began returning. Young men who dreamed of emigrating suddenly found the door to a military career barred to them. The mercenaries, disbanded at the end of the war and the expiration of the French alliance, in 1651, flocked back to their villages and created a surplus of agricultural labour, or what we call an unemployment problem. A miserly soil was forced to feed more mouths. The whole population had to fall back on its reserves.

This was the moment when the ascendancy of town over countryside began to make itself generally felt and resented.

Most of the towns had acquired, through purchase, conquest or a hundred other means, the old powers of the feudal lords over the countryside. To begin with they had exercised these powers with great discretion. The peasant communities often possessed franchises, liberties and privileges with regard to their overlords to which they held tenaciously and which the towns had promised to uphold.

With time, however, they began to be less respectful to these rights. Feudalism, with its manifold complexities, was lost in the mists of time. The towns aimed at simplifying their administrations and suppressing the complications which made them costly and onerous. This was often done with the aim of improving the administration of the rural areas. But it always resulted in greater interference and extortion. Every reform suppressed one of the peasant's liberties and cost him a denier; every progressive measure made him more dependent on the authorities. It was coming to the point where the town-dweller only appeared to the peasantry in the light of a creditor or a tax-collector.

By the mid-seventeenth century the reality of feudal liberties had disappeared. But they were not forgotten. The peasants violently resented their subjection, and they resented poverty still more, following as it did on a time of prosperity.

This prosperity, had, however, given them leaders—rich and educated leaders, for the most part, who resented the superiority of the burgesses. Such men, for instance, as Leuenberger in Berne, Emmenegger and Schibi at Lucerne. The terrible Peasants' War, which broke out in 1653, was primarily an economic and social revolt. But it was not long before it took on a political complexion, at once reactionary and democratic, aiming at the restoration of the old privileges and at peasant control over their administration.

The insurrection spread fast. *Landsgemeinden* were held in farms in the forest cantons at Wohlhusen, Signau, Sumiswald and Hutwyl. An army of twenty thousand men was formed. Before this very real threat Protestant and Catholic cantons suddenly joined forces again, making it clear, in doing so, that power mattered to them more than religion. They united across frontiers and prejudices just as the peasants of Berne, Lucerne, Solothurn, Basle and Aargau had united. The latter were finally crushed at Wohlenswil, Gislikon and Herzogenbuschsee and the repression which followed was merciless.

The collaboration which had suddenly come about between Catholic and Protestant cantons was such a novel phenomenon—almost unheard of for more than a century—that it aroused great hopes. As we know the Confederates had banded together towards the end of the Thirty Years' War, in 1647, to create a federal military organization, known as the Defence Treaty of Wil. Although this act had a limited application, the people of Zurich believed the time had come to extend its implications to the full, on something like a federal scale. The people of Zurich had never quite lost sight of Waldmann's and Zwingli's idea of a uniform federal organization in which each canton would be represented according to its importance, that is to say in which Zurich would finally have triumped over Schwytz and Zug.

The peasant revolt had aroused such alarm in the ruling classes that they thought success was at hand. Bürgermeister Waser, of Zurich, was commanded by the Diet to draw up an outline for a federal pact.

But the Catholic cantons soon took hold of themselves again and realized the risk they had run. At a disadvantage as they were through limited resources and a small population, their one hope of dominating in the Confederation was by pushing the dogma of autonomy in each canton to its furthest limits.

This, precisely, was what exasperated the people of Zurich. As the towns' power and wealth increased—and the outcome of the Peasants' War seemed to them to increase their power significantly—the inferior position to which Zurich, Basle and Berne had been relegated by the second Kappel Treaty appeared all the more outrageous.

The rejection of Bürgermeister Waser's proposals and the Catholic cantons' renewal of their 1586 alliance showed that there was no peaceful solution to this situation. This is why the people of Zurich resolved once again to try their luck at war, and put the peasant cantons in their place, along with the rebellious peasant communities.

The initial cause of the first war of Villmergen—the expulsion of some Protestant families from the Schwytzois town of Arth—makes it look like a religious war at first glance. But the real issue at stake was this question of autonomy for each canton. Was each canton entitled to do as it pleased? The people of Zurich had persecuted the Anabaptists. Schwytz claimed the right to treat Protestants like Anabaptists. It is clear that if the war had given a clear, negative answer to this important question, it would have meant the end of the old federative structure which the Swiss had inherited from the Middle Ages and which they clung to like a fetish. Zurich's victory would have brought forward the advent of modern Switzerland by two hundred years.

But Zurich did not win the war. Extreme federalism triumphed once again. A curious lack of success—partly due to its rivalry with Berne—attended the Zurich armies in their encounters with Schwytz, of which this was the third example in two hundred years. The Zurich troops were defeated at Rapperswil and the Bernese at Villmergen, on 24 January 1656, at the crossroads between the Berne-Zurich, Lucerne-Baden roads, the capital of the bailliages of Aargau.

In its general outline the Baden Treaty recalled the Kappel one. The problem of keeping a balance between Catholic and Protestant forces within the Confederation remained unsolved. It would be certain to crop up again. As for the idea of tightening federal bonds, that had to wait for a hundred and fifty years. The first war of Villmergen, like the Kappel Treaty which it echoed, was one of the root causes of the Revolution.

Once again it was the French alliance which saved Swiss unity after this new battle. The alliance they had entered into with Henri IV had expired 'eight years after the death of his son'—that is, in 1651. Negotiations with a view to renewing it were slow and difficult. The position of the Swiss negotiators was made extremely difficult not only by the fact that they could not agree among themselves but also by the fact that the relative positions of both parties to the treaty were so unequal. It was a far cry from 1516, when the Swiss, even in defeat, could parley with the King of France on equal terms. In that hundred and fifty years each of the two countries had gone its own way, one downwards, the other up. Louis XIV favoured the Swiss mercenaries who contributed so greatly to his victories and renown, but he could do without them. The cantons, on the other hand, who needed an outlet for emigration and trade, could not dispense with the friendship of the French King, or the revenues of mercenary service abroad, without provoking a political, economic and social crisis at home.

The Swiss had hoped that this treaty would give them the right to trade unrestrictedly in France, an increasingly important market in view of their own expanding industry and trade. But the King, anxious to protect and encourage French industry, naturally refused them any such concession. He saw the alliance as a purely military affair. The Swiss realized that agreement was hopeless and that their only course was to give in, which is what they did, one after the other. The alliance was signed at Solothurn, on 24 September 1669, and solemnly ratified in Notre-Dame in Paris on 18 November.

This period of harmony did not last long. Four events soon undermined their cordial relations. These were the conquest of Franche-Comté, the annexation of Strassburg, the fortification of Huningen and revocation of the Edict of Nantes. By the first years of the eighteenth century the alliance was abandoned.

It will be recalled how lightly the Swiss gave up their claim to Franche-Comté, which they had occupied, after the Burgundian wars, in return for a sum of money. They continued to interest themselves in the fate of the province, however, which supplied them with wine, wheat, iron and particularly salt, and there was much traffic across the frontier. In 1512, Franche-Comté was designated a neutral. It was included in the treaties the Swiss negotiated with the Empire, and subsequently, after the Empire fell into the hands of Philip II, with Spain.

Spain was far away. France was very near, and ever since Louis XI, she had had designs on the province. The King of Spain—for the same reasons which were later to make the King of Sardinia demand the neutralization of Northern Savoy—was quite happy to entrust the defence and protection of Franche-Comté to the Swiss.

But the Confederates treated Franche-Comté's neutrality like that of Savoy. They were careful not to make use of it.

Though they claimed the right to invoke it if necessary, the need had not arisen. The religious situation in the Franche-Comté did not favour the Confederates. The Archbishop of Besançon was the Metropolitan of the Bishops of Basle and Lausanne. Catholic Franche-Comté was included in Spain's denominational alliances, which had the effect of making her immediate neighbour, Berne, lose interest in her.

During the summer of 1667 the French threat grew more precise. The people of Franche-Comté, who had their own free and democratic system of government under the distant sceptre of Spain, were not in the least anxious to become French. They hastily sent off envoys to the cantons, led by Jean de Watteville, descendent of an emigrated Catholic branch of the celebrated Berne family.

The Treaty of Aix-la-Chapelle (1668), as we have seen, restored the Franche-Comté to Spain. The arrival of the envoys from Franche-Comté should have been sufficient warning to the Swiss, one would have thought, for they was not at all desirous to have France as a next-door neighbour. And it looked as though the Swiss had taken the hint. The Defence Treaty of Wil was renewed and strengthened in 1668. But when Louis XIV marched into Franche-Comté again, in May 1674, with an army which included Swiss mercenary contingents, the Confederation was as helpless as it had been the first time, for all the terms of the treaties and the prayers and entreaties of the population.

The conquest of the Franche-Comté and its incorporation into the Kingdom of France aroused strong feeling in Switzerland. But Louis XIV set out to win the Confederates round. He granted them economic concessions which amounted to setting up a free trade area.

Good relations between France and Switzerland had been helped by the fact that, if we discount a few kilometres of the Gex region, they had no frontiers in common. But this was no longer the case, and problems were not long in appearing. The annexation of Franche-Comté struck the first blow at the Franco-Swiss alliance.

This was no isolated gesture on Louis' part but a first move which was followed up, in 1681, by the still more alarming annexation of Strasbourg. Strasbourg, as we have seen, had been on close terms with the Protestant cantons ever since the Reformation. Though she had failed, despite frequent representations, to gain admittance to the Confederation as a Canton, she was the recognized ally of Berne and Zurich and was included in the Swiss policy of neutrality. In the latest war Berne and Zurich had provided a garrison for Strasbourg. This proved an effective deterrent against Louis XIV, who had no desire to enter into open conflict against his allies.

Unfortunately, after the Peace Treaty of Nimègue, the Strasbourgeois yielded to French persuasion and sent back their Swiss garrison. Two years later, on 30 September 1681, the town was forcibly reunited with France and the Swiss stood by, helpless to intervene. History repeats itself. Mülhausen and Geneva succumbed, a century later, under almost identical circumstances.

This event caused widespread alarm in the Protestant cantons, particularly in Geneva, who had reason to fear a similar fate. Geneva's welcome of the Protestant refugees from

Strasbourg had caused great displeasure at Versailles, and the Genevans realized that if France were bent on carrying out her threats there was nothing they could do to stop her. The Catholic cantons, meanwhile, were quite unmoved by the fate of Strasbourg. Of the old relations between Strasbourg and the Confederates, all that was left was a somewhat dubious debt and discussions of petty interests which dragged on until 1773.

Meanwhile Louis XIV was building a powerful bridgehead at Hunningen, on the left bank of the Rhine. From there the French cannon had Basle within range. It is difficult now to conceive of the terror which this construction caused, not only to the people of Basle, but throughout the whole Confederation.

It was a nightmare which lasted more than a century. One of the few requests the Diet submitted to the Allied Powers after the fall of Napoleon was that the Hunnigen fortress be demolished.

If Louis XIV had contented himself with measures like these, his relations with the Confederates might not have been seriously impaired. The Swiss had long since renounced any territorial ambitions, making a point of pride and honour of being such a tiny nation. But when Louis revoked the Edict of Nantes, on 18 October 1685, he precipitated a head-on collision with the Protestant cantons in the areas of religious feeling and economic interests all at once. Thousands of refugees came streaming into Switzerland during the next few years—sixty thousand according to report—and most of them arrived totally destitute, without any means of existence. These refugees placed heavy financial burdens on the Swiss Protestants and involved them in incessant wrangles with the French diplomats, who protested at their reception of rebellious French subjects. The following year the Duke of Savoy, imitating the King of France, started persecuting the Vaudois in Piedmont, and this added to the troubles already shouldered by the Swiss.

The Protestant Confederates never forgave Louis for his brutality. The French alliance, for so long the most durable link between Catholic and Protestant cantons, now lost its effectiveness. The Revocation of the Edict of Nantes struck a blow at traditional French policy in Europe from which it has never recovered.

The Protestant cantons were quick to take the hint. On 25 May 1693, a military treaty was drawn up between Zurich and the States General of the Low Countries. This was a move with serious implications, foreshadowing as it did the Protestant cantons' subsequent withdrawal from the terms of the French alliance.

This re-alignment became a fact after the Duke of Anjou's accession to the Spanish throne, following the death of Charles II (1 November 1700). Spain's ally France suddenly found herself allied with the Catholic cantons against the Protestant ones. And the Empire, until only recently the protector of the Catholic cantons, naturally stood to benefit in the ensuing struggle from the sympathy of the Protestant cantons, and the Republic of Berne in particular.

This explains why Berne did not hesitate before sending garrisons to the Black Forest towns to force France to respect their neutrality. After Victor Amadeus, Duke of Savoy, crossed from Louis' camp to that of his opponents, his request for help in protecting Northern Savoy's neutrality against France was well received at Berne. They were not insensible, either, to the offer made by the Duke's ambassador to give up the southern shore of Lake Geneva to them. However, they could not persuade the Diet to share their views. When the Imperial Army under Comte Mercy marched across Basle's territory on 20 August 1709, on its way to attack the Franche-Comté, everyone accused the Berne government of complicity in the move. Finally, at Malplaquet, Swiss fought against Swiss—Catholics in the King's army, Protestants under Anglo-Dutch banners.

France's new attitude towards the Protestant cantons, a complete reversal of her earlier alliance, was shown first of all over the designation of the King of Prussia as Prince of Neuchâtel, on 3 November 1707, and secondly in her separate, secret, alliance with the Catholic cantons on 27 April, 1715.

The designation of the King of Prussia in preference to France's candidate, the Prince de Conti, kept Neuchâtel for the Swiss. The choice turned on the wise political axiom that of two candidates the furthest away is the one to choose. The affair was held to be a failure for French diplomacy.

The French ambassador, M. de Puysieulx, was recalled after this failure, and replaced by a more forceful and intriguing candidate of whom Louis had high hopes, M. du Luc.

The new ambassador turned away from his predecessor's policy of keeping Switzerland united. Borrowing from traditional Spanish diplomatic policy, he threw himself wholeheartedly into fomenting religious discord. The second war of Villmergen was his handiwork. It could never have happened if French policy in Switzerland had not abandoned its old aims. The result was a serious setback for France. After the Catholic cantons' defeat at Villmergen, M. du Luc hastened to offer them, if not the immediate revision of the peace terms imposed by the other side, at least some hope of their being revised. In ways like these the secret alliance between France and the Swiss Catholics of 27 April 1715, with its hidden promises, weighed heavily on federal policy throughout the eighteenth century.

3. *Balance is Restored*

The second national Peace Treaty of 1531 had brought about an artificial balance of power within the Confederation which did not correspond to the real distribution of strength between Catholic and Protestant cantons. Zurich's attempt to put an end to this anomaly in 1656 had been a failure. But it was bound to be renewed sooner or later because life is no respecter of paper barriers.

At the beginning of the eighteenth century, the Protestant position was stronger than it had ever been. The Revocation of the Edict of Nantes had caused them passing inconveniences and expenses, but in the long run it brought them lasting prosperity thanks to the new skills imported by the refugees. It was a very different picture in the Catholic cantons. Contemporary authors are unanimous in describing their economic backwardness and the decay of their industrial life.

As far as one can make out the four Protestant cantons of Zurich, Berne, Basle and Schaffhausen had a population of over 700,000 while the seven Catholic cantons could barely muster 300,000. This is sufficient indication of how inadequately the Diet—where the Catholics could still impose their will—represented the real state of affairs in the country at that time. The disproportion in representation becomes even more striking if one takes wealth, economic activity or quality of administration as a basis for comparison, rather than population figures.

Almost the whole of the Swiss plateau, from Leman to Bodan and from the Alps to the Jura—which meant the whole of the country's productive area—was in Protestant hands. They had industrial towns, great trade fairs, commercial routes and financial strength. The Catholics had none of this. The only resource in their mountains was stockbreeding. They had to go abroad or to their Protestant neighbours for foodstuffs and were forced to buy everything they needed, without actually possessing a single important source of revenue. The inhabitants of the Catholic regions had even fallen into the habit of emigrating to Zurich to work in her industries.

There is no need to look further for the cause of the second war of Villmergen, also known as the War of Toggenburg. The immediate pretext for the war was the road being built between Utznach and Wattwil, designed to give the forest cantons a way out of their economic isolation by creating an exit for them to the north. As far as the disputes between the Toggenburg parishes and the Abbot of St Gallen, begun as far back as 1707, are concerned, it seems unlikely that these would ever have provoked a war if a war had not appeared to everyone at the time, and for quite other reasons, as a national necessity.

The purpose of the second war of Villmergen was to put a stop to a situation which appeared untenable to both sides. Like the first Villmergen war it was a direct consequence of the Protestant defeat at Kappel. It was also, as we have seen, a consequence of French defeats and of the feebleness of French diplomacy during the Spanish war of succession. Thus, the Revocation of the Edict of Nantes finally rebounded against the Swiss Catholics.

Resistance in the Catholic cantons was soon crushed by the Protestants' greater financial strength and superior arms. Wil, residence of the Prince-Abbot of St Gallen, Melligen, Baden, capital of the bailliages, one by one the Catholic fortresses were taken in pitched battle. The decisive confrontation took place at Villmergen, on 25 July 1712, on the very field where the Bernese had been routed by their foes in 1656. This time the opposite happened. The Catholic army lost more than 3,000 men and broke up in confusion before the Bernese troops, which consisted for the most part of French Swiss contingents from Vaud, Neuchâtel and Geneva.

The fourth National Peace Treaty was signed at Aarau, on 11 August 1712. The Kappel Treaty was abrogated, and denominational parity restored in every sense of the word.

The Protestant cantons also insisted on the surrender of certain jointly administered bailliages and this was their big mistake. For, while the restoration of a reasonable balance of power within the Confederation was essential to its further growth, the introduction of territorial feuds and irredentist grievances was bound to poison relations between the cantons and encourage foreign intrigue. This is exactly what happened. In 1715 the French ambassador entered into a separate, secret alliance with the Catholic cantons, known as the Trucklibund Alliance, in which he promised them the restitution of their territorial losses. He thus prevented lasting peace being established in the country.

It took another six years to bring about good relations between the Abbot of St Gallen and his Toggenburg subjects (Peace Treaty of Baden, 15 June 1718). But it is safe to assert that the year 1712 put a final stop to the long period of religious conflict which had begun over two centuries earlier.

Chapter VII

The Patriciate
(1718-1789)

The eighteenth century, which was such a brilliant one for literature, is a blank where Swiss politics are concerned. With the exception of a few riots in the interior, and the solemn renewal of the French alliance on 25 August 1777—an alliance in which both religious parties joined for the first time since 1715—nothing occurred between the Villmergen war and the French Revolution. It is almost as if the Swiss nation had stopped breathing.

This phenomenon is unusual enough to warrant an explanation.

The political development of Switzerland was completed, or rather stopped, which is much the same thing, at the beginning of the eighteenth century. After that the Confederation became a crystallization.

Switzerland had travelled a long road from the admission of Appenzell into the Confederation in 1291—a road which takes us from this shadowy conspiracy of a few people on the Grütli to the close and public alliance of many States. If this process of evolution had not been checked by the Reformation, the Confederation would have taken the step towards federation almost without realizing it. In less than three centuries it would have reached the stage which the United States of America arrived at in a few years, and which was not finally realized in Switzerland until 1847.

But, as we have seen, this evolution was cut short by the second National Peace Treaty of 1531. Until then alliances had been interpreted rather more freely than their texts. The Diet, for instance, had often put decisions to a majority vote and, in 1515, passed a resolution that minority opinion should be overruled. But now all this changed. From now on the Catholic cantons interpreted federal alliances with the utmost rigidity. The evolutionary process which had been eroding the sovereignty of individual cantons in favour of the solidarity of the nation as a whole was permanently checked and overthrown. Particularist interests won the day and pressed ahead.

If Confederate neighbours had carved the country up between them at this point, as happened with Poland, historians would have run out of ink explaining how richly this fate had been deserved. The vacillations of the Diets, their powerlessness to take decisions without consulting each canton in turn and all interested parties in these cantons, together with the cantons' right to withdraw from any decision once taken, added up to a state of affairs which was no better than the Polish *liberum veto*.

Switzerland's allies, whose bonds of mutual interest had been tightening gradually over the last few centuries, suddenly found these bonds loosening and even—as was the case with Constance, Strasbourg, Rottweil, and the Bishop of Basle—being totally dispensed with. The Catholic cantons had had only one aim in view ever since the sixteenth century—to shrink the Confederation's territory as much as possible. On this front too the nation's progress was checked.

Despite efforts by the Protestant cantons, in 1656, to strengthen these alliances, and despite the outcome of the 1712 war, the Confederation never managed to get moving again. It died in 1798 from having ceased to be a living entity in 1531.

A similar phenomenon had occurred within the cantons themselves. For all the complexity of their political affiliations, the diversity of their economic and social conditions and their insurmountable religious differences, the various States which composed the Confederation had all had analogous forms of government. Constitutionally speaking there were not two Switzerlands. The cantons' administrations had developed along similar lines and the differences which could be observed between towns and countryside, corporate and patrician administrations, or republics and monarchies—there were four of these in Switzerland at that time—were caused by differences of method rather than spirit. The strongest proof of the Confederation's fundamental unity is this similarity in its constitutional systems.

Towards the end of the seventeenth century these various States, for economic and moral reasons common to them all, had been obliged to close their doors to further applicants for burgess status, which had the effect of freezing the social mobility of all those not yet admitted to the ruling classes. This measure, which crystallized the social order, led to others imposing a hierarchical structure upon it. In the eighteenth century, social mobility, which had been so common hitherto, became impossible.

Every revolution in history can be explained, more or less directly, by a blockage in the social capillary system—in other words, by the ease or otherwise with which individuals can move from one class to another. This blockage was all the more critical in eighteenth-century Switzerland in that it was a wealthy and enlightened country, which enjoyed an unusually high level of public education and individual prosperity for the times.

The Swiss aristocracies committed the error which many other oligarchies have fallen into before and since. They failed to realize that their sound economic and financial administration, far from being gratefully welcomed by the people, would be their own undoing in the end. Legal measures can check the growth of political systems, but nothing can stop the evolution of a society. The day comes when political systems have to be refashioned to conform to social realities, if necessary by force.

This is the history of the eighteenth century and its sombre conclusion.

1. *The Administrations*

It is no use hoping to understand the old Swiss Confederation by forcing it into the framework of our current concepts and terminology. Eighteenth-century Switzerland was not composed, as the textbooks have it, of thirteen cantons with some allied States and some subject ones. The reality is both simple and more complex: Switzerland was made up of twenty independent States, united by very diverse legal ties, all of which had subjects both separately and in common. No two members of the Confederation were identically situated. But no criterion justifies the claim that 'this one or that one was not part of the Confederation'. To say that the Valais, Neuchâtel and Geneva joined the Confederation in 1814 is to ignore the historical realities of several hundred years.

Even the name 'canton' was not in official use in Switzerland until the French Revolution. The language of the old Confederation was German, and the word *Ort*, *die XIII Orte*, which the members of the old Confederation used to describe themselves, simply means 'place'. We have to fall back on the word 'canton', which is an anachronism—an irritating anachronism in this case, because the word itself is misleading. It evokes the idea of a whole composed of town and surrounding countryside, whereas, in the old Confederation, only sovereign States were members—the town and republic of Berne, for example, or the town of Zurich, represented by their bourgeoisie. The country areas, in these instances, were subjects.

The thirteen cantons were bound to each other by federal letters, all of them different and varying greatly in content, both as to the rights and to the obligations they imposed. But, beside the alliances which were the groundwork for their mutual relations, the cantons were also united by a number of Acts, to which all, or most, of them had been party, and which created a nursery of federal constitutional law. Such, for instance, were the Priests' Charter (*Pfaffenbrief*) of 1370; the Stans Covenant of 1481; the various National Peace Treaties of 1529, 1531, 1656 and 1712; and finally the Wil Defence Treaty of 1647, renewed in 1668.

Each of these thirteen sovereign States had territories which belonged to it and which may be described as subject territory, without, however, seeking to distinguish between the territory owned by the canton at that time and that which may have been taken from it subsequently. The Zurich countryside, for instance, was subject to the town of Zurich; Oberland was subject to Berne, as was the Vaud region. In the urban cantons of Zurich, Solothurn, Lucerne, Fribourg, Schaffhausen, Basle and Zug, all the countryside around the towns was subject. In the forest cantons, part of the countryside was subject to the other, for example Einsiedeln was subject to Schwytz and the Levant to Uri.

It is hard for us today to have a precise notion of these juridical relationships, because we approach them with ideas of legitimacy which were non-existent then, either in the minds of the subjects or their masters.

Apart from these subject lands, which were the sole property of a particular canton, there were others which belonged to several of them at once, in the most widely different combinations. Berne and Fribourg between them owned Schwarzenburg, Orbe, Echallens, Grandson and Murten; Schwytz and

Glarus had Uznach, Gaster and Gams; Uri, Schwytz and Nidwald owned the Riviera, Val Blenio and Bellinzona; Zurich, Berne and Glarus jointly ruled over Rapperswil, Baden and part of Freiamt. The remainder of Freiamt, Thurgau and Sargans belonged to the eight oldest cantons; the Rheintal likewise, plus Appenzell; while Lugano, Mendrisio, Locarno and the Val Maggia belonged to all the cantons except Appenzell.

There was a similarly diverse situation with respect to their allies. The word 'allies', like 'canton', is inaccurate and gives a false impression of the situation. The Confederates were united among themselves by alliances and were therefore allies; on the other hand they had allies who were not part of the Confederation, like the King of France or the Duke of Savoy. The term 'ally' does not make the distinction clear. But we have to use it for want of a better one, because the technical expression *zugewandter Ort* has no exact equivalent.

After the old links with Constance, Rottweil and Strasbourg were severed, in 1548, 1632, and 1681 respectively, there were eleven allies all told: the Abbot of St Gallen, the town of St Gallen, the town of Bienne, the 'Dizains' of the Upper Valais, the Three Rhaetian Leagues, the town of Mülhausen, the principality of Neuchâtel, the town of Geneva and the Bishop of Basle—to which should be added the Abbot of Engelberg and the independent republic of Gersau, on the shores of Lake Lucerne.

We do not intend to take on the almost superhuman task of detailing the various relationships, in fact and in law, of these different allies with the Confederates. They have undergone considerable changes through the years and the text, in these cases, does not always mirror the realities. None of these States was the ally of all the members of the Confederation. Many of them, like St Gallen, Bienne, the Valais and even the Grey Leagues, were in every other respect indistinguishable from the cantons. They were obliged to send troops to the aid of the Confederates, they were a party to their alliances and were allowed to take part in the Diets, a privilege of which they did not always avail themselves.

Others, however, like Geneva, were kept out of the Diet by the opposition of the Catholic cantons. Some of them took part in the Diet, from time to time, whenever a matter which directly concerned them was under debate. In principle, the allies were included in the treaties negotiated by the cantons, but in 1777, the Catholic cantons opposed the inclusion of Geneva, Neuchâtel and the Bishopric of Basle in the French alliance, or the inclusion of their territories under the guarantee of federal territory. Mülhausen, on the other hand, was expressly included—which, unfortunately, has not been of the least assistance to Switzerland.

These allies, like the cantons, had their subject lands, who were treated as part of themselves and shared in the burdens as well as the benefits of the alliance. The Valteline, for instance, subject to the Leagues, was admitted to the Confederation to the same extent, and under the same title, as the Bas-Valaia, which was subject to the Haut-Dizains, or the Toggenburg, subject to the Abbot of St Gallen.

Where their internal systems of government are concerned, there are generally held to be five distinct regimes among the sovereign States—cantons and their allies—who made up the old Confederation. There were the democratic states, Uri, Schwytz, the two Unterwalds, Zug, the two Glarus, and both Appenzells, all governed by *Landsgemeinden*; federative States—the Valais and the Grey Leagues, where sovereignty did not repose in the community as a whole but in its sub-divisions: *dizains*, magistrates and communes; oligarchial States—Zurich, Basle, Schaffhausen, St Gallen and to some extent, Bienne, Mülhausen and Geneva, whose administration was the responsibility of corporations; aristocratic States—Berne, Lucerne, Fribourg, Solothurn, where the sovereignty belonged to an exclusive patriciate; and finally the monarchical States—the principality of Neuchâtel, the Bishopric of Basle and the Abbeys of St Gallen and Engelberg.

It should be remembered, however, that these distinctions are founded on appearances rather than upon the realities of the situation. For, in every one of these States, the real power was vested, by right of birth, in a closed class of people, and to a small number of individuals within that class.

The distinguishing feature of the Swiss constitutions of this period was, as we have said, the closing of the ranks of the bourgeoisies, who were themselves descended from the communal franchises of the Middle Ages and who had always held the real power. So long as the town dwellers and inhabitants of the forest cantons had access to the bourgeoisies, the Swiss States maintained a democratic system of government. As soon as this was stopped, the government became oligarchic and rested upon the privilege of birth. 'Oligarchy,' M. Gonzague de Reynold writes, 'begins as soon as the registers of burgesses are closed in a country or a town, in other words as soon as new burgesses are no longer admitted.' There is no break in continuity, as one might imagine, between these two states—before and after the closing of the registers. The one is the logical outcome and development of the other.

This change took place towards the end of the seventeenth century, for various reasons, most of them economic. All the wealth which accumulated from the fifteenth-century wars, and the property derived from the secularization of monasteries in the Protestant cantons, had accrued to the burgesses. As long as the numbers of the common people went on increasing, and soldiers were needed to defend them and help them prosper, it was easy to gain admission into the burgess class. But, after the crisis which followed on the Thirty Years War, the burgess class found itself suddenly impoverished. Moreover, because of the usual increase in the population during a long period of peaceful existence, the number of those holding civic rights increased enormously, with the result that each individual's contribution to the community dwindled proportionately. In other words, taxes went up and revenues diminished.

While the burgesses enjoyed the revenues and rights they also had to carry the burdens—the care of the poor, in particular, and in Protestant cantons, the upkeep of the cult. It was natural that the beneficiaries among the bourgeoisies should not want these responsibilities to multiply uncontrolled.

This is not the whole story, however, or the most important part of it. In the towns a great number of economic activities were reserved for the burgesses exclusively. To admit new burgesses meant increasing competition. In times of economic crisis such a prospect can hardly have been attractive.

The bourgeoisies in Switzerland closed their registers for the same reasons that the guilds closed all over Europe. For every burgess belonged by law to a guild.

The same thing was happening in the rural areas. An increase in the number of burgesses meant a cut in their share of common grazing lands as well as in the revenues from foreign pensions and the perquisites of office—what were then called, gloatingly, *Bundesfrüchte*, fruits of the State.

The move toward closing the registers became irresistible

towards the end of the seventeenth century, and the dates clearly indicate a causal link with the economic crisis. In 1656 Berne refused admission of foreign artisans to the bourgeoisie. In 1660, it was decided that no new burgesses should be admitted for ten years. In 1694 the register was finally closed. Similar decisions were taken at Uri in 1669, Zurich in 1679, Solothurn in 1680, Fribourg in 1683, Mülhausen in 1705, Lucerne in 1707, Schwytz in 1716, and Basle in 1717. Elsewhere without being legally excluded, admission to the bourgeoisie became more and more infrequent and difficult. Only two burgesses a year were admitted in Appenzell, and only a batch or so every ten years at Glarus. Between 1718 and 1798 Schaffhausen admitted a total of two.

All the cantons provide similar examples. It would be true to say that from this time on, it was no longer possible to get into the bourgeoisie in any Swiss State without exceptional reasons and a great deal of money. Thus the population of Basle fell by several thousands in the course of the eighteenth century, and the bourgeoisie of Lucerne dwindled to one hundred and seventy people, outside the ruling families. Such are the rewards of avarice, when it becomes elevated to a principle of government.

The results of this shrinking of the burgess class were soon apparent in the economic as well as the political sphere.

The refusal to admit new burgesses was bound to alter the future prospects of two large sectors of the population, the peasants on the one hand and the non-burgess town-dwellers on the other.

Hitherto there had been no essential difference between the peasants, subjects of the towns, and their masters. The peasants were always free to move to the towns, marry there and in time become incorporated with the ruling Sovereignty. But now that marriage between subjects and burgesses was forbidden, and entry into the bourgeoisie was ruled out, the state of the subject became a precisely defined and irremediable condition—rendered all the more onerous by the fact that the burgesses displayed an increasing tendency to arrogate all the political and economic privileges to themselves.

At the same time as the bourgeoisie closed its doors to the peasantry, it was also barring them to the first generation immigrant town-dwellers, who were briefly known as *Ansassen*, and their descendants who were known as *Hintersassen*. Before this, subjects were to be found only in the rural areas, but now they were to be found in the heart of the towns as well—and this fact looms large in subsequent political evolution.

There is no greater threat to public order than the existence of elements who have nothing to lose by change. The peasants, isolated in their grievances during the seventeenth century, could now draw on the support of a class of urban malcontents.

Once social categories have been introduced they tend to multiply. The bourgeoisies, who had all the political and economic privileges, soon divided up into a hierarchy of their own, for reasons analogous to the ones which had led to the closing of the registers. A sector of the bourgeoisie only wanted to be left to get on with its work, protected from competition. Public office, honorary in the towns, venal in the rural cantons, required more education, leisure and means than most burgesses could command.

It should be recalled that the number of citizens with the proper qualifications for undertaking these offices must have been extremely limited in the tiny eighteenth-century Swiss republics. What we now call the élite must have represented a very thin layer of society in those days, a tiny proportion of a small population. Under an administration where division of responsibilities was unknown, holding public office was an exacting and onerous business, so much so that, instead of competing for office, most burgesses shied away from it, and gladly surrendered these posts to those who wanted to hold them. In this way an administrative class gradually emerged in all the cantons.

This phenomenon is by no means peculiar to Switzerland. Swiss democracy has always shown a tendency to veer towards oligarchy, and the virtues in the national character are as much to blame for this as the defects. The Swiss place great confidence in their magistrates, and tend to be so taken up with material preoccupations that they prefer to leave the running of the State to the people who enjoy it while they get on with their own affairs. If you tell a Swiss now that public office in the eighteenth century was a life appointment he would be neither surprised nor indignant—even now Federal Councillors are, to all intents and purposes, nominated for life. Such is the continuity of Swiss history.

It hardly matters whether this administrative class was recruited on grounds of birth, as at Berne, Lucerne, Solothurn, and Fribourg, whether it was composed of the leaders of certain privileged guilds as at Zurich and Basle, or whether it was a plutocracy which could offer a higher bid for the posts, as happened in the smaller cantons. In practice, the administrative class was everywhere drawn from the wealthiest members of the population and they invariably recruited themselves, by co-opting further members. The diversity of forms only served to mask identically similar results. The aristocracies came into being in exactly the same way as the peasant dynasties and corporative oligarchies. There seems to be very little difference between the Escher, Meiss and Wyss at Zurich, the Merian, Burckhardt, and Iselin at Basle, the Dollfus at Mülhausen, the Turrettini, Micheli and Pictets at Geneva and the Reding at Schwytz, the Schmidt at Uri, the Wirz and Lussi in Interwald, the Zurlauben at Zug, the Tschudi at Glarus, the Salis, Planta, Sprecher and Travers in the Grisons, or come to that, between the Besenval, Glutz and Sury at Solothurn, the Pfyffer and Segesser at Lucerne, the Montenach, Gottrau and Boccard at Fribourg, the Erlach, Diesbach, Mulinen, Wattenwyl, Bonstetten, Luternau or the Steiger, Fischer, Jenner, Haller, Graffenried or Effinger at Berne. Oligarchy reigned everywhere under different names.

The patriciate, in its earliest form, is often described as the result of natural selection—a superior form of election. This is true—a patriciate like Berne's, completely given over to the art of government, had considerable wisdom to draw upon and good chances of making a success of its task. Unfortunately, though, it did not keep to its original form.

To begin with, as a privileged class, it demanded too large a share of the privileges. The patricians kept all the honours and profits for themselves, as well as the public offices, which included the post of bailiff in subject territories. Berne had some fifty of these to confer, some of them highly lucrative. Then there was a large proportion of ecclesiastical positions, and all the ranking military posts in armies abroad, many of which carried considerable pensions, titles and profits with them. This was too much for the bourgeoisie which was quite content to leave the responsibility of power to the patrician class but would have liked a share in the profits.

In the second place, the patriciate, already an exclusive body, became too exclusive. On the eve of the French Revolution in Berne, out of 67 ruling families, 12 accounted for 132 members of the Council, while 23 accounted for another 181. There were 71 ruling families at Fribourg, 34 at Solothurn and only 29 at Lucerne.

Finally, this already rarefied class began to divide against itself. At Fribourg, a long struggle, fraught with ups and downs and sudden changes of fortune, broke out between the families of feudal origins, who held all the military posts outside the town and drew the titles and pensions which went with them, and the purely bourgeois families dedicated to government and administration. The struggle ended with the defeat of the noble families. The ruling families then ennobled themselves, modelling themselves on the patriciate in Berne and other aristocratic towns. Thus, the patrician class became delimited upwards a well as downwards.

Briefly, society in all the cantons in the eighteenth century was composed of six classes ranging down the social scale. The nobles, who had inherited feudal titles, and were generally few in number and without much influence; an aristocratic ruling class, as jealous of the nobles as of the bourgeoisie; the bourgeoisie who had privileges but no administrative power; natives, inhabitants and subjects.

As we have seen, it was largely for social reasons that the bourgeoisie closed its registers. It was moral reasons which turned this form of government into an autocracy. The Reformation, which fostered liberty in so many directions, was largely responsible for creating an all-powerful State in Switzerland. In the Middle Ages secular powers were constantly curbed by the ambitions of the Church. As soon as State and Church merged, spiritual and secular power were vested in the persons of the magistrates, the State governed souls as well as bodies, indiscipline became a sacrilege, and the notion of the omnipotent magistrate came into being.

One ingredient is lacking to complete the picture—the moral influence of the great foreign monarchies. As we know, the idea of autocracy and the divine right of kings had gradually spread through Europe during the seventeenth century; in France the States General no longer met; the Imperial Diet had lost all its influence. Swiss officers serving abroad, all of whom belonged to the ruling aristocracies, brought these ideas back to Switzerland and tried to put them into practice.

From that moment on the old franchises were no longer respected, subjects ceased to be consulted and the ruling bourgeoisies no longer had their power checked by any external influence.

Under these circumstances, the art of government lay in increasing the privileges of the bourgeoisies so as to make them forget the loss of their political rights, to the detriment of the other social classes, who were not considered a serious threat. This was, in fact, the policy followed by the ruling powers. In Berne non-burgesses were excluded from trade. In Zurich, all industrial activity was reserved for the bourgeoisie. The peasants were forbidden to sell their produce on their own account, or even to cultivate their vineyards. At Basle they hit on the idea of forbidding the peasants to make cheese, so as to lower the price of butter. The net result of this system of privileges was the exploitation of the subjects by the bourgeoisies.

Not all the cantons, however, pursued the same policy towards their subjects. In the aristocratic towns of Berne, Lucerne, Fribourg and Solothurn, the power lay in the hands of the ground-landlords, who pursued an agrarian policy which was in their own interests but which benefited the subjects as well. The most selfish administrations were the corporative ones, Zurich and Basle in particular. The situation they created was one where town systematically exploited countryside. In the forest cantons, where public office was bought, the bailiff's sole aim was to fill his own pockets. But the worst administrations of all were those of the joint bailliages, where an already feeble government was further undermined by federal paralysis.

All the same, the administration of subject territories was not generally of a much lower standard than that of the sovereign states. Lower Valais might be in a state of squalor and destitution, but the Upper Valais, its sovereign, was not much better off. The administration of the Valteline was a reproach to the Grisons, but this was chiefly because the Grisons, with their sovereign free towns, federated into jurisdictions, federated into three leagues, federated among each other, and forming part of the Confederation as well, were cursed with the most burdensome and archaic political system in all Europe.

However, these were exceptional cases. On the whole, the administration of the Swiss cantons in the eighteenth century was as good as and often better than that of their neighbouring countries. The Zurich bourgeoisie was authoritarian towards its subjects; but this was partly in order to get rid of long-standing abuses and unify the administrative system for the benefit of those administrated. As for the Bernese system, it aroused the admiration of visitors from abroad and was quoted as a model by all the 'enlightened' writers of the eighteenth century.

It is no exaggeration to say that the Swiss Confederation, towards the end of the old regime, was the most fragmented nation imaginable. It rested on five main distinctions—between the cantons and their allies, in the political sphere, between the ruling bodies and their subjects, in the social sphere, between the towns and forest cantons in the economic sphere, between Protestants and Catholics, in the religious sphere; and finally there were the language barriers.

These distinctions separated people from each other and made concerted action difficult. They were not all of them equally sharply felt, however. The rivalry between towns and rural areas already belonged to the past, while the language differences were not consciously felt as yet, or were submerged into the conflict between subjects and rulers.

The only reason we have devoted scarcely any space to the language differences so far is that they played a very small part in Swiss history. The Confederation had been thought of as a purely Germanic state for centuries. In 1481, when Fribourg joined the Confederation, the government adopted German for all public announcements and the ruling families Germanized their names. The same thing happened with Switzerland's allies, in Valais for instance. The German language was gaining everywhere.

The conquest of the Italian bailliages and the Vaud region did not change the situation noticeably. German was still the language used by all the ruling bodies—except in Geneva and Neuchâtel. However the Confederation's split from the Empire, the increasingly close relations between Switzerland and France, military service abroad and the impact of French civilization in the seventeenth and eighteenth centuries, had the effect of Gallicizing most of the ruling aristocracies. French was slowly becoming Switzerland's second official language. It even supplanted German in certain public acts—not the ones dealing with the French Swiss subjects of Berne and her allies, but the ones dealing with the King of France. The renewed Franco-Swiss alliance of 1777 was written entirely in French for the first time. The Confederation was moving imperceptibly towards the notion of equal languages, formulated for the first time during the French Revolution.

2. *The Opposition*

This state of affairs, with its virtues and defects, might have gone on for a long time if Switzerland had been a poor and ignorant country in the eighteenth century. But this was far from being the case.

For more than two centuries the Confederation had not taken part, as a nation, in any foreign wars. The country had not suffered an invasion since 1444. Switzerland had soldiers but no army—and her armament industry was a source of profit rather than an expense. During the eighteenth century, the total strength of Swiss mercenaries in foreign armies varied between sixty and seventy thousand men, and sometimes more, with more than eighty officers holding the rank of General. This earned the country considerable revenues—quite apart from the sums paid directly to the cantons by foreign governments in exchange for recruiting rights and the enormous profits made by recruiting agents and officers commanding a regiment.

This long period of peace had allowed the country to leap ahead materially, helped by the effects of the Thirty Years War on the neighbouring countries. Population figures doubled in some regions in a hundred years, indisputable proof of public and private prosperity.

Where agriculture is concerned, the figures for large livestock are set at 740,000 head and those of small livestock at a similar figure. Taking the population figures into account, this is as high or even higher than today's figures. Switzerland then was an exporting country. She exported stock for breeding and slaughtering to France and Italy. Horse breeding was practised on a grand scale and Switzerland provided the cavalry of several European armies with mounts.

Viticulture was important, particularly in the Valteline. This was one of the chief issues over which the economic policy of the various towns diverged. Viticulture was prohibited to the subjects of Zurich. The Berne government, on the other hand, pursued a highly protectionist policy where the Vaudois vineyards were concerned. This was one of the means Their Excellencies used to assure the loyalty of the French Swiss subjects.

Dairy produce was becoming an increasingly important contribution to the Swiss economy. The price of milk continued to rise throughout the eighteenth century because of the increase in cheese production. Gruyère alone exported 30,000 hundredweight of cheese to France per year, Emmenthal and the Oberland somewhat more in all probability, and the canton of Glarus exported 20,000 hundredweight of green cheese (*fromage vert*) to the Scandinavian countries and America.

Swiss agriculture, far from being backward, was an organized export industry. In the course of the century dairy production became concentrated into fewer hands—those of entrepreneurs or co-operatives—and this led to profound social changes in some regions.

Generally speaking, Swiss agriculture was the province of the smallholder. Most of the Swiss peasants owned their own land. If we except the jointly owned territories, latifundia were unknown except in the Lugano region which came under Italian influences. Serfdom still existed, but it was more humiliating than onerous. Feudal levies were not as heavy as they had been and taxes were light, even for the times. It is clear that Swiss agriculture in the eighteenth century, seen as a whole, had nothing to complain of.

Things were equally rosy on the industrial front. Cotton employed something like 200,000 people in eastern Switzerland, 100,000 of them at St Gallen, 40,000 in Toggenburg, and the rest in Glarus and the Grisons. St Gallen manufactured 200,000 rolls of muslin annually and employed 30,000 to 40,000 women for embroidering in the nearby districts and the Vorarlberg. Calico prints were manufactured in French Switzerland, at Geneva and Neuchâtel.

The silk industry had made considerable strides. Silkworms were reared in the Valteline and the Ticino, but most of the spinning and weaving was done in the canton of Zurich. The Zurich bourgeoisie were completely orientated towards trade, since Zwingli had persuaded them against military service abroad. Zurich had created an absolute industrial monopoly for herself where her subjects were concerned. She employed 100,000 workers in her silk industry, who worked at home in their villages and earned more than three million francs a year from France. The ribbon industry in Basle employed more than 2,000 people. Linen, wool, wickerwork, lace, clock-making, jewellery making, leather, and paper, supported a large number of people in various parts of the country. Even the metallurgical industry was beginning to flourish, with the

Jura iron mines and the blast furnaces of Berne and Schaffhausen.

The corollary to all this industrial prosperity was a spate of commercial and banking activity.

From 1740, the Berne government embarked on building a network of roads which were the admiration of its contemporaries, and merited comparison with the royal roads of France. Switzerland drew considerable profits at this time from her transport industry. This explains why the St Gotthard road, inadequate as it was in many places, was constantly travelled by twelve hundred horses.

Unfortunately, the monetary and customs systems were not helpful to commercial expansion. There were as many coinages as there were sovereign states—and the French currency was the only one viable throughout the country. The internal customs barriers, though fiscal rather than protectionist in nature, were another hindrance. Above all, in this mercantile age, the lack of a central government prevented the Confederation from imposing a coherent economic policy which would increase national production, or even protect her interests from foreign competition. All this activity naturally brought a great deal of money into the country. And since the country had not had to deal with any serious catastrophes—the civil wars only had limited effects—the money had stayed there. Over the generations this money had been converted into savings. It had gradually enriched the bourgeoisies in the towns. But this was one area where there were no water-tight divisions and the subjects had ended by sharing in the general prosperity. Administration was carried out at a mediocre level in the eighteenth century. But, generally speaking, the standard of living among the people it administered was higher in Switzerland than in any of the neighbouring countries.

This general prosperity had two results, both predictable enough, one being the outcome of the other. The first was the creation of State treasuries in certain cantons in spite of the low level of taxation. The cupidity aroused by Berne's treasury during the French Revolution is well known. It had become legendary, and this reputation was to play a fatal part in the tragic end of the old Confederation. But Berne was not the only town which had built up a treasury thanks to the accumulated savings of many generations. Moribund political systems frequently make the mistake of thinking of savings as the foundation of the State, overlooking the fact that a sound financial policy is short-sighted unless it is grounded on sound general policy.

The general increase in wealth had one happy result—it encouraged the spread of education. By our present standards the Swiss people would no doubt seem very ignorant; but compared with other nations they were highly educated—particularly in the Protestant cantons where Bible reading was one of the requirements of the religion. The Bishop of Basle himself felt obliged to introduce a system of compulsory education in 1784, in order to keep up with the times. This was a quite unprecedented measure in those times, particularly coming from a Catholic prelate. *Ab uno disce omnes.*

Progress in education was naturally more marked in the towns. Some of these, Zurich, Basle and Geneva particularly, became cultural centres of European fame. Geneva, at that time, might be described as a university supported by a bank. The chief ambition of the Genevan bankers, grown rich by Law's speculations—in which they had not believed—seemed to be to have their sons turn out scholars. This ambition was favoured by the fact that Geneva was a place where English and German influences were both brought to bear on the traditional French culture. Scholarly dynasties sprang up, like the Turrettini, Trembleys, Saussures, Tronchins and many more, whose names lent lustre to the city. The same thing happened at Basle, with the Iselins, Merians, Bernouilli and the great physician Euler; at Zurich, with the Gessners and Bodmers, Lavater, Pestalozzi and Hirsel; at Berne with Albert de Haller, Bonstetter, Muralt and Tscharner; at Schaffhausen with Johannes von Muller, the great Swiss historian, and in the Vaud region with Dean Bridel.

This ferment of intellectual activity, whose influence was enormous, was chiefly Protestant as it tended to be concentrated in the towns. But the Zurlaubens, at Zug, and the Balthasar family at Lucerne, were equally illustrious names. Switzerland, having been an intellectually backward country for so long, was suddenly showing her mettle, once more confirming the maxim that there is no culture without material prosperity.

Great men are not produced in isolation. Scholars and poets need the right context to produce and nourish them. Most of the Swiss writers came from the patrician class. Jean-Jacques Rousseau himself, though of modest parentage, was a citizen of Geneva and thus a member of the Sovereign State. The existence of these men proves that education was no longer the prerogative of one class in the eighteenth century.

It was precisely this spread of education which was to lead to a clash between the greedy materialism of the bourgeoisie on the one hand and the autocratic tendencies of the patriciate on the other. One thing must be made clear, however. Generally speaking there was nothing democratic about these clashes, at least in the sense the word took on after the Revolution. In order to get a clear idea of the nature and extent of these disturbances, some of which were bloody enough, it is necessary to distinguish between those which occurred within the governing classes themselves, and were really party political feuds at a rather elevated level, and the ones which were really directed against the authorities.

Inevitably, in the closed, restricted atmosphere of the eighteenth century Swiss governments, disputes between individuals played a considerable part—especially in the rural cantons. The feud between the Zurlaubens and Schumachers at Zug, the temporary overthrowal of the Reding dynasty at Schwytz in 1764, the rivalry between Schumachers and Meyers at Lucerne, Zellwegers and Wetters in the outer Rhodes, and Geigers and Suters in the inner Rhodes, together with similar events in Basle and Zurich and the exile of Micheli du Crest from Geneva in 1731, were not so much clashes of ideas as clan wars.

The conspiracy of Lemaître and Pierre Fatio in 1708, and the troubles of 1738, 1766, and 1768 in Geneva, the Henzi plot in Berne in 1749, and the Neuchâtel riot of 1768, come into a different category. These movements, originating in the heart of the bourgeois class, were not intended to overthrow the existing order but to extend it. Their instigators wanted more people to share the benefits of power. They approved of the closing of the registers of burgesses. But they resented the fact that they were closed upwards as well, and that the patrician class had become exclusive in turn. They were not seeking progress so much as a return to the old ways, whose advantages the bourgeois class now bemoaned, having paved the way for this turn of events by their own treatment of their subjects.

The real opposition to the patrician class was unlikely to come from people who shared its privileges. It was bound to come from those who felt themselves excluded. Two groups stood out among these, by virtue of their education and wealth—

the natives of the Sovereign States, that is to say the descendants of immigrants who were completely assimilated and were under the same obligations as the bourgeoisie, and the burgesses and landed gentry of the subject regions.

In dealing with these struggles for freedom, Major Davel's attempt in 1723 deserves to be singled out, not so much for its intrinsic importance as because popular reverence was later to attribute a destiny to it and alter its whole character. Major Davel, who was probably an isolated instance of enlightenment in his day, became one of Switzerland's national heroes eighty years after his death.

When the Bernese conquered the Vaud region, in the middle of the sixteenth century, they realized that the only way to govern a people is to make them dependent upon the government. Berne ruled the Vaudois in the fashion of the times, strictly and sometimes harshly but with an eye to the country's needs and a constant care to satisfy them.

The first thing the Bernese introduced into the Vaud region was national unity. Until they arrived, the country had been parcelled out between a mass of feudal lords whose only mutual relations were those of rivalry. The towns of Moudon and Yverdon went to war with each other, on the eve of 1536, over a trifle. Such cases were frequent. The Bernese united the country under one administration, and gave it a national character and way of life. In a word they awoke a nationalist spirit and this was to give rise, later, to a desire for independence.

In the second place, the Bernese troops freed the Vaudois peasants from serfdom. Their arrival in the country naturally led to clashes with the old feudal families, and landed nobility who ruled the men and the land from the safety of their strongholds. Like all enlightened despots, the Bernese invoked the support of the people against the aristocracy. The Bernese administration was a movement of popular liberation, severe only upon the great nobles.

Municipal life already existed but the Bernese encouraged and developed it and it left an indelible imprint upon the Vaudois people. It gave them their sense of identity, their taste for public affairs and that deep culture which is the glory of their peasant class. This was genuine democracy. What did it signify that the power lay with a few families in Berne if all the essential civic rights—election of magistrates, administration of funds, registration of new burgesses—were open to everyone? To those who maintain that a political system cannot shape a whole people we recommend a comparison between the Vaud region and the Chablais—the same people, names, origins, countryside. The difference lies in the contribution made by Berne.

The fourth achievement of the Berne government, closely related to the preceding ones, was the development of the country's material resources. There is no surer way for a conqueror to win over a population than by increasing prosperity all round. Under Berne the roads were improved, travel made easy, the tax system rendered more efficient and viticulture encouraged by protective laws. It is true that some Bernese bailiffs enriched themselves, but this was one by-product of the prosperity they themselves brought to the country. The rural architecture which makes Vaudois villages so distinctive still retains the stamp of Berne's influence in its spreading roofs, silently witnessing the event which brought prosperity to the people and community as a whole.

Lastly, Berne introduced the Reformation to the Vaud region, with the result that, consciously or unconsciously, all the religious powers collaborated in the interests of the State.

The Bernese administration in the Vaud region had the support of the country people, free towns and the clergy. Here they were almost unanimously popular. But they still clashed with the remains of the feudal nobility and the burgesses of Lausanne. Both these groups had been stripped of former privileges and they hankered after their restoration. It was a mistaken policy on Berne's part not to have encouraged these rich and cultured elements to merge with their own bourgeoisie, thus securing their loyalty. This error of judgement can be explained, where the nobles are concerned anyway, by their obstinate loyalty to the Dukes of Savoy and their refusal to enter the Bernese patriciate.

When Major Davel and his troops reached Lausanne on 31 March 1723, without forewarning or preparing the ground in any way, he found himself completely isolated.

His heroic but naive venture met with no response from the Lausanne bourgeoisie, who were naturally on their guard against Berne, or the Protestant clergy, still chafing from the recent trouble over the ecclesiastical consensus. Davel fared still worse in the countryside, where he was not understood at all.

Perhaps he was not very clear himself as to what he wanted to do. The Swiss revere him as a national hero and a precursor. He may have thought of himself merely as a pious man led to revolt by his conscience. Yet his action aroused emotions in the Vaudois people, perhaps an unconscious remorse, which gave birth to the whole revolutionary mystique. Davel achieved his purpose, if he had one.

Events in the other subject countries during the eighteenth century had less lasting consequences. In spite of the feudal dues, now subject to speculation, which set the peasants against the State and the urban capitalists, by and large the peasant populations remained loyal to their rulers. The disturbances in Schaffhausen, in 1717, Werdenberg, between 1719 and 1721, Toggenburg, in 1731, the Bishopric of Basle, in 1740, and the Levant in 1755, were local and sporadic. They occurred at the introduction of new taxes or the reform of old abuses, or were provoked by the fortuitous encounter of a weak administrator and a personality, like Pequignat in the Prentruy, strong enough to take command of an uprising.

If is not until the last quarter of the century that we note the emergence of a new, politically enlightened spirit. Two serious riots occurred, one after the other, which posed a real threat to the authorities and undermined their prestige. These were the peasant uprising at Fribourg, under Nicolas Chenaux, in 1781, and the one which convulsed Geneva, on 8 April 1782, under the command of Isaac Cornuaud. Chenaux may only have been an opportunist, but Cornuaud was undoubtedly the precursor of the revolutionary leaders.

Geneva, home of Jean-Jacques Rousseau, was the setting for the first genuinely democratic upheaval in Europe. It took place in 1764, directly influenced by the *Lettres de la Montagne*. In 1768 the bourgeoisie, having assimilated Rousseau's ideas, obtained an 'edict of pacification' which was at once a triumph for them and a check to the powers of the ruling families. There is a logic in ideas. Isaac Cornuaud invoked the very principles the bourgeoisie had made use of, when he led a rising of the people of Geneva in 1770, and then again on 8 April 1782.

Cornuaud was a genuine forerunner, and it was his inspiration that the Genevan revolutionaries drew upon later, when they styled themselves 'Cornualistes'. He demanded admission for the natives to the Council General together with the economic benefits this entailed. In other words, what he was after, basically, was the wholesale incorporation of the natives into the bourgeoisie.

Their Excellencies in Berne were fully aware of the dangers these innovations exposed them to. With France and Sardinia, who feared repercussions among their own subjects, they dispatched armies to Geneva—6,000 French, 3,000 Bernese and 2,500 Sardinians—to destroy the popular regime triumphantly established there. Henceforth, an aristocratic government would survive in Geneva only with the help of foreign bayonets. Once this support was gone, it would collapse.

All static systems of government are destined to be swept away by force. Those in power tend to think that resistance is the last word in political wisdom when confronted by a rebellious populace. But this is a mistake. Resistance is wise only when accompanied by just concessions. The patriciates of the eighteenth century provided Switzerland, at a given moment, with an administration adequate to the nation's needs. They rendered the country—Berne's especially, which was frugal and honest—indisputable services. But they outlived their usefulness. They failed to grasp the moral and social evolution taking place among the people. They did not see that industrial growth, together with Rousseau's preaching, had robbed them of their justification for existence. They put their faith in resistance and did not have the wisdom to temper it with needed concessions. They perished, as M. de Reynold puts it, through the exaggeration of their own principles.

Chapter VIII

French Domination
(1789-1813)

1. *The Conquest*

The year 1789 is not an outstanding date in Swiss history. In that year nothing of interest happened in the country apart from a riot in Geneva over a rise in bread prices during a severe winter. But 1789 is a crucial date for Europe. For Switzerland as for the rest of the world, it marks the beginning of a new era.

The French Revolution does not seem to have caused much excitement in the Swiss cantons. The meeting of the States General, the fall of the Bastille, even the October Days seem to have been regarded in the light of superficial, external disturbances. Conditions in France and Switzerland were too dissimilar for the Revolution to awaken much response in the Confederation so long as it remained a purely political movement.

The aristocratic system had many faults, chief of which was its static quality. The watertight division of classes on the social front, the selfishness of the ruling bourgeoisies on the economic front, were such as to alienate the sympathy of the subjects from their governments.

Nevertheless, there were many reasons why a revolution should have seemed an impossibility in Switzerland. First, the malcontents were without a leader or a centre of operations. Revolutions are hampered in agricultural countries without big towns, but they are even worse off in highly de-centralized countries like Switzerland under the old Confederation. The French Revolution was made in Paris. It is hard to see where a revolution could have triumphed in Switzerland, a conglomeration of states without a capital and without unity.

The second reason is more important. The numbers of those who stood to gain by the existing regime were very large, even larger perhaps than those who were oppressed by it. The situation in France, Germany or Italy was quite different. The privileged class in France was a tiny proportion of the whole population, whereas, in Switzerland, the burgesses of sovereign towns plus almost the entire population of the forest cantons, and the burgesses of subject towns who had the franchise, made up a total as great or greater than that of the subjects. Numbers are not the whole story though. It should also be remembered that the burgesses had the strength which comes of living in crowded communities, and controlling the power.

Finally, the Swiss aristocracies did not collapse as the French royal family had done. The old regime is said to have crumbled without resistance in Switzerland. This is not true. The only thing one can reproach the aristocrats with is that they underestimated the dangers of their position. They held out too long and too rigidly against legitimate grievances. They still did not realize, ten years after the French Revolution, that the reign of Louis XIV was finished. The aristocracy sinned through too much authority rather than too little.

In any case the Swiss revolution did not occur spontaneously. Swiss historians have sometimes tried to trace a parallel between the crisis of the Reformation and the French Revolution. But the comparison remains superficial. The Reformation came from deep within the country, and foreign influences played almost no part in it. The Revolution, on the other hand, was imported into Switzerland first by emissaries and then armies from abroad. The real troubles did not break out anywhere until the arrival of French troops. The aristocratic governments were not overthrown by their subjects.

This does not mean that events in France awoke no echo at all in Switzerland. Thanks to its position in the centre of the continent, Switzerland could hardly remain aloof from any great European upheaval, especially one taking place in a country with whom she shared several hundred miles of frontier, to whom she was bound by a centuries-old alliance, with whom she had intensive trade relations during the eighteenth century, and whose language was the second mother-tongue of her aristocratic class.

The concept of nationality had not yet acquired, in the eighteenth century, the rigid precision it took on later. No one was surprised when Louis XVI called in a Genevan banker, Necker, to save France's finances. The Gironde did not hesitate either, before entrusting its own affairs to another, Clavière, who had been in exile since 1782. There were more links then between the two countries, France and Switzerland, than divisions.

The French alliance, solemnly renewed in 1777, united the cantons to the person of Louis XVI. The aristocracies were composed of men almost all of whom had served the King of France and remained more loyal to him than many of his own subjects. Tens of thousands of Swiss soldiers served in his armies and lived in his garrisons. Their relations at home followed events in France with intense interest. Life at Versailles was much more familiar to the shepherds of Unterwald than to many a French provincial bourgeois.

It was via the Swiss soldiers serving in the French army that revolutionary ideas first spread, and it was they who introduced them into Switzerland.

On 31 August 1790, the Lullin de Châteauvieux regiment, commanded by a Genevan officer but recruited mainly from the Vaud region, mutinied at Nancy. The motive was not strictly political—the chief reason was delay in their pay. The cantons treated this as a serious stain on the national honour. A Council of War of the Castella (Fribourg) and Vigier (Solothurn) regiments judged the affair as mercilessly as if it were dealing with rebellious subjects. One of the leaders of the mutiny was broken on the wheel, twenty-two men were hanged, forty-one sent to the King's galleys at Toulon and the rest banished for life from the Confederation.

The French revolutionaries, already mistrustful of the cantons because of the way they welcomed emigrés, were appalled by these harsh measures. They saw them as a deliberate act of provocation. The men of Châteauvieux were hailed as martyrs; the red bonnet they wore in the galleys became the emblem of the French Revolution, Lous XVI asked the cantons to pardon the condemned men under the amnesty passed by the Legislative Assembly, 31 December 1791, but they remained adamant, replying that they alone answered for discipline in their regiments. The Assembly's only consolation was to parade the mutineers through the streets of Paris, on 15 April 1792, amid the cheers of the populace.

This incident set the seal on the Revolutionaries' mistrust of the Confederates. The reason why the Swiss Guards were massacred in the Tuileries, on 10 August 1792, and why those that escaped the carnage were savagely butchered in the prisons in September, was not merely that they were the sworn protectors of the King, but because the revolutionaries thought of the Confederation as an enemy. The riots had been started through fear of foreign invasion, and they were aimed at everyone suspected of sympathizing with the invaders. The Swiss, who were harsh with *sans-culottes* soldiers, welcoming to emigrés, loyal to the Bourbon throne and their Austrian alliances, naturally came under suspicion. It was inevitable that they should become the first targets for the fury of the mob.

On the day of 10 August, in which almost six hundred Swiss died, sixteen of them officers, and the September days, in which 200 officers and men were treacherously butchered, passionate resentment was aroused in the cantons. Some of Switzerland's greatest names, the sons, brothers and sons-in-law of syndics, *Bürgermeisters*, *Landammanns*, standard-bearers and magistrates, were among the victims. The three-centuries-old French alliance was destroyed in an instant.

The aristocracies, at this point, found themselves at a cross-roads. Their collapse, some years later, was caused by their inability to make up their minds then. They could have joined the first coalition, making the most of an act without precedent in the laws of men, and dispatched their troops into the Franche-Comté, which was awaiting them. If, after two centuries of inertia and neutrality, the Swiss aristocrats could no longer muster the necessary energy for such an enterprise, they should have set about conciliating their subjects so as to be strong enough to meet attacks from abroad.

The Swiss magistrates overlooked this alternative course of action. They were conciliatory towards France, who already treated them as enemies, and arrogant towards their still loyal subjects. This was their mistake, and the cause of Switzerland's misfortunes.

It is quite wrong to suppose that the French Revolution was messianic in character right from the start. The Constituent Assembly did not have it in mind to assure the happiness of the human race, either by persuasion or by force. Europe, for its part, left them alone. It was the appearance of the Girondists, towards the end of 1791, which led to a series of provocative actions. The Girondists needed a war abroad to consolidate their power and discredit the royal family. But the foreign powers were so determined not to interfere in France's internal affairs that the Girondists were forced to declare war on their own initative, which they did on 20 April 1792.

One of the ostensible reasons for this war was the question of the feudal rights of Imperial princes in Alsace. The Bishop of Basle was one of these princes. Which is why Pruntrut shares, with Avignon, the doubtful honour of having been one of the first conquests of revolutionary France.

The Bishop of Basle had ceased being an ally of the Catholic cantons in 1735. When the French alliance was renewed in 1777, the Catholic cantons opposed the inclusion of the Bishop of Basle to avoid having to extend the guarantee of neutrality to Geneva and Neuchâtel. In so doing, the Swiss designated the first victims of a conquering France. In 1791 the uneasy Bishop brought in Austrian troops to defend Pruntrut. He might have saved himself the trouble because instead of providing him with effective protection, these troops only brought the wrath of the invaders down upon him. Just after war had been declared, General Custine, commanding the Rhine army, occupied the Catholic part of the Bishopric which was not included under the Swiss pact of neutrality. The French army halted at the entrance to the passes leading into Switzerland. There was still some respect for the conventions at this stage. The French founded the Rauratian Republic at Pruntrut. But after Valmy and Jemappes, when they felt they could afford to disregard such formalities, the Rauration Republic became, on 23 March 1793, the Mont Terrible department of France, and this was later merged with the Haut-Rhin department.

France's second offensive took place in Geneva. On 20 September 1792, the invasion of French soil was crushed at Valmy. Almost immediately, General de Montesquiou, who had only been waiting for the word, marched into Savoy. Any power in possession of Northern Savoy inevitably forms designs on Geneva—nature so clearly intended this town as the capital of the Leman basin. Montesquiou advanced on Geneva at the beginning of October.

Geneva was not just another town in the eyes of the Girondist government. It was one of the spiritual capitals of the Revolution—home of Jean-Jacques Rousseau, and also of Clavière, Grenus, Etienne Dumont, François Invernois, Chauvet and many others who played a part in the Gironde, in the revolutionary clubs or the councils of the nations. Some of these men, especially Clavière, the finance minister, were eager to revolutionize their city.

It will be recalled that since 1782, France, Sardinia and the

Berne Republic were all guarantors of the aristocratic government of Geneva. Though deprived of the support of France and Sardinia, who had other things to worry about, they could still count on the support of Berne. That summer, Geneva's deputy to the Diet, Rigaud, finally obtained what the Genevans had been clamouring for for over two hundred years—inclusion in the Swiss neutrality pact. In spite of the reserves with which the Catholic cantons had surrounded the town, this guarantee was once again enough to protect Geneva from invasion. The Berne government at this point was headed by Chief Magistrate Steiger, the only man in the Confederation who knew what he wanted and was not afraid of war. Like Zurich he unhesitatingly dispatched troops to the defence of Geneva.

General de Montesquiou did not dare attack them and thus violate Swiss neutrality. On 22 October he consented to withdraw his troops on condition that Berne did likewise. He was reproached with this action in Paris, where it was considered tantamount to treason. Wrongly however; Montesquiou knew what he was doing. By depriving the Genevan government of the bayonets of Berne and Zurich he was removing its one support. Swiss troops left Geneva on 30 November 1792; on 4 December, the Revolution won over the city.

The debate over this event still continues. Some see it as the salvation of Geneva's independence, because France would never have allowed the town to remain as an asylum for emigrés and a centre for counter-revolutionaries. Others see it as the loss of Geneva's independence because it alienated Swiss sympathies from her. There is something to be said for both points of view. The Revolution was an internal and international necessity to Geneva. Equally it was the prelude to conquest by France.

Though the new government was composed of 'patriots', partisans of independence, it was at the mercy of a sudden French offensive. Geneva's freedom, without Swiss support, was an empty word. Possession of Geneva, on the other hand, is the key which unlocks the Vaud region. The Swiss had discovered this before in the sixteenth century, and they were now to repeat the experience.

During the next few months the revolutionary tide ebbed. With the King's death on 21 January 1793, the war's inner purpose had been achieved. The invasion of Switzerland, which was already half decided upon, was abandoned after the battle of Neerwinden (18 March 1793) which once again opened up the French frontiers to the enemy. The defection of Dumouriez, the intervention of England, Holland and Spain, the surrender of Toulon, the rising in the Vendée and the Terror combined to paralyse the Republican army and draw the fighting away from Swiss frontiers. France's defeat saved the Confederation for the last time.

Austria, Russia and Prussia, meanwhile, were busy carving up Poland—a delicate task requiring a great deal of military and diplomatic vigilance. The war slowed down, and almost stopped. A separate peace between Prussia and France was signed at Basle, in Councillor Pierre Och's house, on 5 April 1795.

Switzerland's oligarchic governments could, if they had correctly interpreted the drift of events, have made use of this lull in the war. But they failed to see the need for making concessions to ideas that were gradually taking hold among the population in spite of all their preventive measures. Repression was the only method which occurred to them, and it was often brutal. The authors of the *Mémorial du Staëfa*, a prudent, respectful, almost timid petition which is a curious mixture of democratic ideas and feudal phrases, were savagely punished in the summer of 1794.

Of all the ideas the French Revolution flung into the world—or rather, gave expression to, since many of them originated in Switzerland—two in particular were peculiarly adapted to social and political conditions under the Confederation—the idea of equality, and the abolition of feudal rights.

The fact that the Revolution found a faint echo in the subject Swiss countries, when it reached the country in the French service waggons, and that it won a measure of sentimental support here and there, had nothing whatever to do with the declaration of liberty, fraternity and unity. The Swiss had no desire to be one and indivisible; a positive thinking people, they had little faith in fraternity; as for liberty, they already had it, or thought they had.

What interested the Swiss peasant in the Revolution was the idea of freedom from feudal servitude and bonds of subjection. It was the explosive phrase delivered by Bonaparte (a massively hypocritical one, coming from those lips) on the occasion of the annexation of the Valteline: 'No people should be subject to another people.' It was the hope, dear to the landowners, of freedom from the payment of dues. The Swiss revolution was an agrarian revolution, because the Swiss people were a peasant race.

Towards the end of the old regime feudal impositions were very diverse, and unequally divided up among the various regions. Individual obligations had almost ceased to exist, except nominally. Serfdom had vanished from the democratic countries centuries earlier. Berne, Solothurn and Zurich suppressed it. Basle abolished it in 1790. It persisted theoretically in Schaffhausen, in the Abbot of St Gallen's possessions and in certain joint bailliages. But it was no longer a hindrance, and scarcely even a humiliation, to the serfs.

The payment of dues, however, was still widespread. Hardly any of the arable land on the plateau escaped paying tithes and these amounted to an average of 8,500,000 Swiss francs annually. Three-quarters of this was the share of the State, and the rest went to private individuals. The latter sum passed from hand to hand; it had lost its feudal connotations and become a moveable chattel. A right to the tithe could be purchased in those days, much as a share in a joint-stock company is bought today. It was the same with the feudal census, which was often in the nature of a mortgage. These taxes, like the 'lods', the right to transfer inheritance, were at once both taxes and securities and they were closely interwoven into Swiss economic life. They do not seem to have been exorbitant. But they shared a tendency to be levied on rural areas, to the exclusion of towns, and on the subject countries, to the exclusion of their rulers. It was this which made them so hateful to the peasants. This is why the suppression of feudal rights, which contained its own promise of equality, became the powerful lever which was to raise the peasant masses of the Swiss plateau to revolt.

The contemporary vantage point is peculiarly suited to studying the events of those decisive years, because almost nothing happened then which has not been repeated in recent history. The French Revolution, which had been driven back behind its own frontiers by the vicissitudes of the war, and threatened to give way before the pressure of its combined enemy, knew intuitively that its one hope lay in making trouble for the whole of Europe. It was not messianism, or an instinctive love of crusading which made the revolutionaries seek to make people happy. They realized that propaganda was their own salvation.

Throughout the world, but especially in Switzerland, French diplomatic agents—Bacher and Mengaud in the Vorort, Soulavie and Desportes at Geneva, Comeyras and Guyot at Chur, Mangiurit in the Valais—played the role of political agitators. Their residences were centres for intrigue against the established governments. Under cover of official correspondence they distributed inflammatory leaflets and hired professional propagandists. French gold, which had supported the aristocrats for centuries, was now being used to undermine their power.

If they concentrated their efforts in the Vaud region—the most proselytised area apart from Basle—this was not, as one might suppose, because of any linguistic or intellectual opposition there to the rulers in Berne. Linguistic quarrels were completely unknown at that time. Modern concepts of nationality were only just dawning. The Vaudois has no complaint against being governed by Germans. The Bernese bailiffs were rejected as aristocrats, not as foreigners.

There were convenient facilities for spreading French propaganda, controlled from Paris by La Harpe, through the Vaud region. But the real reason for its success there was the fact that feudal dues pressed more heavily on the Vaudois people, because of their prosperity, than on other Confederate subjects.

Despite all these favourable conditions, revolutionary propaganda did not have any decisive or startling success. There were disturbances here and there in the Vaud canton, in the Valais, Toggenburg, the Zurich cantons and those of Schaffhausen. But, all in all, it would be true to say that Switzerland was extraordinarily peaceful during the last years of the old regime. It would have been a good moment for the aristocrats to make concessions.

French intrigues, then, had not aroused the expected response among the people. It was different with the Swiss emigrés in Paris.

A Helvetic club had been formed in the earliest days of the Revolution, under the presidency of the lawyer Castella, of Fribourg. Most of the Fribourg exiles of 1781, and the Genevan exiles of 1782, as well as a few Vaudois, Du Roveray, Clavière, Reybaz, Etienne Dumont, Grenus, Rey, Guisolan, Perdonnet, Reynier, Boinod, Schweitzer, were members, as well as a lot of riff-raff. They were joined by other emigrés during the Revolution, among them Frederic César de la Harpe, and de Rolle. These men thought of themselves as patriots despite the fact that sheer distance had made them total strangers to their fellow citizens. They gave the Revolutionary governments enthusiastic support in their policies for the absorption or conquest of Switzerland. At last, in the autumn of 1797, they decided their hour had come.

The Constitution of the year III had charged the government with the task of safeguarding France's 'natural frontiers'—a very elastic concept, as we know. General Bonaparte, that star in the ascendant, went to find France's natural frontiers in Italy. He triumphed at Rivoli. At the preliminary peace talks at Leoben (April 1797) he promised the Austrians the Venetian Republic, a neutral country he had not yet conquered, in exchange for Belgium.

He was fiercely criticized for this disloyal action in Paris by the moderates—who were christened, scathingly, 'the natural frontier faction'. The partisans of a moderate peace and the partisans of conquest came to grips all through the summer of 1797. But the outcome was never in doubt.

France's finances were exhausted. Notes were still being printed, even after the solemn burning of the plate for promissory notes. How could they recall a French army which was being fed by Italy? How were they to pay the volunteers the thousand million francs they had been promised? Bonaparte, with the army behind him, was all-powerful—even before he became invincible. On 18 Fructidor (4 September 1797) he crushed the opponents of a policy of conquest. Barthélémy, a proved friend of Switzerland, was sent to Guiana with Carnot, and replaced by a ferocious personal enemy of the Bernese aristocrats, the lawyer Reubel, of Colmar. This choice told Switzerland the whole story. This date, Fructidor, is a fatal one in Swiss history—the immediate prelude to the loss of their independence.

It is only by seeing them in this context that we can understand the events of which Switzerland was the victim.

A month after the preliminary talks at Leoben, on 29 May 1797, which assured Bonaparte of Lombardy and Austria of Venice, a riot, fomented by French and Italian agents, broke out in the Adda valley, which was subject to the Grisons. The general played the impartial judge. He offered to mediate, an offer neither party dared decline. Months passed, during which the Salis, the real leaders of the Leagues and important landowners in the Valteline, gave the measure of their political inadequacy. But one month after 18 Fructidor and a week before the Peace of Campo Formio, Bonaparte pushed things to a head, confident that his policy of conquest would not be disapproved of in Paris nor hindered in Vienna. On 10 October he announced the reunion of the Valteline with the Cisalpine Republic—including the San Giacomo valley, which had remained unswervingly loyal to the Grisons.

Bonaparte had reasons for acting as he did, and they were the same as Richelieu's during the Thirty Years War. As the master of the Duchy of Milan, though not of Venice, which he had ceded to Austria, the General wanted control of the only route into the Tyrol and thence into Bavaria, where other French armies were in the field. Obviously Valteline was only the first step in this plan to gain control of the mountain passes. France would soon need the Valais, because it led to the Simplon, and the whole of Switzerland, because it was either an obstacle or a link in communications between Italy and Germany. Once started, there was no end to this policy. Unfortunately the cantons did not realize this.

10 October 1797 is an important and tragic date in Swiss history, whose significance has not been sufficiently understood. For the first time for many centuries, federal territory was dismembered. Switzerland had already lost the land she owned by right of conquest or alliance—Ossola, the Chablais, Strasbourg. But this was the first time a piece of her had been torn off in peacetime, and she had been helpless to protest.

The loss of the Valteline was doubly fatal to the Confederation. It proved to Bonaparte that Switzerland was devoid of both pride and power. Appearing at Rastadt in November, he was acclaimed in the Vaud canton and Geneva. It also proved to the subject peoples that they had nothing to lose by revolt. Had not the commander of the Italian army declared, with a fine mixture of irony and brutality: 'A people cannot be subject to another people without violating the public and natural law?'

Fructidor 18 had brought several friends of the Swiss emigrés to power in Paris. Five days later, on 9 September, La Harpe delivered a statement to the Directory. He called the French government to support the people of the Vaud canton, and guarantee the 1564 treaty which had promised the Vaudois their liberty. He was inviting the Jacobins to invade Switzerland in order to uphold feudal law there!

This statement, the work of a fanatical emigré, was disowned by those of La Harpe's friends who had remained in the country, notably Henri Monod. It was signed by three Vaudois and seventeen Fribourgeois, exiled in 1781, all of whom lived in Paris. According to Talleyrand this statement had no standing at all in law, since France had never made any such guarantee. But it gave the Directory the legal platform it needed. Having found an argument, La Harpe had no difficulty in persuading people with other reasons for wanting to become involved in the situation.

The Directory had four, closely related, aims in mind when it envisaged the conquest of Switzerland. The first was to overthrow the oligarchies, whom Paris suspected, with some justification, of harbouring Anglo-Austrian sympathies, and taking in emigrés.

Switzerland, due to its geographic situation, was an ideal rallying place for the enemies of the Revolution. The cantonal governments closed their eyes to their intrigues and gave them their approval, if not their active support. The Directory, being responsible for the country's safety, could legitimately feel itself threatened by these intrigues, and plan counter-measures. Thus the Directory's first ultimatum to the Berne government, 15 September 1797, demanded the return of the English ambassador, Mr Wickham, thought to be organizing a counter-revolution in Switzerland. Mr Wickham left the country voluntarily in order to spare the Confederation further embarrassment.

The Directory's second aim, like the first, was both defensive and offensive. It aimed at depriving Switzerland of her natural frontiers on the western side, so that these could not be used as a jumping-off place by Austria in the event of an attack upon France.

The third, purely offensive, aim to was to occupy Switzerland as a base for an attack against Austria.

The fourth and last consideration was financial. It is sometimes said that France conquered Switzerland to get her hands on the Berne treasury. This is only part of the story. In its desperate financial straits (grossly exaggerated by Vaudois emigrés) it is only natural that the Berne treasury should have influenced the Directory's decisions. Berne's treasury, far from being a protective shield, seemed to be turning into a bait for the enemy. But it was only a fraction of the spoils a conquered Switzerland could be expected to yield. France was at a loss to feed the armies turned loose by peace, until she hit on the idea of sending them to Switzerland for a free meal.

On 17 October, General Bonaparte, now the master of a purged Directory, signed the Campo Formio alliance with Austria. This was the first sharing out of the world. As far as he was concerned, the peace was no more than a provisional truce. He was already preparing for a new offensive. Swiss neutrality, a guarantee to peaceful peoples, is a stumbling block to those bent on conquest. Driven in like a wedge between Italy and Germany, Switzerland effectively blocks their communication lines. On the other hand, Swiss territory is an equally convenient base for attacks against central France, or against Vienna and the Tyrol. The violation of Swiss neutrality, and the conquest of the country, were implicit. They were the logical outcome of 18 Fructidor, essential to the policy underlying the coup d'état.

Bonaparte returned to Paris after the conclusion of the Campo Formio treaty, and had repeated conversations with La Harpe during November and December. Austria had just conceded the Fricktal, as well as all her possessions along the left bank of the Rhine, to France. Bonaparte summoned Councillor Pierre Ochs to Paris, ostensibly to negotiate the transfer of the Fricktal to the canton of Basle. But the Fricktal was scarcely mentioned during these interviews, whereas the invasion of Switzerland came up again and again. It was there Bonaparte spoke the decisive words, which were soon to be translated into action. On 15 December, Gouvion Saint-Cyr marched into the Val de Moutier, Erguel and Neuveville. On 28 December the French government openly extended its protection to political agitators. On 8 January 1798, it sent an ultimatum to the Berne government insisting on the expulsion of French emigrés. Meanwhile French troops massed along the frontiers of the Vaud canton.

Even then, under the nose of the liberators, the expected uprisings just did not occur. The country remained calm and loyal. It took a great deal of propaganda to provoke a riot at Liestal on 17 January, and an uprising at Lausanne on 24 January 1798. Much to the fury of the French generals, who were restraining their impatient troops with difficulty, the Swiss revolutionaries did not think of appealing to them for help.

General Menard was forced to think up a feeble pretext for marching into the Vaud canton, on 28 January 1798.

Some revolts did break out at this moment—at St Maurice, in the Valais, on 28 January, Lucerne on 31 January, the Toggenburg on 4 February, Basle on 5 February, Schaffhausen and Thurgau on 6 February. But they were fewer and less serious than the French, who had been led to believe that the Swiss people were oppressed and eager to throw off their yoke, had anticipated. On 15 February, Lugano, taking William Tell's hat as its emblem, vigorously repulsed an attack by red-bonneted Italians. During the month of February, Berne, Fribourg and Solothurn had friendly discussions with the people about the reforms they judged necessary to the regime, and all the cantons freely liberated their subjects.

As far as the latter were concerned the revolution had now achieved its purpose, and was finished and done with. But the French government did not agree. Sensing that its quarry was eluding it, it decided to precipitate matters. The French armies marched on Berne, from north and south, under the orders of Generals Schauenbourg and Brune; the latter was a creature of Bonaparte's. Fribourg and Solothurn were captured on 2 May. The French were defeated at Neuenegg, but victorious at Fraubrunnen and Grauholz and on 5 March 1798, they entered Berne.

This was the first time foreign troops had ever trodden the soil of this proud republic. Berne might not be the capital of Switzerland, but she was clearly its key stronghold, for the rest of the Confederation collapsed almost at once.

There are many explanations for Switzerland's poor showing at this tragic juncture in her history. Particularism had become chronic since the Reformation. The military organization of the Swiss had declined sharply since the Catholic cantons opted out from the Wil defence treaty. A desire for economy, and mercenary service, had done the rest. Switzerland, so proud of her military reputation, was without an army or armaments.

Moreoever—and this was the chief reason—the fact that the attack was mounted by France, centuries-old ally of the cantons, effectively paralysed Swiss resistance. An Austrian attack would have instantly reunited the Confederates, as in the old heroic days. But the Swiss had grown too used to depending on France to be able to face about, overnight, and oppose her. Finally, the various rulers were no longer certain of their subjects' loyalty, after several years of incessant French propaganda.

Berne's collapse was preceded by Bienne's on 7 February. Bienne was a Confederate ally and part and parcel of her territory since the fourteenth century. This was followed by the loss of Mülhausen on 15 March, and Geneva on 15 April 1798.

Mülhausen, isolated in Alsatian territory, owed its continuing independence since the Peace of Westphalia to the autonomous customs system of Alsace. The Revolution had left the French with a passion for order and symmetry. All the anomalies and divergences tolerated by earlier centuries struck a patriotic French eye as scandalous. Alsace was assimilated into French tariff territory and the Alsace customs authorities knew no peace till Mülhausen was absorbed into their jurisdiction.

After 2 November 1792, when Geneva was under attack from General de Montesquiou, Mülhausen found itself assimilated into foreign territory and encircled by eleven customs barriers which blocked cotton goods from going out, and wheat from coming in. The town was twice reduced to starvation by being prevented from working. Nevertheless it held out for more than five years. French agents had no more success in fomenting disturbances there than in any of the other Swiss towns. The surrender of the free town of Montbéliard, in 1796, was a disquieting omen for Mülhausen, which was in an analogous position. Mülhausen, included under the terms of the 1777 alliance, appealed to the cantons to support it in Paris. This was the last action taken by its centuries-old government. Its fate had been irrevocably sealed by 18 Fructidor. The bourgeoisie of Mülhausen, exhausted by an increasingly stringent blockade, gave in rather than hold out any longer. The annexation of Mülhausen was proposed at the beginning of January, and finally put into effect on 15 March 1798—ten days after the fall of Berne.

Geneva's story is much the same. The Revolution won control there soon after the departure of the Bernese troops on 4 December 1792. Fierce riots broke out in the summer of 1794, and on 25 July, two days before 9 Thermidor, a revolutionary tribunal was set up against the aristocrats. Geneva's Terror began when the Paris Terror ended. But it did not last long. The Genevan 'patriots', with a few exceptions, were real patriots.

Unfortunately, though, the town's economic situation, which

was similar to Mülhausen's, was not viable. As long as Savoy belonged to Sardinia, Geneva found a guarantee of her own independence—outside the Swiss alliance—in the rivalry of her two neighbours, neither of whom wished to drive the republic into the arms of the other. But, with Savoy defeated, Geneva found itself stranded in French territory and forced to depend on France for mercantile outlets and food imports.

A royal edict of 22 December 1775, which brought the administration imposed by Henri IV up to date, had declared the Gex region a 'foreign territory' from the tariff point of view. It was a situation like Mülhausen's, and the only one which could protect Geneva's trading rights. But it was useless to expect a Revolutionary government, obsessed with a desire for uniformity, to respect such an agreement. They erected a tariff wall along the frontier, at Vesenz, at the Carouge bridge, Chatelaine and Secheron. France forbade the exporting of wheat, which forced Geneva to import food from Germany at enormous cost and trouble. The French then transferred their customs post to Ferney. The blockade was formally instituted in December 1797. Geneva could not hope to hold out under these conditions, with a party in the town agitating for reunification, Genevans in Paris plotting against her independence, and no hope of support from the Swiss. On 15 April 1798, French troops entered the town by surprise and forced the citizens to sign a treaty of reunification at bayonet point.

The military, political and economic aims of General Bonaparte and the Directory in the conquest of Switzerland had been achieved. Neutrality, in so far as it might be a hindrance, had been destroyed. The reactionary governments with English or Austrian sympathies had been eliminated. French armies were quartered on Swiss territory, ready to launch yet another attack on the Emperor from there. The day they finally withdrew from Switzerland, they left her deprived of her two strategic operational bases, Geneva and Mülhausen, on each flank, and they left the Jura passes between them open to any future invaders. It was undoubtedly a good day's work, and one whose far-reaching consequences French and Swiss historians alike have been slow to grasp.

2. *Under the Yoke*

The old Confederation collapsed with the fall of Berne, but the conquest of the country as a whole was by no means complete.

Switzerland was never wholly occupied by the French. The forest cantons, Zug and Glarus held out till June and acquitted themselves heroically, under the command of Aloys de Reding, at Wollerau, Rotenthurm and Morgarten. An uprising took place, in August and September, in the small cantons. It was the story of the Vendée all over again. The savagery with which it was repressed, and the atrocities committed by French troops in Nidwald, are remembered to this day. They aroused a hatred and a resentment towards France which has never completely died down. The Grisons, which had not considered themselves entirely Swiss under the old regime, categorically refused to join the Helvetic Republic and were not conquered by Masséna till March 1799.

By now a spirit of resistance was springing up in the wake of the Austrian and Russian armies, who were accompanied by an old Swiss legion composed of emigrés and commanded by a Vaudois, Colonel de Roverea. On 30 March 1799, Archduke Charles addressed a proclamation to the Swiss people promising to restore their independence. With this, revolt broke out at Glarus and spread through the eastern part of the country, including Zurich, Lucerne, Solothurn, the Bernese Oberland, Fribourg and the Ticino. In April French troops were massacred in old Switzerland and the Valais. The former oligarchies spontaneously resumed control. This coalition was victorious at Zurich, on 5 June, and the whole of eastern Switzerland came into the hands of the rebels. But they lost it again at the second battle of Zurich. The Helvetic authorities were now able to establish control over the entire country with the help of the victorious French armies.

The Helvetic Republic was never for a moment accepted as a national government by the Swiss. The name was used abroad as synonymous with the Swiss Confederation, but in the country itself it remained a term laden with opprobrium. Its authority, even in those parts of the country it had freed from subjection, was always precarious. Orbe, the Ormonts, Aigle, and the Enhaut region, Grandson, St Croix, part of La Vallée and the Gros du Vaud had to be brought to heel by force. At Yverdon, a weeping population accompanied the last bailiff of Berne to the harbour. The Aargau troops were loyal to the Bernese government to the last. And the Ticino, with the Grisons, was the last canton to adopt the unitary constitution.

It was the threat of French bayonets alone which kept the

Helvetic regime in power for as long as five years under these precarious circumstances. Revolt followed revolt. When the First Consul decided to withdraw the occupation forces on 12 July 1802, the Helvetic government collapsed like a pricked balloon.

The Helvetic regime was an imported article which remained totally alien to the country. True, on the eve of the French invasion, the Swiss people were clamouring for reforms. But their own form of government had not been entirely discredited as had the old regime in France. Such changes as the people might have wanted to make would never have taken the shape of an artificial and arbitrary unification. An element in the country was dissatisfied with feudal anachronisms and political inequality but the mass of the people still clung to the idea of cantonal sovereignty as the key to freedom and independence.

The revolutionary constitutions have been described as having every virtue—except vitality. This is especially true of the Helvetic constitutions, which were the work of foreign theoreticians.

The first of the six constitutions successively imposed on Switzerland in less than five years created a 'united and indivisible' republic subdivided into cantons whose numbers ranged between eighteen and twenty-three. Executive power, as in France, was vested in a Directory of five members and legislative power in a parliament composed of two chambers: Senate and Grand Council. The Directory, a collegial form of government, was not too far removed from Swiss tradition, but the bi-cameral legislative system was an unprecedented innovation in the history of the country's government.

On 12 April 1798, Citizen Lecarlier, Commissary of the French Republic, and General Schauenbourg set up the Councils of the Nation at Aarau, amid general rejoicing. They did not wait to ascertain whether the whole country was pacified, or even conquered, as yet. These Councils were made up of deputies from a mere ten cantons. It was already apparent three days later that this government must collapse because of two inherent contradictions—it wanted to be constructive without money, and national without power.

Undoubtedly the Helvetic government had some good ideas and carried through some excellent measures. It proclaimed the equality of Swiss citizens in law, equality of languages and freedom of belief and speech; it created a sense of indigenousness which was to be the foundation of Switzerland's modern nationality, and a division of powers, something the old regime had no conception of; it suppressed internal customs barriers and impediments to trade; it instituted a unified system of weights and measures, reformed civil and penal law, authorized mixed marriages, abolished torture and improved the judicial system; it made progress in education and public works. And all this was achieved without experience, without administrative apparatus, staff or the money to recruit staff, and more remarkable still, without bloodshed.

Unfortunately the people were not interested in reforms in education, law or public works. The people wanted one thing only—the suppression of feudal rights. Such support as the Revolution could command in the subject countries hinged on this single measure.

Ever since 4 May the last feudal obligations of a personal nature—that is to say the remnants of serfdom—had been abolished without difficulty. On 31 May and 8 June, two decrees suspended the imposition of tithes. Finally, a law passed on 10 November of the same year abolished tithes, the quit rent and any other existing feudal levies. This must be considered as the most important achievement of the Helvetic government.

This law, a genuine agrarian reform, had serious and unexpected consequences.

Economic, first of all. The tithe, a purely ecclesiastical levy to begin with, had lost this characteristic during the eighteenth century. The greatest beneficiary of the tithe system was no longer the Church, monasteries, or private individuals, but the State. Of the 8,500,000 francs the tithe gathered annually in Switzerland, 6,600,000 went straight into State coffers, and less than two millions into the coffers of charitable institutions or private persons. But the State did not acquire this revenue without corresponding obligations. Most of the money came from the expropriation of Church property, and with it went the obligation for the upkeep of the faith and of the almshouses and charitable institutions.

Thus the State found itself deprived of an important source of revenue with no corresponding diminution of its expenses. On the contrary—the State was obliged to compensate the former owners at fifteen times the annual value of their tithes. It was faced with an expenditure of around 28 million francs at the very moment when centralization of government and all the reforms it had undertaken in the fields of education, public works, the law, army and so on were demanding huge sums of money.

To give the Directory its due, it was warned by events in France, where the promissory note had been a disastrous failure, and did not toy with the idea of creating inflation. But it did create new taxes: a property tax, a tax on capital, a building tax, a tax on drink, on transfer of property, inheritance, and a stamp duty among others. As was only to be expected from the chaotic situation in the country at the time, most of these taxes were not paid. So the State found itself short of money, which only increased its helplessness and unpopularity.

Taxes annoy everyone affected by them whether they pay them or not. The peasants in the small cantons had not been subject to feudal levies since the Middle Ages, and therefore had never been obliged to pay tax. The population was enraged at being called upon to subscribe to the gifts, as it were, now being conferred on the subject countries.

The abolition of tithes and other feudal levies created similar disturbances in the economic field. These levies had been mobile for some time, circulating freely through the economy. They represented a large portion of the nation's wealth. The cost of buying them in, compensation in practice neither being paid into nor paid out by the State, led to considerable discontent in the urban population.

The suppression of tithes caused the value of tithe lands, now freed from the levy, to rise sharply. Proprietors grew rich at the expense of the agricultural workers, a large and significant class of salaried workers, all of whom nursed a dream of one day owning their own land. In fact, far from having the expected democratic effects, the suppression of feudal rights made the rich peasants richer and the poor peasants poorer. This led, as will easily be imagined, to mounting anger and intensifying class friction in the countryside.

In short, the law of 10 November 1798, which was to have been the crowning achievement and cornerstone of the Revolution, had four main effects. It ruined the State, disorganized public assistance and the budget of the free towns; annoyed the beneficiaries, who found their compensation inadequate; infuriated dispossessed proprietors, feudal nobles and urban capitalists alike; and, finally, set the peasants of the mountain cantons and the agricultural workers of the plateau against the government. This theoretically generous law was a disaster which sealed the fate of the Helvetic Republic. It finally had to be rescinded on 15 November 1800; but the only result of this *volte face* was to increase the number of malcontents, and decrease the number of beneficiaries. This state of growing discontent was all the more serious because the country was ruined by war and military occupation.

The Directory certainly had financial considerations in mind when it decided to invade Switzerland. It is difficult to reckon the exact cost to Switzerland of its 'liberation' from the yoke it had borne without too much impatience. But it is safe to say that the price was high. The French army had barely entered Swiss territory when it clapped a levy of 700,000 francs on the Vaud canton. Berne was forced to pay up 24 million francs, in one form or another, some of it levied on the State and some on individuals. The banks and shops of Fribourg, Solothurn, Zurich and Lucerne, were emptied—of some two million francs—and the great monasteries were pillaged, not to mention the war contribution of 16 million francs extorted on 8 April from the former ruling aristocracies and monasteries of Lucerne, Beromunster and Einsiedeln. Most of this money went towards paying the wages and upkeep of the French army in Italy and the cost of the Egyptian expedition. Meanwhile the army of occupation in Switzerland, whose numbers approached 100,000 at times, lived entirely off the country. Over and above these sums, equivalent to many thousands of millions of francs in today's terms, were the extra contributions demanded from the rebellious cantons after their defeat—800,000 from Zurich (30 October 1799), 300,000 from St Gallen, 1,400,000 from Basle and so on.

None of this would have mattered, however, had it not been for the war. The 1799 campaign, which had nothing to do with Switzerland, was only waged on Swiss territory through the fault of the invaders. It cost the people untold suffering and money. The country from Schaffhausen to Gotthard was transformed for several months into one gigantic battlefield. Ragaz, Wallenstadt, Dottingen, Disentis, and many other places were burnt to cinders; orchards, vineyards and fields were pillaged, bridges destroyed, and the population looted. The damage is estimated at some 16 millions in the canton of Zurich, 7 million in Thurgau, $4\frac{1}{2}$ million in Altdorf and correspondingly large elsewhere. As was only to be expected, since the harvest had been destroyed, 1800 was a year of famine, like the one before it. In 1801, Macdonald's army was again quartered on the Swiss people for several months. When the Helvetic government presented France with a bill of 25 million francs, the First Consul retorted that this was not too high a price to pay for liberty.

It is easy to see how unpopular the regime held responsible for all this suffering must inevitably have become.

The Helvetic government's fatal flaw was that it owed its existence and powers to a foreign invader, and the presence of foreign troops was justified by its reliance upon them. Having said this, it must be admitted that the members of the Directory did everything possible to alleviate the heavy burden upon the country.

The French authorities' chief concern, after the conquest was completed on 8 June, was to obtain an offensive and defensive alliance from their puppet government. The chief purpose of the invasion had been to put an end to Swiss neutrality and assure the French of an operational base against Austria. This was something the Helvetians, always somewhat ingenuous about international politics, had not realized. The Directory protested, in the name of what it still, through force of habit, called its sovereignty. Rapinat, the French commissary, laughed in its face—with some reason. On 21 June 1798, two months after the moving celebrations at Aarau, Rapinat dismissed two of the Directors, replacing them by puppets, La Harpe and Ochs, the very men who had called on French troops to invade the country, and drafted the new Swiss constitution.

On 19 August 1798 a treaty of alliance was signed placing the conduct of Swiss foreign relations in the hands of the French government, together with Switzerland's right to war or peace and the guarantee of the Helvetic constitution. Switzerland even undertook, by importing salt at an artificially high price, to pay a tribute to France. In return she received promises of French 'good offices' in helping her acquire the Grisons, which already belonged to her; the Fricktal, which belonged to France; and the Vorarlberg, which belonged to Austria. Any attempt by the Swiss to lay claim to the Vorarlberg would inevitably make her the theatre of another war.

The outcome of this alliance is well known. At the moment the second coalition was established, on 28 February 1799, the Allies were obliged to occupy Swiss territory in order to cut communication lines between the French armies in Italy and Germany. The French, meanwhile, marched into Switzerland to protect them. So the alliance fatally drew Switzerland into another war.

This is not the place to dwell on this appalling campaign which only came to be fought on Swiss territory by accident. The principal events are common knowledge. The Austrians won the first battle of Zurich, on 5–6 June 1799. Then disputes arose between the members of the coalition. The Austrians withdrew across the Rhine, leaving Korsakov to be crushed by Masséna in the second battle of Zurich, fought on 26 September. Suvarov hastily recalled his army from Italy to the aid of his second-in-command, and marched through the St Gotthard pass, but he did not reach Altdorf till late on the evening of 26 September—too late. Finding himself cut off from Korsakov, whose army was retreating northwards, Suvarov had no alternative but to make for the Vorarlberg via the Kinzig, Pragel and Panix passes. It was a march of such appalling difficulty that it has not ceased to astonish later generations. It would probably have failed but for the support and assistance of the mountain people.

Less than two months after the second battle of Zurich, General Bonaparte assumed supreme power in France. Less than two months after 18 Brumaire, on 7 January 1800, the moderates took courage from this event and threw La Harpe out of the Directory, thus bringing the first Helvetic constitution to an end.

It seemed a fitting moment to reaffirm the country's independence. The government wanted to give the people proofs of its patriotism after the crushing years of occupation. Literally interpreting the promises contained in the treaty of alliance, the Swiss government entrusted Escher de la Linth with the task of preparing two reports on the most satisfactory boundaries for Switzerland for the peace talks. These claimed the Valteline, the Tresa line, the Val Ossola as far as Vogogna, Northern Savoy, the Jura, Constance and the Vorarlberg. They laid the groundwork for further work on the subject, in 1814, by Colonel Finsler. They are perfectly sound from a strategic point of view. As the work, however, of a government which owed its existence to French armed support, they stand as a monument of naivety and obtuseness.

Needless to say, the Lunéville peace treaty, concluded on

9 February 1801, brought no advantages to Switzerland. On 25 February, Napoleon sent a note to the Helvetic government demanding the cession of the Valais and the Val des Dappes, in the Vaudois Jura, in exchange for Fricktal whose fate had been hanging in the balance since Campo Formio. This was like exchanging an egg for a cow.

Ever since the dazzling march through the great St Bernard pass in May 1800, which won him the victory of Marengo, Napoleon showed himself increasingly reluctant to part with any of the Alpine passes. The Lombardy plain played a crucial role in his anti-Austrian strategy. He set great store by easy lines of communication with Italy, and the St Bernard, although he had successfully crossed it once, hardly came under the heading of 'easy'. This is why he insisted, after 8 October 1800, that the Swiss construct a military road over the Simplon. General Tureau's troops started work on the road in December, ignoring the vehement protests of the Valais authorities. These protests, however, led him to the conclusion that the Simplon's value would remain uncertain until he controlled the Rhône valley. The Helvetic government, still deluded about its real strength, believed itself in a position to refuse his express demand of 25 February 1801. Lengthy negotiations ensued, inextricably tangled with the constitutional disputes then dividing the country. In May, the government ceded the Valais in return for the First Consul's guarantee of the new constitution which the Swiss had drawn up for themselves. After Napoleon had made various amendments to the constitution, which he considered absurd, the Helvetic government saw fit to make a new proclamation of the 'integrity of the Helvetic Republic', on 28 September 1801.

The declaration was regarded as an act of provocation in Paris. On 28 October 1801, the Swiss government was once again overthrown by French civil and military agents. French troops entered the Valais in November, and treated it as a conquered country. The new Helvetic government tried to get help from the great powers. Seeking help from Europe in the state it was in then was like chasing a phantom. These moves by the Swiss were promptly reported to Napoleon, who profited by the lesson. A new coup d'état—the fifth—on 17 April 1802, overthrew the Helvetic government. The significance of this event was heavily underlined by three events which followed hard upon it and demonstrated that Napoleon was in no mood for trifling. First came the proclamation of the independence of Valais, on 16 May; then an uprising with separatist tendencies in the canton of Vaud; and thirdly, an official announcement of the evacuation of Switzerland by French troops on 12 July.

The Helvetic government was only too well aware that the departure of French troops would be a signal for anarchy and revolt throughout the country. It feared that its efforts to save the Valais might end by losing Switzerland the canton of Vaud. On 27 July the Helvetic Directory yielded to French demands. The Val des Dappes, which, though small, was strategically important, was incorporated into French territory. The Valais was declared an independent republic under the joint protectorate of the French, Cis-Alpine and Helvetic Republics—in other words, of France three times over.

Switzerland had held out for several counter-concessions, notably of the village of Celigny, embedded in her own territory; but she obtained only the Fricktal, Rheinfelden and its surrounding land.

If the Helvetic government counted on winning Napoleon's support by this policy of submission it was soon disabused. It only succeeded in precipitating its own downfall. The cession of the Valais was formally signed on 27 July 1802. On 8 August, French troops withdrew from Swiss territory.

Napoleon was weary of the Helvetic government's prevarications and inefficiency. Six coups d'état, all provoked or encouraged by French agents, and half a dozen constitutions still had not stabilized the situation. France had not succeeded in forming a government she could rely on which would also be acceptable to the Swiss. The First Consul realized that he had made the wrong decision back in 1797, and undertaken an impossible task.

The events of the second war of coalition, on the other hand, indicated that a neutral Switzerland might conceivably be more useful than Switzerland under French occupation. Masséna and Lecourbe had taken huge risks and suffered heavy losses. Switzerland is a difficult terrain for armies, especially when they cannot count on the support of the population. If the allies in the coalition had not fallen out among themselves, who knew how many soldiers Masséna would have had left?

The peace of Lunéville, concluded on 9 February 1801, assured the First Consul of French control over southern Germany. It also expelled the Austrians from Italy and forced

Francis II to recognize the Helvetic Republic. In these circumstances, it was no longer necessary to keep French troops on Swiss soil.

Thus, gradually, the First Consul arrived at the decision to make a fundamental change in his Swiss policy.

This does not mean he was thinking of leaving the Swiss to their own devices. This was unthinkable. A conqueror might toy with the notion, but it was impracticable. France, shortly to become the French Empire, could not permit the existence of a free nation on—almost within—its own frontiers. Napoleon was not the man to underestimate the value of the Alpine passes. He had no intention of abandoning them, he wanted to keep them in his hands but not under constant threat of a national uprising.

Between 29 April, the date of the so-called Constitution of Malmaison, and August 1802, when the French evacuated Swiss territory, Napoleon entertained various schemes. One was to dismember Switzerland, another to hand her over to the Grand Duke of Baden. Gradually he reached the conclusion that it was unnecessary to occupy Switzerland to make certain of her. Quite the contrary. Having arrived at this solution, he proceeded to carry it out, step by step.

On 12 July the First Consul announced his decision to withdraw the French army of occupation from Switzerland. Instantly the whole country from the Jura to the Ticino, was in an uproar. The *Landsgemeinden* met on 1 August in the traditional way, at Schwytz, Stans and Sarnen. In less than six weeks the whole of German Switzerland had been liberated and on 19 September, the Helvetic government, shattered by the fury of the populace, abruptly withdrew from Berne and retreated to Lausanne with all its staff. They were just about to cross the lake when an order arrived from the First Consul demanding that both parties sign an armistice. This took place at Montpreveyres, just outside Lausanne, on 5 October. As far as the Helvetic government was concerned, it was tantamount to abdication.

On 21 October the French army re-entered Swiss territory which they had quitted only three months earlier. On 10 December Napoleon summoned delegates from all the parties and cantons to Paris, but he only involved them superficially in his plans. On 19 February 1803, he promulgated the Act of Mediation, in the form of a French law, under which Switzerland was to regain her internal unity but not her independence.

This act was based on a twofold political concept. The first was that men are more interested in equality than liberty. This was the idea which inspired 18 Brumaire. Napoleon had recognized that the French, though weary of the sterile agitations of revolutionary politics, clung tenaciously to the social conquests of the Revolution—abolition of feudal rights and the division of landed property.

The situation in Switzerland was exactly the same. The peasants were not in the least interested in a one and indivisible republic. But they did not want to return to their former subjection, nor did they wish to resume payment of the former levies that the last Helvetic government had required of them. As long as the existence of the new cantons and the abolition of feudal rights was confirmed, it would be a simple matter to re-introduce oligarchic rule and the most extreme form of federalism into Switzerland.

The second strand of reasoning underlying the Act of Mediation was that the Swiss were more interested in their internal affairs than in international relations. An accurate diagnosis—and one that applies not only to Switzerland, but to countries everywhere. Napoleon determined to interfere as little as possible in Switzerland's internal affairs while keeping the conduct of her international policy in his own hands. After imposing the federal and cantonal constitutions which seemed best suited to their history and temperament, he left them to sort the rest out for themselves.

The Act of Mediation restored all the ancient cantons and gave them back their traditional institutions along with their absolute sovereignty. But it also raised the former subject countries to the rank of cantons. The present boundaries of Vaud, Aargau, Thurgau, St Gallen and the Ticino were laid down at this time. Six cantons, Fribourg, Berne, Solothurn, Basle, Zurich and Lucerne, were to succeed each other annually to the title of *Vorort*; the chief magistrate of the *Vorort* would hold the title of *Landammann* of Switzerland. He would be responsible for treating with foreign ambassadors, but had no power within the country, and the old Diet was resuscitated with all its superannuated procedures and age-old absurdities.

The Act of Mediation is an exact parallel to the policy Napoleon had been following in France. His idea was to preserve everything that could be saved from the past, while upholding all the innovations to which the people were deeply attached. The difficulty lay in making the right choice between all the alternatives. The First Consul, however, went about his task with considerable psychological insight and a real knowledge of people and local conditions. He restored the aristocratic rulers, whose political experience would guarantee their authority. He also restored cantonal sovereignty. He believed in centralization for France, but he recognized the inherent weakness in federalism which made it a convenient form of government for his neighbours.

Instantly all the little inter-cantonal rivalries and jealousies which had paralysed the old Diet sprang up again. These internal divisions fell in perfectly with Napoleon's aim, which was not to let the Confederation acquire any real independence but merely an illusion of independence, enough to deflect it from aspiring to the real thing.

The Swiss people lived with this illusion for the ten years that the Act of Mediation held good. The old *Landsgemeinden*, so dear to the hearts of the mountain people, were back in their old posts. The towns resumed their elaborate electoral procedure and the people were pleased to see men they had come to trust back in power. The new cantons, meanwhile, rejoiced in their freedom—they had achieved the only sort of independence which really means anything to the people, local minuscule independence. Their federalist fervour soon left even the forest cantons far behind.

The Mediation proved a reactionary period where internal affairs were concerned. Most of the Helvetic Republic's achievements, even those which were least controversial and most practical, in the economic field—such as standardization of weights and measures and currencies, and abolition of internal tariff walls—were swept out. The Swiss were intent on scrambling back into the Middle Ages.

This freedom they were so proud of, however, was pure illusion. The Swiss believed that, while they might be at one man's mercy where foreign affairs were concerned, they were nevertheless free to act as they pleased at home. But this was not the case. The magistrates they elected were the men Napoleon wanted, whom he trusted. They would not have been allowed to elect others.

The people might be deceived about the extent of their real freedom, but the rulers, with their inside knowledge, did not have this consolation. They knew how little their own wishes would be worth if they happened to conflict with the desires of the all-powerful Mediator. The grandiose receptions with which Napoleon honoured the deputies of the Diet, on 25 April 1809 at Legensburg, and 27 June 1811 at St Cloud, were primarily intended to remind them of this fact.

The post of Swiss *Landammann* was no sinecure. His chief task lay in trying to find an acceptable compromise between the Emperor's imperious commands and the Diet's vacillating desires. When no compromises were forthcoming it consisted of persuading the Diet to accept the Emperor's will.

Officially Swiss neutrality had been restored by the Act of Mediation. People allow themselves to be inveigled by words and everyone knows how much this one means to the Swiss. But neutrality as understood by Napoleon was not the same thing as the generally accepted meaning of the word. 'As far as I am concerned, neutrality is a meaningless word,' he told M. Hans de Reinhardt on 25 April 1809, 'and its usefulness to you depends on me.' He spoke the truth, and this remark might serve as an epitaph to the tale of the Confederation's foreign relations under the Mediation.

The Mediator's first action, after giving the Swiss their constitution, was to collect the price he had set. On 27 September 1803, the Diet found itself obliged to accept a new French alliance scarcely distinguishable from the 1798 treaty, on which the Swiss people blamed all their present evils. This alliance assured Napoleon of four Swiss regiments of 4,000 men each—not to mention a regiment in the pay of the Batavian Republic and another in the pay of the Cisalpine Republic. In time of war the quota of enlisted men could rise to some 42,000.

The Swiss had never been afraid of foreign service. But it was one thing to enlist under the rarely unfurled banners of peace-loving rulers, and quite another to follow the ever-moving eagles of an insatiable conqueror. Foreign service was a different matter when it became all but obligatory—and the cantons which traditionally supplied most men to the nominated regiments were extremely loath to take part in Napoleon's campaigns.

Swiss soldiers played their part heroically in most of the great Imperial victories, as well as in the Russian campaign, but their heart was not in it. Recruiting became more and more difficult as time went by. This was a source of constant friction between the Swiss *Landammann*, who invoked the fiction of Swiss independence, and the Imperial government, who refused to see why the Swiss should bleed any less than the French. At a time when human raw material was running out in his own empire, Napoleon made service under France obligatory under the terms of the capitulation treaty of 28 March 1812. The cantons yielded even this, but finding it impossible to make up their quota without duress, many of them introduced military service into their penal code as a penalty for infractions of common law. These practices, which elicited protests from the French ambassador, testify to the passive resistance against French military service.

While demanding increasingly large contingents for himself and his allies, Napoleon forbade the Swiss to enrol under the banners of his enemies. He feared, so he said, that the Confederates might find themselves fighting each other. On 18 May 1807, he ordered the Diet to recall any Swiss soldiers fighting for the British, under threat of severe penalties, and in 1808, when the Spanish people turned against him, he placed Spain's Swiss regiments under his own command.

We, with our modern ideas on the subject, might be inclined to congratulate him. But neutrality, as it was understood then, consisted precisely of the equal rights of other nations to recruit soldiers in Switzerland. Nothing could have discredited neutrality more than a monopoly of recruitment.

It is hardly worth mentioning here that French troops crossed Swiss soil on several different occasions, between 11 March and 9 April 1809, before Essling and Wagram, and then on 24 November of the same year, as the army returned after the Peace Treaty of Vienna. The Diet was greatly distressed by these troop movements and sent M. de Reinhardt to Regensburg for talks with the Emperor. It was there the *Landammann* elicited the remark quoted above. Historians have made a great issue out of these frontier violations. This a typical example of a verbal mirage. It is hard to see what difference a few troop movements could make to a State already at the mercy of Napoleon's lightest whim. Switzerland was a toy for him to play with, and she was forced to stand aside and watch the mutilation of her own territory in a spirit of helpless resignation. There would doubtless have been more instances if the Imperial campaigns had not taken place thousands of miles away and if

Napoleon had not taken the precaution of commandeering any vital military routes in advance.

The Emperor had as little respect for neutrality in the economic field as in the military one. His economic war with Britain, and the part this played in his thought and strategy, are common knowledge. In reality Napoleon only fought one war during his reign—against the British. He fought it with all the weapons at his disposal, including those offered by the Swiss.

Napoleon began his ferocious campaign against British products long before the Berlin Decree's official announcement of a continental blockage on 21 November 1806. Ever since 1798, and increasingly since 1803, after the violation of the Amiens Peace Treaty, Napoleon had been working to assimilate Swiss territory into France where customs barriers were concerned. On the other hand he imposed prohibitive import tariffs on Swiss goods entering France. As the Swiss textile industry, the country's chief source of prosperity, depended on England for its raw materials and on France for its outlets, it was ruined twice over by the French customs policy.

The tightening of the continental blockade after the Trianon Decree of 5 August 1810, which extended the embargo to a whole new series of products, had even more serious consequences for Switzerland; only this time they were political as well as economic. Switzerland was unable to import any British goods other than those smuggled through France or allied territory. Nevertheless, with that love of contradiction which characterizes despotic rulers, Napoleon never stopped accusing the Confederation of being Britain's chief trading centre on the continent.

Goods undoubtedly were smuggled into Switzerland. But this went on all over Europe. The accusations against the Swiss authorities were unjust, and in bad faith. Napoleon was demanding that they starve their own country, which was asking altogether too much of human nature. He knew this himself, having failed to do the same thing in his own Empire.

All the same this was the pretext Napoleon chose for seizing more land from the Confederation in 1810.

The idea of redefining Swiss frontiers had occurred to him before. During the talks preparatory to the 1803 alliance he suggested that the frontiers should 'follow the mountain peaks'. But where? Certainly not in the Bishopric of Basle where all the gorges were held by France. Nor in the Principality of Neuchâtel which Napoleon had forced the King of Prussia to hand over to him, on 15 February 1806, only to give it, on 30 March, to Marshal Berthier. These remarks of Napoleon's could only be interpreted one way—as meaning that the frontier of the Confederation should end at the St Gotthard.

In 1809, at Regensburg, Napoleon made a proposal to M. de Reinhardt, which throws light on his conception of Swiss neutrality. The Tyrol and the Vorarlberg had been given to Bavaria, a vassal of France since the Treaty of Pressburg (1805). Rebellions had broken out in both places. Napoleon demanded that the Swiss raise troops to suppress these uprisings, in other words to police their neighbours. In return the Emperor offered to give the Tyrol and Vorarlberg to Switzerland.

Naturally, M. de Reinhardt broke out in a sweat at hearing the peremptory proposal. He was probably right, too, at least as far as the Tyrol was concerned, since she had never known any historical link with Switzerland. Napoleon did not press the matter. This incident shows that while he may have intended weakening the Confederation's frontiers to the west and south, in other words vis-à-vis himself, he also intended strengthening them vis-à-vis Austria, with the idea of making Switzerland into a solid rampart for France.

The Vienna Peace of 15 October 1809 gave Napoleon the title of 'Mediator of Switzerland'—official recognition of his suzerainty over the Confederation—and the fief of Razuns, in the Grisons, which belonged to the Emperor of Austria. On 22 June 1810, Napoleon demanded a small piece of land opposite Hunningen from the Canton of Basle, in order to construct a bridge and bridgehead over the Rhine. But these were merely crumbs, or rather hors d'oeuvres; the worst was to come.

On 30 October 1810, on the pretext of putting a stop to smuggling, Italian troops occupied the Ticino. On 12 November the Valais was incorporated into the Empire, under the name of the Department of Simplon.

The loss was not so severe in the case of the Valais, either to Switzerland or to the Valais itself, since its independence was purely theoretical. But the occupation of the Ticino, in peacetime, and on the most barefaced pretext, was the worst blow which could have been inflicted on the Confederation. The Diet resented it strongly. In spite of its impotence and abasement and the risks attendant upon such a gesture, it continued to protest against the wrong done to Switzerland and the Ticino. Napoleon was incensed by what to us appears to have been very mild and circumspect protests. At St Cloud, on 27 June 1811, he delivered a violent tirade to the delegates of the Diet who had assembled there to congratulate him on the birth of the King of Rome.

The Diet had no choice. It gave way and accepted—at the suggestion of the French ambassador himself—proposals for a 'rectification of frontiers' which would have given Italy the Mendrisiotto and set the boundaries of the canton of Ticino at Lake Lugano. Happily, this proposal was never followed up. Perhaps Napoleon was too busy with the Russian campaign to devote more time to it. Or perhaps, as his appetite grew with eating, he preferred to hold on to the whole of the Ticino, as King of Italy. The Diet's petitions, renewed every year, remained unanswered. The Ticino remained under Italian occupation. It took the disastrous Russian campaign and the battle of Leipzig to free it.

What conclusions may be drawn from these facts? Only one, but an unequivocal one. Switzerland cannot hope to enjoy real freedom whenever Europe passes under a hegemony. Swiss independence and neutrality depend upon a European balance of power. When this is threatened or destroyed, Switzerland ceases to be free.

The Swiss people's guarantee of independence lies in the fact that none of her neighbours can lay a finger on her without uniting all the rest against it. If one of these neighbours is all-powerful, or if Switzerland has only one neighbour, it will dismiss Swiss independence or neutrality as a 'meaningless word'.

A glance at the map of Europe under the Empire shows that Switzerland is hemmed in by France from Basle to the Simplon. French territory eats right to the heart of the Swiss plateau and occupies all the Confederation's natural defences to the west. To the south Switzerland was delimited by Italy, whose king was Napoleon, and from Stelvio as far as Basle, by the German Princes who had declared themselves voluntary subjects of Napoleon. In fact the Confederation was entirely surrounded by France—an enclave.

Her position, politically speaking, was not much better. The great powers already had so many reasons for going to war against Napoleon that the fate of Switzerland did not weigh very heavily in the balance. On the other hand, they him had so many reasons for maintaining good relations with with that Switzerland could hardly stop them. Austria was angry also the Swiss as it was, because of their humiliation, and pursued a hostile policy towards them throughout this period, shown in the illegal confiscation, among other things, of Swiss monastic property in the Vorarlberg.

In short, the Confederation, governed by Napoleon's puppets, found itself politically isolated in Europe and at the mercy of its Mediator, whose title was no vain flourish but a sober reality. Hence the almost servile submission of the Swiss magistrates, which is hard to swallow now, but which it would be unfair to hold against them.

Chapter IX

The Return to Independence (1813-1816)

1. *The Collapse of the Mediation*

The Swiss failed to see the writing on the wall prophesying Napoleon's downfall. In February 1813, just after the Russo-Prussian alliance, the Berne deputy asked the Diet to proclaim Swiss neutrality. The suggestion was haughtily dismissed by the French ambassador and the proposal dropped. On 7 June the Swiss *Landammann*, Hans de Reinhardt, opened the Diet with the customary impassioned eulogy of the Mediator. Even Austria's entry into the coalition in August failed to move the Confederates. The Swiss authorities, lulled by official propaganda put out by the Imperial government, were quite unaware of the mood of dissatisfaction, lassitude and discouragement prevalent throughout the French population as a whole. The façade remained impeccable and superb, and no one in Switzerland dared to peer inside. The Swiss might be divided in their wishes, but they were unanimously convinced as to the likeliest outcome of the European situation. Every European coalition for the past fifteen years had been followed by French victories. Everyone, either hopefully or fearfully, expected a second Austerlitz.

Instead, they had Leipzig (18 October 1813). The Swiss did not grasp the full significance of this event to begin with, any more then they grasped the implications of the German defeats in the summer of 1918. The French ambassador took it upon himself to open their eyes. He hurriedly called for an extraordinary convocation of the Diet to proclaim Swiss neutrality. To the *Landammann's* profound amazement Count Talleyrand came to tell him, at the beginning of November, of the Emperor's decision to evacuate the Ticino immediately and unconditionally. The great débâcle had begun.

On 18 November 1813 the Diet proclaimed Swiss neutrality, authorized the *Landammann* to raise a contingent and decided to send two ambassadors extraordinary to Napoleon and the Allies. But these steps were already invalidated by the talks taking place in the Allied headquarters at Frankfurt-am-Main.

The monarchs had to choose between two plans of campaign before invading France. The first, favoured by Gneisenau and the Prussian government, advocated a crushing frontal assault on Paris. This plan left the Swiss out of account. Schwarzenburg and Metternich, for political and military reasons, favoured a policy of temporization. They did not wish to strike a blow at the heart of France. The Emperor of Austria was unwilling to dethrone his daughter; he merely wanted to impose peace on his son-in-law. The Austrian plan envisaged a slow march by the allied army across Switzerland, and from there, via the Langres plateau, on Paris. By taking the slow way round they would allow time for negotiations with Napoleon.

The Austrians invoked military and moral reasons for violating Swiss territory. The authorities under the Mediation offered no guarantee of impartiality. Napoleon had said that Swiss neutrality was a meaningless word; he never respected it when it got in his way. Swiss soldiers fought in the French armies. It would be imprudent for the Allies to advance leaving Switzerland and Italy in French hands—a double threat on their army's flanks.

England supported Schwarzenburg's plan, and as she was financing the whole coalition, her views carried considerable weight. But the Tsar pronounced himself in favour of the Prussian plan, with a slight modification.

The Swiss believed the reason behind the Tsar's choice was the influence exerted over him by his tutor, La Harpe, and his sister's nurse, Mlle Mazelet, of Morges. But this was erroneous. The arguments of his Vaudois friends might have confirmed the Tsar in his decision. But his choice was essentially dictated by Russian interests. The Russian Emperor was not influenced by promises made to his domestics—as Metternich maliciously hinted. He had already come to a decision before making any such promises.

The reasoning behind Alexander's policy has also been misunderstood. He was not opposed to the Allies marching across Swiss territory, but he wanted to prevent the Austrians occupying the country under pretext of military necessity. In Austrian hands, Switzerland could be used either as a rampart against

France or a base for friendly overtures towards her. In either case, this would mean greater power and security for Austria, and might have enabled her eventually to deploy all her military strength against Russia.

The Tsar may have been concerned about the fate of the Canton of Vaud. But his real concern lay in maintaining the balance of military strength in Europe. His objections were not against Schwarzenburg's plan as such, but against the consequences Metternich wanted to exploit.

Throughout the month of November 1813, Alexander and Metternich engaged in a hard-fought diplomatic match, details of which remain somewhat shadowy. Both sides played on words. The Tsar did not consider that marching across Swiss territory was a violation of neutrality. He was profuse in polite assurances to the Confederates, and promised that their neutrality would be respected. But he did not oppose the sending of two diplomats, Count Capo d'Istria representing Russia and the Chevalier de Lebzeltern representing Austria, to Zurich to secure the right to cross Switzerland for the allied armies. He did not even wait for a reply from the Federal authorities before authorizing Marshal Schwarzenburg to concentrate an advance-guard in the Loerrach region, in a position which clearly implied that the army would shortly be entering Swiss soil.

At the decisive moment the Tsar disappeared on a visit to his family at Darmstadt, leaving Metternich coolly engineering a situation which would make the violation of Swiss neutrality a necessity. The Tsar returned once the deed was done—not too late, however, to make a great show of despair and indignation in public.

If grave doubts attach to Alexander's good faith in this business, there can be none at all about Metternich's duplicity. He tricked everyone. He allowed the Swiss to think their neutrality would be respected; he promised the Tsar that military occupation would have no political consequences; and he promised the Emperor Francis that the Swiss were waiting as one man to welcome the allies.

Prince Metternich was helped in this manoeuvre by the handful of irresponsible ultra-Bernese and Grisons who made up the Committee of Waldshut. The existence of this Committee and its muddle-headed activities enabled Metternich to overcome Emperor Francis' conscientious scruples, by claiming that they represented a summons from the Swiss people themselves.

He was helped still more by the vacillations of the Federal authorities, the inadequacy of their defence organization, the avarice of the Diet, the inefficiency of the *Landammann*, the duplicity of General de Wattenwyl, in command of the Swiss army, and the rivalry between civil and military authorities—in other words, by another attack of the moral paralysis which seems too often to have incapacitated Switzerland at critical moments in her history.

The allied military were growing impatient. The army could not remain inactive in a country which was not supplying it with food. On 15 December Metternich succeeded in forcing Francis' hand. The advance-guard were ordered to march into Switzerland. On 20 December Colonel Herrenschwand signed the capitulation of Basle, and the next day the allied army crossed the Rhine preceded by a magnificent proclamation promising the Swiss people to restore their independence and their former frontiers.

How did the Swiss react to this new turn of events?

As usual, in a highly contradictory fashion. The country split off into three parties. The first saw a victory for the coalition as the end of a hated tyranny. True, the Act of Mediation had assured the Confederation of ten years of internal peace. But what was that compared to freedom?

For this freedom to be complete it had to mean the suppression of the foreign constitution and a restoration of the happy state of affairs before 1798. There may have been few aristocrats so reactionary as to wish for the total restoration of the archaic system of bourgeoisies and patriciates. But most of them saw the newly created cantons as symbolic of the French yoke, and their demotion to subject countries seemed a necessary consequence of an Allied victory.

Barely fifteen years had passed since the collapse of the old Confederation. This is not a long time in which to change the fundamental ideas of a nation. For the aristocrats—many of them back in power under the Mediation—Switzerland was unthinkable except as a union of sovereign states. Sovereigns are not created by law. In their eyes the cantons created by the revolution were in defiance of history. They had no moral claim to existence.

In the new cantons, where these views were known, people sent up fervent prayers for a Napoleonic victory. The burdens of conscription were quite forgotten in the need to defend the only independence which mattered to the people—that of their canton.

The traditionally neutral Confederates, Basle, Shaffhausen Appenzell and Zurich, held views somewhere between these two extremes, not having any territorial claims to press. They hoped an Allied victory would restore Swiss independence. But they also wanted the Act of Mediation maintained, seeing chaos and civil war as the only alternative.

Unfortunately the hopes of moderates and optimists alike were soon dashed by events. At the same time as Metternich was seeking to convince the Emperor Francis, he also sent an agent, Count Senft-Pilsach, on a secret mission to Berne, to persuade the Republic to call in the Allies. Von Senft came up against unexpected resistance from the Mediation authorities. Carried away by zeal, he even went to the lengths of stirring up revolution by promising the aristocratic party help from Austria. On 24 December 1813, the Councils of the old regime seized power and immediately issued a proclamation 'to their loyal subjects in Aargau and the Vaud canton'.

The move towards restoration, once started, was impossible to check. On 29 December 1813, the Diet attempted to prolong the Mediation. But, after various internal upheavals, Schwytz, the Grisons, Solothurn, Fribourg, Lucerne, Uri, Unterwald and Zug broke away one by one from the Diet. It soon represented only a minority of the oldest cantons.

With this, anarchy became rampant throughout the country. The Tsar was forced to issue a categorical order in January to prevent the Grisons separating completely from Switzerland, which would have flung them straight into the arms of Austria. On 2 February 1814, Gersau proclaimed its independence. On 19 February Uri annexed the Levant. On 21 February the old cantons decided to leave the Confederation. On 27 February the free town of Schwytz proclaimed itself sovereign over the surrounding areas and reclaimed its ancient possessions of Utznach and Gaster, which belonged to the canton of St Gallen.

What did the new cantons do to defend their independent status? Thurgau did not feel threatened, the Ticino, which had been under foreign occupation for four years, was powerless to do anything, and the canton of St Gallen scarcely had even the will to survive. Vaud and Aargau, on the other hand began strengthening their positions along their frontiers with

Berne. They started buying munitions and practising espionage. Civil war threatened to break out at any moment.

Learning of von Senft's excessive zeal at Berne and the threat to the Canton of Vaud, the Tsar flew into a violent rage. He had no intention of allowing Austrian diplomacy to exert an undivided influence over Switzerland. He made use of his own disinterestedness and geographical remoteness to intervene in the management of Swiss affairs, which took a turn noticeably favouring the newly created cantons.

The Allied ministers made great efforts to pacify the Confederation during the first two months of 1814. Their efforts were fruitless, however, because the country was hopelessly divided. The fate of Switzerland was being decided, not at Zurich where the Diet officially sat, nor at Lucerne, seat of the Diet for dissident cantons, but at Allied general headquarters, whither all the factions busily tearing Switzerland apart had dispatched their envoys.

The question of whether the new cantons would be preserved or sacrificed became submerged in the broader issues of European politics. Austria insisted upon a negotiated peace with Napoleon. The Tsar refused, determined to settle the sharing of the spoils first with the allies. He had designs on Poland, supporting his claims with the right of nationalities. Austria invoked legitimacy as a reason for refusing him Poland.

These same principles applied to Switzerland. Legitimacy meant Vaud and Aargau to the Bernese, Austrian influence as far as Geneva, thus making the Confederation a glacis of Austria. A country's right to self-determination, on the other hand, of which the formula alone is modern, meant the recognition of the new cantons and the creation of an internal equilibrium between French and Austrian influences. Alexander, for reasons of self-interest, became the defender of the fundamental doctrine of Swiss independence.

The Tsar managed to carry the day with his arguments, at Chaumont at the beginning of March. This was the price he set on his attendance at the Châtillon peace talks, which Metternich was anxious to convoke.

On 16 March, the powers recognized the existence of the new cantons and gave the separate Diet of Lucerne orders to dissolve itself. On 20 March the Berne government solemnly renounced all claims to Vaud, but maintained its rights to Aargau. Finally, on 6 April, the Diet, which is known to history as the Long Diet, succeeded in assembling at Zurich with the participation of all the cantons, to prepare a new pact.

The powers' recognition of the new cantons—which did not guarantee their integrity—did not put an end to hostilities, or to the claims and counter-claims put forward. On 2 May Uznach became united to the canton of Schwytz; on 19 May Sargans proclaimed its reunion with Glarus. The canton of St Gallen was falling to pieces. Federal troops had to occupy it twice, together with the Ticino. Appenzell made the most of its claims to the Rheintal, and Zug likewise to Freiamt, while Uri continued to administer the Levant. Finally, Berne sought to persuade Austria to cede the Fricktal to them, in order to dismember Aargau.

The foreign powers, finding these internal struggles incomprehensible and their outcome debatable, began drawing up plans for the division or subjection of the country. The Prussian cabinet demanded that the Confederation be reunited with Germany, but Metternich opposed this suggestion. The advisability of giving Switzerland a King or *Statthalter* was discussed. No one in Europe thought the Swiss capable of governing themselves wisely or liberally.

The framing of the new pact ran into insurmountable obstacles. The allied ministers, Lebzeltern and Capo d'Istria, joined during the spring by Chambrier d'Oleyres for Prussia and Stratford Canning, for Britain, had taken over the mantle of the French ambassador. In Zurich their word was law. They gave orders to the Diet, re-drafted the cantons' constitutions, and the deputies formed a sort of antechamber in their hotel. The ministers even grew indignant that the Swiss seemed unable to lift a finger without first asking their permission. Habits of tyranny are rapidly acquired, and relinquished with difficulty.

The Swiss, though cowed, were not entirely docile. The ministers could not persuade them to adopt the Pact of Restoration until they finally deleted, after five abortive attempts in eight months, everything appertaining to cantonal frontiers, and the compensation claims the various cantons were making against each other. These litigations had to be postponed until the Congress which was due to meet soon afterwards in Vienna. Even then a further ultimatum, couched in more imperious terms than the one before, was needed to persuade the Swiss to accept the Pact destined to unite them for more than thirty years.

The Swiss have no cause to be proud of their conduct at this time. The question of what would have happened to the country if the Allies had not intervened remains unanswerable.

2. *The Revision of Frontiers*

Simultaneously with the entry of their armies into Switzerland, the Sovereigns issued a proclamation to the people promising to restore the Swiss frontiers demolished by Napoleon.

They had two reasons for going this. Firstly, to win the Swiss round with this promise as a bait. This was a psychological error on their part. Secondly, to stir up trouble in the neighbouring French regions. In this respect their plan was entirely successful. News of the Austrians' entry into Basle caused a great commotion among all the Confederation's traditional allies. Memories of the past survived under the Imperial yoke and Switzerland was still a powerful magnet to the people who had once belonged to her.

Even before the Austrians entered the Bishopric of Basle, the Jura valleys spontaneously turned to Berne for protection. Bienne gave General Haugwitz's troops an enthusiastic welcome on 23 December. That same day, a group of people in Neuchâtel sent a courier to the King of Prussia, at Freiburg-im-Breisgau, asking him to take possession of his principality again. On 28 December, Colonel von Simbschen occupied the Department of Simplon, which the French prefect had evacuated only the day before. Finally, on arriving at Lausanne, General von Bubna, commanding the Austrian advance-guard, found a delegation awaiting him from a Committee for Independence formed in Geneva. On 31 December the Austrian army entered this town—the first French fortress they had so far encountered—without a blow being struck and amid touching scenes of rejoicing.

Tribute should be paid to the courage of the men who took part in these demonstrations, at a time when Napoleon had not yet been defeated. They by no means enjoyed the unanimous support of their fellow citizens. They were accused of taking on responsibilities no one had entrusted to them, and exposing the country to terrible reprisals. They were criticized for taking advantage of public misfortunes to restore the old aristocratic governments, for reawakening bad old memories, for paving the way for new conflict, in short for furthering the cause of their party.

Their machinations were founded on two hopes alone. One, that they might succeed in lightening the burdens of a military occupation. This explains the serious attention the reconstituted authorities in Bienne and Geneva gave to requisition orders throughout that spring—quibbling over what seem to us to be trifles.

The second was that they might obtain recognition of their independence, and admission into the Confederation. With this in mind they sent delegations to the Diet at Zurich, and to the allied sovereigns at Basle.

They were coolly received at Zurich. The Swiss had had enough of internal problems and had no wish to complicate them further with international ones. Besides, imbued as they were with a purely local patriotism and absorbed with their own private quarrels, the Swiss never seriously considered whether the Confederation might stand to gain by increasing the number of its members. Just as their ideal form of government was one restricted to as few members as possible, so their ideal fatherland was one which shared out its benefits among as few people as possible. They thought of these particular Confederates as Frenchmen, and had no desire to offend Napoleon, who might well become powerful once again, in order to please them. In other words they refused to admit that they might owe these rediscovered brothers anything in the way of support or hospitality.

In Basle, where the sovereigns remained during the whole of January 1814, the delegates met with quite a different welcome. The Allies knew what they were about when they promised to enlarge the Confederation. It was in their interests to contain France, strengthen her neighbours and protect Germany with a string of secondary states. It also accorded with their principles, which were to restore the people subjugated by Napoleon to their former independence.

The sovereigns made no mystery of their intentions. They wanted to enlarge the Confederation and strengthen its frontiers to enable it to defend its neutrality against French encroachment. 'The idea is,' wrote Pictet de Rochemont, 'to make Switzerland into a formidable Confederation.' The monarchs said as much to the federal deputies, assembled to greet them on behalf of the Diet, and to the countless delegates sent by all the cantons, parties and liberated regions.

The Genevans came with a timid request for recognition of

their independence and a small 'enlargement' which would allow them to present Switzerland with a compact territory. The Tsar asked them brusquely what they wanted in Savoy. Pictet de Rochemont made his first diplomatic overtures. He improvised a statement outlining the various possible solutions to the Genevan frontier question: one followed the mountain peaks, from the Jura, to Vuache, Salève and the Voirons; the other took in the Leman basin, as protection for the Simplon, and divided Chablais between Geneva and the Valais.

Paris fell on 31 March, without the Swiss having made the slightest effort to turn these favourable proposals to their own advantage. On 5 April the Allied ministers asked the Diet to raise troops to occupy the territory which the Allies intended for Switzerland; the Diet did not stir. On 22 April the Ministers returned to the subject with increasing impatience. But it was not until 18 May that the cantons managed to raise twenty companies. Meanwhile Napoleon had abdicated, France had recalled the Bourbons and pledged all its fortresses to the Allies. Now that the latter no longer had anything to fear from France, they could dispense with Switzerland. The hour of goodwill was past.

The months of April and May 1814 were decisive ones in European history. The conquerors spent this time drawing up the future frontiers of France. These were decisive months for Switzerland, too, because she shared frontiers with France. But this never occurred to the Diet. They neglected to send a representative to the Congress being held in Paris. The one deputation they did send was to Louis XVIII, to congratulate him on his accession and negotiate a military treaty of capitulation with him. The Allies found this display of zeal untimely, to say the least, and it was a black mark against the Swiss.

The Diet took only two peace measures. It demanded the dismantling of the Hunningen fortress, and directed Colonel Finsler, the Federal Chief-of-Staff, to draw up a report on the optimum frontiers for Switzerland. These frontiers left out Mülhausen, Pruntrut and the southern part of the Ticino, but they included the Fort of Joux, the Val des Dappes, the Gex region, Northern Savoy, Ossola, Valteline, Constance and some free towns north of the Rhine. They would undoubtedly have been excellent frontiers to have, and astute diplomacy might possibly have secured them. Their mistake lay in the fact that they were purely theoretical, unrelated to any concrete political thinking by the Swiss people or the Diet. The Diet merely forwarded Colonel Finsler's proposals, on 3 May 1814, to a commission.

The Diet had finally acted on the Ministers' advice and ordered the occupation of the Valteline on 27 April. It was not an occasion for congratulation. The opportune moment, between the armistice and the Milan revolution when the country was a no-man's land, had passed. The Austrians were now in control and the Grisons troops encountered them as soon as they marched down the Bregaglia valley towards Chiavenna. The Swiss retired so as not to have to fight with their allies.

The occupation of the Bishopric of Basle, which was ordered on 6 May, did not go smoothly either. Swiss troops found themselves dragged into the intricate intrigues tearing the region apart. Bienne expected to be treated as an equal, and not to be 'occupied' like the rest of the region. The partisans of France, the Prince-Bishop, the governor, Baron d'Andlau, Berne and those who wanted an autonomous canton were all quarrelling furiously among themselves and the unfortunate Swiss officers, entangled in a situation they did not understand, did not know where to turn.

Meanwhile, the real decisions concerning the Swiss frontiers were being taken in Paris, in the absence of Confederate representatives, but in the presence of, first, a Bernese deputation who wanted to obtain the Fricktal for internal political reasons, secondly, a deputation from the Valais, which had come to ask that their country should not be united to Switzerland, but remain independent, a concession they failed to get; and thirdly, a deputation from Neuchâtel which obtained a slight revision of their frontiers, thanks to Prussian influence, but were refused an extension going as far as the Doubs; and finally, a deputation from Geneva and one from Savoy, at loggerheads with each other. In fact Pictet de Rochemont was the only man who stood up for the best interests of Switzerland in Paris, without having even been asked to do so.

Geneva's history since the Middle Ages hinges on the town's need to remain united to the countryside which fed it, and the countryside's fear of becoming isolated from the town which absorbed its products. The uniting of Geneva to the surrounding area was the one benefit conferred by French annexation in 1798. The idea that this unity might now be broken was unpopular with all the tradesmen, particularly the clockmakers, who were influential in Geneva, and most of whose parts came from the Gex region and Savoy.

For similar reasons the people of Savoy and the Gex region were mostly anxious to uphold a regime which had brought them undeniable benefits over the past fifteen years. The Central Commission of the Geneva Department, which represented their case, kept pressing on their behalf for the union between the town and its economic zone to be preserved.

But this idea had its opponents, both in Geneva and elsewhere. In the eyes of the party headed by the Mayor, Ami Lullin, it was Protestantism which had saved the city's independence under Imperial domination. Geneva's only justification for existence was as a strictly evangelical city and it should beware of an influx of Catholic citizens. This was the view of Protestants and old aristocrats alike.

The relative strength of the two currents of opinion in Geneva varied according to military and diplomatic events. But the Genevans were united on three points.

First, that Geneva should accept as much territory as would be necessary to join her to Switzerland. The Genevans, like the Allies, were under the illusion that the Swiss would like to expand their frontiers. The second was that the canton of Geneva should retain its name, armorial bearings, motto and Protestant character. For this reason 'contingency laws' were drawn up whereby the Catholics were assured of certain rights, but not of equality with the Protestants.

The third was that Geneva should avoid a clash with France. Even in defeat France remained a powerful neighbour. The ideal thing would have been for France to cede the land freely, and without rancour. Which is why Pictet de Rochemont was instructed to ask, not for a cession, but for an exchange, of territory. In return Geneva planned to offer Mülhausen. This town had been occupied by Austrian troops in January 1814 'as part of the Swiss Confederation'. Mülhausen, which had been conquered in 1798, did not fall within the 1792 frontiers to which France was to revert.

The Genevans did not trust Austria, a deeply Catholic power with Sardinian connections. The Austrian agents at Geneva, Count von Bubna, General Zuchmeister and Count d'Ugarte, had sounded a somewhat ambiguous note. Nevertheless Austria supported Geneva's claims at the Congress of Paris.

On the other hand, the English and Russians, whose support

Geneva had relied upon, deserted them. The Provisional Government wrote assuring the British Prince Regent: 'Geneva is the most British town on the continent.' This was true. The Genevan aristocracy was steeped in English culture, and had had the courage to display these sympathies even under Imperial rule. Geneva thought she would be able to count on British support in return. As for the Tsar, he was the ruler of a remote and disinterested country, known to be generous towards the oppressed, and European eyes turned towards him at this period with much the same fervour that they later displayed towards President Wilson.

At first, everything went well. On 1 May the Allied ministers at Zurich wrote to the Provisional Council to congratulate them on their return to power, and to promise them an extension of their territory. On 12 May 1814, M. de la Forêt signed a protocol on behalf of King Louis XVIII, promising the cession of the Gex region.

The Emperor of Russia had made promises to the King. He was given a million subjects and the 1792 frontiers. But where was the line to be drawn? The King wanted it in the north, to keep the fortresses of Flanders. That was why he ceded the Gex region. The English, who wanted to take these fortresses from the French, insisted that the additional territory be taken somewhere else. So the French King was given the Gex region and Mülhausen, and part of Savoy. On that day Geneva found herself footing the bill for British security and the Tsar's generous promises.

The Paris Treaty of 30 May 1814 was only a preliminary peace. The great problems posed by a total reorganization of Europe were reserved for the Congress which was to meet in Vienna on 1 August 1814 and which finally opened on 1 November.

The reason the Swiss appeared uninterested in the Paris Congress was that its sole purpose was to revise the French frontiers. All the same, the Paris treaty defined Switzerland's western frontiers for at least a century, and probably permanently.

Mülhausen was handed to France without compensation. The whole of the Bishopric of Basle was detached from French territory. Neuchâtel obtained a slight adjustment of its Jura frontier. Otherwise frontiers between the two countries remained unchanged. The treaty allowed Geneva to join itself to Switzerland, and made the Versoix road a neutral zone, but did not give it any additional territory.

South of Geneva, it created a bizarre frontier between France and Sardinia which has not survived the test of time, but which contemporaries considered definitive. The result of this was considerable agitation in Savoy. The fate of the countries separated from France was to be settled by the Congress of Vienna. The population set about making its wishes on the subject known to the major powers. Savoy had been loyal to Napoleon. But now that the Empire had fallen and the frontier was defined, Northern Savoy was left with a choice between Victor-Emmanuel and Switzerland. All the elements in the Chablais, Faucignys and the Genevois which were neither aristocratic nor clerical were passionately eager for unification with Switzerland. Petitions comprising thousands of signatures were presented to the Diet. The Diet, however, taken up with cantonal relations with the Courts of France and Sardinia, decided not to follow them up but to await the decisions of the Congress of Vienna.

Meanwhile, the Provisional Council in Geneva, dissolved in February after the French army's advance, was back in power. This time it had the unanimous support of the population. On 18 May Austrian troops evacuated the Republic's territory and the rest of the land destined for Switzerland. On 1 June the Fribourg and Soleure contingents reached the city amid general acclaim.

On 17 May the Diet decided to recommend that the cantons approve Neuchâtel's request to be admitted into the Confederation. It came to the same decision, on 18 June, with regard to the Valais—where opinion was not so unanimously pro-Swiss—and on 19 June with regard to Geneva, 'in deference to the wishes of the great powers'. Finally, on 12 September, Neuchâtel, the Valais and Geneva, were officially received into the Confederation as cantons.

One would have preferred the Confederation to show more enthusiasm. But to be fair—the decision to enlarge the Confederation by three French-speaking cantons at one fell swoop, thus profoundly affecting the linguistic and denominational equilibrium of the country, was pregnant with consequences.

3. *The Congress of Vienna*

The Swiss Confederation, which had not been officially represented at the Paris Congress, sent more than twenty delegates to Vienna: three federal deputies with a secretary, four Grisons, two Bernese, three Genevans, three from the Jura, one from Aargau, Bienne and Lucerne, two deputies from the Valteline, not to mention the Swiss minister at Vienna, the Bishop of Basle, the Abbot of St Gallen, a large number of private individuals and a quantity of Swiss in the English, Russian and Austrian delegations.

None of these men agreed about anything. Most of them were there to contradict and argue with each other. The various factions had been carefully represented in the Federal deputation. M. Wieland of Basle was in favour of the new cantons. M. de Montenach, of Fribourg, was an ardent aristocrat and the Swiss *Landammann*, Hans Reinhardt, of Zurich, was only concerned to protect his canton's interests. As it turned out, these deputies, who had no bonds of personal sympathy to unite them, did nothing but intrigue against and betray each other. The Berne deputy, Zeerleder, became neurasthenic by the end of the Congress. 'All in all,' wrote Pictet de Rochemont, 'this delegation is a pity'.

The Diet's instructions to the deputies were to obtain recognition of Switzerland's perpetual neutrality, and restitution of the territories seized from her—the Bishopric of Basle, the Val des Dappes and the Valteline. They also laid claim to Constance, the natural capital of Thurgau, Campione, the German enclaves in the canton of Schaffhausen and a slight amendment to the frontiers of Geneva and the Valteline.

The Diet's representatives were also to abstain from taking sides in the internal disputes of the various cantons. But this recommendation was fated to be ignored because recognition of neutrality immediately raised the question of independence, and this in turn raised the question of a constitution. The powers were ready to recognize neutrality, which served their own interests, but only as long as Switzerland was capable of defending it. And this meant that the country's external frontiers must first be decided upon.

In the matter of external frontiers it did not seem as though there would be any serious difficulties over Valteline. The Allies had formally promised that reunion would take place and the Grisons had undeniable historical claims. Constance was a trickier matter because there was no reason why the Grand-Duke of Baden should hand over the town for nothing. Finally, in the case of Geneva, the French frontiers had been definitively established at Paris.

If they put their request for a territorial concession to the King of France they would be involved in paying compensation. Any remaining territorial extensions would have to come from Savoy, from the territory which the 30 May Treaty had left outside the French frontiers.

But right does not rule the world. Europe had been at war for twenty-two years, and people were desperately weary. What they wanted from the Congress was peace, not new difficulties. Diplomats dislike changing the map, taking territories from one side to give them to another, forcing this party to make way for that. These operations are risky, and statesmen detest risks. In politics the easiest way out is always the most popular. Wherever possible a congress will choose the status quo rather than make changes.

A perceptive observer would have had no difficulty in foretelling the outcome of the Congress in the autumn of 1814. The Confederates would be allowed to keep the territories they already possessed; they would not be given those they had neglected to occupy—the Valteline and Savoy—though they would have been allowed to keep them if they had already moved in. Internally, it would be the same story, with the frontiers left unchanged. This is precisely what happened.

The Swiss had no sooner arrived in Vienna than they found themselves swept away on a tide they could not control. They had been under the illusion that they could manage their affairs for themselves, but they found that these were inextricably entangled with the larger issues before the Congress.

The Tsar, who wanted Poland, played the democrat and kept roundly invoking the principle of nationalities. He had promised Prussia by way of compensation to seize Saxony from its King, guilty of too long a loyalty to Napoleon. Neither Austria, Russia's neighbour, nor England, her rival, wanted to see the Tsar's territories and power increased. The King of France, meanwhile, whose only claim to the throne was that he was Louis XVI's brother, made himself the champion of legitimacy and refused to deprive the King of Saxony of his throne. On 3 January 1815, England, Austria and France signed a secret alliance against Russia. This is a date to remember, because it was a decisive one for Swiss history. The Congress is divided, where Switzerland is concerned, into two periods—before and after 3 January 1815.

The reasons why the Tsar should have been interested in supporting the Swiss case have already been stated. La Harpe's influence and Capo d'Istria's goodwill may have played some part in forming his attitude. But the real reason was that Russia did not want Austria to extend her hegemony over Switzerland, and use the country as a base for operations against France. Alexander was the friend of everyone who wanted real independence for the Confederation.

Austria, on the other hand, wanted to exploit this unique opportunity to consolidate her influence over Switzerland. Her plan was to strengthen the canton of Berne, whose aristocracy she felt she could trust, and create an Austro-Bernese hegemony within the Confederation.

As long as Russia remained influential at the Congress, and the other powers were concerned to placate her, everything went well for Switzerland. In December the Committee for Swiss Affairs decided to reunite the Valteline to the Grisons canton, as a fourth League. On 12 December Prince Talleyrand agreed for the second time to exchange the Gex region for Pruntrut. Finally, the Committee recognized the integrity of the new cantons. After this, discussion revolved around the compensation Berne should be paid for the loss of Aargau. It was finally decided to give the Bishopric of Basle to Berne, or rather force her to accept it, because the Bernese did not want it.

This was the basis for Capo d'Istria's report to the Congress. Unfortunately, when the document was submitted to the plenipotentiaries of the great powers, the diplomats were aghast. The report was returned to the Committee and rewritten from beginning to end by the British delegate, Stratford Canning, and the French delegate, the Duc de Dalberg. Talleyrand withdrew his offer of the Gex region and Pruntrut was added to the Bishopric of Basle as Berne's compensation. The Valteline was simply handed over to the Austrians.

The blame for the loss of the Valteline lies first with the Grisons, and secondly with *Landammann* de Reinhardt—a limited and timid man. Outward circumstances only aggravated the results of their mistakes. The Swiss were never once in agreement throughout this highly important negotiation. The two Grisons delegates were from the de Salis family, whose properties had been confiscated in 1797. They were far more interested in the return of their own property than in their country's, and calculated that they would find it easier to wring compensation from the Austrians than from the inhabitants.

The Swiss had interminable discussions among themselves, right up to the time the Committee started sitting, as to the place Valteline should occupy in the Confederation. No soner was everything apparently settled than M. de Reinhardt voiced new objections.

The very able representative of Valteline, Count Guicciardi, who came from the country's nobility, had pro-Austrian sympathies which he did not dare to declare. Instead, his strategy was to claim the status of canton for Valteline, Bormio and Chiavenna. He was in a very strong position. To the very last moment, as late as February, the Swiss could have acquired this magnificent stretch of country simply by admitting it as a twenty-third canton.

Such a move would have immensely benefited the internal stability of the Confederation. Many of Switzerland's problems stem from the fact that the Italian element is not strong enough. One curious fact—which proves how little linguistic preoccupations mattered at this period—was that this particular argument was never invoked one way or the other. M. de Reinhardt, however, categorically refused to admit another Catholic canton into the Confederation. Sectarian fervour prevented the Confederation from taking in a population which was partly at least—in Val Bormio and Val St Jacques—passionately pro-Swiss. On this occasion the exclusiveness which characterized the Swiss Catholics for three hundred years rebounded against them.

The same, or very nearly the same thing happened over Savoy, at the other end of the country. When Geneva's representatives at the Congress, Pictet de Rochemont and François d'Ivernois, found themselves deprived, for the second time in eight months, of all hope of receiving the Gex region, they turned their attention to Savoy. The Treaty of Paris had imposed a very curious French frontier in this region. United to Piedmont, Northern Savoy became almost impossible to defend and almost impossible to govern because its only communication with Piedmont was via high mountain passes.

Before the Congress got under way the Sardinian plenipotentiary, M. de St Marsan, made approaches to the Genevan deputies. He seemed favourable to the idea of making Northern Savoy into a Swiss canton, under the sceptre of the King of Sardinia—under the same conditions as Neuchâtel. Failing this, he wanted Savoy—which was inaccessible to the Sardinian armies for most of the year—to be included under Swiss neutrality, and he was willing to pay for this by a concession of land to Geneva.

The Genevan representatives, eyes clamped on the Gex region at this juncture, did not pursue these proposals for fear of upsetting Talleyrand. M. de St Marsan then turned towards France. He suggested an exchange of Carouge for Montmeillan to Talleyrand, which would establish a communication route between the two parts of the kingdom. When the Genevans resumed discussions, after they had lost the Gex region, the atmosphere was much less favourable.

No one can tell how the talks on Swiss affairs would have turned out if they had been allowed to continue. But with Napoleon's landing on 1 March at Golfe-Juan, and war imminent once again, the whole thing had to be concluded as rapidly as possible. The protocol ending inter-cantonal disputes by a negotiated settlement was signed on 20 March 1815. The integrity of Switzerland's internal frontiers was guaranteed but right to compensation was allowed to the despoiled older cantons. The Confederation's neutrality was recognized in principle by the great powers. The Valteline was not mentioned in this act.

On 29 March the protocols whereby Savoy agreed to hand over the free towns on the shores of the lake as far as Hermance and those of the Salève foothills to Geneva, against certain guarantees for the Catholic community, were signed too. In return Northern Savoy was to be included under Swiss neutrality.

The Congress of Vienna, if one takes all the circumstances into account, does not seem to have deserved the criticisms levelled at it. It was not entirely successful as far as reorganizing the world went. But the Vienna treaties, which endured for a century, stand comparison very favourably with the achievements of our own generation. Despite the inadequacy of the Swiss delegates—excepting Pictet de Rochemont—their rivalries and limited outlook, the decisions taken by the Congress assured Switzerland of internal and external equilibrium—in other words, tranquillity within and peace without.

4. *From the Military Alliance to Perpetual Neutrality*

Napoleon disembarked at Golfe-Juan, after sailing from Elba, on 1 March 1815. The news reached Vienna on 9 March, and Zurich on 10 March, the day that Napoleon entered Lyons. It was received with consternation everywhere. Talleyrand, in Vienna, found himself instantly isolated and without influence. The coalition reformed, Napoleon was declared an outlaw, and Stratford Canning was sent to Switzerland to persuade the Swiss to enter the new alliance. The Diet, at Zurich, raised a contingent and appointed a General Bachmann, of Glarus, Commander of Swiss troops in France. In its proclamation, which made no mention of neutrality, it stressed that these measures were of a defensive nature.

These decisions bear the stamp of compromise. Once again Switzerland was divided against herself at a time of crisis. Vaud and Aargau turned Bonapartist again. Basle and Geneva—whose attitude shocked the Allies after so many petitions—were in favour of neutrality because they felt themselves endangered. The aristocratic cantons, on the contrary, with Berne at their head, felt that the Swiss should do everything possible to help bring down the usurper. Though she might take up a neutral position between France and her enemies, she could scarcely do so between Napoleon and Louis XVIII.

There were powerful arguments on both sides. It certainly seems strange that the first act of the great powers, after recognizing Swiss neutrality, should have been to violate it, and Switzerland's first act to renounce it. But neutrality presupposes independence. Real independence for the Confederation can only come from a peaceful and stable Europe. It was in Switzerland's interest that France should be peaceful. Napoleon stood for war and the Bourbons for peace. So, they must needs go to war to save their neutrality.

This was the Allied argument. During the months of March and April they stepped up the pressure. The Tsar made repeated appeals to Vaud and Aargau and threatened to withdraw his goodwill if they did not join the coalition. After Stratford Canning, General von Steigentesch came to plead the same cause on Austria's behalf, along with Colonel Leake for England and General de Damas for Louis XVIII.

Napoleon, who had enough enemies already, made approaches to the Swiss. He sent friendly messages and agents, recognized the frontiers defined in the Paris Treaty and the

Confederation's neutrality. At the same time he ordered the Hunningen fortress to place itself in readiness to bombard Basle 'to reinforce the neutralist party'.

All in vain. On 3 May the Diet, yielding to the combined pressure of the diplomats and the military, agreed to negotiate an alliance which was duly signed on 20 May 1815.

Had the Swiss been able to reach an agreement based on a common policy, rather than a compromise, this imposed alliance could have turned out very usefully for them. The powers were prepared to make considerable concessions to obtain the Confederate's collaboration, or merely for permission to cross their territory. If the Diet had taken this opportunity to put forward the requests presented to the Congress of Vienna—for the Valteline, Constance, Campione, the frontier of the Doubs, Valserine, Rhône and Usses—it might have been successful. But the Diet asked for nothing. Its chief concern was to reduce the number of military routes and hospitals. It sacrificed the future to the present. Since the Allies were secretly resolved to ignore these restrictions, what the Diet in fact let itself in for was the full burden of military occupation without any ensuing benefits to the country.

Once the alliance was signed, Switzerland's juridical position became a puzzle. Was she neutral or ally, at war or peace with France? Heads were in a whirl at Swiss military headquarters. General Castella, general chief-of-staff, who—like Bachmann—was an officer in the service of France, made an offer to the allied military attachés to send the Federal army into Franche-Comté without waiting for the Diet's instructions. General Bachmann, more punctilious, asked for instructions but did not receive them. Napoleon alone seemed to have reached some conclusion as to what lay behind Swiss behaviour. He profited from it by putting a stop to all traffic along the Versoix road and the length of the frontier.

The alliance was ratified by the cantons on 12 June 1815. On 18 June, Napoleon's power was finally shattered on the field of Waterloo and Confederate collaboration lost most of its value in the eyes of the Allied Coalition.

The Swiss chose this moment to display aggression. The first Austrian units had crossed the Simplon on 17 June and the bulk of the army started crossing Basle on 25 June. Basle was bombarded in retaliation on the 28 June by Hunningen fortress. The French launched a series of small attacks along the Franco-Swiss frontier. Finally, the response which greeted the Allies' first entry into Switzerland in 1813 occurred again. Various French free towns asked the Swiss to occupy them to avoid an enemy occupation.

At this the Swiss military leaders forced the politicians' hands and went over to the offensive. The Federal army took the fort of Blamont on 3 July, Jougne the day after, Morteau on 7 July; St Hyppolyte, Ornans, Pontarlier, the fort of Joux, the Rousses and Gex were likewise occupied by the Swiss army, which had now reached a position before Besançon and Salins. Finally, under the command of Archduke Johann, it participated in the siege of Hunningen.

This military escapade was neither long nor glorious. On 8 July a mutiny took place among the troops from the neutralist cantons of Aargau, St Gallen and Ticino. On the same day Louis XVIII and the Allied coalition signed an armistice in Paris. Bachmann and Castella, who saw themselves as servants of the King rather than leaders of the Swiss army, instantly suggested that the troops be demobilized and tendered their resignation on 22 July. Only Jougne, the Rousses, the fort of Joux, Blamont and Gex, remained under Federal occupation till October.

The Swiss have no cause to be proud of this campaign, which began with insurbordination on the part of the high command, moved into the offensive only when it was safe to do so, and collapsed in mutiny among the troops. Still, this was Switzerland's last campaign fought on foreign soil and it cannot be erased from history. It is interesting to note that the Swiss people have almost entirely forgotten it.

On 12 August 1815, the Diet sent Pictet de Rochemont, of Geneva, to represent Switzerland in Paris at the Peace Congress—a conspicuous honour for a native of the Confederation's most recently admitted canton.

Pictet de Rochemont was loaded with instructions—conflicting of course—from the Diet and the Genevan government. Genevan opinion had been disappointed and annoyed by the conditions relating to the Catholic community imposed by the Congress of Vienna in return for the cession of certain free towns in Savoy. Besides, it was chiefly to obtain admission into the Confederation that the Genevans had accepted territorial extensions. Having achieved this they had lost interest in the annexations. The 'Little Geneva' party had definitely gained the upper hand in the town's Councils.

The opposite was true of Zurich, where David de Wyss, an open-minded and far-seeing man, had succeeded Hans de Reinhardt. Now that Napoleon had been thoroughly beaten the Diet no longer had to fear a counter-offensive from France. It was decided that Switzerland might now take part in the sharing out of the spoils—as long as she did not appear to be doing so.

Pictet de Rochemont soon realized that he would not obtain the restitution of the Valteline, or the cession of Constance and Campione. The Allies had no intention of footing the cost of France's defeat. But he managed to get the Congress to accept the western frontier he had suggested—which followed the Doubs as far as Brenets, then the Valserine, Rhône and Usses—without too much difficulty. That was at the beginning. The Allies submitted these conditions to the French government on 19 September. Gex was restored to Switzerland, for the third time in eighteen months.

What happened next is common knowledge. Louis XVIII recalled Talleyrand, who had lost his influence with the Allies, and replaced him with the Duc de Richelieu, who was on very close terms with the Tsar. This was when the real battle started.

At the first Congress of Paris the Allies extended France's frontiers to please Louis XVIII and strengthen his authority. At the second Paris Congress, they abandoned their previous intention to reduce France's territory, in order to please the Duc de Richelieu and keep him in power.

Pictet de Rochemont was a personal friend of Richelieu's. But he found the friendship not a help but a hindrance. How could one stand up to a man who claimed to be one's friend? And when would he find support? The Tsar, enchanted by Richelieu's nomination, could think of nothing but scoring personal triumps at Paris. He was ready to do anything which might strengthen France and already envisaged a time—which he anticipated by almost a century—when the balance of power in Europe would rest on a Franco-Russian alliance against Germany.

England, in 1815, as in 1814, was only interested in Flanders and was ready to sacrifice anything in the south which might gain her something in the north.

Austria, on close terms with Sardinia, had lost interest in Switzerland since she had been forced to abandon all idea of establishing a dominant influence there. Prussia, finally, who advocated a merciless policy with regard to France, had too much on her own plate to take much interest in anyone else's claims.

Pictet de Rochemont was in an extremely difficult position. The fact that he was not more successful was not due to lack of effort or astuteness on his part. Pictet de Rochemont has been unfairly accused of being opposed to accessions of territory. His personal sympathies lay with the Great Geneva party. The fact that he did not achieve more should be blamed on his vacillating superiors, French opposition and Allied apathy.

In the midst of almost incredible complications, he did finally manage to achieve the following:

(1) The cession of certain free towns in the Gex region.

(2) The free town of St Julien.

(3) The promise of support in obtaining a further cession of territory from Sardinia.

(4) The establishment of a special tariff system for the rest of the Gex region. This was by way of compensation to Geneva for the loss of a territory which had been promised, ceded and withdrawn three times over. It imposed a heavy, unilateral mortgage on France, in return for the possession of the territory itself.

(5) The extension of Northern Savoy's neutrality—even though she had lost most of her justification for existence and usefulness to the King of Sardinia by the restoration of French Savoy to the Sardinian Crown.

(6) The dismantling of the Hunningen Fortress.

(7) War compensation amounting to three million francs.

These achievements met with a very diverse reception in Switzerland. Pictet de Rochemont has often been criticized for not obtaining anything for his native town, Geneva. It should not be forgotten, however, that he personally redrafted the act by which Switzerland's perpetual neutrality was recognized by the powers. Even those who are not disposed to exaggerate the benefits of perpetual neutrality must concede that it assured the country of a whole century of peace and a position of incomparable moral strength throughout Europe.

The idea of perpetual neutrality was not Pictet de Rochemont's own; its roots stretch far back into Swiss history. But, for the first time, in 1815, neutrality became a principle of European international law based, *expressis verbis*, on the interests of the great powers. The mere fact that Swiss neutrality was not simply recognized henceforth but written down and contractual had considerable repercussions in the juridical sphere as regards the evolution of the whole concept of neutrality

The Paris Treaty of 29 November was not severe upon France. If one remembers that this country had kept Europe in a turmoil for over twenty years, and that it had just welcomed Napoleon with almost universal enthusiasm, it is scarcely to be wondered at that Europe should have taken precautions against a fresh outbreak of French imperialism. But these precautions were by no means excessive. Neither French power nor French territory suffered vitally.

The Treaty of Paris still left one loophole to be stopped up in Switzerland's frontiers—Jussy was left as a Swiss enclave in Savoy territory.

Pictet went to Turin, in January 1816, to wind up this affair. It might have seemed like a mere formality, but this was far from being the case. Negotiations were held up, to start with, by a divergence of opinion between Switzerland and Sardinia as to the correct interpretation of Northern Savoy's neutrality. The Sardinian government maintained that Switzerland was under an obligation to defend Savoy in time of war, and did not see why Sardinia should cede part of her territory unless Switzerland promised to be responsible for the defence of the rest. As the Federal government saw it, this was a purely optional right of the Confederation and had no connection with the cession of territory.

After this dispute had been shelved—but not settled, because it dragged on throughout the nineteenth century—the extent of these cessions had to be gone over inch by inch. The Paris protocol provided for the restitution of the lake shore between Vesenaz and Hermance to Sardinia, in exchange for the freeing of Jussy. The Genevans were prepared to accept this condition but the Federal government refused. This territory, which was officially part of Switzerland, struck the government as essential to the security of navigation, and the freeing of Jussy seemed inadequate compensation for the loss of the lake shore.

Pictet de Rochemont finally succeeded in both directions,

by reassigning to Sardinia the free town of St Julien, minus Perly-Certoux, and a strip of land at the foot of the Salève where a road could be built, and by adopting a conciliatory position over the tariff question. Although the Genevans found this solution unsatisfactory it was the best that could be achieved under the circumstances. The Turin negotiation, crowned by the Treaty of 16 March 1816, may be considered Pictet de Rochemont's greatest diplomatic success.

Switzerland's troubles were not over yet. The occupation of the territories ceded by Savoy, on 23 October 1816, gave rise to incidents. It was not till 1824 that the Neuchâtel frontier, defined under the first Paris Treaty, was definitely settled. Finally, negotiations regarding the Val des Dappes, which had been clumsily initiated by a protocol of which Pictet de Rochemont knew nothing, dragged on until 1862 and even then was only settled by a transaction.

However, by 16 March 1816, Switzerland's territorial limits were finally consolidated and the period which had begun with the Battle of Leipzig was ended. Some readers may find it surprising that so much space should have been given here to this brief period of Swiss history. But the significance of historical events is not measured by their duration. These thirty months, which laid the foundations and fixed the frontiers of modern Switzerland, had more vital impact on the country than some of the previous centuries had had.

Switzerland had lost some of her historic possessions: Mülhausen, the Valteline. She had not obtained the geographical and military frontiers which had been solemnly promised to her. But she had got back most of the territory Napoleon had taken from her, she now had solid frontiers and the will and means to defend them.

France's hegemony was crushed and—this was the important point—no new one rose up to replace it. Under the old regime, Switzerland had really had only two neighbours, Austria and France, with Spain and the secondary powers supporting first the one and then the other.

Henceforth the Confederation would have no less than six neighbours, all of them independent of each other: France from the Rhine as far as the Rhône; Sardinia from the Rhône to the Ticino; Austria from the Ticino to Lake Constance; Bavaria; Württemberg, and the Grand Duchy of Baden.

The equilibrium among Switzerland's neighbours gave the

Restoration a chance to build up the country's position internationally in a short space of time, despite its own weakness. And a balance of power among the cantons, which had been created by the dismemberment of Berne, allowed the government to achieve a state of internal harmony and tranquillity unknown to the Confederation for some time.

Chapter X

From the Holy Alliance to the Sonderbund (1816-1847)

The second Treaty of Paris finally put a stop to the long war France had been waging against Europe since 1792. But it did not put a stop to the consequences of this war, after-effects of which were felt till as late as the mid-nineteenth century.

There are striking analogies between the aftermaths of all the great European struggles. The Thirty Years War was followed by an economic and social crisis which recalls, in more ways than one, the one from which Switzerland has just emerged. The men of the Restoration were witness to similar phenomena, springing from the same causes, and leading, as in the seventeenth century, to civil war.

All the energy of Europe, for centuries past, had gone into building up its wealth by securing peace. To produce more than one consumes, in other words to economize, and to use these savings for the improvement of one's physical well-being and moral development—that is what we call progress.

These aspirations were interrupted, at least once every century, by great convulsions during which the peoples of Europe lost their savings and had their progress checked. These convulsions were followed by times of economic exhaustion, social stagnation and political reaction. After the curb, the stick. The Restoration is one of these times.

In the course of the wars of the Revolution and the Empire, wars longer, bigger and more shattering than any in history, Europe had run through all its material reserves. The national treasuries were empty.

The populations were ruined and their purchasing power reduced. Economic trends were upset by the continental blockade and revision of frontiers. Foreign exchanges were unbalanced, trading capital destroyed and individual production at a low ebb. The misery of unemployment was added to the hardships created by war.

Europe needed may years of peace for these wounds to mend.

Communities weary just like individuals. After Waterloo the nations were in a state of exhaustion. Twenty years of upheaval had left them wanting only one thing—peace and calm. The Restoration, far from being imposed upon the people against their will, answered the needs of the time. Only prosperous people want to govern themselves. Dictatorships are created by economic crises, just as these are the creation of war.

Situations like these are necessarily temporary. A population is made up of individuals and individuals have an irrepressible tendency to improve their lot. When men are suffering, they start looking for a way out, they adapt. It was the great upheaval of the Restoration which launched, or at least advanced the machine age. This resulted not merely in economic renewal but in a series of social transformations which led to the emergence of new political needs.

A society may come to a temporary halt in its evolution; but the evolution of a society cannot be stopped. This was something the Swiss at that time did not understand. The lesson of the eighteenth century was lost on them. The men of the old regime believed, now that they were back in power. that they could once again fix the country in one eternal pattern. They did not see the gulf opening between immutable institutions and a society in movement. As soon as the gulf had opened wide enough, they tumbled into it, without understanding why.

This is the history of the Restoration. The economic crisis caused by the war gave rise to two contradictory needs—the need for stability, and the need for re-adaptation. The authorities, who answered to the need for stability, failed to observe that the people were changing. The old constitutional forms no longer corresponded to the new social structure created by industrialism. Since they did not incorporate any revisionary clauses they were fated to be overthrown by violence.

In this chapter we propose to examine the economic crisis, its extent, various aspects and consequences. We shall then pass on to the internal and external policy of the Confederation. Finally, we shall show how the institutions were forced to adapt themselves to the facts, or in other words how the Federal State was born in 1848.

1. *The Economic Crisis*

1816 was a terrible year, with snowfalls every month, and flooding everywhere. All the harvests were ruined—wheat, hay, potatoes, vegetables, fruit, wine. During the winter the price of bread rose by 800 per cent. In Glarus people were eating excrement. In Appenzell half the population was on public assistance. In St Gallen the number of deaths was double the birth rate.

The reason eastern Switzerland was hit particularly hard by the worst famine the country had known for several centuries was that the agricultural crisis there was paralleled by an industrial one.

Swiss agriculture had become industrialized with the passing of time. Large stretches of land which had formerly been worked and sown had been converted into pasture land to support the dairy industry. As a result the agricultural population had dwindled and surplus workers were diverted into industry.

Everything went well while prosperity lasted. But Swiss industry, at the beginning of the Restoration, was suffering the effects of a crisis provoked by the introduction of machinery on the one hand and the stoppage of commercial outlets on the other.

Towards the end of the old regime textiles employed a hundred thousand spinners in eastern Switzerland; by 1815 this figure was considerably smaller, while productivity had gone up. Switzerland's traditional industries, particularly flax and hemp spinning, were endangered and almost disappeared, as a result of the continental blockade. They were only partly replaced by cotton spinning and weaving. Freed from British competition Swiss cotton products managed to dominate part of the European market. But this boom was artificial.

As soon as the embargo on British goods was lifted, Swiss industry lost most of its outlets. It could not compete with the Lancashire industry, which was more concentrated and better supplied with plant and had built up enormous stocks during the blockade.

One by one, the other continental nations were driven to impose high duties and import restrictions, in order to replenish their public finances and protect their own industries. On 28 April 1816, France, which had accounted for almost two-thirds of the Confederation's foreign market, all but shut down on Swiss imports. The Low Countries followed suit in October 1816, Spain in January 1817, and Austria in September 1817. The south German States, Baden, Württemberg and Bavaria, with whom Switzerland had close commercial ties, then Sardinia and the Kingdom of the Two Sicilies, joined in. Soon the only outlets left to Switzerland were England, her chief rival, and a few tiny Italian states.

The agricultural and industrial crisis brought the usual evils with it, unemployment, wage reductions, poverty and emigration. In the absence of statistics it is difficult to estimate the numbers of unemployed during this time. But the extent of unemployment can be gauged by the massive relief programme introduced. The authorities embarked on public works schemes to cut down unemployment figures; the cantons bought wheat to distribute among the starving population; public subscriptions were opened, soup was distributed. Public and private charity did what it could. But it could not stop emigration, very often so badly organized that it usually ended in disaster. The cantons and the Diet did all they could to prevent it, but in vain, because it is impossible to exercise a hold upon starving people. In 1819, the canton of Fribourg alone lost 1,600 people, who emigrated to Brazil.

Relief programmes, work for the unemployed, emigration, are not remedies for an economic crisis; they are merely palliatives. Unfortunately the Federal authorities were powerless to take any real measures to fight the crisis, and the measures taken by the cantonal governments only served to aggravate rather than reduce its intensity.

Switzerland, under the 1815 Pact, resembled Europe today. The cantons had sovereign rights, and were in complete control of their economic policies. Switzerland then had no less than eleven foot measures, sixty types of ell, eighty-seven grain measures, eighty-one for liquids and fifty different weights. Alongside the Swiss franc, equivalent to ten *batz*, and the Helvetic nickel coinage, French francs, the French *écu*, worth six Swiss francs, as well as the *écus* of Brabant, Bavaria and Württemberg were all legal currency. The cantons, unable to agree on a common policy, multiplied their offensive tactics against each other. Almost all the mistakes we have seen committed latterly in Europe have precedents in the Confederation under the Restoration.

Attempts to adopt a policy of reprisals in answer to France's prohibitive measures collapsed before the resistance of the commercial cantons and those which preferred French pensions to prosperity for their fellow-Confederates. The retaliatory agreement, which the Diet quashed on 28 August 1822, was only effectively carried out by six cantons and was officially abrogated on 27 July 1824. Efforts by the south German states to draw Switzerland into their customs union also failed. Finally, two successive decisions taken by the Diet with a view to introducing a semblance of order, if not unity, into the internal tariff system were hardly more successful.

The cantons, unable to agree on a common tariff policy towards France, waged economic war upon each other instead. Switzerland had more than 400 taxes on the traffic of goods, cantonal, communal and even federal taxes, seventy more than there had been in 1803. They were to be found everywhere except along the external frontiers. Not a bridge nor a road was built without a toll being imposed on its users. The canton of Ticino levied no fewer than thirteen taxes along the Gotthard route, with the added imposition of having to unload the merchandise each time to weigh it. The Valais imposed differential duties along the frontier with Vaud, with the aim of encouraging traffic through Savoy. The canton of Berne slapped what amounted to customs duty on Vaudois wines, on the pretext of imposing a tax on drink. The failure of the retaliatory agreement, by angering certain cantons, only multiplied the number of tolls and reprisals. Bearing in mind that this system was rampant on a tiny, divided territory, it is not hard to imagine the results. In most cases foreign products were better off making a detour round Switzerland than attempting to cross it. The St Gallen industrialists sent their goods to Geneva via Besançon and to Italy via the Brenner pass. A country which was handsomely endowed by nature for the transport industry, and equipped with a network of excellent roads, was completely depriving itself of an important source of revenue through the fault of its institutions.

However, some comforting conclusions may be drawn from an objective appraisal of the situation. The example set by Switzerland under the Restoration proves two things. Firstly that every situation, however bad, in fact the worse the better, has its corresponding remedy. To create European unity now is not so much more difficult than it was to unite Switzerland a hundred years ago. In the end this task was accomplished in less than thirty years, despite prejudices, opposition and conflicting passions.

The second is that there is no policy pernicious or powerful enough to crush individual initiative. Good comes out of evil. Swiss industry, abandoned by the authorities, was rescued by the people.

They had no alternative. They were too numerous for their small and infertile country, and they had to import food or starve. Having no raw materials they could only buy food with the products of their own labours. Industry is a necessity for Switzerland.

Swiss cotton goods, debarred from France, Austria and Southern Germany, began to make headway gradually—via Trieste and Italy—in Egypt, the Levant and even the Far East. The United States, Mexico and South America saw the opening of Swiss consulates and Swiss trade there made great progress. The country's extra-European trade relations date from this period.

These relations required a far-reaching transformation in the technical conditions of manufacture. Spinning machines were introduced into the cotton industry in 1801. The house of Escher-Wyss, a spinning-mill before it began to make machines, was founded in 1805. But it was under the Restoration that the textile industry went over to mechanization in a big way. In 1814 Switzerland had 700 machines producing 630,000 pounds of spun yarn. These figures had doubled by 1835, and were six times as great in 1850. Between the end of the old regime and 1848, the numbers of silk weaving looms rose from 1,800 to 12,400, of workers from 3,000 to 16,000, and production from 3 to 22 million. The weaving of tulle by machine began around 1825 and started to boom in 1830. The Jacquard loom was introduced to Basle in 1816, St Gallen in 1821, and Zurich in 1824. By 1836, there were more than 300 in this town and in 1845 more than 1,200 in St Gallen.

About the same time, mechanical methods of printing cloth and chemical processes for bleaching it began to be used. All the industries concerned benefited greatly from this, including the mechanical construction industry, which had started about 1810. The industries which did not know how, or were unwilling, to adapt themselves to the new demands of the market, like the lace-making and flax and hemp weaving industries, were seriously jeopardized.

Switzerland's most intensive industrial development, it should be noted, took place in the period immediately preceding the introduction of steam power. This made its appearance in St Gallen in 1839. Until then, Switzerland, with almost unlimited hydraulic power at its command, possessed a considerable advantage over its rivals.

This time too saw the growth of another branch of what is not strictly speaking an industry—but something which brought the country considerable earnings—tourism. The Romantic movement was a great help in this respect, and the services rendered to Switzerland by the first poet-travellers, like Lord Byron and Shelley, should not be underestimated. The fame and prosperity of the shores of the Geneva, Oberland and the Lucerne lakes date from this period, preceding that of the mountains themselves, which were still inaccessible.

This economic development led to a considerable increase in the population figures, and far-ranging social changes. An industrial proletariat came into being, leading lives of wretched poverty because wages were very low and the cost of living relatively high in Switzerland. The number of children employed in industry was very high, and their exploitation was rife.

These workers were recruited from among the old artisans and home workers, victims of mechanization and from the old peasantry, victims of the agrarian revolution. In each of these categories the least skilled, that is to say the poorest workers, became the proletariat.

The first important industrial establishments were built beside rivers or communication routes, some distance from the regions where the poor were most numerous. The bulk of eastern Switzerland's work force was drawn from people from the barren mountainous regions of the country, which led to a flow of immigrants from abroad and to internal migration.

These shifts in population, and the increased traffic of goods which resulted from them, together with the growth of industry in general, made certain needs more sharply felt. These needs were not new but till then they had not played an important part in the collective life of the country. The free circulation of people and goods, and freedom to set up new industries, the suppression of internal tariffs, the creation of a customs barrier along the national frontiers, unification of currencies and weights and measures, had already existed under the Helvetic Republic. All these progressive measures had since been dropped and everything had reverted to chaos. A Swiss was once more a foreigner anywhere outside his native region. There had been moves to re-introduce the economic conditions of the old regime in 1803, and in 1815, but by then circumstances had changed.

These needs gave rise, around 1830, to the great movement of ideas known as the 'Regeneration', as opposed to the Restoration. When the workers of Zurich who had come together in a popular assembly at Uster on 22 November 1832, to demand a revision of the canton's constitution, were incited to set fire to a spinning-mill, they probably only intended to express their hatred of the machine which took bread out of the workers' mouths. In fact, however, this fire demonstrates the close ties between the industrial movement of the first quarter-century and the political revolution of 1830.

2. *The Political Evolution*

The Restoration, authoritarian at home and irresolute abroad, had the paradoxical effect of building up the country abroad and weakening the State at home. Its external achievements were the strengthening of Swiss independence and neutrality. Its internal consequences were revolution and civil war.

The Restoration was authoritarian at home because this was what the country wanted. In all the cantons there was a passionate, and often puerile, harking back to the ideas and ways of the past. The aristocrats, who were so proud of their legitimacy, nevertheless had a confused sense that their fifteen years' absence had in some way undermined it. So they lost no chance which came their way to reaffirm their authority. Traditional forms became the base and essence of a regime for which the only justification was tradition.

The most archaic legal codes, particularly that of Charles V, were exhumed. Torture was re-introduced, and practised with new refinements of cruelty, censorship was applied with meticulous thoroughness, innovations forbidden, education was suspect and a stranglehold exerted on the press. The cantonal governments trembled at the slightest breath of publicity and feared all criticism. Secrecy became a dogma. No commercial or industrial enterprise today could be half as confidential about its books or processes as was the nomination of a Swiss rural policeman a hundred years ago.

This mystery was not a cloak for evil-doing. On the contrary. In a few years the country's finances were rebuilt, and public works were forging ahead. The foundations for a solid military organization had been laid, and the Federal general staff, which was created at this time, helped to strengthen nationalist feeling. The 1815 regime was a restoration in every sense of the word.

The work of internal reconstruction slowly gave the country a renewed sense of power and dignity. This was the worst possible thing which could have happened for the aristocracies, who had meanwhile shown themselves incapable of any national policy-making either at home or abroad.

The reactionary spirit, which found support in popular sentiment in the cantons, overreached both the needs and the possibilities of the time at a Federal level. The Pact of 7 May 1815, whose very name suggests some kind of treaty, had destroyed central authority and given all the power back to the cantons. The latter, feeling their sovereignty threatened by social changes, interpreted their duties in the most overweening fashion. Exactly the same thing has happened before our eyes in the international sphere. In 1515, the Diet had resolved to abide by majority decisions. Three centuries later it was incapable of pushing anything through, for lack of unanimity.

The only power which had succeeded in exerting a preponderant influence and occasionally steering common policy under the old regime, the republic of Berne, had been dismembered. The Confederation might be better balanced within, but this only made it all the weaker. All transactions, even the simplest, had to be settled by way of concordats, in other words by treaties between twenty-five sovereign states. The result was appalling chaos in such a tiny country. Cantonal sovereignty gave proof of its own impracticability by its excesses and abuses.

Things fared worse still in the diplomatic field. How could a consistent foreign policy be framed, without an organ capable of doing so? How could the various authorities, hypnotized as they were by cantonal affairs, by small, trivial, petty matters possibly arrive at a world outlook?

The Swiss only came to adopt their fundamental charter thanks to foreign influence. Most of the clauses in the Pact and the cantonal constitutions had been framed by Capo d'Istria and Stratford Canning. By invoking the mediation of the great powers at Vienna, the Swiss implicitly placed their government under their guarantee.

Services are soon forgotten by the people who benefit from

them. The Swiss soon forgot the good offices of the Allied Ministers on their behalf. But these, and their governments, remembered. Where the Allies had at first proffered their good offices, they now imposed them; their assistance became guardianship.

In opposition to revolutionary, Napoleonic France, the aristocracies seemed to enshrine the country's spirit of independence. But faced by the great powers at the Congress, to whom they were bound by too many ties, these same men were far from successul in upholding their country's dignity. The way in which they had organized Switzerland was not conducive to a sound foreign policy. Unconsciously, the cantonal governments allowed themselves to become the instruments of the great powers against their own people.

This capitulation was evident on two fronts—the military capitulations and the right of asylum.

No sooner were they back in power than the aristocratic governments set about making new capitulation treaties with various countries. France, Holland, the Kingdom of Naples, Sardinia, England and Spain all maintained Swiss contingents under the Restoration, not to mention the Pontifical Guard, founded in 1832. The number of soldiers involved totalled some 30,000.

While the capitulations might revive the old forms of foreign service, they were unable to resuscitate the spirit or the living reality which had traditionally animated it

The French Revolution worked a total change in the country's way of thinking. Under the old regime mercenary service was not argued about. The Swiss people were proud of their regiments and foreigners admired them. Under the Restoration, on the other hand, mercenary soldiers began to suffer from unpopularity. The Swiss no longer understood why their fellow citizens should choose to become expatriates rather than serve their own country. Foreigners did not see why exceptional privilages—immunity from the law for instance—should be accorded to troops who were Swiss only in name.

Mercenary service had long been an economic necessity for the cantons. But now, thanks to industrial progress, the country could support all her sons. The capitulated regiments came to be formed more and more of foreigners. Only the officers were genuinely Swiss.

Having lost its national character, mercenary service gradually became a caste institution. As far as the Swiss people were concerned the only point of the capitulated regiments was to provide careers for the sons of aristocrats. To foreigners, their only point was to protect the aristocracy against liberalism. Once an institution, with an ancient and glorious history, changes character to this extent, it has outlived its usefulness. The only thing left to it is to disappear.

If the aristocratic policy with regard to the capitulated regiments was unpopular with the people, their attitude to the right of asylum was still more so.

On 27 January 1817 the Diet yielded to the overpowering insistence of Russian diplomacy, and joined the Holy Alliance. This alliance, in the beginning, was formed for no other purpose than to maintain peace in Europe. In this it served Swiss interests as much as any others. The statesmen of Europe, however, soon came to identify peace with the preservation of their own handiwork. The Holy Alliance worked to conserve the status quo. Now that treaties were threatened not from without, by the ambitions of rival governments, but from within, from the peoples themselves, it was against these that the Holy Alliance went into action.

Switzerland was suspect. For centuries now she had offered a spectacle of constant anarchy and civil war. Quite recently a number of her cantons had openly declared their admiration of Bonaparte. In spite of all their precautions, it had not been possible to erase every trace of popular government from their constitutions. Enough remained to make the aristocratic powers, who felt threatened by it, uneasy.

Switzerland, situated as it was, was bound to become the chosen place of refuge for refugees from Germany, Italy, Austria and France. The weakness of her central institutions made it impossible to take swift, concerted action against conspirators who only had to move to another canton to put themselves out of reach. It was not the authority of the Swiss government which caused the right of asylum to be respected in the country under the Restoration, but its weakness.

Political refugees caused the Confederation serious trouble on two occasions. The first time was between the years 1820 and 1825, the second between 1833 and 1837.

During the first of these two periods Switzerland came under criticism from the German authorities because of the presence on her soil of certain important refugees, including Snell,

Volker, Herbst, the Follen brothers, and several more, most of them professors in her universities.

This was the time of the Congress of Karlsbad (1819), Laybach (1821) and Verona (1822), the time of the Spanish Revolution and the Italian troubles. To the uneasy rulers there appeared to be revolutionaries everywhere. The Austrian, Prussian, Bavarian and Sardinian cabinets inundated the country with spies and agents provocateurs and dispatched several threatening notes to the *Vorort*.

The Diet was forced to yield to their demands in order to avert more direct intervention. On 14 July 1823, the Diet voted for the adoption of stringent measures against the press and against foreigners, and enforced the application of them on the cantons.

The Diet, so helpless to take measures in the national interest, suddenly recovered its strength when it was a question of going against Swiss interests and complying with the great powers. This contradictoriness was its undoing and did more to discredit the regime than all the liberal speech-making.

Though the 1823 *conclusum* on the press and foreigners had less immediate impact than the July 1830 rulings of Paris, it still played a similar role in Switzerland. It showed up the fundamental vice of her institutions and provided all their adversaries with a common objective.

The liberal movement which shook Europe between 1820 and 1830 had a pronounced nationalist character. This was the time when the Swiss people, fired by Gabriel Eynard, shared in a common enthusiasm for the rebellious Hellenes. Philhellenism became an affirmation of principle against Metternich and the Holy Alliance.

Meanwhile the Helvetic Society, the Swiss Society for Natural Sciences, the Zofingen Society, the Swiss Rifle Society, the Federal Societies for singing, shooting, gymnastics, the societies of doctors, officers and others, all helped to kindle the federal spirit. In their annual assemblies Confederates from all the different cantons rubbed shoulders with each other. They proclaimed the glories of their fatherland and sang the praises of solidarity and unity. Each one of these assemblies was something of an event, an implicit protest against the abuses of cantonalism, and against the Diet's complaisance towards the foreign powers.

The 1823 *conclusum* was nullified in 1829 as a result of public pressure. But it was too late. Already several of the cantons, Schaffhausen, then Appenzell (Inner Rhoden), Lucerne and Vaud, had introduced liberal modifications into their constitutions. A revolt broke out at Ticino in 1829. The trouble spread to Basle, Zurich, Aargau and Thurgau. News of the revolt in Paris, in July 1830, only served to give added impetus to a movement whose origins were national.

There were three causes for the Regeneration. The intellectuals were dissatisfied with the country's decline, the absence of authority at a federal level, and the arrogance of the aristocratic caste. The workers were exasperated by economic barriers and the spread of mechanization. The peasants, finally, were protesting against the continued privileges accorded to the towns. This was the most powerful movement of all, without which the others would have come to nothing, and through it the Regeneration's roots plunge far back into the most ancient national traditions.

Between 1830 and 1833 some ten cantons, Aargau, Thurgau, Zurich, St Gallen, Solothurn, Lucerne, Fribourg, Vaud, Schaffhausen and Berne all introduced liberal modifications into their constitutions. Glarus followed suit, in 1830, and put an end to the denominational sub-divisions which had existed there since the Reformation.

Though these modifications were very diverse in detail, they did inspire some general ideas.

In 1815 no one had dared to restore the institutions of the old regime in their entirety, in so far as they applied to the formerly subject countries. Nevertheless the reins of power had been handed back to the bourgeoisie, or rather to the aristocracy which formed its core. The former subjects had succeeded in sending representatives to the Great Councils. But these had been carefully kept in the minority while the real power was transferred to the Little Councils. In this way the peasants had come to exercise next to no influence in the government of the country.

All countries at that time held that an elective system needed to be stabilized by guarantees which would tend to place power in the hands of those best qualified to exercise it. The electorate was the magistrature, not a universal franchise. This was a reasonable attitude at a time when public education was far below the standard it has reached today. Traces of the attitude survive to this day in the exclusion of women from the right to vote. Switzerland has never generally adopted an electoral system based on property qualifications but she achieved the same result by different means. The towns, more influential and better educated than the rural areas, obtained certain privileges for themselves. It was these privileges which sparked off the revolts between 1830 and 1833. Using different means, the liberal movement of 1830 achieved the same result as in France, which was the extension of the right of suffrage.

The essential ideas behind the liberal constitutions of 1830 were, first, to transfer the real power back from the Little Councils to the Great Councils; second, to make these properly representative; third, to give the people themselves sovereign power by calling for their vote on constitutional reforms.

Direct democracy was not a new idea for Switzerland. It had been in operation for centuries in the forest cantons and the Helvetic Republic was an attempt to apply it at a national level. But its introduction into the big cantons of the Swiss plateau marks a turning-point in Swiss history.

The main consequence of all these innovations was to take the power out of the hands of the urban bourgeoisies. Thus, in a single day, the centuries-old authority of the Bernese patriciate was destroyed. Emmanuel Friedrich von Fischer, eighty-eighth *avoyer* (chief magistrate) of Berne, was replaced by magistrate Neuhaus, a small businessman from Bienne.

Nevertheless, the men who took power after this were not peasants. Keller, at Zurich, was a professor. The Pfyffer brothers, at Lucerne, were aristocrats. They had no contact with the real populace, whom they claimed to control. Their rule was necessarily a transitional one, and it proved brief. A counter-movement was launched in Zurich before 1840, and it soon had imitators in many other cantons.

The liberal movement came up against insuperable obstacles, meanwhile, in the three cantons of Neuchâtel, Schwytz and Basle.

In Neuchâtel, armed bands under the leadership of Lieutenant Bourquin came down from the valleys and made two attempts, on 13 September and 17 December 1831, to seize power and declare the canton a Republic. They nearly succeeded. But the net result was failure. Encouraged by this success the Royalists in the chief town took the opportunity to vote, on 16 February 1832, for the Principality's separation from the Swiss Confederation. Luckily, the King of Prussia was unwilling to challenge the 1815 treaties and involve himself in international complications. Besides it was in his own interest to have the Swiss protect and defend his principality. He vetoed the decision of subjects more royalist than himself.

In Schwytz, the outlying districts, annoyed by the refusal of the inner districts (Schwytz and Muotta) to revise the constitution, held a separate *Landsgemeinde* on 25 February 1831. On 27 March 1833 they obtained the Diet's recognition of their existence as a demi-canton, the 'regenerated' cantons now being in a majority there. However, during the summer, Schwytz forcibly reconquered the outlying districts. Federal mediation finally resulted in a revised constitution, on 29 September, which restored peace, but a fragile peace.

In Basle events took a still more serious turn. Riots and battles followed each other in quick succession from 9 January 1831, the date of the first peasant attack against the town, till 17 August 1833, date of the Diet's recognition of the demi-canton of Basle-Campagne. Most of these battles, particularly the Pratteln struggle, were bloody affairs. Instead of exerting a pacifying influence, the Diet only stirred things up by coming down resolutely on the side of the peasantry against the town. The Diet was responsible for a solution which did not spring from necessity and which the majority of the population, even in the rural part of the canton, did not agree with.

The Restoration had been essentially a cantonal affair. The Regeneration, on the other hand, had largely national aims. It took over power in the cantons with the idea of 'regenerating' the Confederation. This was a sound and patriotic ambition. But its first effect was to split the Diet into a majority and minority party, thus hopelessly undermining an already tottering institution. The second was to set the Confederation against certain cantons, and the third was to set it against foreign powers.

The hostility between the regenerated and conservative cantons took a turn for the worse after the 1830 revolution. On 17 March 1832, Aargau, Berne, Lucerne, St Gallen, Solothurn, Thurgau and Zurich signed a concordat—known as the Concordat of the Seven—with the aim of mutually guaranteeing their constitutions. This concordat was not strictly speaking a separate alliance, and was not contrary to the pact, but it was both pointless and dangerous. Pointless, because the popular constitutions were not in any way threatened—the conservative cantons accepted the dogma of cantonal sovereignty in all its manifestations. Dangerous, because it created a precedent. On 16 November that same year, the cantons of Uri, Schwytz, Unterwald, Valais, Neuchâtel and Basle concluded an alliance of their own, the *Sarnerbund*, and agreed to keep out of the Diet as long as it admitted the Deputies from Basle-Campagne and Outer Schwytz.

On 17 July 1832, the Diet yielded to pressure from the regenerated cantons and decided, in principle, to revise the federal pact. This decision, however, remained a dead letter as the cantons rejected two successive proposals for revision.

The idea of revision met with resistance not only from the cantons but from the great powers as well. The cantons of the Sarnen League, particularly the forest cantons, would not allow of any tampering with their absolute sovereignty, which they saw as the one safeguard of their existence. They considered that the 1815 pact, like the old alliances, was a treaty and could not be altered without the consent of all the contracting parties. Such unanimity was chimerical, so all revision of the pact was out of the question. In a moving world Switzerland alone was destined to stand still.

The great powers shared this view, seeing themselves as the guardians of the achievement of 1815. In their eyes, the guarantee of the pact was part and parcel of the guarantees of neutrality and independence. The federal pact was sacred and intangible, not because the Swiss people thought of it as their own national creation, but, on the contrary, because they had adopted it under external pressure, because it was the creation of the great powers and an integral part of the European fabric.

'Regenerated' Switzerland was born of the humiliation inflicted on the country by the Holy Alliance in 1823. From the very first it was fated to meet with opposition from these same powers. And the conflict would be sparked off again, as it had been ten years earlier, by the question of the right to asylum. The 1830 revolutions, whether defeated or triumphant, had left a wake of troubles and political persecutions across Europe, all of which started a new wave of refugees making for Switzerland and the right of asylum.

But the situation had changed, particularly from the international point of view. During the first fifteen years of the Restoration, the balance of power in Europe had been upset by the artificial solidarity of the powers involved in the Holy

Alliance. The progressive weakening of this alliance, as it allowed international forces freer play, made for the greater independence of Switzerland.

Within the country, the Restoration's cantonal governments were basically in agreement with the powers and hostile to the revolutionaries. They might practise the right of asylum but it was grudgingly, and because they lacked the means to take rapid, concerted action.

The elective governments, on the other hand, who had replaced aristocratic rule in many of the cantons between 1830 and 1833, sympathized with the liberal, revolutionary aspirations of their neighbours. In 1833, for instance, the Berne government admitted a troop of 400 armed Poles and allowed it, in violation of Berne's international obligations, almost publicly to mount an expedition against Sardinia.

The Young Europe movement, whose headquarters were in Switzerland, the intrigues of Mazzini, the Steinholzli rally in Berne (1834), the murder of the German spy Lessing (1835), and the arrest of the French agent provocateur Conseil (1836), all involved Switzerland in serious diplomatic difficulties. The worst of these however was provoked by the presence of Prince Louis-Napoleon Bonaparte on Thurgau soil in 1838.

The future Napoleon III, a gifted conspirator, had been accorded, in highly irregular circumstances, the title of 'honorary citizen' of the canton of Thurgau. This exceptional distinction, conferred upon a man who displayed no gratitude for it later, says very little for either the perspicacity or dignity of the Thurgau authorities. But the Swiss people refused to abandon one of their citizens. When Louis-Philippe insisted that they expel the Prince, they responded by mobilizing the army. On the eve of war with France the Prince fortunately decided to leave the country.

The Louis-Napoleon Bonaparte affair marks a turning-point, from two points of view: firstly, as to the feeling of national solidarity, and secondly, as to Switzerland's attitude towards the great powers. It was the first time, for many many years, that the Swiss people felt themselves strong enought to resist foreign pressure and take military measures against a foreign power. In 1815, Switzerland recovered only a semblance of sovereignty. But in 1838, she showed that she had once more acquired a sense of her own dignity, which is much more important, as it is the only sure foundation of independence.

3. *The War of Secession*

The Sonderbund war was only outwardly a religious war. Religious questions were fortuitously involved with constitutional problems. But the real cause of the struggle was political.

By 1830 the 1815 Pact no longer corresponded to the needs of the nation. From day to day the numbers of people thwarted by a complete lack of central authority was growing. The spread of new ideas, the increasing numbers of Swiss transplanted from one canton to another, and thereby deprived of legal rights, the necessities of the country's economic life, and above all, a concern for the country's status vis-à-vis the great powers, all made revision of the 1815 Pact a necessity.

Revision, as we have seen, collapsed before the resistance of the small cantons and the great powers. The cantons insisted that a pact is an international act and cannot be altered without the unanimous consent of all the contracting parties. The Powers felt that they had guaranteed the Pact and that it could not be modified without their participation.

These views were juridically tenable ones. But, from this time on, it meant that the Pact no longer survived by reason of its own virtues but because of foreign support. A nation cannot live under ossified institutions. There was no legal way to revise the Pact, or practical possibility of doing so. So the revision was destined to be put into effect by force.

In law, Switzerland was a Confederation of States. In reality she had gone beyond this stage. The Sonderbund war was intended to make the law fit the facts.

A crisis was inevitable. But there was no reason why the political problem should be complicated by a denominational one. This was a great misfortune. Neither the Concordat of the Seven, of 17 March 1832, nor the League of Sarnen, of 16 November of the same year, had had a denominational character. Lucerne's inclusion in the Seven, as well as Basle's and Neuchâtel's in the League, is sufficient proof of this. These were purely political groupings.

But the situation changed when, on 20 January 1834, the delegates from the seven cantons of the concordat adopted a programme of ecclesiastical reform at Baden. This was to include a Swiss archdiocese, the introduction of a synod into the Catholic Church, permission from the authorities for episcopal letters, guarantees of mixed marriages, a reduction in the number of religious holidays, surveillance of monasteries and convents and so on. As a whole, there was nothing reprehensible about the programme. No doubt some of the recommended reforms could have been carried through after negotiations with the Church. But it was sheer ignorance of history to suppose that the Holy See would be disposed to allow a programme of reform like this to be imposed from without. The Baden proposals were formally condemned by the ecclesiastical authority on 17 May 1835.

These proposals, which the cantons of Aargau and St Gallen rushed to put into practice, were the big mistake made by the growing radical movement. They gave a religious tincture to disputes which might have been purely political, and which could have been settled in a friendly spirit. They were the principal cause of the Sonderbund war, and the radical leaders must be held responsible.

There is an inexorable logic about the events which followed. On 9 January 1841, a revolt broke out among the clergy at Villmergen. The Aargau government, by way of reply, believing itself to be taking legitimate defensive action, suppressed the canton's eight convents with one stroke of the pen, on 20 January.

This action, however, was contrary to the ruling of the Pact. Clause 12 of the Pact expressly guaranteed the existence of these convents. Swiss Catholics saw this violation of their rights as a threat and an outrage. Both parties took up their positions and the split between them became irreconcilable. The small cantons had always been against any revision of the Pact because they felt it would undermine their influence in the Confederation. They were in a position to prevent it since any alteration of the Pact required unanimity. The only hope of winning them round would have been for the radicals to reassure them as to the programme they planned to carry out if they achieved power. But convincing them that any lessening of cantonal sovereignty would be followed by violation of religious rights was a sure way to make them quite intractable. After the Aargau convents were suppressed any hope of founding a federative state by peaceful means went out of the window.

Catholic indignation turned against the radical regime at Lucerne first of all. On 1 May 1841, the people of Lucerne adopted a new constitution and gave power to the men who were later to be the leaders of the Sonderbund: Siegwart-Muller and Bernard Meyer.

Catholic Switzerland's protests in the Diet about the suppression of the convents did not have the expected result. The Catholics had the impression that a majority vote in the Diet would go against the maintenance of the Pact, so they decided to take the offensive. A proposal to suppress the Jesuit Order had been put to the Diet on 19 August 1844. On 24 October, the Lucerne government decided to give the Jesuits in their canton charge of the canton's leading schools.

The liberals' detestation of the Jesuits was probably a hangover from the past. In the sixteenth century, the Society of Jesus was the incarnation of the Counter-Reformation. As time passed the Society had lost most of this militant spirit and very little remained to distinguish it from other religious orders. But this scarcely mattered, because liberal hatred of the order was an established fact. Lucerne's summons to the Jesuits was seen as a deliberately provocative action throughout Switzerland, which in effect it was.

The liberal reaction was nevertheless deplorable. On two occasions bands of men, almost publicly recruited in Berne and Aargau and supplied with weapons from government arsenals, invaded Lucerne's territory. This happened on 8 December 1844, and again on 31 March 1845. On 20 July one of the most popular leaders of Lucerne's peasant and clerical democracy, Leu Ebersoll, was assassinated in mysterious circumstances. Now it was the turn of the Lucerne government to feel not merely offended, but threatened. As a result of these events the Sonderbund was secretly concluded on 11 December 1845 between the cantons of Lucerne, Uri, Schwytz, Unterwald, Zug, Fribourg and Valais. The reformed cantons which had joined the Sarnen alliance thirteen years earlier did not take part in the Sonderbund.

Both parties had wrongs on their conscience. The radicals felt guilty about the ill-advised Baden proposals, about the suppression of the Aargau convents in violation of the terms of the Pact, and about the expeditions against Lucerne, an unpardonable outrage against a Confederate canton. The Catholics, for their part, had taken a step fraught with grave consequences in calling upon the Jesuits. So far, however, they were within the law.

Was the Sonderbund a violation of Article 6 of the Pact, as the Diet ruled on 20 July 1847? It all depends on the intentions with which it was formed. The Catholics have always maintained that it was a purely defensive measure directed against unjustified attacks, like the expeditions against Lucerne. On the other hand, its secret nature, and the military preparations and intrigues of its leaders abroad, are sufficient proof that the existence of this alliance was irreconcilable with Switzerland's interests, if not with the Pact.

It was inevitable that the Sonderbund should seek help abroad from the clerical nations, Austria and France, as had happened in the sixteenth century after the formation of the Borromeo League. This was precisely what they did next, and Switzerland was only saved from foreign intervention by two fortuitous circumstances—Great Britain's opposition to concerted action by the great powers, and the February 1848 revolution in Paris.

To begin with, opinions were divided, even in the Protestant cantons. The Geneva government, created by the 1841 revolution, and the highly reactionary governments of Basle and Neuchâtel, did not consider the Sonderbund illegal. It required a further revolution in Geneva, on 7 October 1846, and a political reshuffle in St Gallen, in the spring of the following year, before the Diet was able to pass a resolution dissolving the Catholic alliance on 20 July 1847. The fact that James Fazy's seizure of power in Geneva was made with the help of Catholic peasants proves that, even at this stage, the issues at stake were not purely denominational ones. It is one of history's ironies that it should have been the Sardinian and French communes, established in Geneva in 1815 and protected by the treaties, which enabled the radicals to dissolve the Sonderbund and transform Switzerland into a federative state.

After this, events followed thick and fast. On 16 August 1847, The Diet decided to revise the Pact. On 8 September, it ordered the expulsion and suppression of the Jesuit order. On 4 November it ordered arms to be taken up against the Sonderbund.

Thanks to the energy and restraint of General Dufour, who was entrusted with the execution of this order, the war was a short one. Fribourg surrendered on 14 November, and Zug on 21 November. On 23 November, there was fighting all day long at Gislikon and Roterberg. The following day federal troops entered Lucerne, and on 30 November, all the Sonderbund cantons had capitulated.

The Catholics may perhaps have had the letter of the law behind them in this struggle. But the realities of life were against them, and this is why they were defeated. The question now confronting Switzerland was analogous to the one which split the United States, several years later. This was whether the sovereignty of the part is greater than the sovereignty of the whole, whether an individual State can override the interests of the Confederation. But the situation was more serious in Switzerland than in the United States. If the South had won two nations would have been created. But if the Catholics had triumphed in Switzerland, the probable outcome would have been the country's disintegration.

It is indeed hard to imagine how, in the mid-nineteenth century, it could ever have been possible for a conglomeration of twenty-five sovereign states with scarcely any links between them to have survived in the heart of Europe, surrounded by four major powers. The change to a federative state had become a necessity of survival for the Confederation. It is highly fortunate that the Confederation was able to achieve this transformation unaided, thanks to the speedy victory of General Dufour, and before any foreign power could intervene.

It is more fortunate still that the winning side knew when to exercise restraint. This would probably have been impossible after a long-drawn-out and bitter war. But the losses sustained by both sides were slight, and the Sonderbund cantons had elected new leaders, so the Diet contented itself by imposing fines on them.

The important thing was not vengeance, but the work in hand. Now that the resistance of the Catholic cantons had been crushed, the Diet was able to draw up a new federal constitution speedily, and put it into effect on 12 September 1848. Modern Switzerland had come into being.

Chapter XI

Modern Switzerland
(1848-1914)

1. *The Spirit of Institutions*

To understand what the men of 1848 achieved it is essential to know what they set out to do.

With the collapse of the Helvetic Republic as a warning, they did not attempt to turn Switzerland into a unitary state. Their aims were not revolutionary. They did not seek to break with tradition but to take a step further in the direction it indicated. They were convinced of the need to centralize power, but they realized that the cantons must retain not only their juridical powers but their own vitality. The Swiss like local autonomy. They like their government on their doorstep, and they like to know their magistrates. If you distance power from the people, you distance the people from power. The only real political cell, endowed with the reserves of strength and prestige which only centuries of survival can give, is the smallest one. In Switzerland supreme power can only be sovereign by delegation.

The Helvetic Republic was inspired by the mathematical concepts of the French Revolution. The 1848 constitution shows Anglo-Saxon influences, but it is primarily the fruit of experience. It bears the stamp of the practical race which conceived it and for which it was destined. It was not the work of doctrinaire theoreticians but of the cantons' statesmen, who were careful to tailor the sacrifices they would have to impose on the cantons to the minimum required to further their collective undertaking. Their constitution, though founded on compromise, welded the country into a durable shape from the start.

In endowing Switzerland with the federal institutions which answered the needs of the time, previous generations rendered the country a signal service. But this would not have lasted long or been of much value if they had committed the mistake of previous regimes and tried to make these institutions immutable. The men of '48 avoided this error. They were not persuaded of their own infallibility, nor did they assume that the world would stop evolving after them. They inserted a revision clause in the federal constitution and insisted that all the cantonal constitutions should do likewise. The experience of 1830 was of value here. Thanks to this precaution Switzerland has been completely free—with the single exception of the Ticino episode of 1890—of troubles, coups d'état and revolutions ever since. In three-quarters of a century the foundations of these institutions completely altered, and the reason this happened without conflict is that these developments were foreseen and the legal means for expressing them already existed.

The article in the constitution which made the greatest, though not the most obvious, contribution to the unification of the country was the one placing cantonal constitutions under federal guarantee with the reservation that this could be withheld, a check which had not previously existed. The effect of this clause was gradually to eliminate the divergencies between the regimes in the different cantons. After 1849, Zug and Schwytz gave up their *Landsgemeinden*; in 1854 the Grisons abandoned their federalism. At the present time, though the cantonal constitutions may vary as to detail, they all bear a strong family resemblance. The cantons all have a collegial executive power and a representative legislative power, tempered by considerable experience of direct democracy. It is only here and there in the realm of the judiciary that certain original institutions have subsisted.

Thanks to its evolutionary format, the 1848 constitution did away with Switzerland's political problems. For better or worse, this is a fact. Critics may argue that a country needs conflicting ideas to keep it alert. Or that material preoccupations will tend, in the long run, to shrink an already naturally small horizon. Or that these same material preoccupations were at the bottom of the divisions which split the country at times of crisis. There is some truth in these contentions. But it would be completely to misunderstand the later stages of the Confederation's history not to realize that this is the history of economic rather than political evolution.

It was no accident that the new Confederation found itself confronted by urgent economic tasks right from the start. This was the precondition of its birth. The fundamental purpose of the 1847 revolution was to give Switzerland the economic unity which is the basis of a modern nation. The federal constitution was not born of an idea but of a need. If this revolution had not occurred, or had failed, Switzerland, with its growing flood of foreign imports, would have lost its independence almost without realizing it. Economic unity emerged, in the mid-nineteenth century, as the chief condition of the Confederation's existence. This necessity gave rise to political unity and it was then the task of those concerned to set about creating economic unity.

A nation requires one thing above all if it is to succeed in its economic tasks—and that is continuity. The Federal Council enjoyed a stability unknown in any other country, and it was because of this that it was able to become a powerful institution and gradually acquire for the Confederation some of the functions which the constitution allotted to the cantons.

Between 1848 and 1928 Switzerland had fifty federal councillors, which averages out at about eleven years of office for each. One of them, M. Schenk, of Berne, remained in office for thirty-two years. Only one, during this period, M. Challet-Venel, of Geneva, was not re-elected, in 1873, although he stood for office.

This stability is less surprising than it appears at first sight. It is in accordance with Swiss tradition. The Swiss have never been able to admit that their magistrates might be unworthy of their position. They believe them to be perfectly honest. The magistrates do their jobs to the best of their ability, as would others in their place. Besides, Switzerland has always been a democracy veering towards oligarchy. The patriciates, destroyed in the fourteenth century, reappeared during the centuries which followed, only to come to grief again in the eighteenth.

Stability in the Federal Council accords with the aim of the State, which is to develop and protect the people's material assets. The Swiss government saw its functions as those of an administrative council given over to the solving of technical problems. Its ruling preoccupation is the good of the enterprise. What an assembly asks of an administrative council is vigilance and honesty, or, in a word, efficiency. The Federal Council has always possessed these qualities to a high degree. In return the assembly was able to assure the Council of continuity, which is necessary for the efficient management of technical problems.

If the 1848 constitution had not functioned along these

lines it would never have functioned at all. The Federal Council is elected by the Federal Assembly, for four years. The Assembly cannot overthrow or dissolve the Council. If any dispute were to arise between the two ruling bodies, it would be insoluble and would end logically in either a coup d'état or a revolution. It required exceptional confidence in their fellow-citizens on the part of the constituents to risk putting a constitution into force which could never have worked in most of the other countries of the world.

It worked admirably in Switzerland. No dispute ever arose. This is primarily due to the naturally moderate tendencies of Swiss public opinion, and their dislike of speculative debate. Instinctively, the Swiss avoid conflicts of principle and look for positive solutions.

But the real reason must be looked for in the Federal Council's moral ascendancy over Parliament. Of these two powers, whose falling-out could have jeaopardized the whole undertaking, the former, of national origins, instantly took the lead from the other, which was an imitation of a foreign institution.

The one institution which goes right back to the earliest days of Swiss history is the collegial system. Unlike the United States, which has adopted the personal power system, the Swiss have never known anything but collective power. When they found a model for their executive organ in Swiss traditions, rather than across the sea, the men of 1848 assured the government of real and considerable authority.

The Federal Council, which is not controlled and cannot be dissolved, enjoys almost absolute power. The only curb on the will of a Federal Councillor is the will of his colleagues. The Council is king so long as it is unanimous and the Councillors are kings in their own sphere.

The Federal Assembly came into being in quite a different manner.

Faced with the task of reconciling the sovereignty of the people with that of the cantons, the federalist principle with centralization, the men of '48 thought they had found a solution to this difficult problem in the example of America. In the eighteenth century, Switzerland provided a model for the institutions of the United States. However, the latter progressed through the stage of a Confederation of States in six years where it took the Confederation more than five hundred. In this way the United States came, in their turn, to provide a model for the Swiss. The Swiss Federal Parliament was created along the lines of their own; one chamber represents the people as a whole, and by giving preponderance to the many has, if anything, a centralizing effect. The other represents the cantons, with two deputies from each; this provides an element of resistance, a curb on over-rapid progress towards unity.

At the time this was thought to be a happy solution. Most of the authors of the constitution, Rüttimann, Druey, Kern, James Fazy, and more besides, were proud of having thought of it. Good ideas are never short of godparents.

It was a novel solution and one with no national precedent to recommend it. The Helvetic Republic had certainly attempted a bi-cameral system, but no trace of that experiment remained in the people's political consciousness.

Switzerland provides yet another instance of the law that imported institutions never, or rarely, have the vitality of indigenous ones. The Council of States has not achieved all that was hoped for it. Unlike the American Senate on which it was modelled, the Council has proved weak in the face of an exceptionally strong executive, the most active agent of centralization.

The American Senate concentrates most of the powers of the State within its hands, and has a tendency to monopolize all of them. The Council of States, on the other hand, has played scarcely any part in Swiss political history. Though it was conceived of as an organ of opposition and control, it rapidly showed itself as governmentally minded as the National Council, and sometimes even more so. It is made up of magistrates from the cantons, who understand the problems of power and have generally tended to identify themselves with the Federal Council. The Council of States has been drawn into the very current it was supposed to fight against.

The National Council's conception of its role is not very different. It was dominated from the start by a compact majority who advocated consistent support of the Federal Council. Unable, constitutionally, to dissolve or revoke the government, the deputies are also deprived by their own statutes of the right to personal initiative in parliament and the right to raise individual questions in the chamber. As far as bringing pressure to bear on the government is concerned, the only means left to them are the budget vote, the examination of the administration and the blocking of re-election. But these means have been allowed to grow rusty through lack of use. Far from being an effective opposition the popular chamber has turned out to be a solid foundation for the executive power.

This was one of the most unexpected effects of direct democracy. Once the people got supreme control over legislation they lost interest in designating their representatives. They disown them and then re-elect them. The deputy does not feel, as he would in other countries, that he is under the constant control of the electorate. The voters entrust him with small matters and reserve the right 'to settle the important ones themselves. This is one of the reasons for the high proportion of abstentions in the elections, something which would normally seem surprising in a decentralized nation. In Switzerland, direct democracy has gradually undermined representative democracy and tended, indirectly, to strengthen the executive arm.

The chief concern of any democratic constitution should be to protect individuals against the encroachments of power. In the case of a federative constitution it is the member-States who have to be protected.

The 1848 constituents realized this. They wanted to create a strong federal power to carry out the economic tasks facing the new Confederation. But they took care to provide the cantons with a double guarantee.

The first was contained in the principle that all non-delegated power should belong to the canton. The federal constitution should be interpreted restrictively and the Confederation could only function from a basis of unanimity.

In the second place, sovereignty should not reside with the people alone but with the people and the cantons at once. Thanks to the double majority system, which is needed to revise the constitution, and to the institution of the Council of States, Uri, with its 12,000 inhabitants, has as many rights as Berne, which then had 300,000 inhabitants and in 1928 had almost 700,000.

In practice, however, these guarantees proved illusory. The two majorities have always taken the same side. The Council of States did not play the role it was created for. Lastly, the constitution was revised thirty-four times between 1848 and 1928, almost always with the aim of increasing the Confederation's powers. This will continue to happen even more easily and frequently, as a consequence of direct democracy in action.

As the population increases it will be increasingly easier to make use of the right of referendum and initiative, and the guarantee against abuse will be that much less reliable. When the 1874 constitution fixed on the figure of 30,000 as the number of signatures needed to request a referendum, this figure represented approximately five per cent of the electoral body. By 1928 it represented barely three per cent. Similarly the figure of 50,000 signatures needed for an initiative, which was eight per cent of the electorate in 1891, represented in 1928 only five per cent.

The period from 1848 up till the present time has been characterized, in the economic and social field, by an astonishing expansion of industry and commerce and by an increasing tendency towards migration within the country. Whereas almost two-thirds of the Swiss lived in their native town in 1850, by 1920 this number had shrunk to less than one-third. The proportion of those indifferent or favourable to centralization had increased in the the same ratio. This phenomenon of migration, together with immense progress in the communications field, reveals the forces at work which have tended to undermine the cantons in favour of the Confederation.

In 1849, federal spending rose to 6,400,000 francs; in 1860 to 21,900,000; in 1879 to 35 million; in 1890 to 73 million; in 1900 to 103 million; in 1911 to 167 million; and in 1924 to 304 million. These figures illustrate the progress of centralization.

Over these eighty years then, centralizing elements clearly prevailed over the federalists. For all its authors' intentions, for all their desire to keep continuity with previous regimes, the 1848 constitution was a revolutionary work. Cantonal sovereignty counted for very little by 1928.

Nevertheless, while direct democracy may not have hindered centralization, it does not seem to have assisted it as much as one might have expected.

First of all, it favours the coalition of minority groups. Direct democracy is a guarantee for opposition movements. In isolation the French Swiss, the Catholics and the Socialists are powerless. It would be very difficult for them to carry out a common policy in Parliament. As a coalition before the electorate, however, these minorities frequently managed to make their point of view prevail over the radical majority of the Chambers.

French Switzerland, which accounts only for a third of the population, is often said to be without political influence. But this is quite untrue. The views of a united French Switzerland can predominate over those of a German Switzerland which is, more often than not, divided. French Switzerland, thanks to its lucidity of mind and imagination, exercises a considerable influence over the country's policy, one quite out of proportion to its numerical strength.

In the second place, direct democracy tends to be a somewhat conservative institution. Democracy is often confused with progress. In reality, democracy is nothing but government according to the will of the people. If the people are conservative, their democracy will be conservative. The Swiss people, a largely agricultural population, are highly suspicious of innovations. In a country like Switzerland giving the people their rights slows down rather than speeds up evolution.

Without dispensing value judgements which the future may not uphold, it can be said that direct democracy has yielded good results in Switzerland. If one stands back far enough to take a dispassionate view of the principal federal votes, one would be justified in maintaining that the sovereign power has hardly ever committed a serious error of judgement.

This does not mean that the same institution would give the same results elsewhere. The federal constitution testifies to the legislator's confidence in the nation. Such a regime could not work unless the mass of people were 'enlightened' in the eighteenth century sense of the word. Education is not enough. The people must be interested in public affairs and understand what is going on. This requires a long democratic history, and a high standard of living generally, which are the fruits of a long period of peace. And this is where direct democracy relates to a policy of neutrality.

2. *The Evolution of Federalism*

National unity in Switzerland did not issue from the instinctive preferences of the people, nor from the thinking of an elite. It was imposed on the country by economic realities, progress in communications and population movements. It was born of the same needs which, seventy years later, imposed the League of Nations on Europe.

This is why most of the New Confederation's activities were given over to the economic unification of the country. Hence the passing of a law, 4 June 1849, concerning the award of appointments, followed shortly afterwards by a law concerning customs duties, intended to provide the Confederation with the resources it needed. The monetary system was unified in 1850. Finally, on 28 July 1852, a law regarding the railways was passed. The implementation of this law was to dominate federal politics for a long while to come.

Switzerland had fallen behind her neighbours in this respect. England had had railways since 1825, Germany since 1835, France and Austria since 1837, Italy, the Low Countries and Russia since 1839, but Switzerland had not progressed beyond a line between Basle and St Louis in 1844, and one linking Zurich and Baden in 1847, twenty-five kilometres of track in all. Europe's most centrally situated country, heart of the transport industry for centuries, was in danger of being cut off while the commercial traffic of the continent flowed past its frontiers.

Switzerland risked paying heavily for her smallness at this stage. The cost of building a vast railway network was far beyond the resources and capacities of the Confederation. Though the estimate for a line between Constance and Morges, the one indispensable line, was as low as 113 million francs this was considered exorbitant, and in any case paying off the debt would have swallowed almost the whole federal budget.

Thus, in the teeth of expert advice and the centralizing and state-oriented wishes of the majority, the federal Assembly decided, in 1852, to place the construction and control of Swiss railways in the hands of private enterprise. This was a definite falling away from the ideal of 1848. After four years' existence the Confederation was already finding itself obliged to relinquish one of its most important economic functions to the cantons. This sparked off a conflict which has gone on ever since between state-mindedness and liberalism, centralization and federalism. Liberals and federalists had won the first round.

This decision had the result of setting off the old cantonal rivalries once again. Vaud planned a Morges-Yverdon-Murten line; Fribourg wanted to provide for traffic to her chief town via Oron. The eastern cantons wanted to tunnel through the Lukmanier, the central cantons wanted a line over the Gotthard.

Partisans of longitudinal lines clashed with supporters of transversal lines. And the foreign powers took advantage of these quarrels to step in and resume their age-old role of meddling in Swiss affairs.

What all these disputes ultimately boiled down to was the rivalry between two towns, Berne and Zurich, and between the radical views on one hand and moderate views on the other of two men, Staempfli and Escher, whose feud more than once threatened to bring down the party in power.

Setting aside the obstacles these disputes threw in the way of setting up a Swiss railway system, they were on the whole beneficial to the country's development. They distracted men's minds from denominational and political questions, and substituted regional for party disputes, and thus helped the country calm down and forget the civil war.

In spite of all these problems, the building of the railways pushed ahead rapidly. In ten years, from 1854 to 1864, the Swiss network jumped from 38 to 1,300 kilometres. This development brought the different cantons closer together, improved relations between them and produced great shifts in population throughout the country. It thus gave rise to a need for further unifying measures.

The 1848 constitution had only partly regulated the rights of domicile of Swiss outside their native cantons. Jews had been pointedly excluded from these provisions. France was more progressive in this respect and the Confederation was obliged in 1864, at the conclusion of a commercial treaty with France, to give French Jews the right to settle freely in Switzerland, which was something Swiss Jews did not yet possess.

This was the point of departure for a partial revision of the constitution in 1866. The people voted for the equality of Jews by a small majority. But all the other reforms proposed at this stage were rejected, some by the Federal Assembly and some by the people. Parliament refused as premature and dangerous such measures as the transformation of the demi-cantons into cantons, introduction of a popular veto and referendum, direct election of the Federal Council, the non re-eligibility of Federal Councillors, unification of the business and penal codes. The people likewise rejected—because of the coalition of the French Swiss, the Catholics and the eastern cantons, who were upset by the Gotthard tunnel—all measures relative to the voting rights of Swiss from other cantons in cantonal and communal affairs, together with a series of less important projects.

The dicussions preceding this federal ballot—the first since 1848—had focused attention once more on political problems. The excitement over the railways, though still in the forefront of polemical questions of the day, was beginning to die down now that the network was almost completed. The economic measures which the people had expected of the 1848 revolution had been put into effect and were beginning to show results. No important new industrial invention had cropped up in the meantime. More machines were in use and production had been stepped up, but without any radical change of character. However, the changes resulting from mechanization, and from the creation of a proletarian class, were beginning to make themselves felt.

The political expression of these changes took the form, in some cantons, of adopting direct democracy. The 18 April 1869 constitution which was adopted in Zurich after a series of disturbances introduced the initiative, the referendum, and popular election of the government and State councillors. These institutions had hitherto existed only in the small agricultural cantons. The adoption of pure democracy by the largest industrial canton of the plateau set off a chain reaction through the whole country. Several other cantons, Thurgau, Berne, Solothurn, Lucerne and Aargau followed suit almost immediately, giving fresh impetus to the move to revise the federal constitution which had proved abortive in 1866.

Two events which occurred outside the country but had enormous influence there—the Vatican Council and the Franco-Prussian war—gave the movement irresistible force.

The war, and occupation of the frontiers, brought the Swiss of different cantons into closer contact than usual. It also showed the need for centralization in a sphere which the 1848 constitution had left to the cantons—the army.

The Vatican Council, meanwhile, with its proclamation of the dogma of papal infallibility, stirred up new denominational troubles. Half-dormant memories of the civil war were reawakened. The evil days of the Sonderbund seemed to have returned. Radicalism, exhausted by the effort of carrying out its programme of reform, went back to its sources for re-fuelling. Switzerland was once more divided into two camps. The civil war which ensued was not bloody, but it was genuine enough.

The anti-clerical movement which this produced brought many men into the government, from the various cantons, who were determined to battle for the rights of the civil powers whether they encroached on the clergy in the process or not. At the same time it led to the founding of a new church in Germany which soon found its adherents in Switzerland. Calling itself Catholic, though not Roman Catholic, this creed demanded the right to worship in Catholic churches and insisted that its priests be recognized by the ecclesiastical authorities. The latter refused and the radical governments of Berne and Geneva took strong action against the Bishop of Basle, Mgr Lachat, and against Mgr Mermillod. The Federal Council joined in, expelling Mgr Mermillod from Swiss territory and returning his passport to the Papal Nuncio, Mgr Agnozzi.

Following this, several cantons brought in laws for the organization of the clergy which they were unable to compel the clergy to accept. Thus, in Geneva, the new religion found itself endowed with many places of worship but scarcely any worshippers. Even the eloquence of Father Hyacinthe Loyson failed to kindle the spark and it soon died out. Soon, all that remained of all this skirmishing was a definite split between the Catholic Church and the State.

Passions ran high in both camps, and the Catholics found themselves thrust back, where the Confederation was concerned, into the sterile posture of opposition from which they had only just emerged.

Under these circumstances, the Federal Assembly decided on a total revision of the Constitution. 'One law, one army.' The new constitution was influenced by ideas which the German victory in France had made fashionable. It succeeded in almost completely centralizing the country's juridical and military institutions. This two-fold unification, however, was too much in advance of the thinking of the time. And for this reason it failed, being defeated by a small majority on 12 May 1872.

The advocates of centralization were not discouraged, however, and returned to their project almost immediately. The plans for the unification of the law and the army which had roused opposition in French Switzerland were modified. The anti-clerical measures, on the other hand, were stiffened. In this way the radical party succeeded in driving a wedge between the two minority parties, Catholics and French

Swiss, whose coalition had led to the failure of the revision programme of 1872, as well as that of 1866. The plan for the constitution was accepted by the people, on 19 April 1874, with only the Catholic cantons voting against it.

The importance of the new constitution did not lie, as contemporaries believed, in the new proposals for centralization which it put forward, or in those which it ignored. Its most lasting innovation was the introduction of direct democracy at federal level.

The 1848 constitution was founded upon a rather strict and inflexible division of State competencies between the Confederation and the cantons. The 1874 constitution completely altered the situation by introducing a convenient means for modifying it at any moment.

Experience teaches that there can be no innovation within a Confederation without further centralization. Progress requires that the federal constitution be constantly revised in a centralizing direction.

In speaking of direct democracy, we are referring to three different institutions: the obligatory referendum in constitutional matters existed since 1848; the optional referendum, in legislative matters, existed since 1874; and the initiative was introduced in 1891. Since 1921 all international treaties of a certain duration are treated like laws and submitted to the optional referendum.

In practice these distinctions have lost some of their importance. The right of initiative can only be invoked in constitutional matters. But no precise definition of the constitution exists, there is no criterion to distinguish it from the law, so these notions are purely formal ones. The people therefore can always make use of their right of initiative by framing their request in the form of a constitutional article. In this manner, clauses were introduced into the constitution which should never have figured there.

Curiously enough, the first reform submitted to the people, in 1879, the suppression of the suspension of capital punishment, was a federalist move, and it was accepted. But many further centralizations were rejected. However, the Confederation was consistent in its aims. Most of the rejected proposals were taken up again later and accepted in a modified form. The monopoly of bank notes, rejected in 1880, was accepted in 1891; the protection of inventions, which had been rejected in 1882, was voted in 1887; the right to legislate on jobs, which was refused in 1894, was accepted in 1908. The people slowed down centralization but they did not stop it. The process could be seen still more clearly were one to make a detailed study of the federal laws and the administration's acts, which often succeeded in bringing in reforms in a roundabout way which the electorate would never have passed.

On the whole the people do not seem to have been too critical of the constitutional revisions submitted to them. Between 1879 and 1925, they accepted twenty-six and only rejected seven. As one might expect, the projects which were put to the referendum and those which emanated from the popular initiative had less success. Of the former, thirteen were accepted and twenty-three rejected; of the latter, five were accepted and fifteen rejected.

Despite what the defeated party tends to say after one of these popular votes has taken place, the Swiss people are not guided in these matters by sentimental or irrelevant reasons. On the contrary, their verdicts show a high degree of consistency and their judgements are invariably balanced.

The people will accept personal sacrifices if they can be made to understand that these are necessary—for instance: the vote for military law in 1907, the banning of absinthe in 1908, and the two votes on the war tax in 1915 and 1919. But they will not permit any attack on property rights, as was proved by the rejection of a capital levy on 3 December 1922 by 737,000 votes to 109,000.

The people are not systematically opposed to centralization. Most of the constitutional projects submitted to their vote conferred new powers on the Confederation, and most of them were accepted. For example, we could quote the monopoly of banknotes and alcohol, of the water and forest police, of foodstuffs, the re-purchase of the railways, the unification of civil and penal law, legislation on the arts and trades, on hydraulic power, automobiles, and aerial navigation. But while they may grant the Confederation new powers freely enough, the electors are hostile to monopolies and thoroughly examine the suggested laws of application. Many of these have been dropped as a result.

The same is true of the social sphere. The people are not against progress here, but they are suspicious of it. In 1890 they accepted the constitutional article relating to accident and sickness insurance. But in 1900 they rejected a law giving the State control over its application. In 1877 the electors accepted a law regulating factory work, which was making great progress at that time. But in 1894 they rejected legislation on jobs and the right to employment, and in 1920, a law relating to the conditions of work undertaken at home. On the other hand, once a step forward has been made, they are reluctant to go back on it, as the two votes of 1920 and 1924 instituting an eight-hour day go to show.

The people are in favour of extending popular rights, but not blindly so. In 1891, they accepted the right of initiative and in 1921, an extension of the referendum to include international treaties. But in 1900 they rejected direct election to the Federal Council and did not accept proportional representation until 1918, after two former attempts, in 1900 and 1910, had failed.

Finally, the people are hostile to all encroachments upon the freedom of the individual, to superfluous restrictions of cantonal sovereignty and to any vaguely expressed project which might confer indeterminate powers upon the Confederation. In 1882, they rejected the proposal for a schools inspector; in 1884, the federal penal code; in 1896 proposals for disciplinary sentences in the army; in 1903 dispositions making incitement to insubordination in the army a punishable offence; in 1922 and 1923 two measures against revolutionary meetings.

On the whole, the Swiss people have been equal to the heavy task which direct democracy imposes upon them. Their seriousness and sense of responsibility in public affairs was exemplified by the 1920 campaign for entry into the League of Nations. Swiss citizens try to arrive at a considered opinion about the matters submitted to their vote. Switzerland's example proves that it is easier for an educated people to choose ideas than to choose men.

Nevertheless, direct democracy has had one unfortunate result on Swiss politics, and this is to diminish Parliament's importance and the people's interest in legislative elections.

This flagging interest gave one party complete control of the Federal Assembly for three-quarters of a century. The radical party, strictly speaking, had no unity either in space or in time. There were considerable differences between the radicalism of Geneva, Vaud or German Switzerland. The party had developed greatly. It gradually absorbed its right-wing opponents and took over their ideas. Progressive at first, it gradually became conservative where social issues were concerned.

Radicalism drew its strength from the fact that it was a party without class or regional connotations. It represented big industry, commerce and agriculture all at once. Compared with the Catholic party, whose basis was denominational, the liberal party, mainly representing urban and bourgeois interests, and the socialist party which spoke for the proletariat, radicalism had a comprehensive character.

The radical party had uncontested control of Parliament from 1874 to 1920. During this time it shouldered the full burden of power. This position appeared briefly threatened by proportional representation. Not only was the socialist deputation greatly strengthened, but a new group formed within the radical party itself, a peasant and bourgeois party. The radical party lost its absolute majority in the national Council and one might have supposed that this would lead to a profound transformation of Swiss politics. But there were two reasons why this did not happen.

The first was that the peasants were carrying out the same policy as the radicals under a new name. They were exclusively preoccupied with economic problems, and they continued to follow the Council's lead in any field which did not impinge on their own interests.

The second is that the strengthening of the socialists led to a rallying round the Federal Council on the part of the bourgeois elements.

As far as the Catholic conservative movement was concerned, this was nothing new. It dated from the entry of M. Zemp of Lucerne into the Federal Council in 1891. This date marks the end of the *Kulturkampf* and the anti-clerical tendencies of the radical party. It also marks the end of consistent opposition from the conservatives. M. Zemp followed a centralizing policy over the railways. From this time, though the Catholic party stuck to its federalist guns on certain points, it was no longer hostile to central power on principle.

The liberal party, meanwhile, found the number of its deputies steadily diminishing. Its fear of socialism was stronger than its opposition to the Federal Government. The socialist party alone followed a policy of determined opposition in the Chambers and it is to this, no doubt, that it owed an increasing number of votes.

Parliament, and the various parties, however, do not account for all the political forces in the country. The Swiss Peasants' Union, the *Vorort* for industry and commerce, and the Union for Arts and Crafts, for instance, to mention only the principle economic organizations, exerted considerable influence over federal policy.

During the last decades of the nineteenth and the first decade of the twentieth century, the industrialization of Switzerland proceeded by leaps and bounds. Between 1887 and 1913, export figures soared from 653 to 1,376 million, 80 per cent of which represented manufactured goods, while only 35 per cent of manufactured goods were imported. In 1914 there were more than 8,000 factories and more than 500,000 workers.

The traditional industries, embroidery, textiles, silk, clock-making and mechanics, had been joined by others, industries producing foodstuffs, shoes, chemical products and electrical appliances. The development of water power made up for the country's inadequate supplies of natural fuel. Electricity made industry possible in the remote mountain valleys, with a consequent upheaval in the social structure of these regions.

This progress is all the more remarkable in that Switzerland, to all appearances, was lacking in all the requisites for success, particularly in the century of steam and coal. Her great achievements are due to the long, hard labours of a race accustomed to the toiling mountain life. The Swiss people contributed hard work and high standards to their imported raw materials and this won them new markets and earned them money.

Switzerland does not produce the raw materials she works on; she does not consume the products she manufactures, and her countryside does not feed its inhabitants. She depends on foreign countries for food supplies, raw materials, and markets for her products. Without these, the country cannot eat, buy or sell. In other words she cannot live. All the European countries are interdependent, and it is this which led to their uniting in the League of Nations. But Swiss industry, which is over-developed for the national market, labours under particularly difficult conditions.

Switzerland's wealth at the beginning of the twentieth century was seen in the improved standard of living among the lower classes, and in the increase of public education. By dint of hard work and thrift, through generation after generation, enough savings were accumulated to improve the crops or permit the children in a family to rise in the social scale. Each generation started life on a higher rung of the ladder than the preceding one.

This phenomenon is not peculiar to Switzerland. But the high standards of administration, the efficiency of her public services, the luxury of her official buildings, and the attendance of her secondary and special schools, attest to its intensity in the country.

The flaws in the system, however, were already apparent before 1914. An exceptionally prosperous and well educated population finds it difficult to stoop to menial jobs. In an over-wealthy society, certain social functions find no takers. Thus, Switzerland became a country of immigration and emigration all at once. Intellectuals, businessmen, technicians and skilled workers left the country rather than fill inferior posts. Meanwhile Switzerland was obliged to recruit foreign workers to do these jobs. The number of foreigners in the country, which had reached 71,570 in 1850, soared to the astonishing figure of 552,000 in 1910, equivalent to 15 per cent of the population. There were 62,000 Germans in Zurich and 42,000 in Basle; 42,000 Italians in the Ticino, 36,000 French in Geneva, not to mention the floating population attracted by the booming hotel industry.

This disproportionately large foreign population, which accounted for forty-two per cent of Geneva's population and over fifty per cent of Lugano's, created serious problems which would have got worse but for the First World War.

Switzerland, about 1910, was a prosperous and flourishing country and her politicians were well pleased with themselves. But signs of a moral unrest were apparent among the people. Already over-populated and now invaded by growing numbers of foreigners, dependent on other countries for food, raw materials and outlets, Switzerland was beginning to wonder whether, in the chaos of contemporary Europe, she still retained any real independence.

It was this problem which the Convention of Gotthard put before the nation with exceptional urgency. And it was to this problem that the Nouvelle Société Helvétique, founded in the spring of 1914, was seeking to find an answer when the First World War erupted.

3. *Neutrality in Practice*

In 1848, when the federal State was born, Switzerland's international situation was being affected, in fact rather than in law, by two circumstances.

The first was the outcome of the creation of the State itself. Till then, Switzerland's foreign relations had always been controlled by the sovereign cantons or by the Diet acting in their name. The absence of a central power which could make rapid and effective decisions had weighed heavily upon her foreign policy. Although the Federal Council, a seven-headed government, is by its very nature somewhat slow-moving when it comes to diplomatic action, its very existence and the continuity it imposed on the country's international relations made for a considerable improvement in Switzerland's position.

The second fact, which is equally important, was external to the country. This was the formation of the great modern nations.

The alignment of nations which resulted from the 1815 treaties strengthened Switzerland's independence and allowed her to rediscover an international autonomy which she had lost sight of. The movement of ideas which resulted from the 1848 revolution had a similar effect.

The principle of nationalities was to dominate the policy of the major powers. France, under the sceptre of Napoleon III, became its champion and this permitted the unification of Italy, first of all, and then Germany. This principle, as it was understood then, and often is still, is the negation of Switzerland. If nationality resides, not in the will of the people, but in the language they speak, there is no place in Europe for a nation like the Swiss Confederation. No country has adhered more consistently to the people's right to self-determination, or is more contradictory to the principle of nationalities. With some justification, therefore, the Swiss saw a threat to their independence in the events of 1859 and 1860.

People are often astonished that Switzerland has managed to survive the centuries despite her linguistic diversities. But this astonishment is based on a misapprehension. Language problems are an entirely modern phenomenon. Formerly, people hated each other because of their religion rather than the language they spoke. Our forefathers were neither embarrassed nor astonished by the fact that they expressed the same ideas in different words, and Switzerland was not endangered by this situation in any way until the mid-nineteenth century.

When Italy and Germany became united, the Swiss felt that the only safe course for their country was strict neutrality. The Confederation could never have survived in the midst of countries imbued with the notion that a language makes a nation, if they had offended them in any way or if they had not seemed trustworthy. The Swiss saw a steadfast and impartial policy as the condition for survival.

Pictet de Rochemont, whom the Swiss honour as the founder of the country's perpetual neutrality, observed that this neutrality was 'in the interests of Europe'. This is perfectly true and explains why it survived. The great powers saw Switzerland's integrity as the *sine qua non* of European equilibrium.

Conversely, the existence of four great countries of comparable strength along Swiss frontiers was the thing which made neutrality practicable. As long as Switzerland's neighbours were numerous and unevenly matched, some scarcely more powerful than herself, there was a strong temptation to get involved. Whereas no one in Switzerland in the mid-nineteenth century seriously contemplated playing the role of a great power.

This attitude was dictated by circumstances. However, a formula had yet to be evolved to define it.

It is a mistake to think of Swiss neutrality as something ancient and unchanging. Neutrality, as understood by the Swiss on the eve of the First World War, dated, not from 1516 or even 1815, but from 1860. Neutrality under the old regime was denominational, whereas under the new one it was primarily political and linguistic.

Swiss neutrality, as a concept, was still not satisfactorily defined. There were two divergent concepts of it. Abroad, Swiss neutrality was seen as having been guaranteed by the great powers in 1815, and this limited the international sovereignty of the Confederation.

Swiss jurists did not accept this theory. To them neutrality was restrictive. It should be interpreted first and foremost in Swiss interests. The powers recognized but did not guarantee it, and this gave them no rights to intervene in the Confederation's affairs. Neutral Switzerland claimed the right to make alliances and make war or peace; in other words she claimed full sovereignty.

To us today this debate seems astonishing because these

arguments have not been used since 1860, though Swiss rights are still asserted. As it turned out, the Swiss authorities accepted the foreign jurists' definition, in practice—the very one Swiss jurists were attacking in theory.

The situation was different in 1848. Radicalism gave expression to a movement of revolt against the great powers' interference over the refugee question. At the time of the Sonderbund, the memory of which was still vivid, the Swiss people had been very conscious of the threat posed by these rights which the foreign powers claimed to possess. The question of whether neutrality had been guaranteed or merely recognized was not yet pressing. It was a party question. On this point radical doctrine was straightforwardly nationalistic.

The year 1848 was a year which sowed troubles and revolutions throughout Europe. On 18 March a revolt broke out in Milan. A week later, Sardinian troops, who had rushed to support the uprising, entered the town.

The King of Sardinia found himself obliged to deploy all his forces to the east and he was uneasy about Savoy. He was afraid of invasion and insurrection both at once. He turned to the Federal Diet, which was still extant, and suggested an alliance against Austria in a note of 4 April, 1848.

This suggestion was not, as one might expect, indignantly rejected by the Diet. It was rejected, but by only fifteen votes to seven. Berne, the Ticino and the French-speaking cantons—headed by Druey and Staempfli—favoured the alliance, or in other words a violation of neutrality from which they hoped to gain territorial compensations in the Chablais and Faucigny.

This was an adventurous policy. On the other hand there was much to be said for the arguments favouring occupation of Northern Savoy by federal troops. The King of Sardinia had hoped, in 1815, to guarantee the security of his possessions by including them in Swiss neutrality. Now that Sardinia was at war Switzerland was obliged, or at least entitled, to occupy Savoy and it would have been easy for her to obtain some recompense for this service. Thus the Swiss missed a chance to put the King of Sardinia under an obligation to them and instead adopted a course of action which aroused his lasting resentment.

The next few years were taken up with innumerable disputes over refugees which brought Switzerland into conflict with all her neighbours and even, in 1850, within a hairsbreadth of war.

With Jakob Staempfli's arrival in the Federal Council in 1854, Swiss politics took a much more active turn, particularly in the Neuchâtel incident of 1856 and that of Savoy in 1859.

Neuchâtel's juridical position had been vague since 1848. On 1 March 1848, the republicans seized its principal town and declared the place a republic. This movement won the support of the federal authorities. The efforts of Neuchâtel's conservative government to break away from the Confederation, together with her abstention from the Sonderbund war, had angered the radicals, and there was a general feeling in Switzerland that the principality's hybrid position could not be maintained much longer. For this reason the Diet resolved, on 3 April 1848, that the federal guarantee would only be granted to cantonal constitutions if they were on republican lines.

The King of Prussia refused ever to accept the legality of what happened in Neuchâtel and kept up a stream of complaints to the great powers against what he described as 'spoliation'. The Protocol of London, 8 May 1852, gave formal recognition to his rights in return for a promise that he would not attempt to impose them by force.

This was how things stood when, on the night of 3 September 1856, a royalist revolt broke out in Neuchâtel. After a brief moment of triumph, the rioters were put down and their leaders imprisoned.

This affair set the wheels of European diplomacy in motion. Prussia demanded the release of the prisoners and a complete amnesty, but without promising to abandon her own claims in return. The Federal government, which had gained some unexpected hostages from the affair, refused to negotiate on this basis. Repeated approaches by France and the other powers, both collectively and separately, had no result.

Tempers meanwhile were rising in Switzerland. Prussia had embarked upon military preparations, so the Federal Council mobilized part of the army and convoked the Federal Assembly. On 27 December 1856, the latter appointed G. H. Dufour as general.

Europe became uneasy. There was no telling where the business might end, thanks to the collective nature of their guarantee of Swiss neutrality, if war broke out between Prussia and Switzerland. Moreover the powers no longer felt as reluctant as they had before 1848 to tamper with the 1815 treaties.

A formula was finally arrived at. Switzerland released the prisoners and a diplomatic conference was held in Paris to give formal recognition to Neuchâtel's independence of the King of Prussia.

The treaty of 26 May 1857 gave a happy ending to an affair which had incurred grave dangers for Switzerland. The way the business had been settled in 1848 had not been above reproach and it had needed a favourable conjunction of circumstances to obtain the King of Prussia's renunciation, without counter-claims for compensation. One can imagine what would have happened if this affair had dragged on a few years longer and come into Bismarck's hands!

Unfortunately the success which a tough policy had achieved in the Neuchâtel business went to Staempfli's head. This led to the Confederation suffering a serious setback, three years later, over Savoy.

The invasion of the Franche-Comté in 1815 and the diplomatic campaign of 1860 were Switzerland's last attempts to expand and regain her natural frontiers.

For several centuries, Switzerland had avoided any expansion of her new territory. She let slip some excellent opportunities, in 1814 and 1815. But in 1860, the expansionist spirit suddenly took hold of her. The Federal government, with almost unanimous public support, did not hesitate to resort to aggression in an attempt to secure Northern Savoy, which the Diet had not even been interested in in 1815.

The 1859 Franco-Austrian war had changed the nationality of two regions near Swiss frontiers, on both of which she had historic claims—Valtellina and Savoy.

The Confederation, as we know, refused to recognize Valtellina's separation from the Grisons. In 1815, Switzerland and the Grisons made repeated official protests against the seizure of Valtellina, reserving their claims for a future date.

It seems likely that Austria, in 1859, after being forced to cede Lombardy to an enemy power, would have jumped at the chance of separating Valtellina—whose strategic importance she was well aware of—from it. Sardinia, expanding at an unprecedented rate, and not yet in possession of this territory, might well have considered relinquishing all claim to it. France might not have been averse to distracting the attention of the Swiss from Savoy. Thus, quite unexpectedly, the diplomatic stage seemed set for a Swiss territorial coup.

The amazing thing is that no one realized this. The Swiss were too obsessed by Savoy to give a thought to Valtellina. The matter was not raised at the peace congress and the Zurich Treaty, 10 November 1859, transferred a region to which the Swiss had not as yet renounced their claims, to Italy, without so much as a word of protest from them.

It was a totally different matter where Savoy was concerned. Why? No doubt because the leader and prime mover of the *Grands Suisses* party, the Bernese Staempfli, was inspired by the historic traditions of the Republic of Berne, with its political expansionism to south and west.

The Confederation could summon three arguments in support of its claims on the Chablais, Faucigny and the Geneva region as far as Usses. It used them one after the other.

The first leaned on the interests of Geneva. This town's prosperity and security depend to some extent on whether the neighbouring territory belongs to one country or two. It was greatly to Geneva's advantage that the Leman basin should be divided between two powers. France's annexation of Savoy was a threat to Geneva for which the Swiss felt justified in demanding compensation.

The second argument was the 1564 treaty between Berne and the Duke of Savoy, whereby the Duke undertook not to cede the land restored to him to any power other than Switzerland. Ironically enough, the treaty invoked by the Federal Council in support of its claims on Savoy was the identical one used by La Harpe in 1797 to bring the French into the Vaud region. This claim was much weakened, it must be added, by the Swiss failure to have their right of pre-emption recognized by the Congress of Vienna in 1814.

The strongest card the Swiss could play was the wishes of the Savoyard population itself. Petitions circulated through Northern Savoy in February and March 1860 collected more than 12,000 signatures in the space of a few days. To stop any manifestation of popular sentiment it was necessary to organize a plebiscite which gave the inhabitants no opportunity of voting for union with Switzerland.

Assuming that perpetual neutrality does not preclude the right to make territorial claims, the Federal Council had valid arguments for demanding France's cession of North Savoy. Had they set about the matter more adroitly, they might even have succeeded.

Unfortunately, the Federal Council did not know how to tailor their policy to the means at their disposal. It is impossible for a Swiss not to feel ashamed of the hopeless blunders they perpetrated.

The first of these was to have neglected occupying the territory they claimed, which they were legally entitled to do under the terms of the treaties. They failed to implement their claims, even while insisting upon them! They even allowed France to dispatch troops bound for Italy across this neutralized region, an oversight which understandably drew protests from Austria, and earned them no gratitude from the French.

Had Switzerland occupied the area militarily she would probably have gained possession of it without too much trouble. Napoleon III was not, at first, resolved against her acquiring it. He even made some remarks which could have been interpreted as promises. However, the Federal Council went to extraordinary lengths to antagonize the Emperor by making their mistrust of him pointedly obvious, and by insisting on a guarantee. After protesting, in advance, against the French annexation of Savoy, the Federal Council then demanded to be admitted to talks, and finally, on 10 March, asked for the intervention of the other great powers.

The feverish activity of Swiss diplomats, making urgent approaches to right and left, and some ill-timed displays of public feeling, at length provided the Imperial government with a pretext for breaking its promises. Switzerland's passionate protests and claims at last evoked some response in Southern Savoy. A deputation of forty-one Savoyard dignitaries was sent to Paris to protest against the annexation of their country. They were received on 21 March 1860, by the Emperor, who did not conceal the fact that they had arrived 'almost' too late. He had already given verbal assurances in Switzerland's favour, he said, to the three cabinets of Berne, London and Turin.

These assurances, however, were not allowed to stand in his way. On 24 March, Sardinia ceded the entire region to France. On 22 April, the cession was ratified by a plebiscite which obtained, from the Northern Savoyard arrondissements, 46,076 votes of 'Oui et zone', 14,354 'Oui' and 160 'Non', with 3,874 abstentions. Voting papers marked 'Suisse' were declared null and void.

The way the choice was framed left the population no way of

expressing its real wishes in the matter. The creation of a great zone, represented as a concession to Switzerland, was really in French interests as it caused a definite swing in popular sympathy towards France. Napoleon III, who was a free-trader, wanted to try out his tariff policy there.

Further, the Imperial government had realized that in enlarging the 1816 zone, it would be giving the area strength to resist the natural attraction exerted by any economic capital over its surrounding area.

On 5 April, too late, the Federal Council made a last attempt. It proposed convening a European Congress. But as far as the cabinets were concerned the matter was settled and their suggestion was not taken up. On 14 June 1860, the annexation of the disputed territory to France was officially proclaimed by the imperial council responsible for creating the great zone. On 18 June the Federal Council lodged a last protest, and this put an end to the whole business where Switzerland was concerned.

In 1862 the old Franco-Swiss dispute over the Val des Dappes was settled by a compromise. It will be recalled that, in 1815, the powers restored the territory which Napoleon had seized to Switzerland. However, in a secret agreement, they also promised the French to try and get it back for them. Pictet de Rochemont did not know of this promise, and the Swiss government refused to be bound by it. This led to a dispute which dragged on for almost half a century. The Second Empire, its foreign policy dictated by a constant search for spectacular successes, was impatient with Switzerland's stubborn resistance in this matter.

The dispute was finally settled by a compromise on 8 December 1862. The Val des Dappes was shared out. Switzerland yielded the road between Faucigny and Morez—the real bone of contention—and received, in exchange, a territory of comparable size but without economic or strategic value.

Jakob Staempfli, who inspired the Confederation's foreign policy during the Savoy affair and was the last exponent of an active foreign policy, left the Federal Council on 31 December 1863. The following year, thanks to the initiative of a few eminent Genevans, the Geneva Convention was set up, on 22 August 1864, founding the International Red Cross. This date marks the beginning of a new era in foreign relations.

The Red Cross, whose central idea is the neutralization of

wounded and ambulances, is the offspring of perpetual neutrality. Conversely, its great merit from the Swiss point of view is that it gives an aim and a meaning to Swiss neutrality. Till then, it had been purely negative. Now it became active. The Red Cross gave Switzerland a purpose in every war to come. The Red Cross and the Swiss army are the two safeguards of Swiss independence. It made Switzerland, helped by the geographical situation and the development of the railways, into an international centre of the first importance.

Gradually it became the custom for international organizations, whose numbers multiplied steadily during the last quarter of the century, to establish themselves in Switzerland. The oldest of these, the Bureau des Telegraphes, dates from 1868, which indicates its affiliation with the Red Cross. After the Alabama affair Switzerland also became the cradle of international arbitration. Finally, it was the Red Cross and the prestige it gave the country which attracted the League of Nations to Switzerland.

It was in 1870–1871 that Switzerland, as a nation, adopted the Red Cross motto for the first time: *Inter arma caritas*. The great wave of public and private beneficence which greeted the internment of France's eastern army in Switzerland probably did the country's reputation more good than her refusal to accept Mülhausen from Bismarck's hands. This was the third time in ten years that Switzerland had to stand by while one of the territories lost at the beginning of the century slipped through her hands yet again. Before it had been Valtellina, and then Savoy, now it was Mülhausen.

The Council has often been praised for refusing a gift whose acceptance would have risked implicating Switzerland in Germany's destiny. All the same, it was a hard sacrifice to make and the Swiss have perhaps tended to make too light of it. Mülhausen was snatched from the Confederation, seventy-two years earlier, in peacetime, after having been in its possession for almost three hundred years. Had its inhabitants been consulted in 1870, they would undoubtedly have chosen Switzerland in preference to Germany, and it would not have been difficult to renew ties which had grown up over three centuries.

It is arguable whether the Federal Council, on this occasion as later over the Vorarlberg, interpreted the Federal Constitution according to the letter of the law. The Constitution gives the people the right to decide on territorial matters, and it is arguable whether the government ought to withhold such an important decision from the people by means of a negative decision.

After 1870, Switzerland's foreign as well as her home policy were ruled by economic considerations. There were three reasons for this: Switzerland's industrial expansion was forcing the country to seek foreign markets, while protecting the home market against foreign imports; the progressive adoption of protectionist policies by her neighbours made the Confederation's free-trade policy, dating from 1849, impossible; lastly, Article XI of the Frankfurt Treaty increased Switzerland's dependence on Germany.

In 1891 Switzerland adopted a strictly protectionist policy, which immediately led her into a tariff war with France lasting from 1893 till 1895. Every subsequent tariff revision intensified protectionism further, sometimes on behalf of industry, sometimes of agriculture.

Whether the Confederation could have acted differently under the circumstances is arguable. Protectionism is essentially damaging to Switzerland's fundamental interests. The purpose of a tariff wall is to ensure national production of its home market. But the home market, in Switzerland, takes second place to the growth of industry. Scarcely any other countries in the world export such a high proportion of manufactured goods. Therefore a policy with the long-range effect of sealing off foreign markets in order to protect the home market may be inflicted by circumstances but it would hardly be recommended by economic theory.

It was Germany's industrial expansion in the last quarter of the nineteenth century which imposed this policy on the Swiss, and it is one of history's strange ironies that the result should have been to sow conflict between Switzerland and France.

Article XI of the Frankfurt Treaty assured Germany of preferential treatment from France. Since Germany was Switzerland's chief rival in the most important branches of its industry, this provision operated against the Swiss. Had they not contracted various industrial agreements with Germany assuring them of advantages in some fields, the French market would have been closed to them.

During the First World War the French often reproached

Swiss bankers and industrialists for too close an association with Germany. There were grounds for this attitude, but it was still unjust. The Swiss could not be held responsible for the French defeat in 1870 which left them overwhelmingly open to German influence for over forty years.

Germany not only dominated Swiss industries, thanks to Article XI. She controlled the country's supply of raw materials through her coalfields, and, via the Rhine, Switzerland's chief communication route to the outside world, the British Empire and the United States in particular.

Neutrality, as we have pointed out more than once, requires a balance of power in Europe. As soon as one of the powers becomes too dominant the Confederation is drawn, reluctantly and almost unconsciously, into its orbit. This happened under the Second Empire. French-Swiss opinion correctly interpreted the national interest in 1870, when it opted to support Prussia instead of France, as being the more distant and therefore less formidable of the two powers. But Germany's prodigious rise to power in the last quarter of the nineteenth century was to create a new danger for Switzerland.

The Gotthard Convention of 13 October 1909 was the clearest but not the only expression of this preponderant influence. The Swiss government has often been sharply criticized for this situation, and not without reason. But the historian cannot help seeing that Germany, with European politics as they were at that time, was in a position to bring irresistible pressure to bear on the Swiss.

Public opinion was dimly aware that the Gotthard Convention's significance was far greater than that of a mere railway conference. That is why the country as a whole took such a lively interest in it. After the ratification of the Convention by the two Chambers, an initiative demanding that international treaties be put to the referendum was launched (1913) and rapidly adopted.

The First World War broke out soon afterwards, while the impression left by these events was still fresh in people's minds.

Chapter XII

The First World War

1. *The War*

The declaration of war, at the beginning of August 1914, caught Switzerland unprepared, both morally and materially. Only the army, which was mobilized immediately, was ready.

After a long period of tranquillity and peace the Swiss had lost the taste for foreign politics. They had fallen into the habit of thinking that what went on in other countries was none of their business. They took a purely speculative interest in external affairs. Generally speaking, the Swiss people overlooked the fact that Switzerland is situated at the heart of Europe and that all nations are interdependent. They had forgotten that Switzerland had never succeeded in remaining outside any major European catastrophe, and that she had shared in the consequences of all the revolutions and great wars.

Most of the Swiss press works under difficult conditions. With a small readership and not much money or staff, they tend to look for news and ideas in foreign newspapers written in the same language. It is so much easier and cheaper to cut something out than translate it. This tendency was intensified, during the first days of the war, by the disorganization of editorial staff and communication services following the call-up.

This was not the only reason for the two sections of the country losing moral contact with each other. Economic and financial considerations, and the presence of foreign colonies on Swiss soil, also played their part. But a sector of the press was quick to capitalize on these growing misunderstandings.

German Switzerland took the moral standpoint which it felt was most becoming to neutrality. It reserved judgement. The causes of the war, the invasion of Belgium, and the atrocities never impressed the German Swiss as being sufficiently well documented, sufficiently clear and comprehensible to justify their condemnation. A demand for immediate peace, which the Allies did not want, seemed to them to be the only admissible national policy. German Switzerland was not, as has been irresponsibly suggested, Germanophile but it was dreadfully neutral.

The French-speaking cantons, meanwhile, were unanimous, despite varying shades of opinion, in their involvement in the name of justice and the national interest. They did not want to be morally neutral. What Switzerland has most reason to fear is the creation of a continental hegemony. The destruction of Belgium and a German victory would have created a Europe where there was no room for a free Switzerland. For as long as the war lasted the French-speaking Swiss never stopped berating their Confederates for letting neutrality blind them till they were unable to discriminate between justice and injustice, between the country's temporary and long-term interests. The French Swiss were indignant that anyone could remain neutral between Germany and Belgium, the aggressor and the victim. On the other hand, the German Swiss reproached the French Swiss for sacrificing neutrality to their prejudices and incurring grave dangers for Switzerland.

A government which had given the people clear directives, and canvassed public support for an active policy, might have succeeded in smoothing over if not ironing out these misunderstandings. But the Federal Council abstained from all intervention in party warfare. The policy it adopted towards the belligerents was one of never making a gesture to the right without immediately following it by one to the left. This sort of balancing trick was not likely to have a calming effect when what was needed above all was moral appeasement.

The circumstances in which Colonel Ulrich Wille was appointed as commander-in-chief; the tendencies displayed by the high command on various occasions; the Federal Council's refusal to express an official opinion on the rape of Belgian neutrality, the affair of the Colonels, and then the Hoffman affair, all contributed to a growing feeling of exasperation in French Switzerland, aggravated rather than alleviated by the anger aroused in German Switzerland by various untimely demonstrations and the explosive language of a section of the French-speaking press.

These conflicting views created a split between the two sides which has been called the 'trench'. The depth of the trench however has been greatly exaggerated. The disputes between the Confederates were never as serious as those occasioned by the Thirty Years War. There were no armed soldiers to be seen, as there had been in 1815, along the frontiers between Berne and Vaud. German Switzerland, moreover, was not unanimous in its sympathies, as the many demonstrations made by the Nouvelle Société Helvétique or the historic speech made by Switzerland's greatest writer, Carl Spitteler, at Zurich on 14 December 1914, would suggest.

It is undeniable, however, that moral contact between the parties was temporarily severed. What was serious about this split was that it appeared along the linguistic frontier, thus dividing the country into two compact camps. Was Switzerland, after wars between towns and countryside, Catholics and Protestants, democrats and aristocrats, now to be torn by wars of language and race?

In the material sphere Switzerland was no better off. As we have already pointed out, the country supports a population out of all proportion to her natural resources. Her survival depends on importing raw materials and re-exporting them in the form of manufactured goods. Pre-war, Switzerland's external trade figures were around 1,000 francs per head of the population, which was the highest in any country. Finally, not having any outlet to the sea, Switzerland must rely on her neighbours, not only for outlets but for transit facilities. Without their permission, she cannot sell, buy, eat, or work.

No one had an inkling, to begin with, of what the war would be like, particularly from the economic point of view. The Federal Council believed it had taken care of the country's food problems by reaching an agreement with France over wheat supplies, and a similar agreement with Germany over coal supplies. As for the rest, it was felt that neutrality would take care of everything.

But this was not the case. Economic neutrality was not, and and could not be, respected. Once the war became a protracted affair, and was fought, not with a stockpile of armaments accumulated in advance, but with newly manufactured weapons, economic considerations became of the utmost urgency for all the belligerents. Under Napoleon, Switzerland had been forced to participate in the continental blockade. She was unable, for the same reasons, to withdraw from the blockade of Germany.

The Confederation's position, which had been difficult from

the first, was further aggravated by the intervention of Italy, who sealed off her last frontier in the spring of 1915. It became almost desperate when the United States, which had been supplying the 200 freight cars of wheat Switzerland needed daily, joined the alliance. Fortunately, a mission to the United States in the course of the summer of 1917 succeeded in interesting President Wilson in Switzerland's fate and the country was not forced to take any desperate measures. But the Allies were in effective control of all the country's communication routes and almost her entire intake of foodstuffs and raw materials—with the exception of a few essentials like coal and potatoes.

This circumstance, while causing the Swiss serious difficulties, was the saving of their neutrality. If Switzerland had depended exclusively on the Allies, and the Germans had had nothing to give her, she would have risked being sucked into the orbit of the countries she depended on. But the Allies had nothing to gain from taking over the entire provisioning of the country. Swiss industry supplied them with an appreciable range of goods needed for the war, manufactured, partly at least, with German coal. At the price of certain concessions to Germany, to which the Allies shut their eyes, while officially deploring them, the country was able to keep up its economic activity for the five years' duration of the war. The S.S.S.—Société Suisse de Surveillance Economique—which began life in the autumn of 1915, was the expression of this policy, which allowed Swiss industry to expand considerably. Without the manufacture of war materials, and without compensation, Switzerland would not be where it is today.

The Federal Council decided, on 3 August 1914, that the situation was serious enough to warrant taking exceptional measures. It got the Federal Assembly to grant it full powers, which were renewed on several occasions and did not end till long after peace was declared.

It is difficult to make a fair appraisal of this economic and political dictatorship. It assured the country's survival and this is an inestimable achievement. But one cannot help wondering whether it was necessary. The Federal Council's influence over the Chambers would doubtless have allowed it to exercise as much authority as it needed without resorting to exceptional powers. In any case, the powers accorded to it should not have been so extensive or long-lasting. They had serious effects on the country. They left the people unaccustomed to the practice of pure democracy at precisely the moment when the government needed the backing of determined public opinion.

By making home affairs subservient to European questions, the war strengthened the Confederation at the expense of the cantons. The full powers had the further effect of concentrating all the competencies within the hands of the Federal Council, or rather the Administration, at the expense of people and Parliament. The normal functioning of the Constitution was thwarted in two directions at once. These exceptional powers finally turned against the Federal Council itself. It was forced to accept all responsibility, with no support to fall back on. It was unable to say no either to foreign governments, or to socialist ultimatums. The Federal Council was weakened rather than strengthened by its vast new powers.

Without seeking to canalize public opinion in any positive direction, the government tried to limit freedom of expression by censorship. A fruitless undertaking, which only succeeded in alienating a section of the people and the foreign governments. The Federal Council, omnipresent and all-powerful, had to answer for everything.

One should not examine events from a negative standpoint only. This extraordinary period of history gave the Swiss people a chance to render inestimable services to the belligerents. No previous war had involved so many people or caused so much individual suffering. The toll of dead and wounded, the length and hardship of captivity, the numbers of dispersed families, occupied territories, deportations of entire populations, the blockade of several great countries, all these things made the war a terrible ordeal for hundreds of millions of people. Thanks to the Red Cross and the Prisoner of War Agency, Switzerland was able to act as intermediary between the belligerents, give families news of prisoners and prisoners news of their families, improve internment conditions, arrange for the repatriation of refugees and send food to the starving. Finally, thanks to the internment of prisoners of war, Switzerland was able to shorten the captivity and save the health of a great number of soldiers. Switzerland's charitable efforts earned her a great debt of gratitude. The price she paid for this could not have been too high, though it meant sheltering a large number of undesirables for five years and becoming a centre for countless intrigues.

But the war went on too long for Switzerland, as well as for the belligerents. Public opinion, resolute to begin with, and even enthusiastic at the time of the general mobilization, was beginning to weary. By 1918 the people's moral resistance had been exhausted.

Exhausted by moral uncertainty to begin with. In French Switzerland, where people congratulated themselves on knowing the difference between justice and injustice, feeling remained staunch right to the end. But neutrality, a negative concept, is hardly suited to arouse and nourish a great collective enthusiasm. German Switzerland, which saw nothing more than a conflict of interests in this giant struggle, was gradually losing heart.

Exhausted, in the second place, by privations. The Swiss people, poorly nourished for five years, restricted by the cost of living and official regulations, did not have the grand ideals and hopes animating the belligerents to sustain them. They were suffering for a cause which was not their own, which could bring them no advantage or benefit, and which, up to a point, they did not even understand.

Moreover, the sudden industrial boom and rising salaries created a great demand for manpower in the towns. Huge fortunes were being made rapidly in armaments and speculation. Agglomerations of dubious moral worth were formed, composed to a large extent of foreign deserters. They proved ideal soil for subversive propaganda, helped by the fact that in 1918 Bolshevism still exerted a very real fascination over the working classes.

The hardships and temptations of civilian life were reflected in the state of affairs in the army. The army carried out its thankless task magnificently during these four years. But each successive mobilization, with their long periods of inactivity and uncertainty, only added to the country's ailments.

The uncertainty which chequered relations between the civil powers and the military command undermined national morale still further. Finally, the great scandals which erupted in the course of 1916 and 1917 gave a shaky situation the last push towards chaos.

There was a tendency in French Switzerland, at the start of the war, to criticize the Federal authorities for their excessive neutrality. So its disgust was all the greater when the affair of the Colonels, followed by Federal Councillor Hoffmann's secret missions to Petrograd, revealed that this apparently scrupulously maintained neutrality had not been as impartial as people had been led to believe. This conclusion, while not altogether just, was readily accepted by a weary and jittery public.

It was the combination of all these circumstances which precipitated the general strike of November 1918. At the very moment when the whole of French Switzerland was sharing in the allied celebrations, the revolutionary wave sweeping across eastern and central Europe suddenly broke on Swiss soil. This was a consequence of Switzerland's geographical situation and a striking illustration of the division in men's minds at a critical time. The social trench now appeared deeper than the moral one. Most of the German Swiss bourgeoisie gave up the struggle; they had been infected by the spirit of defeat. The country was saved by the energy of French Switzerland, for whom the war had a real meaning and who had no intention of letting victory be swamped by revolution.

2. *Peace*

Peace arrived almost as suddenly as the war had done and found Switzerland almost as unprepared. But what country was prepared for peace?

Modern Switzerland's status rests on the 1815 treaties. So it was inevitable that the Peace Conference, which has the task of rebuilding Europe on new foundations, should be confronted with a series of questions directly or indirectly involving Switzerland.

These included: the League of Nations, perpetual neutrality, the neutrality of Northern Savoy, administration of the zones, navigation of the Rhine, the Gotthard convention; finally, one last problem, the Vorarlberg, arose in the most unexpected way.

Changes in the European balance of power could hardly fail to affect a country located in the centre of the continent and surrounded by four great powers. It is hard to determine from our present standpoint how much the dissolution of the Austro-Hungarian empire, Germany's defeat and France and Italy's victory affected Switzerland's diplomatic standing. But one thing is certain, the Federal Council would never have agreed to the zone Convention before the war. They would never sign another Gotthard Convention, nor a Germano-Swiss trade agreement.

Switzerland, not having been a belligerent, was not asked to take part in the Peace Conference. However, Federal Councillor M. Catonder went to Paris in February and March 1919 at the head of a mission which included Alfred Freg, Max Huber and William Rappard, to discuss questions arising out of the League of Nations. M. Gustave Ador was sent to Paris in April to negotiate the terms of the zone agreement. In the meantime, Professor Rappard was in close touch with President Wilson and the English and American delegations. Just as Pictet de Rochemont had turned to Russia and England, a century before, Switzerland now, in similar circumstances, turned to the most distant and disinterested powers for help.

Few countries can have given more thought to postwar international organization than Switzerland. Apart from work undertaken by private individuals and societies, an extra-parliamentary commission was set up by the Federal Council in the autumn of 1919 to prepare a detailed report for the League of Nations. The report was the basis for recommendations submitted by the Council's delegates to the Peace Conference Commission in charge of drafting the Pact, during two sessions held in Paris on 20 and 29 March 1919.

One of the decisions made by this commission was of particular interest to Switzerland, and this was the proposal that Geneva should be the League's headquarters. Two reasons for this choice are worth mentioning. Not having taken part in the war Switzerland was not haunted by painful memories and thus seemed to offer a serene atmosphere where the League of Nations would stand a better chance of pursuing its task of reconciliation. Geneva herself, as the headquarters of the Red Cross and the Prisoner-of-War Agency, seemed a fitting symbol for this work of reconciliation. This is the likeliest explanation for the choice.

The most serious question the founding of a League of Nations raised for Switzerland was whether she should maintain or abandon her position of neutrality. Recognition of Switzerland's perpetual neutrality by the great powers dated back to the 1815 acts, so it was reasonable to wonder what would become of it now. Would the new treaties weaken it? Did the League of Nations, whose aim was the coalition of peaceful nations against those which disturbed the peace, preclude the very existence of perpetual neutrality?

A movement began among certain French Swiss intellectuals favouring the abandonment of neutrality. But the mass of Swiss people saw neutrality as their best guarantee of independence. The Federal Council was anxious to placate popular feeling on this point, because it feared that otherwise the people would settle for a neutrality which assured them of peace, and refuse even to consider exchanging it for a newer institution whose aims might be the same but whose effectiveness was as yet unproven. This is why the Federal Government's chief concern, during the spring of 1919, was to get the powers to confirm Switzerland's perpetual neutrality. It even went to the lengths of sacrificing important interests to achieve this end.

In the first place the Federal Council agreed to renounce the dispositions in the treaties regarding Northern Savoy's military neutrality. The right to occupy this territory in the event of war, conferred by the Vienna and Paris treaties, had originally been thought of as a duty for Switzerland and a guarantee for Sardinia in return for the cession of certain territories. But Switzerland had always refused to exercise this right during the nineteenth century, even when it might have been profitable to do so, as in 1848 and 1859.

After Savoy became French this right ceased to have any point or value for Switzerland. But it represented a claim on the territory and the Federal Council felt justified in asking for a positive advantage in return for surrendering it. This was recognized by France when she promised to support the move to retain Switzerland's perpetual neutrality.

Unfortunately, negotiations did not end there. France dragged the question of free zones into the matter of Northern Savoy's neutrality and tried to get the powers to authorize the suppression of these small zones resulting from the treaties of Paris and Turin. In this the French government was seeking to consolidate the measures it had taken along its political frontiers during the war, and which it had adhered to ever since in spite of the Federal Council's protests.

Switzerland successfully opposed this move and the proposed French wording was altered.

The revised draft, Article 435 of the Versailles Treaty, was completed by an exchange of notes between Switzerland and France. The Swiss note of 5 May, anterior to the communication of the treaty to the German delegation, stated the Federal Government's adherence to Article 435 under certain conditions which were contested in the French note of 19 May. Both notes were inserted into the treaty and the result was protracted litigation.

The Versailles Treaty contained other dispositions affecting Swiss interests. It nullified the Frankfurt Treaty, Article XI included. Article 354 and those following it revised the agreements controlling the navigation of the Rhine. Switzerland was allowed to send representatives to the Rhine Commission but she failed to obtain assurances that the river would be kept open for navigation as far as Basle. Finally, Article 374 permitted the abrogation of the 1909 Gotthard Convention.

The Versailles Treaty had scarcely been signed when a new territorial question cropped up along Switzerland's frontiers. The dismemberment of the Austro-Hungarian empire, decided upon by the Allies during the war, had never met with general approbation in Switzerland. Switzerland had had no cause for complaint about her relations with the Viennese Court for a long while back, and she had no particular reason for wanting to see it dissolved. Moreover, Swiss public opinion was anxious lest the dissolution of the Dual Monarchy should lead to Austria uniting with Germany. The Swiss did not want to see one of their neighbours disappear, only to increase the mileage of their common frontier with another, more powerful one. Federal Councillor Motte declared in an official speech that such an eventuality would alter the balance of power along Swiss frontiers and affect the country's vital interests.

On 3 November 1918, the Vorarlberg proclaimed its independence. During the winter a movement started up there pressing for unification with Switzerland. Despite the difficulties of communication in snow-bound mountainous country a petition collected thousands of signatures. On 15 March 1919, the National Assembly, recognizing the force of this movement, decided to organize a plebiscite, held on 11 May; 47,208 votes opted for union with Switzerland and 11,248 against. All the communes, with two exceptions, yielded majority votes—overwhelming in most instances—in favour of unification. The opposition came chiefly from Austrian functionaries. The indigenous population was almost unanimous.

The head of the Vorarlberg government, Dr Ender, went to St Germain with the Austrian delegation to present the case for unification. After the leader of the Austrian delegation, Chancellor Renner, had prevented him from making direct contact with the Allies, Dr Ender decided to leave St Germain.

On 10 August 1919, large demonstrations were held in the country during which Switzerland was generally acclaimed. The people of the Vorarlberg decided to address themselves directly to Clemenceau, on 17 August, in a telegram signed by Pirker and Neubner.

The telegram had some effect. The Conference's Territorial Commission discussed it and decided to organize a plebiscite in the Vorarlberg. The wishes of the country seemed on the point of fulfilment. But now the Federal Council stepped in and swung the balance in the opposite direction.

The aspirations of the people of the Vorarlberg did not meet with unanimous approval in Switzerland. Although a sector of the press came out in favour of unification, there was some opposition among the agrarian population, afraid of the competition of Vorarlberg agriculture, among the radicals, afraid of the influence of a Catholic population, and in French Switzerland where the people of the Vorarlberg were unpopular because they spoke German, because they had formerly been Austrian and had fought against the Allies.

The Swiss government, unofficially consulted on several occasions, refused to take any active interest in this affair. Once again, as in 1870, it acted as if the Federal Constitution gave it the right to interpret the people's wishes in advance and take negative decisions on territorial issues without referring them to the sovereign power.

The powers concluded, in the circumstances, that there was no reason why they should be more attentive to Swiss interests than the Federal Council and they incorporated the Vorarlberg with Austria, against the almost unanimous wishes of its inhabitants.

3. *The Postwar Period*

When peace was concluded, after a war so hideously destructive of men and materials, Switzerland shared the illusions of the rest of Europe. She believed herself at the start of a period of great prosperity, where the only check to public purchasing power and industrial production could be a shortage of manpower or decreased productivity.

This was in fact the picture during 1919 and 1920. Prices went up, and salaries with them, an eight-hour day was introduced with the bosses' approval. No sacrifice which could check the progress of Bolshevism and provide industry with the manpower it needed was too great. Suddenly, in the spring of 1921, everything changed and one of the most desperate economic crises in history hit the country.

The crisis, which had several points of resemblance with those which had occurred after all the major wars in the past, had a triple cause.

The first was the general crisis sweeping across Europe. The war had given an extraordinary impetus to industry everywhere. Europe had greatly increased its productivity. The other continents, deprived of European products for five years, had done likewise and stopped importing Swiss manufactured goods. So European industry found itself with considerable production capacities and export markets which had either shrunk or been closed altogether. In selling less Europe found itself unable to buy; and being unable to buy, it could not sell.

The second contributory factor was the unbalanced state of foreign exchanges. As long as certain neighbouring countries were living on inflation, their cost prices were much lower than Switzerland's, which made competition in foreign markets difficult.

The third and last cause was the need for Swiss industry to re-adapt to the situation of the market. New frontiers had been drawn up, new countries created, new customs barriers imposed; the old commercial patterns were shattered. Besides, Swiss industrial installations had been developed in haphazard fashion during the war. It was now necessary, under the most inauspicious circumstances, to transform industries geared to war production into peacetime concerns and find new outlets for them.

These problems were not peculiar to Switzerland but they hit her harder than any other country because of the proportionately higher number of inhabitants employed in her industry and because of the vital importance of exports to her commercial activities as a whole. The remedies designed to improve matters only made them worse. The other countries closed their markets to Swiss products while the Swiss authorities reluctantly imposed higher import duties and restrictions in order to preserve the national market for Swiss industry.

Economic nationalism and protectionism throughout Europe only aggravated existing problems. For a country like Switzerland, whose home market is tiny and which lives by her exports, these methods were bound to be fatal. In our era of mutual interdependence, it is impossible to secure the economic independence of any country, however big or however isolated. But it really is futile to seek economic independence for a country whose prosperity entirely depends on the international exchange.

The economic crisis had the usual consequences in the social and political spheres. The first was unemployment; the number of unemployed rose in 1922 to more than 130,000, which, together with their families, was almost a fifth of the total population and an even higher proportion of the urban population.

In a society like Switzerland's, unemployment is an extremely serious matter. When industry was still relatively recent, and the urban workers still felt close to the land, urban unemployment simply diverted more manpower to the countryside. But this was no longer the case. Peasants and workers belonged to completely separate classes. The unemployed, whom the economy could not use, had to be supported by the community. All the countries in the world, whatever their political regime, were obliged to maintain men like these, who wanted work but could not find it, at the expense of the State. The result was that the effects of unemployment, a new form of war wastage, were not felt by the unemployed alone but by the entire population.

If the world believed that it would be able to spend money during these years without regard to men and property and then find itself back where it started, it was under a serious misapprehension. If the neutrals thought they could escape the agony and look on serenely while other countries fought, they were still more sadly mistaken. The cost of mobilization in Switzerland was more than a thousand million francs, or three hundred francs per head of the population. She had liquidated her reserves and upset the balance of her economy. She had lost money all round, through the war and inflation abroad, and through the economic crisis and unemployment at home.

The Swiss stock-holders whose securities were depreciating and incomes dwindling; the businessmen whose businesses were at a standstill; the workers whose pay was cut or whose working hours increased; all the citizens whose taxes soared—all these people were badly hit by the consequences of those terrible years. The war devoured the savings accumulated during a century of prosperity by four generations of Swiss.

In the field of diplomatic relations, the three most important issues raised by the first six years after peace were Switzerland's entry into the League of Nations, the zone dispute and the economic alliance with Liechtenstein.

The Federal Council finally succeeded, on 13 February 1920, in getting the League of Nations Council in London to recognize that perpetual neutrality was not incompatible with the terms of the Pact. It rendered assurances, in return, that Switzerland would not evade the obligations resulting from Article 16 of the Pact, where economic sanctions were concerned.

In other words, Switzerland's right to stand aside from military sanctions, and above all prevent foreign troops crossing her territory, was recognized. But economic neutrality, which the First World War had proved to be impracticable, was officially abandoned.

These were the circumstances under which the Swiss people were finally called upon to decide whether or not Switzerland should join the League of Nations. A vote was held on 16 May 1920, and the result was affirmative, by 416,000 votes to 323,000, and by eleven and a half cantons to ten and a half. These figures demonstrate how controversial this issue was.

The Swiss people are the most enlightened people in the world where practical democracy is concerned. But they are, perhaps, less experienced in questions of foreign policy.

As a weak country encircled by strong ones, the Confederation has everything to fear from war. She has a vital interest in furthering, through her participation, all enterprises directed at maintaining peace and organizing international society. Great countries can, at their own risk and peril, afford the luxury of absolute and intransigant sovereignty. For small nations like Switzerland, whose very existence defies the principle of nationality and the evolution of modern Europe, it is better to have a limited sovereignty than to lose it altogether. Far from diminishing the international importance of the secondary nations, the League of Nations offered them, via the rule of unanimity, a way of defending their interests and effective protection against abuses of power.

This is an instance where Switzerland's ideals and interests were in agreement. The League of Nations sprang from the same spirit of international collaboration which formerly gave birth to the Confederation. The cantons came together to defend their independence, guarantee their territory and increase their collective prosperity. Europe's preoccupations were not very different.

The League of Nations was a confederation of nations, still somewhat loosely attached but growing progressively closer. It respected the full sovereignty of its members. It was based on the same political concept which had, throughout the course of history, given birth to Switzerland's federal and cantonal institutions. So one might have expected the country to give an enthusiastic welcome to an organization which was an extension of its own principles.

Nothing of the kind happened. Not only did Switzerland hesitate before joining the League, the decision to enter resting on a small majority vote, but her co-operation was frequently hedged about by reservations. The Vilna expedition, the interpretation of Articles 10 and 16, the international conventions on labour, opium, and so on, all demonstrated how hard the Swiss and their government found it to accept the need for certain sacrifices in the common interest of all nations. On the other hand it is only fair to note that, thanks to Federal Councillor Motta, the Confederation was well to the fore in the field of arbitration and international law.

On 7 August 1921, after various fruitless attempts to persuade France to accept the interpretation of the Versailles Treaty which seemed closest to historical truth, the Federal Council finally decided it was tired of the struggle and yielded. It concluded an agreement which did away with the free zone arrangement. In return France agreed to preferential treatment for products manufactured in Geneva over a period of ten years.

By virtue of the new constitutional article giving the people the right to vote on any international treaties covering a period longer than ten years, a referendum was demanded by 56,000 Swiss citizens to protest against this agreement. This right, which had come into being as a result of the indignation aroused in the country by the Gotthard Convention, was invoked for the first time over a treaty negotiated with France.

The Zone agreement was rejected, on 18 February 1923, by 414,000 votes to 93,000. The Swiss people gave the government to understand, by means of this poll, that they had no intention of bartering permanent rights for temporary advantages which the depreciation of French currency rendered illusory from the start. Until the meaning of Article 435 was established by an impartial lawsuit it was hopeless to try and build a contractual system upon it. Inevitably, one of the parties would consider they had been unfairly done by.

On 10 November 1923, the French government, headed by Poincaré, extended its tariff wall as far as France's political frontier without previously consulting the Swiss Federal Council. The latter immediately protested against these strong-arm tactics which placed Geneva in a highly disadvantageous position, economically speaking. Though it did not succeed in having these illegal measures revoked, it was not averse to signing a new agreement with France, on 30 October 1924, after the fall of Poincaré. The settlement of the legal questions arising from Article 435 was referred to a judicial proceeding and the settlement of the practical issues postponed until the law had been clarified. This had always been Switzerland's proposal, as well as being the one most acceptable to the population of the zones.

The negative decision with regard to the Vorarlberg had left the 13,000 inhabitants of Liechtenstein in a difficult position. Although united to the Austro-Hungarian Empire since 1852 by close economic ties, the principality had always retained its independence in law. After 1866, it refused to make peace with Prussia. During the great war it was a non-belligerent, and did not supply soldiers to the armies of the Empires.

During the first years of peace, the economic and financial ruin of Austria had grave repercussions on the small country of Liechtenstein. Dependent on Switzerland for food imports, the country suffered more than any other part of Austria from the depreciation of the krone.

One day during the year 1920, Liechtenstein businessmen began refusing payment in Austrian currency and insisting on payment in Swiss francs. This move, which spread from person to person, soon involved the whole population and even the Prince's government.

The latter was obliged to enter into negotiations with the Federal Government to regularize the situation. On 29 March 1923 an agreement was signed incorporating Liechtenstein in Switzerland's customs zone, and giving the Federal administration control of the principality's public services. Furthermore, since the League of Nations had refused membership to Liechtenstein, the principality entrusted Switzerland with the task of defending its interests abroad.

This treaty was not materially important. The addition of a population of 13,000 to Swiss economic territory was unlikely to have much influence over the country's future. But it was significant morally because it harked back to the system of alliances which had been Switzerland's traditional method of extending its influence for four hundred years.

The First World War left Switzerland with three great problems to deal with in the social, political and international spheres.

On the political side, two phenomena should be borne in mind, of totally different origins and character—the crisis of parliamentarianism, as manifested in certain neighbouring countries, and the need to re-adapt Swiss institutions to actual conditions.

Anti-parliamentarianism is not a Swiss tendency and has little appeal for them. The attempt to introduce it to Switzerland arose from a confusion of ideas. The Swiss were not familiar with the abuses against which it was directed—the parliamentary system, unstable government, a weak executive or corridor intrigue.

In any case this crisis was short-lived. Post-war periods tend to favour authoritarian government. Populations who willingly entrust themselves to a dictatorship when the problems in hand are too complicated to deal with, tend to swing back to democracy, sometimes through violence, once these problems have been solved.

Switzerland's political crisis was of quite a different nature. Her institutions had in the past, like those of so many European countries, undergone the influence of the individualistic concepts of the French Revolution. The Swiss, unlike the French, had not done with all the intermediary political cells between the State and the individual. This was their salvation. They nevertheless shared in the belief that the will of a nation was the sum of the opinions of its individual inhabitants, and that this could be ascertained by counting votes.

The question is, whether this belief is well founded. Is the will of a nation founded on the opinions of its citizens or the interest of groups? There are few isolated individuals within a society. Individuals represent nothing. It is collective entities which matter—families, professions. The fact that there are more peasants than workers in Switzerland is fortuitous. If there were suddenly more workers than peasants, the will of the country would change. Nevertheless, its real interests, which are permanent, would remain the same.

Democracy, it would seem, is the search for a means of weighing up collective interests, rather than counting up individual opinions.

Democracy, which was going through a critical time in the political field, was nearing the end of the road on the social front. The organization of industry had lagged behind that of the State. Notions of authority and obedience, which characterized the patriciates, still ruled at work. However, the spread of education, the rising standard of living among the masses and the growth of trade-unionism, all pointed to a need for certain reforms in the management of industry. One cannot raise the standards of living and education of a population during a whole century without accepting the logical consequences of such a policy.

On the international front meanwhile, the world appeared to be locked in a contradiction. Realities moved in one direction and ideas in an opposite one. Economic needs forced governments to become more and more internationally minded. Peoples became more dependent upon each other day by day and were obliged to search for a joint solution to the problems confronting them. The League of Nations was the expression of this need.

But men failed to recognize this. Nationalism, which the war had frustrated, surged up around and in Switzerland and began a desperate struggle against the realities which it did not yet understand.

These nationalistic movements would ultimately be crushed. Facts always triumph over ideas. But the struggle would halt world progress in the meantime. Surely Switzerland's role, having acquired six centuries' experience in these matters, is to show other peoples the path which leads through international co-operation to the formation of a Confederation of States and a federative State, or in other words an increasingly perfect United Nations?

Appendix

At the request of my colleague, Georges-Henri Martin, I have undertaken to write a chapter covering the period between 1928 *and the present day as an appendix to this* History of Switzerland. *I have done so with a feeling of gratitude and reverence towards the great independent journalist and clear-sighted historian, William Martin, who guided my first steps in our common profession in* 1929. *I hope to remain faithful to the spirit which animates his work and to his own teachings, and I trust I have not been unworthy of this fine and challenging task.*

Pierre Béguin

Switzerland since 1928 by Pierre Béguin

1. *Remarkable Material Progress*

Over the past thirty to forty years Switzerland's economic situation has developed in a truly spectacular fashion. There was a time when the study of statistics led certain observers to conclude that it was embarked, despite its lack of natural resources, on a steady and a triumphant journey towards material prosperity. There seemed no limit to its possible expansion, even over-expansion. The alarming consequences of the 1963 inflation forced people to take a more realistic view of the situation. Nonetheless, remarkable progress has been made.

In 1930, Switzerland's population was just over 4 million. Eleven years later, it had increased by 200,000. In 1950, helped by the high birth rate of the war years, it had risen to 4.7 million inhabitants. The most recent census, in 1960, shows that it has risen to more than 5.4 million, a jump of more than fifteen per cent in ten years. And these figures do not include the foreign seasonal workers, who arrive in tens of thousands year after year to work in the building trade, agriculture and the hotel industry. At all events, it is thought well within the bounds of possibility that the total population of this small country will have reached or even topped the ten million figure by the end of the century.

Over the same period Switzerland's foreign trade has developed at a rate exceeding all expectations. In 1929, the last year of prosperity before the economic crisis, Swiss imports cost

2.7 thousand million and her exports fetched 2 thousand million francs. In 1964 these figures were, respectively, 15.5 and 11.4 thousand million. Even taking the devaluation of 26 September 1936 into account, and the general rise in the cost of living, which had almost doubled, the fact remains that national production had increased by 150% since 1938. To quote a typical instance—in the years before the Second World War Switzerland exported from 12 to 17 million watches annually. By 1964 this figure had reached the record total of 34 million. Another telling example: the port of Basle handled merchandise equivalent to 187,000 ten-ton wagons per annum immediately before the war; in 1963 this figure had reached 828,000. Production of electrical power almost tripled during these thirty years, which went a long way towards easing the political and economic dependence weighing on the country at the time when Switzerland relied on Germany for its coal imports.

The national income, under 9 thousand million in 1938, was nearly 46.5 thousand million twenty-five years later, which represents—taking the rising cost of living into account—a real gain of more than 120%. The population's material welfare had greatly improved. In 1930 for instance, the Swiss placed 300 million francs in insurance premiums in the hands of private insurance companies. By 1963 this figure had risen to 2.2 thousand million, and this figure does not allow for the 1,100 million realized annually by obligatory pension and life insurance policies, or the 160 million in benefits in the form of fiscal receipts. Nor does it allow for the sickness benefit scheme, introduced in 1960, which absorbs an annual sum of 200 million. And we should not forget—another test—that between 1930 and 1964, the number of automobiles in circulation rose from 60,000 to 780,000. In other words, there was one car to seventeen families thirty years ago, whereas there is one car to two families now. The number of motorcycles, mopeds and scooters rose from 46,000 to 450,000 over the same period.

2. *The Economic Crisis*

One might suppose that Switzerland, in achieving results like these, must have benefited from exceptionally favourable circumstances, above all from a long period of international peace. Yet this leap forward was checked at the outset by the world economic slump which did not hit Switzerland till three years later, around 1932 and 1933, and whose effects were still felt in 1939. Then it was brought to a complete halt by the Second World War from 1939 to 1945, years during which Switzerland was forced, through lack of adequate imports and exports, to develop her own resources and make the most—albeit in the most artificial manner—of every means of feeding her population and creating work for all. In fact, 1930 marked the end of a period of noticeable prosperity. Fifteen difficult years were to follow. The return to prosperity is a post-war phenomenon. It did not begin until 1945, when Switzerland drew full advantage from the 'miraculous' immunity she had enjoyed during the war which had left her production apparatus intact and allowed her kinetic energy to expand quite spontaneously.

The economic crisis of 1931 and the ensuing years did not merely halt the country's industrial and economic development. It also led the country's general policy into quite new channels, channels from which it has never been able to free itself completely since. Above all, it changed the Swiss people's way of thinking, and their traditional view of the role of the State.

Before 1930, the idea that the State should rush to the rescue of private banks which had crashed or got into difficulties would have struck everyone as highly improper. Nevertheless, while the large banks held firm and the small private banks kept going thanks to their traditional rules of management, which were models of prudence and wisdom, various public loan-societies of middling importance had been founded which, in the euphoric atmosphere of the great American speculative boom, had embarked on hazardous investments. They were helped to the tune of millions—not always successfully—because the country's financial credit must remain intact, and—more important still—the State took upon itself, at a time when unemployment was reappearing and incomes dwindling, not to abandon the investors to their unfortunate plight. By the same token, before 1930, no one would have thought of taxing the State with the responsibility of setting to rights an industry threatened by a production and export slump; yet this was what happened with the clock and watch making industry which received its first statute of general organization very early on, in September 1931; the same thing happened again when the State, anxious to prevent new competitors starting up in the midst of the depression, issued laws prohibiting the opening of new commercial enterprises or the expansion of existing ones, as for instance in the heart of the footwear industry and in the large stores and chain stores, in this case with the idea of protecting the small shopkeeper. Likewise, it was a new departure to give the State powers to share, with industry, the financial risks inherent in exporting to countries with a reputation for defaulting on payments, or whose currency was unstable. And it was an innovation, yet again, to abandon the traditional free-exchange policy, and authorize the government to restrict imports and arm itself against the countries where traffic in payments was regulated by adopting the same methods: compensation, quotas, clearing, etc. A man like Schulthess, presiding genius of the Swiss national economy from 1912, was able to make the best of this situation without too much difficulty because he was first and foremost a pragmatist. His successor, Hermann Obrecht, however, felt less at ease in a situation which required him to legislate and govern rather more actively than the constitutional norms allowed for. Therefore, while continuing to act and take whatever precautions seemed necessary, he devoted the bulk of his time to an attempt to put the fundamental law of the State in step with modern times. Though he did not have time to achieve all this, the influence of his thinking can be seen in the new Constitutional articles, passed in 1947, which bear the imprint of the depression and the war.

This crisis was at the root of another, much more important, development. There were many influential men who suggested, in accordance with time-honoured economic theories, that the depression should be allowed to develop till crisis-point was reached, with the idea that the task of setting the economy back on its feet could then be left to the free play of economic laws. This was the time when there was much talk of deflation, austerity, cuts in wages and salaries, largely due to the influence of Jean-Marie Musy, who was then in charge of Federal finances. Of course, aid had to be given to industries to prevent them collapsing altogether. Of course, the unemployed needed help to tide them over till better times returned. But it was soon apparent that this policy, quite apart from the fact that it did not seem to be succeeding, was against the wishes of the public as a whole. And this led to two important measures.

First, devaluation. The Swiss franc was devalued in September 1936—a painful step in a country where maintaining the currency at its legal value was seen almost as a moral obligation, but a clearly unavoidable measure if the Swiss were to remain in line with other national economies, and if Swiss industry was to be able to compete on foreign markets. It was a measure which left a large sector of the population—there are more savings books in Switzerland than inhabitants—with very mixed feelings, but it did pave the way for a better understanding of the fact, now generally accepted, that while monetary manipulations may improve matters temporarily, the aim of a nation should not be to maintain the gold standard at all costs but rather to concentrate on a consistent improvement of living standards, of real as opposed to nominal salaries.

On the other hand, it was a great step forward when—about 1934—people realized that pouring out unemployment benefits was not the real answer, which lay in giving every citizen the chance to be active and earn his own living. The psychological and moral problems of unemployment, it was now realized, far outweighed the material ones, and the best remedy for the situation was to pursue an active policy directed towards creating more opportunities for work. The Swiss people's refusal to lower civil service salaries, in May 1933, a gesture of solidarity on the part of all job-holders, and the socialist launching of an *initiative de crise*—emphatically rejected on account of its ideological character and extreme planning—were not inconsistent with the birth pangs of a new policy. It would not be incorrect to date Switzerland's abandonment of Manchesterian liberalism in favour of a liberalism grounded on community interests from this period.

In this respect the economic crisis—together with the Second World War, which will be dealt with later—left a deep impression on the country. It might be described as a turning-point in the national life of Switzerland.

3. *Political Stability*

One might have supposed that major events like the economic crisis and the Second World War and the new ideas and attitudes to which they gave rise would have affected the relations between the political forces in the country. But this was not the case. Switzerland's political map, which is at the mercy of the system of proportional representation, an essentially conservative system which does not allow for strong swings in public opinion, has not undergone any noticeable changes in the past thirty years. Another reason for this is the Swiss people's loyalty to their representatives, whom they freely disown but regularly re-elect. To be sure the Radical Party, the governmental party par excellence under the majority system, had become a party like any other despite its services to the country, and lost its preponderant influence. Its deputation to the National Council has slowly fallen from fifty-cight to fifty-one seats between 1928 and 1963, but it still remains comfortably installed as Switzerland's second largest party where votes are concerned. The Catholic Conservative Party is very solid: though its deputation has only increased by two seats—from forty-six to forty-eight—over the same period, its followers have increased to a much greater extent, which can be explained by the fact that its members, originally from peasant regions, now turned urban workers, have stayed loyal to it. As for the Agrarian Party, it has seen its deputation to the Council drop from thirty-one to twenty-two seats as a result of a 'young peasant' splinter group after 1935, but it seems to be holding its ground at present. A new 'independent' party was formed in 1935 on the fringes of the 'national' or 'bourgeois' coalition, under the leadership of Gottlieb Duttweiler, an exceptionally dynamic personality.

This party holds ten seats in the National Council. Essentially a party representing economic interests, it benefited to a certain extent from the radical losses, but it also helped curb a too-rapid advance on the part of the socialist left-wing. The Labour Party, the country's largest since 1931, has not made as much progress as one might have expected in view of the industrial boom, urban concentrations and increase in the numbers of employed. Between 1928 and 1963 its deputation to the National Council increased from fifty to fifty-three seats. The general situation shows shifts of emphasis rather than real changes.

The composition of the Council of States, while it does not entirely reflect the respective positions of the political forces, because of the way its members are elected, nevertheless shows more signs of change. The Catholic Conservative Party has been in the lead there since 1935, with eighteen members out of a total of forty-five, but the radicals, in the majority between 1922 and 1925, have dwindled to only thirteen seats. The party which gained most from these losses was the Socialist Party. Though excluded from the Upper Chamber between 1928 and 1931, it has since succeeded in getting three of its representatives elected. The liberals, meanwhile—thanks to French Switzerland, where strong personalities can carry the day without a strong party machine behind them—have also managed to gain three seats, although they only hold six out of 200 seats in the National Council. This disposition of political forces has undoubtedly encouraged the Council of States to pursue a moderating role, to become a gathering of eminent men rather than an assembly of politicians. This political prudence has shown itself too in the silencing of certain voices—particularly clamorous on the political left—calling for diminished powers for the Helvetic senate, and even for its suppression. This move was soon quashed and the bi-cameral system, the authentic expression of federalism, no longer seems threatened.

Such political stability is doubtless due to the regime's skill in surmounting problems arising from the economic crisis, and the still more formidable ones—since national independence and life itself had to be kept going behind tightly bolted frontiers—arising from the war. These events did not leave a legacy of bitterness or rancour. None of the parties in power could be accused of incapacity or disloyalty. It is noticeable, too, that there were few scandals during these troubled times; a few irregularities perhaps, on the part of officers in charge of interning foreign prisoners during the war, of entrepreneurs entrusted with the building of fortifications and of certain parties benefiting from the subsidies to viticulture. There was also the Mirages affair, to which we shall refer later. But none of these were of a calibre seriously to undermine the regime.

The growth of the Socialist Party was a determining factor in maintaining this stability. For a long time, by virtue of its revolutionary theories, loyalty to the ideal of dictatorship by the proletariat, and profound anti-militarism, the Socialist Party remained on the fringes of Swiss politics. It was avowedly an opposition party and the outbreak of the general strike of 1918 provoked by some of its leaders was a serious indictment of its political responsibility. But the threat of Italian Fascism, plus the far more serious and direct menace of Hitlerism, combined to achieve its conversion. By slow stages, implicitly at first and then openly, the party subscribed to the major principles of liberal democracy and approved the national defence measures. After 1936 the Socialists became a party like any other. Its new programme even goes so far as to recognize the virtues of private enterprise and, while it may call for more planning, it does not advocate systematic nationalization or more State interference in the economy. It is a frankly reformist party, scarcely surprising in a country where upward social mobility has taken any real sting out of the term proletariat. It no longer stands aloof and is no longer kept in political quarantine. Thus, while the left wing may continue to alternate between opposition and participation, Swiss political life presents an unusual picture of majority and opposition parties with very flexible lines of demarcation between them, where all the parties, with the exception of the extreme left wing, play the game according to the same rules. During the last few years the only real differences and clashes between the left-wing moderates and the centre and right-wing parties arose over military questions, the rising cost of the national defence budget and the prohibition of atomic weapons.

One other cicumstance has contributed towards this astonishing political stability. Over the past thirty years, Switzerland has seen more and more ideological debates yielding to the pressure of professional and economic interests. The parties still have their doctrine, ideas, tendencies, and an ideal to which they subscribe. But in order to stand a good chance of being elected a candidate needs another string to his bow: he must represent a particular social milieu, a trade association, an association representing employers, workers, artisans, agricultural or business interests. The pursuit and furthering of sectional interests is more important now than political discussion as such, and the country's political organizations depend far less on a political programme or an ideal conception of society than on the practical necessities of sound economic management for their inspiration. This development is not without its dangers, in the sense that the political parties do not stand for themselves as much as for certain great economic associations like the *Vorort* for industry and commerce, the Union for Arts and Crafts, the Peasants' Union, the trade unions, and so on. Were it not for this split between political appearances and professional realities, there would not have been such a repeated demand, in many different quarters, for an economic chamber where the various interests could fight it out on the sidelines of political power itself which would sit in arbitration over the disputes. Meanwhile, the fact that none of the parties coincides with a particular sector of society—that the Socialists for instance do not have a monopoly of the workers' votes or of trade unionist support, that workers and employed are found among Radical and Catholic ranks, that peasants are not all Agrarian but often Conservatives or Radicals, that artisans are scattered through all the so-called 'national' or 'bourgeois' parties—all contribute to the spirit of collaboration shown by the various parties at the parliamentary and even governmental levels.

From this point of view, the changes which have taken place in the composition of the Federal Council itself are highly indicative. From 1919 to 1929 it was composed of five Radicals and two Catholic Conservatives and thus represented a national coalition with radical leanings. In 1929, the need to strengthen their ranks against the Socialist left, still hostile to national defence schemes and only partially in sympathy with the country's democratic institutions, led to the appearance of an Agrarian, Minger, within the Council. After that the Confederation was governed by a tripartite coalition with radical leanings. But in 1943, thanks to the Socialists' impeccable loyalty in the face of external dangers, and by reason too of the left's increasing influence in cantonal governments, the Radicals gave up one of their seats to a Socialist, this losing control of the government. This formula (three Radicals, two Conservatives, one Agrarian and one Socialist) lasted for ten years. When Max Weber, Socialist, retired from office in 1953 after the people had rejected his financial and fiscal programme, his place was taken by a Radical, thus re-introducing the formula the Council had known between 1929 and 1943. But this was only for a year. Since 1954, Radicals and Conservatives have both held three seats, with one seat apparently permanently in the hands of the Agrarian Party. But everyone realized that this was only a temporary disposition of strength and that the time was rapidly coming when power would be divided equally between Radicals, Conservatives and Socialists, who had openly declared their intention of returning to the Federal Council with, not one, but at least two seats. This happened in December 1959. Since then the four chief political parties in the country have shared the responsibilities of executive power according to the rules of proportional representation: two Radicals, two Conservatives, two Socialists and one Agrarian. This is something of a departure from Swiss tradition and the teachings of experience, which demand that the executive be controlled by a coherent group. But it is an innovation which suits a State whose first aim and even duty is the wise furthering of collective interests.

By the same token, it is worth noting that in several recent governmental elections, many well-known politicians put forward as candidates by their parties were rejected, and men chosen in their stead who were not particularly distinguished by the colour of their political beliefs, but struck the electorate as qualified—because of their technical expertise, independence of character, or moral and intellectual pre-eminence—to deal intelligently with the major problems confronting the country, which were the problems of a society in the throes of transformation.

Thus, from the point of view of personal qualifications the level of the central government has remained consistently high. This is a reassuring and fortunate circumstance. It proves that Parliament goes about one of its most important tasks—the election of members to the Federal Council—with discernment and success. But it should be noted that the current distribution of seats between the parties, the famous and to some people definitive and even sacred formula of 2-2-2-I, is beginning to incur increasingly outspoken and persevering criticism and objections. In 1965, when a replacement had to be found for the outgoing F. T. Wahlen, it became clear that his successor had to be a Bernese and an Agrarian. This was no reflection on the personal qualities of Rudolf Gnaegi, but it was evident that the freedom of choice of the principal electors, the members of the Federal Assembly, was irksomely restricted. One deputy without party affiliations, a man of unorthodox and non-conformist views, publicly protested against the almost automatic nature of this election which, in his view, gave more weight to the decisions of a party committee than to those of the National Council or to the assembled Council of States. While taking into account the extremist nature of his arguments, it must be admitted that his views were favourably received by a large section of the population. This should be sufficient proof that the political composition of the Federal Council and its very necessary internal cohesion have become the subject of ardent debate.

This would probably not have happened if the 'Mirages' affair had not erupted eighteen months earlier, with national repercussions which have not yet been smoothed over. This unfortunate business—which some people tried to blow up into a scandal, quite wrongly, since no suggestion of dishonesty could be imputed to anyone involved—focused the country's attention on a series of facts which several observers of Swiss political life had already remarked on, but which the population as a whole had refused to acknowledge. These are the essentials. The army high command, in this case the chief of the Military Department and the National Defence Committee, proposed to buy a hundred aeroplanes of the French Mirage type. The Federal Council, then the Chambers, raised the necessary funds, 870 million francs, a considerable sum. Three years later, Parliament was asked to increase this sum to 1,350 million. The surprise this occasioned was proportionate to the figure. The deputies objected. They insisted on knowing the reasons for this spectacular increase, in detail. A committee of three technical experts was appointed and set to work. Without waiting for the results of their investigation, the Chambers elected a Commission of Enquiry, presided over by National Councillor Furgler, of St Gallen, a Catholic Conservative. The Commission pursued its investigations and interrogations with a speed and dispatch to which Swiss political life is not accustomed. And finally the facts came to light.

The general rise in price was obviously the most important question at issue. It transpired that the original estimate had been fixed on somewhat offhandedly by the top army officials who agreed that they would raise the money, as had often been done in the past, by an ulterior request for supplementary funds which would be raised by mobilizing the bourgeois groups against the socialist opposition, still suspected of anti-military tendencies. Next, the army technical experts, anxious to perfect the type of aircraft chosen, had requested so many improvements and modifications from the makers that they had run through the allotted funds to purchase an aeroplane fundamentally different from the one originally chosen and approved. They had known all along that the bill was getting larger and larger, but had not bothered to calculate the exact cost of the operation or, still more important, to obtain the extra funds involved from the authorities. Had they been allowed to persevere in this policy the final bill for 100 Mirages would not have been 870, or even 1,350 million, but two thousand million francs. What made matters worse was that the officials responsible for the undertaking from the start had been guilty, at the very least, of negligence. Instead of insisting on a stage by stage report, they had entrusted and more or less delegated responsibility to a subordinate service. Neither the Federal Council nor the military committees of the two legislative Chambers had been kept fully informed of what was going on. Finally, the Furgler Commission fixed on a compromise settlement which cannot have pleased them much: the number of aeroplanes was reduced from 100 to 57, and the necessary credit cut from two thousand million to 1,750 million.

This affair was pregnant with consequences. To begin with, it came to light at a time when there was a growing feeling in the population that Switzerland's military expenses were exorbitant, and that they were not justified by the international situation or the balance of strength between the great powers. This, too, at a time when the country was faced with the need to make massive investments to build motorways, develop scientific research, expand the universities and train a numerous and well-qualified élite class for the future, to take measures against water pollution, to develop the country's amenities, to launch a programme for producing nuclear power, among other things. At the same time there was indignation in parliamentary circles, where it was felt that they had not been in a position to exercise their right to control governmental activities. They went so far as to demand an extension of these rights, even if it meant breaking with the tradition which had always allowed considerable powers to the Federal Council. The latter was criticized for a lack of unity and allowing too much autonomy to the seven ministerial departments without attempting to co-ordinate their activities sufficiently. It was generally admitted that the collegial system did not work as well as it had once done. The crisis reached such a pitch that it would be impossible today for William Martin to write of 'the Federal Council's moral ascendancy over Parliament', a factor which he held to be essential to the proper functioning of the Swiss State. He would no longer be able to claim that 'the Federal Council, which is not controlled and cannot be dissolved, enjoys almost absolute power' though he might have reminded them that 'the Council is king so long as it is unanimous'. This authority of theirs, a distinguishing feature of Swiss democracy, and a counterweight to possible parliamentary excesses, had been thrown into disrepute. At first, when the crisis first erupted, the deputies started by claiming these extra powers for themselves, thus giving themselves the right directly to control the administration, which is an absurdity since the administration is controlled by the Executive and Parliament's role is to control the administration of government, which is quite a different thing. But, after a period of re-appraisal, the more clear-sighted people concerned began to cast around for ways of restoring the authority and internal cohesion of the Federal Council. Suffice it to say that the formula 2-2-2-I came under discussion once again. Some people have suggested that, in order to arrive at a more flexible and effective formula, the number of departments should be increased from seven to nine, or even eleven, and this idea seems to be steadily gaining ground. Others make the reasonable suggestion that the Federal Councillors should re-organize their working methods, delegate the onerous task of settling hundreds of petitions to the sort of juridical administration which Switzerland still lacks, surround themselves with a cabinet of colleagues, create a special department in charge of co-ordination, and thereby restore the authority and prestige of the Federal Chancellery. At the time of writing, the beginning of 1966, the strongest opponents of these innovations are the Federal Councillors themselves who hold that the present system has proved itself, and see no reason to introduce fundamental changes in their working methods. Nevertheless, an attempt should be made to cut down their administrative work as such, to allow them to devote more time to strictly political tasks. Whatever delaying tactics are resorted to, the problem has been tabled. From this aspect the 'Mirages' affair, painful as it was, did the country a great service by confronting it with problems it tended to overlook.

4. *Extremist Tendencies*

It should be remembered, however, that Switzerland's political stability was frequently threatened by extremist movements which, had they not been rapidly and firmly checked, might well have undermined the country's internal equilibrium and independence. It all seemed quite harmless at first. Certain young people, mostly university students, were evidently fed up and irritated with the regime and the political parties. They felt oppressed by the conformist atmosphere of the country. In their view, Swiss stability was a largely negative posture, incompatible with their yearning for movement, initiative and innovation. The disintegration of the Weimar Republic and the incessant French political crises had the effect of disenchanting them with the values of a liberal democracy. They wanted to go beyond the old struggle between capital and labour, between employers and the proletariat. They were attracted by corporatism, whether Italian or Austrian. They were tempted to subscribe to authoritarian formulas, hoping that a strong regime would put an end to the dullness of Swiss political and parliamentary life.

These young people, some of them following in the footsteps of the traditional parties, others belonging to new groups, got together briefly to attempt to bring about a total revision of the federal constitution. But they were hopelessly defeated, and the Swiss people rejected their proposal in September 1935 by an overwhelming majority. Some of them learnt their lesson from this defeat and returned to the traditional political groups, but others threw themselves into desperate enterprises and, in their disappointment with their own country, turned increasingly for salvation to the new regimes in Italy and Germany. The harm was not great in French Switzerland where National Socialism, with its vague and irrational appeal, never aroused strong sympathies. German Switzerland was more deeply affected. 'Fronts' had been in existence since 1933. They achieved some success, supported in various places by the bourgeois right wing who imagined that Hitlerism was a solid bulwark against communism. But it soon became apparent that the same people who talked so loudly about 'renovating' the country from within, and making it fully autonomous, were rapidly becoming the puppets of a foreign regime. Though they insisted that Switzerland could retain her *Eigenstaatlichkeit*, or in other words remain an independent nation, they equally insisted that she should join the 'new European system' which Hitler desired. From this deliberately ambiguous position to outright treachery was only a step. This became clear during the war when a rash of treasonable activity broke out in a country which had always been able to depend, hitherto, on the absolute loyalty of her citizens. There were cases of espionage, passing on information, denunciations. Political cells were formed, individuals fled abroad or placed themselves at the disposal of governments whom Switzerland had every reason to fear. Thus the military tribunals were led to pronounce nineteen death sentences, of which sixteen were executed, thirty-three sentences to life imprisonment, 202 sentences of imprisonment of varying duration. And though Switzerland was a country where banishment was hitherto unknown, the government was forced, as a warning, to deprive several Swiss nationals of their citizenship. As far as one can judge, these troublemakers were a tiny minority, numerically speaking. But it is easy to imagine what would have happened if the country had been occupied—they would have served as a rallying-point for the politically luke-warm, hesitant, timid or adaptable.

These tendencies were clamped down on. Even at a time when Hitler seemed assured of victory, the political authorities unhesitatingly suppressed the 'fronts', along with any groups which had taken their place, prohibited demonstrations, kept their meetings under surveillance, and blocked their efforts to win back popular support. The government's staunchest ally in this policy was the sane, proud, dignified and inflexible attitude of the mass of Swiss people, who were totally opposed to any compromise with political regimes which would, had they gained control over the country, certainly have undermined or abolished the institutions and liberties they cherished. Italian fascism won some support in the country because it appeared to have genuinely constructive aims at first, particularly on the social front, and because Mussolini, at the height of his power, made a great parade of his pro-Swiss sentiments and seemed eager to avoid being left with a single German neighbour to the north. But National Socialism, almost from the first, was viewed with horror by the Swiss, particularly the German Swiss, who felt themselves cut off from their intellectual and spiritual roots and were appalled at the way in which the civilization they belonged to was being perverted and betrayed. This spontaneous revulsion was as marked among the Swiss socialists whose German friends were being persecuted, as among the Catholics and Protestants whose fellow believers in Germany were confronted by the spectacle of all their most cherished beliefs mocked and reviled by Hitlerian nihilism. This unanimity was one of the cornerstones of Swiss national unity during the Second World War.

While the National Socialist fronts have been completely eradicated from Swiss political life, and no political groups espouse their ideology, communism has shown itself more resistant to the measures taken to suppress it. It is noteworthy, too, that none of the members of the Swiss Communist Party has even been prosecuted by the government for treasonable actions, despite the fact that their first allegiance is to a foreign power. Some of them have been taken to task for unpatriotic behaviour, such as publicly attacking Swiss governmental policy abroad. The Swiss people have a great distaste for anything that smacks of sick thinking, and communism therefore is not discredited to anything like the extent of 'Hitlerism'. And while communism has operated since the First World War in independent cells in many of the large German Swiss industrial cities, for many years it represented the extreme left of the French Swiss socialist party, only splitting off from it at the beginning of the Second World War, and openly revealing its identity at the end of the conflict.

Swiss communism, under active and skilful leadership, has chiefly concentrated on creating an atmosphere of unease, a climate of uncertainty, in the country. Everything has been grist to its mill—anti-fascism, the economic crisis, difficulties abroad and social injustices at home. As a direct result, a whole new body of legislation has had to be introduced to deal with, not the perpetration, but the planning of illegal acts, with illegal intentions rather than actions directly infringing the constitutional code. Hence the law for the protection of public order which was rejected in 1933 thanks to the combined efforts of communists, socialists and fascist 'renovators'. The rejection of the law led to the resignation of its author, Federal Councillor Haeberlin, who was tired of being left without legal means of enforcing constitutional order, and the retirement, for totally different reasons, of Federal Councillor Jean-Marie Musy, who had hoped that this failure would lead to his adoption as leader of an anti-communist movement supported by the traditional right wing and the 'fronts'. Other legislative and administrative measures were brought in for the same purpose; arrests for breaches of national security, the formation of a Federal political police force, prohibition of communist groups in certain cantons on the eve of the Second World War. In each case it was a question of preventing conspiracies against the regime rather than punishing infringements of public order. Thus communism, because of its ideology and methods of achieving power, was almost completely eradicated from Swiss political life by the eve of the Second World War, and again during it. This was doubtless a wise move in the situation Switzerland found herself in during the five years of the war, which was that of a besieged fortress. But these somewhat arbitrary measures were never really popular and aroused considerable unease even among those most vigorously opposed to communism, and with every reason to fear its expansion.

This became apparent after the war, when these various prohibitions were abolished, in some cases by deliberate action on the part of the Federal Council, and in others by a popular vote in the cantons where communism was outlawed. The communists made the most of the chance to appear as martyrs, and their cause was greatly helped by the sympathy which the Russian people's struggle against Hitler, and the French communists' activities in the Resistance, had aroused in the Swiss people. The communists were returned in force in various city and cantonal councils. But their success was short-lived. After what happened in Prague, Korea and Hungary, public opinion right down the social scale swung right the other way, indignant at the machinations of international communism and its Soviet leaders. Communism has been almost entirely eliminated from German Switzerland. It only keeps going in a limited fashion in French Switzerland because of the clevely sustained confusion in the popular mind between totalitarian Marxism, which nobody wants, and the old French-inspired libertarian tendencies which have no other mouthpiece.

Increasingly, in recent years, the Swiss communists have desisted from quoting the Eastern 'popular democracies' as an ideal, and ideological considerations have almost vanished from their propaganda literature. Their efforts are chiefly devoted to backing up their claim to be Switzerland's only opposition party. Their position has been somewhat strengthened by the fact that the Socialist Party, in espousing the government cause, has lost much of its appeal. So the communists demand reforms, and put forward claims for social legislation which, though innovatory, are only mildly revolutionary. This policy has brought them some success latterly in the Geneva, Vaud and Neuchâtel cantons. If a severe economic crisis seemed to be on the way, however, they would certainly instantly revert to their old style of approach.

5. *Profound Changes in the Population Structure*

Switzerland, as we have said, enjoys remarkable political stability despite the threat posed by extremist movements, a threat which any sudden upheaval—another economic crisis, a war—would most likely re-introduce. This stability is the more remarkable, paradoxical even, in that the country has undergone tremendous demographic, social and industrial changes over the last thirty years. Some statistics will be revealing here.

Switzerland, a country built on the reconciling of differences, is understandably proud of the fact that she has managed to induce populations of different race and religion to live together so harmoniously that no real minority problem—with the exception of the Jura affair—has ever emerged. This stubborn preference for national unity over linguistic or denominational loyalties is one of the most valuable constants in the country's history. It is the touchstone of her neutrality, which may be defined as a refusal to seek assistance from powers of the same religious persuasion or social origin. Nowadays, with Europe no longer divided by religious feuds or narrowly based nationalist creeds, one can only hope devoutly that the same reflex would come into play if the country were ever confronted by a choice between East and West, between communism and the free world. From this point of view, neutrality is still the cement which holds the Federal State together.

Nevertheless, Switzerland's denominational balance is constantly changing. Protestantism (57.5 per cent in 1920, 52.6 per cent in 1960) is progressively losing ground and Catholicism continues to make progress (40.9 per cent in 1920, 46.2 per cent in 1960). This phenomenon is accentuated by the influx of foreign workers, two-thirds to three-quarters of them Catholics. A similar phenomenon can be discerned in the country's linguistic configuration: the number of German-speaking Swiss has increased from 73 to 74.4 per cent over the past forty years, that of the French-speaking Swiss has dropped from 21.7 to 20.2 per cent, while in the Ticino things have stayed as they were; but taking the figures for the population as a whole, foreigners included, it becomes apparent that German is on the decrease from 70.9 to 69.3 per cent, French from 21.3 to 18.9 per cent, whereas Italian is making gains—as a result of the influx of workers from the south—from 6.1 to 9.5 per cent. Yet the number of German Swiss living in Latin Switzerland and continuing to speak German increases all the time—13.3 per cent in Geneva, 11.9 in Neuchâtel, 11 in the Vaud region, and 9.4 in the Ticino. If this tendency continues at the same pace, the powers of assimilation of the indigenous populations will be jeopardized and a progressive Germanization of the country could upset its internal balance. This problem may not come to a head for a long time yet, but it is worth noting.

Far more important, from the point of view of the country's political evolution, is the general mix-up of the Swiss population pattern. In 1850, almost two-thirds of the Swiss lived in the town or place where they were born. Because of the freedom to settle anywhere, the speeding-up of transport generally, and the attraction of the industrial centres, this proportion has shrunk rapidly. It was only one third in 1920; since the 1960 census it has fallen to 25.2 per cent. The pattern remains the same at cantonal level. In 1860, 91 per cent of Swiss lived in their native canton; in 1930 only 72.7 per cent, and after the 1960 census—the most recent figures available in this connection—it was only 55.9 per cent. And these figures do not tell the whole story. It is becoming increasingly easy and rapid for foreigners to become naturalized and for Swiss nationals to acquire rights of citizenship in their chosen domicile. This is an irreversible trend which only the nostalgic will bewail, and then without much justification. We mention it here by way of explaining the widespread tendency towards juridical unification and centralizing of power. Under the circumstances federalism and the rights of individual cities have lost much of their meaning and value; with predictable results.

The poulation's economic structure has shown some even more noticeable changes. The exodus of countrypeople to the urban centres accelerates with very year that passes. The proportion of Swiss engaged in agricultural labour has fallen from 25.8 per cent in 1920 to 11.2 per cent in 1960. Large properties of over 30 hectares are getting fewer in number and area, and becoming sub-divided progressively, but it is the smallholdings of less than 5 hectares which are disappearing most rapidly, becoming absorbed into properties of between 5 and 30 hectares, which is the norm today. The small peasant holding is no longer viable. The upper Alpine valleys, in particular, are becoming depopulated as the farmers leave the mountains to go into industry on the plain or take part in dam-building projects. Thus, to quote only two examples, Fribourg, for a long time attached to a stationary rural economy, is now rapidly going over to industry. This is bound to be a severe test of its traditionally conservative political regime. The Valais has jumped three centuries, from its old domestic economy into an industrial civilization, in twenty years. There have been some attempts to check the exodus—such as founding industries in the remoter valleys where the workers can revert to agricultural work during certain seasons of the year—but these appear to be palliatives without much future.

Meanwhile industry goes from strength to strength.

The proportion of the resident population working in Swiss factories and workshops in 1960 was 49.5, almost half. The consistent increase in population figures always benefits industry, so that the number of people employed in this vital branch of the economy rose from 360,000 in 1937, to 727,000 in 1964. The increase was particularly noticeable in this period in the following industries—chemical (12,000 to 37,000), metallurgical (39,000 to 100,000), machine (68,000 to 181,000), clock and watch (37,000 to 63,000). This increase could never have occurred without drawing on foreign labour forces. In August 1964, Switzerland employed 720,000 foreign workers, a record total which dropped off considerably after the Federal government adopted restrictive measures as part of its anti-inflationary policy. All the same 138,000 foreign workers were employed in the machine industry in August 1964, while further large contingents filled the menial or uncongenial jobs the Swiss are increasingly reluctant to take —18,000 in agriculture, where the worker's situation compares unfavourably—as far as man-hours and accommodation are concerned—with the urban worker's, 186,000 in the building trade, 76,000 in the hotel trade, and 25,000 in domestic service. The high standard of public education and vocational training has gradually turned the Swiss into an élite of highly skilled workers, and it was inevitable that labour forces from less advanced neighbouring countries should be recruited to fill the gap. This essential requirement is not always properly understood, with the result that immigrant workers have not always been given the welcome to which they are entitled. They are treated as intruders in some areas, and xenophobic tendencies have increased at an alarming rate despite the eloquent warning conveyed by Henry Brandt's films at the 1964 Lausanne Exhibition. Using foreign workers is not an entirely satisfactory solution, perhaps, but before condemning it, it would be as well to ask ourselves what would happen if deflation or partial unemployment forced the Federal government to send the foreign workers home and oblige the Swiss to return to jobs to which they have become unaccustomed, and frequently despise? And what would happen if a move towards European integration, which did not include Switzerland, should have the effect of attracting the predominantly Italian southern labour force elsewhere, now that it has become an essential part of the manpower which it would be incorrect to call 'Swiss'?

Furthermore, it should be noted that the number of people employed in banking, commerce and insurance has risen from 7.9 to 13.8 per cent, and the number of civil servants, including those engaged in national defence, from 1.4 to 3.1 per cent. In private business, as in State administration, the number of people employed in managerial and administrative capacities grows constantly. This is a world-wide phenomenon. We mention it here only to underline the fact that the 'independents' are diminishing rapidly in favour of the 'dependents', the employers in favour of the employees. This should be enough to explain why the country's general policy is chiefly orientated towards satisfying a need for security rather than an uncompromising defence of individual liberties.

6. *Political Pragmatism*

In spite of this demographic evolution, which could well take on the characteristics of a profound revolution if it continues unchecked, the Swiss people have shown a solid loyalty to both their institutions and their traditional structure. We have already seen, in 1935, how they opposed the plan to revise the constitution. It is unlikely that a similar proposal now would meet with greater success, even though the 'Mirages' affair highlighted the organizational problems of the upper echelon of public administration, and even though certain German Swiss circles seem to doubt whether the technical and specialist society is suited to a long-term regime of direct democracy, taken to its logical extremes. In 1942, the people refused to back a demand for reform of the National Council, and election of the government by the people. The Swiss appear to view their constitutional institutions as somehow untouchable. Until these have been shown to be inadequate, they will never change them. It was typical of this ultra-conservative outlook that representatives who had abused the crisis clause in the economic crisis were sharply called to order in 1939. And while the Swiss may have accepted the government's assumption of full powers during the war, they insisted in 1949 on dismantling these extraordinary measures which the ruling powers showed an inclination to protract after the need for them had gone. But refractory as they may appear to a total application of the direct democracy system, they have consistently refused, since before the Second World War, to submit the country's legislature to a judicial power created expressly for the purpose of determining the constitutionality of the law. The Swiss people, as guardians of their acquired rights, evince the deepest repugnance, apparently, for anything which smacks of juridicism, or the submission of practising politicians to the guidance of jurist theoreticians.

Indeed, the Swiss seem positively fearful of touching existing institutions. The Jura question is a case in point. Since 1948, certain areas in the French-speaking part of Berne canton had been agitating for independence, for their right to split off into a separate canton. This movement aroused some sympathy in the French-speaking cantons, but German-speaking areas hoped fervently that the business would not be taken seriously. Not so much because they felt sentimental about the ancient structure of the canton of Berne, but because they were alarmed at the thought of the Confederation's existing structure undergoing a radical alteration. While the obstinate resistance of the Berne authorities in this affair is open to criticism, the separatists also failed to arouse much sympathy in German Switzerland and forfeited goodwill even in the French-speaking areas, for their exaggerated polemic, their refusal to condemn various unfortunate acts of violence, and frequent appeals to foreign intervention won them a reputation for unco-operativeness and even extremism. Fear of change is so deeply ingrained that women's suffrage—fought for with great persistence by the various women's associations over a number of years; proposed in countless cantonal polls since 1946; rejected at federal level in February 1959 by a two to one majority, but since then accepted in several cantons—has progressed but slowly; the pace nevertheless is now quickening, since the issue will again be placed before the federal electorate in 1971, this time with every chance of success.

The country's political circles are undoubtedly examining their consciences on this issue. They are perfectly well aware that civic equality for men and women must come in the foreseeable future, but they are apprehensive of jumping the gun. Resistance to this measure—as shown by various cantonal opinion polls—comes largely from country people, who uphold the traditional view of marital authority, and from workers who are deprived of the joys and responsibilities in an increasingly dehumanized working context, and wish to preserve their exclusive right to citizenship at least, *vis-à-vis* their families. However, conclusive experiments in French Switzerland have helped dispel most of these anxieties, with such success that Basle-Campagne have partially resolved the problem, Basle-Ville and Zurich are beginning to tackle it seriously, and youth organizations of all political shades actually managed to take it to the level of a popular initiative in the Ticino, without success unfortunately, as it was rejected by a far smaller majority than on two earlier attempts. Finally, while on the subject of tidying the Constitution, the curious fact that no one dares voice the question of the role of professional organizations seems worth mentioning. Their role grows larger all the time. It parallels and even clashes with that of the political parties who are increasingly the mouthpieces for the views, claims and interests of the various corporations. Sooner or later a clear distinction between the function of professional associations defending private interests, and the function of political powers intended to act as impartial arbiters, will have to be drawn. But this is a problem no one, a few theoreticians excepted, has dared to raise. In modern Switzerland, which worships pragmatism and practical efficiency, structural reforms, even when designed to translate a reality into constitutional law, are permanently deferred until tomorrow.

Under the circumstances, it is hardly surprising that federalism has lost ground. Its advocates failed to gain support in 1938, when they tried to oppose the adoption of a unified penal code for Switzerland. Centralization continues to make great progress in the fiscal sphere. It is not accepted in principle, because there is still a strong sentimental attachment to the country's traditional structure. Nevertheless, each time the people are called upon to vote for federal taxes, they tend to accept them for a limited period, with the result that the fiscal system is gradually becoming centralized, balanced by rebates to the cantons whose sovereign rights are to some extent being bought in. This tendency has become such an accepted fact that one wonders whether it would ever be possible to reverse it.

At all events, in 1950, when the Chambers drew up a tentative financial and fiscal statute, designed to allow federalism more scope, it was a total failure. Even at a time of prosperity, with federal returns greatly in excess of the State's immediate needs, and the national debt cut down from the 1946 figure of 8.7 hundred thousand to 5.1 hundred thousand in 1964, it has not been possible to suppress direct federal taxation. The State's expanding role in the economy, the regulation and distribution of subsidies, and the system of social insurance have all helped to weaken the cantons' influence and importance. The general view is that efficiency, the first law of a modern economy, makes this inevitable. And even French Switzerland is no longer the sturdy bastion of federalism she was thirty years ago. An interesting study could be made of the change which has slowly taken place in people's values, and which has perhaps been too readily accepted: in the old days it was understood that all powers not expressly accorded to the Confederation remained with the cantons; nowadays most constitutional innovations have the effect of conceding greater powers to the central government, which then delegates some of them to the cantons to carry out in its name and on its behalf. There is a fundamental difference here.

As we have seen, the Swiss have little inclination for speculative debate, theoretical discussion or abstract problems. They are interested in practical measures destined to improve their lot, organize and stabilize the economy, and achieve a more equitable distribution of the national income. They approve measures like these. But in these matters they are invariably governed by their traditional moderation, wisdom and common sense. Hence the failure of a whole series of initiatives which struck them as being unrealistic, pursuing some ideological red herring, or quite simply demagogic: rejection, in 1935, of a socialist crisis move to introduce a planned economy, rejection in 1952 of a communist move to suppress the turnover tax, rejection that same year of a socialist move designed to step up taxation, rejection in 1946 and 1947 of such vague and impracticable measures as the 'rights of work' and the 'right to work', rejection in 1958 of a plan to make a forty-four hour working week absolute in the Constitution.

Other examples of this common sense and moderation can be found in the failure of certain projects designed severely to restrict economic freedom, where these restrictions could not be backed up with convincing arguments. This was particularly marked after the Second World War, a long period in which the Swiss people accepted a mass of new regulations and prohibitions with remarkable self-discipline and civic spirit. But equally this tendency is a re-affirmation of their profound attachment to liberalism. Thus, in a series of memorable popular votes, the people opted for the removal of restrictions from the transport industry and the tourist industry which wanted to enlarge existing hotels and open new ones, against the introduction of a certificate of competence for certain trades, and against empowering the government to build a second sugar refinery or subsidize a factory for making saccharine out of wood in the Grisons. In each case, the general consensus was that the State was overstepping its mandate, and that private enterprise should take over, or at least assume a leading role in the solution of economic problems. At the same time (1952) however the people approved a legal overhaul of the tobacco industry, because otherwise the workers in the smaller factories would have risked being out of a job. They also, that same year, unanimously passed the law relating to agriculture, because the Swiss peasantry cannot survive without considerable State aid. The same spirit no doubt made them so reluctant to launch a referendum attacking the statute relating to the clock and watch industry. But, to save this industry, greater flexibility in the regulations was obviously necessary, chiefly to encourage a new flow of workers into the trade. This fundamental love of freedom accounts, too, for the difficulties the Swiss authorities run into every time they try to introduce legislation to safeguard public order. The communist and 'frontist' extremists would never have succeeded on their own, even with socialist support, in bringing about the rejection of the 1934 law. This required the active co-operation of everyone who spontaneously and instinctively repudiated the suggestion that political opinion should be a punishable offence in Switzerland. And it should be remembered that all the measures brought in during the most critical wartime and post-war periods—such as censorship of the press, political police, the threat of losing their citizenship for Swiss nationals suspected of disloyalty to their country—were put into force by the government without the active co-operation or express approval of the sovereign. Communism was outlawed in certain cantons but these interdictions were lifted after the war. Finally, when—long after the war ended—the Federal Council decided to sack civil servants and employees in state departments whose political activities cast doubt on their loyalty to these institutions, the measure was received with considerable unease and some protests, even in circles least sympathetic to communism and its activities.

True to this spirit of liberalism and instinctive dislike for anything which seems to encroach upon individual liberty, the Swiss people have always opposed any attempt at over-regimentation. In the middle of the war, when national defence was top priority, they cast an astonishing vote against compulsory military training for the young (December 1940). At the end of the war, Fritz Wahlen proposed to extend the law for compulsory labour. There was such unanimous and spontaneous public protest that any similar projects had to be hastily abandoned. In 1949, a small group of citizens brought about the rejection of a law pertaining to the anti-tuberculosis campaign because its enforcement would have meant permanent invasion of people's private lives. And more recently, in 1957, the people voted against a civil organization for protection against air attack because it involved mobilizing women and most people felt that the citizens' voluntary services would be more valuable than their compulsory integration into a sort of second army. Nothing is more unpopular in Switzerland than State regimentation, even when officially sanctioned by the national interest.

7. *From Liberty to Security*

As William Rappard has shown, the first aims of the federative state created in 1848 were to lay solid foundations for democracy and liberty, create closer ties between the formerly highly independent members of the Helvetic family, unify the principal legislation, and centralize the administration to meet the requirements of a State in the midst of the industrial era, a State with great new national States being formed right along its frontiers.

But after 1874, as he points out, while still insisting on Switzerland's autonomy, strengthening her defences and pursuing a strictly neutral policy, the Confederation's principal efforts went into improving the material well-being of the population. Since then, Switzerland's internal history can be summed up as a persistent effort to better the lot of all its inhabitants. Once the problems of individual liberty had been settled—though it has needed considerable vigilance to prevent them from being taken for granted—problems of social security became the most pressing on the agenda.

This trend has definitely speeded up over the last thirty

years. We saw how the economic crisis of the '30s left a permanent mark on Switzerland's national life: state intervention in the economy, made necessary by external circumstances, became an accepted thing. People recognized, too, that human problems take precedence over purely material ones. One might argue that the Second World War had a less lasting effect on the country, in as much as the Swiss people showed themselves determined, as soon as circumstances would permit, to throw off the controls, regulations and prohibitions willingly accepted so long as the country was marooned like a fortress under siege, in the heart of Europe. Rationing, though exceptionally intelligently organized and motivated by imaginative social considerations, was dispensed with as soon as possible. There was never any question, except in a few muddled minds who saw permanent rationing as a move towards greater social justice, of retaining the system indefinitely. The same applied, as we have noted above, to the compulsory labour service. Nor was there any question of putting a long-term agricultural improvement scheme into practice, and the government's subsequent policy has concentrated on encouraging farmers to balance production through indirect methods like incentives and subsidies rather than by direct orders. Recently, an effort was made to check depopulation of the countryside by encouraging mergers of small properties, and putting modern equipment within reach of peasant purses. The peasants' position has improved considerably over the past few years thanks to greatly increased productivity and a long overdue collaboration between the property owners. Unfortunately, the debt of 8.5 thousand million francs, the highest in the whole world, is a heavy burden on Swiss agriculture and undoubtedly slows down the work of reorganization and streamlining now well under way.

The Second World War, however, created a psychological climate in which it was possible to take certain important steps in various branches of the legislature, whose clauses and terms are all designed to satisfy the general craving for security. Thus the principle of a national pension scheme was entered into the Constitution in 1925. But an act putting it into force was rejected by popular vote in 1931, because some people thought it would involve too much state control, and others too little. A solution was eventually found, and an extensive organization created to deal with the situation in 1947, but this was the outcome of a decision made by the executive powers exercising their wartime full powers: after 1940 non-mobilized workers were compelled to pay two per cent of their income over on behalf of the men who had been called up on active service and the bosses likewise; this is how compensation funds were built up. Once this idea was generally accepted, it was relatively easy after the war to transform it into an old age pension and dependants' scheme; these same funds, increased by subsidies from the State and the various cantons, were used to pay allowances to the aged, widows and orphans. This scheme is still in the development stage. However, it has been able to build up important reserves and increase the size of its funds several times over, thus greatly enlarging the number of its beneficiaries. Recently, the cantons have co-operated by instituting a complementary pension scheme, and their allowances to the less well provided-for have been increased by a large federal subsidy. In 1960 a sickness benefit scheme was introduced, which had been adopted as a constitutional principle way back in 1925. And it is not out of the question that a maternity benefit scheme—the third stage in the state social security programme—will be brought into force in the next few years. A new attitude to social security has come into being. The idea used to be that the State should guarantee a minimum degree of security and the rest was left largely to individual initiative and foresight, but now some left-wing circles are suggesting that Switzerland follow the example of other countries—France and Italy for instance—where public contribution schemes and allowances of all sorts play a much more important part in social security programmes. The Swiss people will be called upon to make an important decision in this respect in the near future. However, contrary to what might have been expected, the state insurance schemes seem to have given new impetus to private saving in all its forms, particularly private voluntary insurance policies, so it seems more than likely that left-wing policy in this respect will not ultimately be successful.

One noteworthy circumstance—on the same day in 1947 the Swiss people adopted the new economic articles of the Constitution, though admittedly by a far less comfortable majority. Had it not been for the economic crisis and the Second World War, or the growing dislike of the free play of economic laws, public opinion might not have been ready to approve what is now the cornerstone of Swiss social policy—any branch of the economy which seems threatened is now entitled to State aid, not to the extent of artificially prolonging its life over a period of years, but long enough to tide it over the worst of an economic crisis, and for its workers to find alternative employment. The same ballot laid down the responsibility for maintaining a flourishing peasant population as one of the fundamental laws of the constitution. But for the self-discipline shown by the peasants during the war, their refusal to exploit the situation by exorbitant price increases, and their consistent efforts—despite long periods of active service when wives and families undertook most of the work—to increase production and compensate for falling imports, in short, but for the town dweller's gratitude for this eminently responsible attitude, agriculture would never have benefited from this statute, which gives very real guarantees to the farming population. And the 1952 legislation which put these principles into effect would never have been carried by such a large majority.

The war left other marks on the social sphere. Legislation designed to protect tenants was introduced at the time of devaluation, in 1936. It was reinforced during the war. It has since been abolished, because this well-meaning regulation, which only applied to the tenants of old apartments, has greatly increased the difficulties in the way of a solution to the general housing problem. Precisely because of state control, the cheaper apartments were not always accessible to the people with least money, young married couples in particular, whereas people in better financial situations continued to reap the benefits. The authorities have gone about reversing this trend by a series of gradual encroachments, allowing certain rent increases year after year, and finally substituting a system of surveillance which prevents abuses, and which is only in operation in the towns where the housing problem has not been satisfactorily resolved. All the same, it looks as if real estate has taken a permanent knock. As far as most Swiss citizens are concerned, the right to draw reasonable interest from investments sunk into old buildings is not on the same scale of importance as the social principle which ordains that everyone has a right to a roof over his head. This change in outlook would not have been possible without the war.

Also a consequence of the war, fiscal policy has taken a quite new direction. The expenses arising from national defence and active service, plus the need to assure the country of adequate food supplies and maintain the essential functions of the economy, all led to the imposition of much heavier taxes: a tax on war profits, a capital levy, a considerable increase in direct federal taxation, a tax on luxury goods. Some tax concessions have been made since the war but the revenue from taxation is still much higher than it was pre-war, as these figures demonstrate. Between 1938 and 1964 the revenue from direct taxation at federal, cantonal and commune level rose from 567 to 5,200 millions a year. Purchase tax meanwhile rose from 373 to 3,400 millions over the same period. The rise in the cost of living (over 120 per cent) and the diminished purchasing power of money are not by any means the only explanations for this development. The increased burden of taxation is very largely the expression of general government policy: social works, insurance schemes partially financed by taxation, economic subsidies are all seen today as a means of adjusting and re-directing the redistribution of national wealth. Furthermore, taxation now provides the government with a means of influencing the laws of supply and demand and curbing inflationary tendencies. Here again, we have an example of a fundamental change in the conception of the role of the state which would have been impossible but for the international events of the past thirty years.

Twenty or thirty years ago, when the likelihood of increasing state control first became apparent, some perceptive observers feared that the State, in assuming so many tasks, enlarging its powers, and fulfilling the general need for security, would become too powerful, to the detriment of all the intermediary units such as family, cantons, communes and professions, leaving the individual dangerously helpless in face of the powers-that-be, and stripped of his sense of personal involvement and responsibility. These fears appear to have been well grounded. The State has certainly gone a long way towards guaranteeing the security of the community as a whole and the political powers—parties, government, parliament—have not always made the imaginative effort needed to popularize less schematic solutions which would have encouraged a sense of individual responsibility and given citizens an incentive to become the architects of their own salvation. It is certainly true that with a bit more initiative and inventiveness the State could have founded its social programmes on the intermediary and traditional bodies—

family, cantons, communes and professions—rather than upon a necessarily anonymous administration.

Nevertheless, by adopting this critical view of the present situation, there is a danger of ignoring one extremely important aspect of it. We have already seen how the Swiss people, just after the war, brushed aside certain anti-liberal proposals, and how they evinced their determination to keep the national economy flexible. There is another factor. This is the immense effort on the part of professional associations and trade guilds to organize themselves into autonomous bodies, without State assistance and without waiting for the government to give their decisions legal weight. No doubt these organizations are tending to re-introduce the closed shop and the old oligarchies in a new form, and restricting competition and freedom in their own interests. The Swiss people grasped this point clearly when they repudiated summary laws against cartels at the beginning of 1958, on the express condition that any abuses committed by these cartels should be checked by a more flexible legislation. This was subsequently put into effect, though without as yet showing any very tangible results. In spite of everything, the legitimacy of professional associations was overwhelmingly supported on that occasion. The average citizen realizes that he has a right to ensure that economic liberalism does not lead to the law of the jungle. He also knows how much the community owes to the various agreements reached—without State interference—between employers and workers' organizations, agreements which have set the seal on a social peace, which found its most eloquent expression in the *paix du travail* negotiated in the metallurgical industry in 1937, a model for many similar agreements. Since then such matters as working hours, holidays with pay, retirements and salaries have been settled more and more frequently by direct negotiation between the interested parties. By making personal contact inevitable, this has helped trade union leaders to keep abreast of the needs of free enterprise and employers' representatives to form a clearer view of the workers' problems. The age-old disputes still crop up from time to time, but we have seen these negotiations between equals maintaining social and economic stability under difficult circumstances, as for instance with the 1947 agreement stabilizing prices and wages. The fact is, at precisely the moment when the State was extending its province, various intermediary units of a new sort have evolved and are now working towards a better deal for everyone thanks to their knowledge of social and industrial realities which no administration could hope to rival.

Once again it was a case of a liberal reflex emerging at a timely moment. There seems little doubt that this innovation will be of the greatest importance as a protection from the dangers of excessive state regimentation. None of this—especially the trade unions' better understanding of the advantages of free enterprise—would have been possible thirty years ago.

At the beginning of 1963, it seemed reasonable to hope that these freely negotiated agreements between professional bodies, with the guidance and encouragement of the State, would provide a useful check to the alarming effects of economic over-expansion and the anarchic investment policy which threatened to plunge the country into inflation. The warning signals were unmistakable and it should have been obvious that, failing a resurgence of public-spiritedness and discipline on the part of those responsible for the national economy, the State would inevitably be forced to take its own measures to stabilize the situation.

This hope was disappointed. Faced with inflation, a steeply rising cost of living, unprecedented quantities of foreign capital seeking investment in Switzerland, and speculation in real estate and building developments reaching scandalous proportions, the Federal Council was forced to act. Its appeals to public restraint and self-control had gone unheeded. It passed two decrees at the beginning of 1964: the first limiting the volume of construction work, the second introducing a credit squeeze. The people approved both measures at once. The first measure was repealed, but the second was to remain in force. until 1967. One way or another, the brake has been applied. Property speculation has been curbed, at least for the time being. The country's financial growth has been slowed down. It is still expanding, but no longer suffering the effects of over-expansion. This is partly due to the two government measures, but still more to simultaneous measures which cut down the quota of foreign workers employed in the various industries. Their numbers are definitely shrinking.

Effective as this policy has been in most respects, it has had two disappointing results. The first is the continued rise in the cost of living and the fact that the country is still locked in a wage-and-price spiral. The other was that it proved impossible to engage the great economic associations in really fruitful collaboration. Prosperity is still so real, and future prospects are so bright, that everyone is intent on protecting his own interests rather than adapting them to the needs of other economic branches or social groups. Furthermore, the Federal Council, the only body capable of inspiring a stabilizing policy and conducting an economic dialogue of this sort, remains extremely sceptical about the real value of such interviews or the need for them. However, it is fairly certain that such a dialogue will eventually take place. Switzerland's ablest and most liberal economists agree that the inflation might have been avoided if Switzerland had got down to some long-term planning in advance. The problem still remains unsolved. Already, faced by gigantic tasks and steadily rising expenses, the government are trying to draw up an investment plan for the Confederation, cantons and free towns. This is an essential move. The funds needed for such projects as building motorways, fighting water pollution, granting federal aid to the universities, encouraging scientific research, developing new sources of power, bringing agriculture up to date, developing the land, building cheaper housing for the less well-off—will have to be spread out over a number of years. In any event, the requirements of State and private enterprise should be reconciled as far as possible, so that the credit demands can be spread out over several years, and the man-power available distributed to best advantage without the need for imports of foreign workers. At present Switzerland's preference for economic liberalism is so strong that the mere suggestion of planning causes anxiety and alarm. But public opinion will change when the present impasse takes a turn for the worse. And that will be the moment to start top-level discussions on economic strategy once again.

8. *The Second World War*

In our broad outline of Switzerland's political development in the preceding chapters we have already touched on various topics related to the Second World War; such as, rationing and the compulsory labour service, the peasants' war-effort, the threat to morale posed by extremist groups, the unavoidable fiscal measures, and above all, the long-term effects of active service on Switzerland's internal development. But we shall have to return to them again to show the conditions under which the country entered, and endured, this critical period in her history.

Luckily, during the years before 1939, the Swiss people had closed their ranks against the menace of National Socialism and the country was united as it had not been for a long time. The threat of totalitarianism hanging over Europe strengthened the people's faith in the fundamental beliefs which had gone to the making of the modern Swiss nation. Thanks to the Socialist left wing's grasp of the principle of and need for a national defence programme, there could be no doubt of the swiss people's determination to defend themselves against aggression. In defiance of their northern neighbours, who wanted the purity and superiority of the German 'race' proclaimed, the Swiss stood by the principle of different races living in harmony and the rights of minorities: the elevation of Romansh to the fourth national language (1938) was done for no other purpose.

The German attempt to put their national culture at the service and under the control of the State led the Swiss government, in defence, to take various steps to protect their own rich and varied culture and ensure that Switzerland's intellectual and spiritual inheritance was accessible to all. The National Exhibition at Zurich, just before the war, is one example. The *Landi* was more than a mere inventory of the country's material prosperity and technical progress—it was an eloquent reminder of the ideals so central to the life of the country and the human society which lives there. All these official efforts and achievements were nothing but the expression of national tendencies at work in a climate of perfect security. It was this which enabled Switzerland to confront the difficult war period with high morale, and cope successfully with the signs of discouragement and vacillation which appeared occasionally later.

No doubt all this went with a mood of insularity which is not without its dangers. There was a tendency in certain circles to believe, rather too readily, that Switzerland could be self-sufficient and had no need of contributions from abroad. This led to 'Helvetism', a movement inspired by many pure and noble sentiments, but which, if practised too zealously, would undoubtedly lead to the impoverishment of Swiss national life. Switzerland, a country founded on three cultures, needs to refer to the source of these three cultures for spiritual and intellectual nourishment. And the fact that German Switzerland is no longer closely linked to Germany, while the Ticino maintains only the loosest ties with Italy, is an alarming one, though readily explicable in the light of the alienation resulting from the war.

The country also made great strides in the military sphere in the pre-war years. The Federal Council had been requesting larger and larger allocations, ever since 1930, for this purpose. Prime mover in this was Minger, Head of the Military Department, who rendered the country an invaluable service by curbing the activities of a blindly pacifist movement, ensuring that the troops were adequately equipped with up-to-date weapons, and extending their training periods. In 1936, despite intervening devaluation, the national defence loan was beginning to show remarkable results. True, many of the defence projects were still at planning stage, or only beginning to be put into effect, at the onset of war in September 1939. And General Guisan could complain, in his final report, that nothing like an operational plan had been available at military headquarters. Nevertheless the will to defend themselves—a wholehearted, positive and unwavering determination—was implanted in the people more strongly than ever before. The moral climate for call-up had been prepared. The same could not be said, as William Martin has pointed out, in 1914.

Moreover the country was not divided by conflicting loyalties as it had been a quarter of a century earlier. The Swiss knew which side would respect their independence and freedom. What is more, in the face of external danger, the country had at last awoken to the need for a strong national policy. The part played by General Guisan, by his personality, convictions and public appearances, was highly important in this respect. He inspired the people with a confidence which no one in Switzerland has ever equalled, and their loyalty remained unshakeable. His declaration on the field of Rütli, in 1940, before all the higher-ranking army officers, of an inflexible determination to resist whatever danger might arise, gave the country a lead and inspiration. No one else could have won approval for the 'national redoubt' plan, which involved the concentration of troops in the Alps, in a position to maintain a corner of free territory. If the country were invaded by powerful forces, it was a position from which her ideals could be preserved, and eventually restored to her.

Equal foresight had been shown in planning the wartime

economy. Obrecht, Head of the Department of Public Economy, had created a militia system instead of a new administrative department to mobilize the industrialists, businessmen, exporters and civil servants responsible for feeding the country and ensuring a fair distribution of available supplies. This organization proved both exacting and authoritarian. It propagated a mass of new regulations and restrictions. It interfered everywhere. But it was efficient, and not just restrictive, seeking to keep the national economy functioning in adverse circumstances rather than merely hedging it round with superfluous regulations. Above all, it served the cause of social justice. Instead of the 1914–18 situation, when the population was divided into a poor class suffering serious hardship and a minority busy making their fortunes, the Second World War was a time of public-spiritedness even in the economic sphere. This fact not only helped keep up morale during the war but facilitated a smooth return to the conditions of normal life afterwards.

9. *The Development of Neutrality*

Switzerland could scarcely claim a foreign policy at all until the First World War. While the balance of power in Europe was maintained and the country encircled by four powerful nations, the policy of total neutrality was relatively easy to pursue—an exclusively military neutrality, that is. It never occurred to anyone that the commercial relations of such a small nation could be interpreted as a gesture of commitment to one or other side in time of war.

Switzerland joined the League of Nations when it was founded. She made various reservations in doing so, limiting herself to applying economic and financial sanctions to countries who violated the Pact, while maintaining her neutrality intact. This was the period of differential neutrality. The step seemed a reasonable one because everyone realized that the League of Nations was a genuine effort to organize international relations within a strict juridical framework, and because the League subscribed to ideas dear to the Swiss: equal rights for small nations, recognition of their sovereignty, the peaceful settlement of international disputes, the illegality of force, and the maintenance of collective security.

Motta loyally supported these principles and this policy for many years, despite the fact that the rule of law did not permit compensation claims on behalf of Swiss who had suffered losses or war damage, and despite the fact that arbitration resulted in a disappointing solution to the vexatious free zone problem. In any event a whole new series of events soon claimed the attention of the men responsible for Switzerland's foreign policy. There was an outbreak of incidents involving Italy and Switzerland: espionage, unjustified arrests, demonstrations by the irredentist party. Swiss public opinion grew indignant. The government showed considerable tact and flexibility in dealing with isolated incidents, but resisted attempts to draw the Ticino into the wake of 'Italianism'. However, a deliberate policy of friendship between the two nations was entered into, and was re-affirmed from time to time. People readily accommodated the view of Mussolini as an adroit politician rather than a megalomaniac, who supported all the different camps in turn, who only paraded his military strength —overrated anyway—to spare himself the necessity of using it, who seemed to entertain genuinely friendly feelings towards Switzerland, and was chiefly concerned, at a time of rising German nationalism, to maintain a balance in Europe and prevent Germany's emergence as the single neighbouring power to the north. These illusions led the country into some uncongenial byways: over-hasty recognition of Italian sovereignty in Ethiopia, and of the Franco regime in Spain, which was supported by Italian troops. It needed the *Anschluss*—which happened on a spring day in 1938 when Mussolini was on holiday and incommunicado—and the attack on France in June 1940, finally to strip the scales from many people's eyes.

The Swiss never entertained similar illusions about Hitler's Germany. Comparable, but more serious incidents, occurred between their respective governments. It was useless for Motta to bring back soothing reassurances from Goebbels in September 1933, or for the former Federal Councillor to engage in cordial talks with Hitler himself in February 1937. No one believed a word these two men said. Besides, the pressure exerted by the Third Reich was much more formidable than anything brought to bear by the Italians in the Ticino. The totalitarian regime to the north was openly trying to stir up support among the Germanic majority in the country. German nationals in the country were organized into efficient Nazi party cells. After Gustloff's assassination, the group previously under his command was limited to a purely local affair, and the Federal Council was pressurized into giving the party's leadership to a member of the German Legation in Berne. This made an already dangerous movement more dangerous still by allowing it to operate under cover of diplomatic immunity. Then, German protests against the critical, indignant and sometimes hostile reactions of the Swiss press gradually took on such a threatening character that the government felt impelled, as early as 1933, to embark on a policy of controlling the press. This started as fatherly supervision, but grew into full-blown censorship during the war. The day on which censorship was first introduced—wisely, the government did not make this public—was the day Switzerland turned her back on the wise view of neutrality as a maxim of the State which does not interfere with the private opinions of individual citizens. A spanner had been thrown into the works.

The affair of sanctions against Italy was a turning-point in Swiss foreign policy. The Federal Council agreed to apply the sanctions, though still believing in Italy's good faith, but in a very qualified form: the sale of arms to either Ethiopia or Italy was forbidden; commercial relations between Switzerland and Italy were not interrupted, but a 'clearing' was set up with the aim of balancing imports against exports so that Italy should not derive any financial advantage from her trade relations with Switzerland. There was no reason why Switzerland should strictly enforce the law where other powers, among them the most powerful in the West, were cunningly circumventing the sanctions while paying lip-service to their underlying ideals. Nevertheless, the disputes arising in the League of Nations committees proved that the Swiss notion of differential neutrality was not accepted by the powers, particularly France. Swiss delegates to the League of Nations were given to understand that while there was no question of involving Swiss troops in punitive actions, the country itself must allow the passage of armies going to the assistance of victims of aggression. This condition was all the more unacceptable in that the League of Nations was showing itself increasingly powerless to enforce the law of collective security.

In fact, the conditions which led to Switzerland joining the League of Nations no longer existed. The sacrifice of certain aspects of neutrality was no longer compensated for by a guarantee of strictly maintained international order. Meanwhile, two of Switzerland's neighbours, Germany and Italy, had left the League, and a third, Austria, was under occupation. It was at this point that Motta decided to proclaim Switzerland's return to total neutrality. He succeeded in getting the League of Nations as well as the two totalitarian regimes to recognize this. Switzerland was back in her pre-1920 situation. This statute, which Switzerland decided upon quite independently, proved extremely useful during the Second World War.

This neutrality rested upon something like equilibrium in Europe, illusory no doubt, but which no one as yet expected to see violated in the most tragic and sudden manner. Things went fairly well during the first few months of the war, until Italy entered the conflict in June 1940. Throughout the 'phoney war' Switzerland, who still had one door to the world open at Gênes, was able to refuse to take part in blockade and counter-blockade measures, and even prevent herself being too badly hit by them. Her right to keep 'normal avenues' of trade open was recognized. She agreed not to re-export merchandise bought from one camp to the opposing one. The authorities' freedom of movement was restricted, but not abolished.

France's defeat completely altered this situation. Switzerland, henceforth, found itself surrounded on all sides by fascist-controlled territory. Germany and Italy had so positioned the dividing line between the two French zones that Switzerland was only left with a narrow loophole through the outskirts of Geneva into so-called Free France for trading with non-Axis powers. The Third Reich was imperious in its hour of triumph. An order was conveyed to the Swiss that all relations with the British Empire must cease forthwith. The Reich had two potent threats up its sleeve for use against an isolated country struggling to survive, to keep up production for the sake of public morale and—most important of all—procure the raw materials needed for its own armament industry. They could cut off coal and iron deliveries and prevent commercial traffic to and from Scandinavia. The price paid for an uninterrupted flow of essential consignments was heavy—credits to Germany, tight control on all merchandise sent via France to the Allies. The British reaction was sharp and immediate. The authorities responsible for the British blockade adopted a hostile policy which they kept up for the duration of the war. Food supplies were now arriving in driblets from the West, and the Swiss were forbidden to build up more than two months' reserves. Even after the tide of war turned, with the United States' entry into the war in December 1941, and the North Africa landings and Stalingrad defeat, by which time Germany was less and less able to meet her obligations and deliver iron and coal against a clearing credit of more than a hundred thousand francs, and the Hitlerian authorities were forced to allow Switzerland more freedom of movement, it was already too late. Great Britain, thanks to American aid, was no longer interested in buying Swiss products or even accepting the credit arrangements which the Federal Council, anxious to be fair, was offering. It must be said that Britain's lack of concern for a small country struggling to preserve its political independence against heavy odds, rather like a besieged fortess, had the effect of increasing Swiss dependence on Germany. This state of affairs took a turn for the worse when Mussolini was removed from power in July 1943, and Switzerland found herself for the first time in her history with, practically speaking, only one neighbour. She had to sit out this encirclement till the day in August 1944, two months after the Normandy landings, when the first American soldiers reached Switzerland's western frontiers.

As Switzerland's military neutrality was never threatened, apart from the dark days of May 1940, and, to a lesser extent, in the summer of 1944, it must be acknowledged that Swiss neutrality was only compromised in the economic sphere. This happened involuntarily, without the slightest connivance, simply because a fortress under siege can only receive food supplies from its immediate neighbours. In fact, neutrality was only just saved. The winning side in the Second World War did not fully comprehend how much moral courage it took to refrain—apart from certain indispensable concessions—from any sign of capitulation. There were long negotiations, at the beginning of 1945, before the Allies were persuaded that Switzerland had never given the Axis powers real or tangible aid. In fact, the country's exports to Germany and Italy, as well as to the countries dependent on them, had totalled 5.3 thousand million francs while their imports had reached 7.1 thousand million. On the other hand, thanks to an infinitely skilful network, it had been possible to supply the Allies—through the Geneva loophole—with goods worth 1.7 thousand million francs whereas imports from Allied sources had totalled 2 thousand million. Was it fair to expect much more of a small encircled country apparently at the mercy of its formidable neighbours?

Switzerland's correct, if not heroic, policy throughout the war has finally been generally recognized and criticisms levelled at the country in 1945 and later have long since been silenced. All the same, the wall of misunderstanding which the Swiss authorities came up against for a time led them to make various gestures of appeasement which were not, to say the least, entirely orthodox or legal: for instance, the mass expulsion of Italian and German nationals who were far from being war criminals, refusal of asylum to political refugees, seizure of German property, and so on. All this is minimal in comparison with the sufferings other nations endured. If this is the price of immunity, it is not exorbitant. All the same, the Swiss policy of neutrality, worthy enough in itself, might have acquired a further moral justification in the eyes of the countries which did suffer had the Swiss thrown their doors open more generously to the refugees, victims of hideous persecutions.

Switzerland was able to resume normal and increasingly confident relations with the Allies fairly rapidly. A proposal to re-establish diplomatic relations with the USSR was rejected in November 1944, which led to the resignation of Marcel Pilet-Golaz, head of the Political Department—who had to take the blame for the unpopular policy of 'possible co-existence' with the Axis, though in reality only safeguarding the country's independence—but this normalization of relations with one of the great Allies finally took place a year and a half later in March 1946.

Post-war, Switzerland has retained its entire neutrality in law. But this is in appearance only. In fact, her foreign policy has developed a more varied and lively character—what Max Petitpierre, the new Head of the Political Department, calls 'neutrality and solidarity'. These are not mere words. True, Switzerland has not been able to join UNO because its charter does not allow neutrality to be practised by one of its members. But she was never eager to join an organization conceived, from the start, as a club for winners. Prudent as ever, Switzerland never felt much faith in an international organization which, unlike the League of Nations, never succeeded even for a few hopeful years in rallying the world around a common moral law, universally practised principles or a system of collective security strong enough to prevent the bending of rules which invariably accompanies relations between countries.

All the same, Switzerland has adopted a broader interpretation of neutrality, and come out of her traditional shell. For instance, she collaborated in the Armistice Commission in Korea, and played a discreet but effective role in the settlement of the Algerian question, proving that she is less afraid of commitment than formerly. Also, since the war, she has played an increasing part in the technical organizations which strive to impose some order and stability on the world. At a time of integration and national re-grouping, Switzerland has realized that a policy of keeping oneself to oneself is no longer practicable. Attached though the country may be to the traditional neutrality which has allowed her to keep out of mortal conflicts for so long (Swiss public opinion seems to be trying to make neutrality a taboo) the country realizes that its future lies in association and collaboration rather than in a touchy sovereignty which is beginning to seem out of date. She sees, dimly still, but more clearly than before, that it will not be very long before she pursues a policy unlike her previous one, even while still maintaining her neutrality. There is already a move afoot to get Switzerland to join UNO. And it is typical that the government should contribute, by means of fairly large credits, to maintaining the military forces responsible for keeping the peace in Cyprus. Only a few years ago it would have seemed unthinkable for Switzerland to send her troops for a task of pacification. But nowadays this suggestion is often mooted, and it seems quite reasonable—which fact alone indicates the change taking place in the Swiss outlook. This will be the fourth re-working of a permanent concept which must have periodic revision if it is to remain a living one. The Common Market and European Free Trade Area discussions are so typical of the new direction of Swiss thinking that they deserve some space to themselves, because their outcome will affect the whole future of the country.

10. *European Integration*

If we are to see this problem in perspective, and understand what it means to contemporary Swiss, we must remember that Switzerland has a vocation, a passion even, for independence. Other nations have sought and found other means of satisfying their need for aggrandizement. The Confederate bond stemmed from the need to defend themselves against foreign ambitions and pressures, and a wish to pool the slender resources of many small States to this end. The desire to live in harmony with each other and build an ever more closely linked national community came later. Since Marignano, still more so after the Treaty of Westphalia, juridically since 1815 and constitutionally since 1848, the Swiss have always seen armed neutrality as the surest way of ensuring, defending and winning respect for their independence. These things are deeply ingrained in people's minds. The tradition of independence is so old and so faithfully subscribed to that it still dictates Swiss reflexes and reactions at national level whenever the problem of Switzerland's right and proper place in the world arises. The country's inhabitants are all the more attached to this policy in that it has been a successful one. It is hardly astonishing that neutrality has an almost sacrosanct quality for many people, who see its simplicity as the answer to everything, or that it should have all too often become a taboo and led to a somewhat sterile intellectual complacency. People are reluctant to abandon a tried and proven formula for something still vague, less clearly defined and full of unknown quantities and potential misadventures.

Certainly the policy of neutrality has been modified and adapted to the changing European situation, which has undergone abrupt revolution as well as slow evolution, and a perpetual revision of its equilibrium. It is understandable that inaction often strikes the Swiss as the highest form of wisdom since this cherished immunity has allowed them to escape the worst of the dramas which have befallen their neighbours. Basically, the Swiss were never deeply involved in these events. While neutrality has needed revision and modification to fit the fluctuations of continental history, its fundamental principle has never really been questioned, even at the time of the League of Nations, because Switzerland's membership of the League did not involve any real or important sacrifices of sovereignty.

From this point of view, European integration poses an entirely new problem for Switzerland, one she has either never been confronted with before or succeeded in evading. If the European countries go further than economic co-operation, progressive demolition of tariff barriers and encouragement of free trade, and create a structure which does away with their old confrontations, and is too closely united to permit war, if they organize themselves politically, the logic of events will lead them from alliance to association, then to a Confederation of States, finally to a Federative State, and a United States of Europe. In this light, it seems to many observers that an irreversible process has been set in motion, though it is now evident—especially after the checks applied by Gaullist policy—that it will take much longer to achieve than the advocates of integration had supposed. This phenomenon is nothing new to the Swiss. This was how Switzerland took shape, with the difference that it took her six centuries of patient effort to achieve what the founders of European integration hoped to bring about in a few years. However, with history accelerating so fast, her slow progress in this respect may be less pertinent than their haste.

The result of all this is that Switzerland will have to embark in the relatively near future on a whole series of agonizing re-appraisals, which she has always managed to avoid until now. The truth is a policy of isolation, even relative isolation, would be catastrophic for Switzerland at a time when all the other nations were uniting, and forging closer bonds between themselves. The problem, as far as Switzerland is concerned, lies in ascertaining whether it will be necessary to abandon the beliefs and principles which have guided her long history in order to escape this isolation, or whether she can still salvage an appreciable part of them.

The notion of European integration was bound to awaken a sympathetic response in the country. The idea of Europe treading the very paths the Swiss had chosen, and followed, for so long, was agreeably flattering. When Sir Winston Churchill chose Zurich, just after the Second World War, to launch his first appeal for continental unity, the Swiss were inclined to see this as a gesture of homage towards the men who created Switzerland. Later, when the first European organisms—the Council of Europe, which Switzerland finally joined after more than fifteen years of doubts and scruples—were set up, cohorts of young Swiss intellectuals flocked to Strasbourg on a wave of enthusiasm, upsetting a few frontier-posts along the way. For some time voices had been heard abroad saying, and repeating, that if Europe—especially now she no longer led the world—wanted to ensure her safety, consolidate her independence and once again play a role commensurate with her past and her civilization, she would have to become 'Helvetic'. The men who spoke these words were generous:

the Swiss were inclined to think them far-sighted as well. For some time past the Swiss too, giving rein to their pedagogic instincts, had been counselling their neighbours to imitate them by banding together in a solidly constructed whole. The application of Switzerland's proven formulas at a European level seemed to them the surest way to guarantee lasting peace and promote closer co-operation. As long as European Federation remained an idea, it was extremely popular in the world's most federalistic country. When the idea began to take flesh, however, and it seemed as if it might be put into effect in the foreseeable future, the old national reflexes came into play again and public opinion grew dubious, if not downright mistrustful of it. Once again there was much talk of neutrality and Switzerland's right to benefit from her own peculiar situation. European reaction to the Swiss attitude, it appears, was one of disappointment and disillusionment. Apparently, while Switzerland can draw on immense moral credit thanks to the many humanitarian undertakings she has engaged in, as well as reserves of genuine friendliness and goodwill, her political life, the principles she stands by, and the complexities of her internal structure come up against a wall of blank indifference. This has been blamed on her lack of public relations. This lack became painfully obvious when she began negotiations with the integration-minded countries of Europe.

Ever since the war, the Federal authorities have shown their willingness to co-operate actively in the sphere of economic and technical collaboration. This spirit of co-operation was only to be expected of a small country whose wealth is entirely derived from her productiveness and inventiveness, whose livelihood depends wholly on her foreign exports and who has consequently made liberalism the first law of her economic life. Her adherence to the European Organization for Economic Co-operation posed no problem. This group of seventeen States agreed to free trade restrictions, cut down or even abolish the quota system, and any other obstacles to the free development of foreign commerce. Political questions did not enter into these proposals, so the problem of Swiss neutrality did not really arise. Moreover, all decisions taken by this organization had to be unanimously agreed upon, which gave the small nations, anxious to preserve their full independence, a comfortable sense of working on an equal footing. Switzerland would have continued to support the organization after its main task had been accomplished if the organization of European relations, meanwhile, had developed along similar lines. She would have wholeheartedly supported a large free trade area. The Swiss government has always maintained that the chief problem in this connection is the organizing of a huge market of 300 million Europeans. As long as there was no question of sacrificing political sovereignty it felt quite happy about the whole project.

It is important to note, too, in this connection, that the Swiss leaders, together with the top men in the national economy, considered it self-evident that Europe would not proceed beyond economic co-operation, at least for a long time, and that political integration was only a very distant possibility. It was therefore agreed, with only a few dissenting voices, that a special study of this aspect of the question was neither urgent nor necessary as yet. Thus the projected European 'leap forward', and even the Messina conference, aroused so little excitement that it never even occurred to the Swiss rulers that they should take part. Consequently, the signing at Rome, on 27 March 1957, of the treaty founding the European Economic Community, in other words the Common Market, came as a great surprise. Six countries, Switzerland's three most powerful neighbours among them, had committed themselves to pushing their economic integration to its furthest limits. What is more, the political intentions of this new structure were clearly apparent. Though the shape and scope of the political organization had not been very precisely defined, it seemed as though political integration was on the cards in the near future.

Though the Common Market was conceived as an open organization, and the admission of new members had been allowed for, there was never any question of Switzerland joining the new group. The political institutions which were to control this new European community were still undefined. But whether it would have involved the setting up of supranational authorities, or a looser system where one important country would have had the presiding voice, the envisaged solutions appeared quite incompatible with Swiss neutrality. True, the Gaullist conception of a 'Europe des patries' aroused some response in Switzerland, in as much as it seemed to involve only a limited loss of sovereignty. Nevertheless, if this proposal won the day, it would have implied a French dominance seriously threatening Swiss independence, even if

France shared the leadership with the Bonn government. Supra-national authorities as conceived in the Common Market were not much more palatable, because small countries would inevitably have had very little say under these conditions. At all events it appeared that no one, after the Treaty of Rome, seriously considered the possibilities of European federalism, federalism as the Swiss understand it at any rate, where the weight of demographic masses is compensated for by the fact that all the nations concerned, large or small, have an equal voice. There was never any serious consideration, during the talks about Europe's political structure, of a regime with the slightest resemblance to the Swiss bi-cameral system founded on the twofold reality of the people and the States. Which is why the Federal authorities, abandoning the idea of rapprochement or private agreements with the Common Market, enthusiastically welcomed the proposal for a large free trade area extending the narrow sphere of operations of the Six. Then, when this project failed, the Swiss fell back on a partial, limited and temporary solution; the setting up of a small free trade area—EFTA—by seven European countries, Great Britain, Switzerland, Sweden, Austria, Norway, Denmark and Portugal. This was inaugurated in Stockholm at the end of 1959, to take effect from 1 July 1960. It was envisaged as an organization devoted purely and simply to promoting economic co-operation, each of its members retaining absolute control over its political destiny. While abolishing tariff barriers and favouring trade among themselves, the seven countries concerned retained complete freedom of action in foreign markets. However, the founders of this new organization were perfectly aware that its life was a limited one, and that its chief purpose must be to foster an economic liberalization parallel to that undertaken by the Common Market, with the idea of constructing a bridge between the two groups, in the event of an association, or the organization of a larger free trade area comprising the Six and the Seven, or the nations, in other words, prepared to accept political integration and those which, for very diverse reasons, were not.

It was in the nature of things and the logic of events that the more dynamic and powerful organization should wield more influence and exert more attraction than the smaller and less effective one. Though the small free trade area is a living reality, and has made some headway, the Common Market has made such spectacular progress, so fast, that the signatories to the Stockholm Convention felt obliged, rather sooner than they had expected, to reach some agreement with the Brussels group. Great Britain asked to be admitted to the Common Market as early as the summer of 1961, with the proviso that her partners in the Seven—with whom she intended to remain linked—must be allowed to make their own parallel agreements in accordance with their own wishes and requirements. This move led quite naturally to a chain reaction among the other members of the Seven, requesting admission to or association with the Common Market group, as being the more substantial, and powerful, and the one with the most promising future.

These approaches, however, did not receive the unequivocal welcome hoped for by those concerned. They had begun by standing aloof from the enterprise on the grounds of their fundamental beliefs, or particular situations. They were now prepared to move a step nearer, while still claiming special recognition of these beliefs and situations. The members of the Common Market were not of a mind to subscribe to elastic formulas, exceptions or reservations. They feared this would weaken their own organization. To their way of thinking, any country wishing to work hand in hand with the Common Market should be prepared to accept all the obligations entailed. They also feared, and in this they had strong American support, that any loosening of the ties of European integration would permit Germany, sooner or later, to opt out of a Western European organization and yield to the attractions of neutralism. Besides, the negotiations were undermined from the start by the fact that while the Common Market countries might insist that European integration was a reality, its political organization had barely been sketched in and no major decisions, in this connection, had been made. France, under General de Gaulle, still insisted that the first step was to learn to live and work alongside each other, that experience should be gained in this respect before bringing in constitutional measures to consecrate in law what had been achieved in practice, and she continued to make her special relationship with Germany a cornerstone of her policy, clearly intending to secure leadership in European affairs for herself, but the small Benelux countries remained the advocates of the pure doctrine of a politically integrated continent directed by supra-national authorities. They wanted a date fixed for the creation of these authorities and declared they would not accept a delay of more than three years. In the meantime, however, French or Franco-German ambitions left them so uneasy that they received Great Britain's request for admission with relief, hoping that this great country would provide a counterweight and exert an influence at least as great as France's. This was enough to stiffen French opposition to the proposal, because France sees integration as part of a larger design—escape from unpopular American domination and her own reinstatement as one of the leading powers in the Atlantic Alliance. The Common Market carried on negotiations with Great Britain lasting eighteen months. Then, out of the blue, de Gaulle's government engineered a breakdown of the talks, fearing no doubt that Great Britain, with her traditional Anglo-Saxon bias, would help to keep Europe under the thumb of the United States. The breakdown of negotiations has postponed political integration for several years.

At first sight this breakdown should have been welcomed by the Swiss authorities, since it is the political aspect of European integration which constitutes the great stumbling-block in their eyes. But it is clear that no progress can be made so long as Great Britain's position—and she still heads the list—has not been decided upon. Under the circumstances, Switzerland's request for association with the Common Market, first announced a year after the British move, and set forth at Brussels in September 1962, four years before General de Gaulle's press conference led to a breakdown, was adjourned *sine die*, postponed till a more favourable occasion. Thus, the Swiss government's primary concern at the beginning of 1963 was to tighten the bonds between the Seven in such a way that their liberalizing measures took place at about the same tempo as those adopted by the Common Market, and that the gap between the two organizations should not be too large when the time came to make a bridge between the Six and the Seven. This need was so generally recognized that the members of the Seven overcame their previous reserve and went so far as to envisage some co-ordination of their commercial policies, and embarked on some co-operation in agriculture, which they had at first avoided while the Common Market had arrived at a common agricultural policy, which leads however to unbearable surpluses, and at the preliminary stages of a common commercial policy.

The Swiss request for association, of 1961, still remains

highly interesting since the two delegates from the Federal Council made a real effort to depart from the traditional Swiss aloofness and think up really practical and positive solutions. They made, together with Sweden and Austria, the proposal that a Council of the Association be set up which should assemble all the members and associates of the Common Market whenever subjects of mutual interest were on the agenda. This was a real contribution, because it must be remembered that while the Treaty of Rome provides for association by countries which do not want to become full members, it never clearly defined what was meant by this term. Though the Swiss delegates made express reservations as to their relations with non-Market countries, they declared themselves in accord with a progressive and far-reaching co-ordination of commercial policies with regard to these countries. They still demanded special treatment for Swiss agriculture—which has to maintain an appreciable production level despite the peculiarly unfavourable conditions under which it labours—but they explicitly asked for Common Market help in solving this thorny problem. Finally, the most important reservation expressed by the delegates concerned the possibility of Switzerland's breaking off her Common Market agreements, in the case of a serious international crisis for instance, or a war, when she would need to safeguard her neutrality or ensure food supplies. On the one hand, the Rome Treaty does not allow for the possibility of termination, and its provisions have no time limits. From a purely practical point of view, one may wonder whether it would be possible to stop the wheels of an integrated European economy from functioning, given the fact that this will lead to a rigorous division of labour and unprecedented specialization, and that it will be attended with such complex intermeshing of the various national economies that for one country to extricate itself would not be easy.

Some of the motives underlying the official Swiss attitude have scarcely been touched upon, but they may perhaps be the most important of all. Firstly, it is generally accepted that in an integrated Europe with which Switzerland would merely be associated, certain decisions would be taken by the Common Market authorities, as regards commercial, social, financial, economic or fiscal matters. The Swiss delegates would participate in these decisions and present their country's view, and they might even exert some influence. But it is undeniable that certain areas now released from cantonal sovereignty would become the appanage of the central government, that federalism would be weakened thereby, and that direct democracy would not be able to function as broadly as it does now. To say this—and it was implied at Brussels—is not to invite alarm and despondency. It is simply looking facts in the face and defining some of the choices which association with the Common Market would impose. Any modification of federalism and direct democracy implies changing the institutions which have been the mainstay of Switzerland's internal equilibrium for so long, and a change in the values to which the inhabitants of the country are profoundly attached. When the time comes, this dilemma would have to be clearly explained to the people, the only power competent to decide what they want to preserve at all cost, and what they are prepared to give up.

Added to this there is another cause for unease, which is no less real for not having been openly, or rather, officially, expressed. As we mentioned at the beginning of this chapter, the Swiss united to give themselves a better chance of dealing successfully with external dangers, and their internal cohesion, nourished by a common cult of individual liberty and respect for differences in language and religion, came later. From this point of view, the Federal bond is curiously akin to a marriage of convenience and the Swiss live in constant fear that it may prove vulnerable and its centrifugal forces blow the whole arrangement apart. They do not talk about this because people are reluctant to admit their weaknesses. However, it is understandable that men burdened with heavy responsibilities should fear for Switzerland's internal cohesion once the country, integrated into a larger whole, is forced to relinquish the historical constants which conditioned its birth and permitted its survival. This is worth noting in view of the obligations which the Swiss will be called upon to fulfil.

The presentation of the Swiss case aroused marked interest at Brussels, precisely because it took a constructive line on many points and seemed a new departure from the traditional Swiss negativism and dubiety. It would be foolish to ignore the fact that the Common Market countries, despite their differences, are reluctant to accept anything which might weaken their organization. They are primarily concerned with maintaining its effectiveness and they evince a spontaneous and marked mistrust of qualified solutions. Finally, surprising as it may seem, Switzerland is undoubtedly the most misunderstood of the three neutral countries which have asked for associate status. She is constantly reminded of the fact that her neutrality was the outcome of the old balance of power in Europe, and that it was justified so long as there was danger of war breaking out between her neighbours, but that it no longer serves a useful purpose now that they are all closely and lastingly united. Austria's neutrality meets with more sympathy because this is the one country from which the Soviet occupying forces withdrew as a result of Vienna's declaration of neutrality. As for Sweden's neutrality, it is well known that this is conditioned by a fear of compromising her friend Finland, and by the desire to make the Baltic a secure and peaceful area. These variations are all permanent ones and they are bound to reappear when negotiations are resumed, after Britain's case has been settled one way or the other.

Earlier than most observers assumed, prospects for European integration changed fundamentally. President de Gaulle, who for a decade was the most influential statesman in Western Europe and who was furthermore particularly successful in impairing certain developments of European integration, suddenly retired on 28 April 1969. The day before, the French people, in a referendum, had rejected his proposal for a certain change in the institutions of government. This was not so much due to de Gaulle's proposal, but rather to the discontent of a large section of the French population with de Gaulle's policy since the crisis of May 1968.

De Gaulle's retirement facilitated a more favourable French attitude towards the issue of an enlargement of the Common Market. However, France's position in international politics had already been weakened by the 'events of May' when France had to ask for financial support from the United States and the Federal Republic of Germany. It is not surprising that de Gaulle, such a proud man, hesitated to draw the conclusions from France's unlucky situation.

On 1 October 1969, the European Commission submitted its opinion on the applications for membership of Great Britain, Ireland, Denmark and Norway to the EEC Council of Ministers. In this document the Commission had spelled out the general conditions for membership under the new circumstances, which suggest a high price for entry:

—the treaties and all the regulations have to be accepted without reservation;
—the 'political aim' has to be accepted;
—stronger institutions and more intensive co-operation in economic policy.

At the Hague summit conference of presidents and prime ministers of the Common Market countries on 1 and 2 December 1969, the future programme for the Community was formulated: The 'political aim' of the Community and the aim of establishing an economic and monetary union was reaffirmed. It was also stated that the enlargement of the Community was considered desirable and the participants of the conference did not fail to express their willingness to start conversations with the countries that did not apply for membership. In May 1970, the European Commission submitted to the Council a report on the Community's attitude towards those countries of EFTA which did not apply for membership in the Common Market. On 8 June the Council decided to start conversations with these countries in the autumn. On 30 June negotiations between the EEC and Britain, Ireland, Denmark and Norway were formerly opened.

Switzerland expressed her desire to start exploratory talks with the Community as soon as possible. There is, however, a difference in the approach of the neutral countries, Switzerland, Sweden and Austria, towards the Common Market in 1970 as compared with 1961. In 1961, these countries proposed a certain form in which to join the Common Market, an 'association' as mentioned above. On the basis of this application negotiations took place only with Austria because among all the EFTA countries it was only Austria who insisted, after the breakdown of the British negotiations in 1963, to pursue her application for negotiations. However, these negotiations were not successful. Furthermore, it seems as if the old concept of an 'association' between the neutrals and the Common Market is bound to fail because, as a matter of fact, in most cases the neutrals could not but accept community decisions which they would be unable to influence.

Contrary to the approach in 1961, the neutrals now wish to clarify, in conversations with the Community, in which form they could join the Common Market, compatible with their neutrality. The outcome of these exploratory talks still remains to be seen. Council and Commission are fully occupied by projects for the further development and the enlargement of the Community, and particularly by the case of Britain. In the Community the problems of the neutrals do not arouse much interest. These conditions enhance the danger that, should there be an enlargement of the Community, a solution for the neutrals would not be found in time. The statements by the EEC and EFTA Councils of Ministers, in which the interest was expressed that the enlargement of the Community should not destroy present free trade among EFTA countries, is certainly a consolation to the neutrals, Finland included, and Portugal, but should not be overestimated. It is up to the neutrals too, to reduce the dangers of their isolation in the future European integration process. They could do so by formulating a common concept which takes into account new conditions, particularly the failure of the old association concept, the decrease in the 'supra-nationality' (no majority votes for important questions) and the diminishing ambitions for *real* political unity. The Swedes are considering a 'membership under reservations of neutrality'. This is so far the only form for joining the Common Market with the neutral as a full participant in the decision-making process. It is doubtful, however, whether the Swiss people would go that far. They will presumably do so in the next few years because they are just not yet prepared for such a far-reaching step. Besides this important psychological factor, there are also difficult internal problems, as mentioned above: federalism, direct democracy, agriculture, mobility of workers. It should be made clear, at least, that permanent neutrality does not exclude membership in the Community under reservations of neutrality. If this solution does not come into being, it will be for other reasons than neutrality. A particular problem poses a rather doctrinaire approach and wishful thinking on the part of the Community: in the name of a doctrine, the aim of 'political unification' of Europe, certain politicians and officials of the Community are apparently inclined against the Swedish suggestion of a specific membership for neutrals. However, it does not appear feasible that the Community could achieve its 'political aim', which it has not yet even defined clearly enough, during the next two or three decades. There is apparently a contradiction in the policy of certain Community countries: on one side, they are supporting East-West *détente*, on the other, they are showing but little understanding for some small neutral countries which are fervent advocates of Western democracy. In the case of the neutrals' position towards the Community, its member states will get the opportunity to demonstrate how 'European' they really are.

In recent times, officials of the Brussels Commission have put forward the idea of a multilateral association between the Common Market and those EFTA countries which did not apply for membership. There have not been official reactions on the side of the neutrals, but it seems that they appreciate this proposal. One has to assume that conversations between the Community and the neutrals will concentrate on this type of solution. The main problem will be to what extent the associated countries will be able to influence decisions of the Community which they have to execute.

Bibliography

I

The bibliography reproduced here is a slightly abridged version of the one compiled by William Martin, which accompanied the first edition.

We have no intention of compiling a complete bibliography of Swiss history. This has already been published by Barth and Brandstaetter and runs into several volumes. We will confine ourselves here to giving a few notes on source material used in writing this book, so that readers can acquaint themselves with the salient points as rapidly as possible.

Swiss historiography comes into three categories—general histories, histories of the cantons, and monographs.

Among the general histories a distinction should be made between educational and more strictly scientific works. There are a large number of Swiss histories written for schools. We would like to mention here Oechsli's work, *Schweizergeschichte*, Zurich, 1912, and Suter's, translated by Professor Gaston Castella (Benziger 1915). These works are recommended to readers who require Swiss histories for rapid consultation, containing most of the principal events and a brief commentary on them.

Swiss historiography can also boast of many great, comprehensive works. Some of these, Tschudi's for instance, might seem a little dated to a modern reader but mention must be made of the classic *Histoire de la Confédération suisse* by Jean Müller, in 18 volumes, translated and completed by Monnard (1837).

More recently Dierauer published a *History of the Swiss Confederation* in six volumes (Librairie Payot, Lausanne) which may still be usefully consulted today. Finally, in 1925, the same firm published a French translation, in two volumes, of Gagliardi's *Histoire de la Suisse*. The Swiss war office is publishing a Swiss military history, in instalments. Lastly, we should mention the *Dictionnaire historique et biographique de la Suisse* (Attinger, Neuchâtel) which is an inexhaustible fund of information.

Where the different periods of Swiss history are concerned, we would like to draw attention to certain seminal works and to some of its more important phases. The first is the founding of the Confederation.

This is a matter on which historical theories are not in full agreement. The above mentioned general works were of course unable to make use of the latest discoveries in this field. For these readers would be well advised to consult Professor Karl Meyer's work, *Der Alteste Schweizerbund*, published in the 'Revue d'histoire suisse' in 1924, also that of Professor von Below, which appeared in the same publication in 1923, entitled *Die Enstehung der schweizerischen Eidgenossenschaft*, and the replies to this by Dr. Leo Weiss in the Nouvelle Gazette de Zurich, *Die Anfange der Eidgenossenschaft*, and by Professor Hans Nabholz: *Die nueste Forschung uber die Enstehung der schweizerischen Eidgenossenschaft.*

With regard to modern times, we should mention M. Oeschli's work *La Suisse au XIX siècle* and the highly interesting studies by Professor William Rappard of Switzerland's economic history which have provided us with useful material: *Les Origines de la Démocratie en Suisse* (Agriculture in the eighteenth century) and *La Révolution Industrielle* (The origins of legal protection for the workers). In the same field of study, we should like to mention Professor Garel's work *La Centralisation économique de la Suisse* and M. Antony Babel's *Essai sur les causes et le développement de la législation du travail en Suisse.*

Our own chapter IX on the reconstruction of Switzerland's frontiers is partly based on documents found in the archives of London and Vienna and partly on unpublished material.

Finally, one of the chief sources of material where Swiss history is concerned are the local and cantonal histories. Notably those of Daendliker with regard to Zurich, and von Tillier with regard to Berne.

II

Some works on recent Swiss history:

La Suisse, a national annual published by the Nouvelle Société Helvétique (36 volumes published).

L'économie de guerre suisse, 1939–48. Edited by the Centrale Fédérale pour l'économie de guerre. Berne 1950.

Pierre Béguin: *Le balcon sur l'europe.* A short history of Switzerland during the 1939–45 war. (La Baconnière, Neuchâtel 1950).

William E. Rappard: *La Constitution fédérale de la Suisse* 1848–1948, *ses origines, son élaboration, son évolution.* (La Baconnière, Neuchâtel 1948).

William E. Rappard: *L'individu et l'Etat.* (Editions polygraphiques Zurich, 1936).

Andre Siegfried of the Académie française: *La Suisse, démocratie-temoin.* (La Baconnière, Neuchâtel 1948).

III

Some further recent books:
E. Bonjour, et al., *Short History of Switzerland.* (Oxford University Press, London, New York, 1952).
Dominique Fabre, *Switzerland.* (Viking Press, New York, 1961).
George Thürer, *Free and Swiss: the story of Switzerland.* (Oswald Wolff, London, 1970).

Index